Praise for *Forging Latino Power*

"*Forging Latino Power* is a major contribution to Latina/o political science. With their unique ringside views and firsthand experiences in helping shape what they call the "Latina/o political empowerment project," Ayón and Pla have established themselves as the preeminent scholars of Latina/o American political development. To understand the historical and contemporary ebbs and flows of progressive Latina/o politics, read this book!"

— **Chris Zepeda-Millán,** UCLA Labor Studies Program Chair, Associate Professor of Public Policy and Chicana/o & Central American Studies, Strategic Research Lab Faculty Director, author of *Latino Mass Mobilization: Immigration, Racialization, and Activism*

"*Forging Latino Power* spotlights the changemakers who have taken brave steps to speak up for Latino communities and have used their newfound political power to right the wrongs of history, creating generational change for marginalized communities in the process. The political landscape has been forever changed for the better because of the inclusion of Latino voices. I thank George and David for taking up the task to document and share this history."

— **Karen Bass,** Mayor of Los Angeles

"*Forging Latino Power* is a testament to the enduring strength, vision, and influence of Latino leaders in American democracy. From their unique insider vantage point, Ayón and Pla illuminate the strategies and unwavering courage with which Latinos have insisted on justice, resisted marginalization, and persisted in shaping the nation's future. This compelling work is essential reading for anyone seeking to understand the heart of US history and the promise of its political future.

— **G. Cristina Mora,** Chancellor's Professor of Sociology, Co-Director of the Institute of Governmental Studies at the University of California Berkeley, and author of *Making Hispanics: How Activists, Bureaucrats, and Media Constructed a New American*

"For a rising generation of Latinos, this book is a mirror, a map, and a movement—all in one. It's a bold, unapologetic celebration of Latino identity, civic rise, and resistance in the face of exclusion. For every young person who has ever felt unseen or underestimated, this book says: *you belong in the rooms where decisions are made.*"

— **Dr. Mike Muñoz,** Superintendent-President, Long Beach City College

"As a Mexican diplomat who has had the privilege of serving in California over the past three decades, I have witnessed firsthand the remarkable evolution of Latino political power in this state, its growing impact on the national stage, and its critical role in US-Mexico relations. With clarity, depth, and historical perspective, George Pla and David Ayón once again deliver a landmark book. *Forging Latino Power* is a compelling chronicle of how Latino political influence has taken shape, adapted, and expanded. It is also a timely reminder that progress is never linear. As this powerful narrative reveals, every advance has been hard-won, every breakthrough met with backlash, and every setback answered with renewed determination and audacity. A must-read for anyone seeking to understand the evolving role of Latinos in American democracy."

— **Ambassador Carlos González Gutiérrez,** Consul General of Mexico in Los Angeles

"*Forging Latino Power* is an exquisitely nuanced follow-up to the seminal book, *Power Shift*. Once again, Pla and Ayón skillfully remind their audience of the possibilities that exist within and across the Latino political, ideological, generational, and demographic diaspora. In this compelling narrative, the authors highlight the critical convergences of opportunity and acts of informed resistance that continue to define the ongoing political evolution of Latinas/os, underscoring their growing influence and enduring promise for the future of the American enterprise."

— **Juan Sánchez Muñoz,** Chancellor of the University of California Merced

"*Forging Latino Power* is an important new book, meticulously tracing the rise of Latino political empowerment from its complex rural and urban lineages in California to its florescence in the nation's capital, Washington, D.C. The authors take us from farm-labor organizing and consumer boycotts to immigration reforms and voting rights in the diverse sites throughout the United States that forged Latino political power."

— **Ramón A. Gutiérrez,** MacArthur Fellow, Professor Emeritus of US History at the University of Chicago, coeditor, *The New Latino Studies Reader: A Twenty-First Century Perspective*

FORGING LATINO POWER

Books in the Power Shift Series

Power Shift: How Latinos in California Transformed Politics in America
(Berkeley Public Policy Press, 2018)

FORGING LATINO POWER

The Politics of Inclusion, Backlash, and Resistance

David R. Ayón and George L. Pla

Berkeley Public Policy Press
Institute of Governmental Studies
University of California, Berkeley
2025

Forging Latino Power : The Politics of Inclusion, Backlash, and Resistance

978-0-87772-463-6 (hardcover)
978-0-87772-464-3 (paperback)
978-0-87772-465-0 (eBook)

Publisher's Cataloging-in-Publication
(Provided by Cassidy Cataloguing Services, Inc.)

Names: Ayón, David R., author. | Pla, George L., author. | Schiff, Adam B., writer of foreword.

Title: Forging Latino power : the politics of inclusion, backlash, and resistance / David R. Ayón and George L. Pla ; [foreword by Senator Adam Schiff].

Description: Berkeley [California] : Berkeley Public Policy Press, Institute of Governmental Studies, University of California, Berkeley, 2025. | Includes bibliographical references and index.

Identifiers: ISBN: 9780877724636 (hardcover) | 9780877724643 (paperback) | 9780877724650 (ebook)

Subjects: LCSH: Hispanic Americans--Political activity--California--Los Angeles. | Hispanic Americans--California--Los Angeles--Social conditions. | Power (Social sciences)--California--Los Angeles. | Social integration--California--Los Angeles. | Los Angeles (Calif.)--Politics and government. | United States--Politics and government. | BISAC: BIOGRAPHY & AUTOBIOGRAPHY / Hispanic & Latino. | POLITICAL SCIENCE / Political Process / Campaigns & Elections. | SOCIAL SCIENCE / Cultural & Ethnic Studies / American / Hispanic & Latino Studies.

Classification: LCC: F869.L89 S75 2025 | DDC: 979.4/9400468--dc23

Marcha, 2021 cover art by Jose Ramirez, ramirezart.com.

Who lives, who dies, who tells your story?
—Lin-Manuel Miranda, *Hamilton*

In memory of the *Power Shift* pioneers
we lost during our work on this book,
Richard Alatorre and Gloria Molina.

Contents

Foreword

BY ADAM B. SCHIFF

OVER THE LAST DECADE, DEMOCRACY has come under unprecedented strain. Time and again, America's core institutions have been attacked and our fundamental values and principles violated. When I was elected to the US Senate in 2024, I joined my colleague Alex Padilla on the Judiciary Committee—our nation's first line of defense of the Constitution, the rule of law, and our democracy—with these well-known challenges clearly in mind. Even so, I was genuinely shocked, as was most of the country, when on June 12, 2025, Senator Padilla was forcibly removed from a press conference held by the Secretary of Homeland Security in a federal building in Los Angeles—the senator's hometown—and pushed to the floor.

If there is any image that captures the enormous progress of Latino empowerment in the last century, and the fierce backlash it has prompted, it is this: a Latino US senator from the largest state in the union on the floor with his hands cuffed behind his back. That this son of immigrants, themselves a short-order cook and a housekeeper, would graduate from MIT, become the youngest City Council president in LA history, and later the state's first Latino US senator, is a story only possible in America. But his treatment by the current administration is all too familiar in repressive regimes anywhere. It is also a harbinger of a dangerous and difficult new period that the Latino community—and the country—is struggling to overcome.

As George Pla and David Ayón detail in *Forging Latino Power,* the story of Latino political empowerment in California and the country is one that cycles through periods of tremendous advancement and intense backlash, realignment, and then empowerment again. It is also the story of the diversity of the Latino community, which is often painted with the same broad brush. The authors reveal communities that are deeply complex, and where personal paths to power are as dissimilar as they are woven tightly together.

When I ran for the California State Assembly in 1994, I shared a political consultant with a young and energetic labor organizer named Antonio Villaraigosa, who was also running for the state legislature. His district was overwhelmingly Democratic, while mine was lean-Republican. He won. I lost. Nationally, it was a very strong GOP year, but in California, there was more to the Republican surge than a national trend. Proposition 187—a deeply xenophobic and anti-immigrant ballot measure—was Republican Governor Pete Wilson's ticket to reelection. I opposed it, and I vividly recall the sensation of standing on railroad tracks, my feet tied to the rails, and recognizing this train was going to run over me. The proposition passed by a large margin. Wilson won his reelection, but the long-term consequences for the GOP were severe. If supporting civil rights legislation in the 1960s cost Democrats the South, Republicans' support for rolling back Latinos' rights cost them the West Coast.

I was elected to the state Senate two years after my abortive run for the Assembly, and Villaraigosa went on to become Assembly Speaker and then mayor of Los Angeles. In my time in the California Senate, the US House of Representatives, and now the US Senate, I've been blessed to work with many of the people whose stories fill these pages. What was often a lonely journey through the corridors of power for early Latino leaders is not so lonely now. Their ranks are filled with talented representatives from all over the state and country, and no longer confined to a handful of Latino districts or neighborhoods. As recounted in *Forging Latino Power,* so many of the political leaders chronicled here came of age in the 1980s, '90s, and early 2000s. They came from Southern California and the Valley, the Coast and Northern California, rising from often humble beginnings to challenge the establishment, disrupt the status quo, reframe how issues were discussed, and bring much needed change to the halls of power. The issues that they champion go well beyond traditional concerns over immigration, to the whole panoply of challenges facing the community and country.

I became active in politics just as some of the original power brokers of the Latino community were handing over the reins to a new generation of leaders who have redefined what it means to be a Latino leader in California. That generation has given way to yet another, like Pete Aguilar, a young mayor from Redlands whom I once helped persuade to run for Congress, and who is now the third-ranking Democrat in the House of Representatives. Or Robert Rivas, the grandson of farmworkers who emigrated from Mexico in search of the California Dream, and who now serves as California Assembly Speaker. Their stories inspire, but they also demonstrate the power that Latinos have built in Sacramento and Washington, and the ability to turn that power into real legislative victories.

The struggles chronicled in *Forging Latino Power* are uniquely Latino, but they also tell a broader story about the pluralistic nature of our democracy and how the accomplishments of our predecessors build on each other. And while their origin stories differ, they are deeply familiar to me—not just because I know many of these leaders personally. My grandparents fled Eastern Europe at the turn of the century; some of the family who stayed behind were lost during the Holocaust. When they arrived in the new world, they were not always welcomed at universities, in social clubs, at workplaces, in housing, or in politics. But early Jewish political leaders emerged and paved the way for others to follow. Sharing that common experience of immigration, discrimination, and hardship, it should come as no surprise that the early generation of Jewish political leaders so often found common cause and friendship with their Latino counterparts. That tradition proudly continues. And given the tremendous challenges facing both communities, it needs to, more than ever.

As this book shows, it took a century for Latinos in California to establish an electoral foothold, initially based on the sustained organization and mobilization of a single community. From there, one community after another was empowered, until Latinas and Latinos developed the leadership and built the clout needed to make government address their needs. As we organize to overcome current and future backlashes, their stories of struggle and achievement give me confidence that we will succeed.

* * *

ADAM B. SCHIFF serves as a US senator for California, is former chair of the House Intelligence Committee, and led the first impeachment trial of Donald J. Trump. Schiff previously served as a California state senator and as an assistant US attorney in Los Angeles. He is the author of the best-selling book *Midnight in Washington: How We Almost Lost Our Democracy and Still Could.*

Preface

Latino Politics in Transition

THIS BOOK IS OUR SECOND "deep dive" into the US Latina/o political-empowerment experience, emphasizing roles of community, leadership, participation, representation, and policy achievement.[i] Sustained Latino empowerment had multiple, independent origins across the country, at different times and in varying circumstances.[ii] Here, however, as before, we trace the current of American political development that we argue most shaped Latino politics—and especially Latina/o political leadership—over the last half century. That current emerged in a diverse Eastside *barrio* of Los Angeles in the late 1940s, evolved in significant ways over time, and contributed fundamentally to empowerment in the state and beyond. Top-tier California Latina/o leadership in the last decade, however, has transitioned away from those distant barrio origins to second and third generations predominantly not from LA, and it is now confronting unprecedented national political challenges.

To take into account key recent inflections in Latino politics, we had to reframe this book following the 2024 elections—much as we had to reframe our first collaboration after the elections of 2016. We started on that previous title, *Power Shift: How Latinos in California Transformed Politics in America*, early in Barack Obama's first presidential term and Antonio Villaraigosa's second term as mayor of LA—both historic and seemingly definitive breakthroughs.[iii] *Power Shift* highlighted the origins, rise, and contributions of a "top ten" selection of LA-based Latina/o leaders we dubbed *Los Diez*, who pioneered their community's *politics of inclusion* at every level.[iv] From that perspective, the story of Latino empowerment was of a people who through a lifetime of struggles acquired a "civic voice" in Los Angeles, supported the formation of a professional political leadership class in California, and triumphed over systemic exclusion and invisibility in the US.[v]

As we neared completion of that project, however, Donald Trump was elected president. We adapted to that challenging turn by emphasizing at the book's outset that Latina/o political empowerment has been marked by recurring cycles of progress, backlash, and resistance, with progress eventually resumed. Indeed, we noted that effective *politics of resistance* has also spurred substantial progress, as we saw in the 1994 experience with the anti-immigrant California Proposition 187, which passed in a landslide but was followed in 1996 by a dramatic Latino-led comeback that helped fundamentally change state politics.[vi]

We undertook this follow-up book amid the social and political upheavals of 2020 to further document consequential advances in Latina/o empowerment. Generally speaking, greater Latino representation and organization strengthened the capacity of leaders, their communities, and ultimately the state to resist policies contrary to "California values," and to continue making further social and political progress.[vii] More specifically, they contributed to the Democrats retaking control of the US House of Representatives in 2018 and to the efforts to recover the presidency. Those developments, combined with the growing importance of Latina and Latino leaders besides the *Los Diez* pioneers, provided ample need and motivation for another book. Success in helping end the first Trump presidency, accompanied by unprecedented LA Latino representation in the new cabinet and US Senate, strongly confirmed that effective resistance can result in historic progress. These achievements consolidated the understanding that Democratic governing coalitions at both state and national levels must include a major role for Latinos.

We needed to delve further into the rise of the second and third generations of Latina/o leaders who had become the new players in these roles. That meant capturing their growing diversity and political and policy assertiveness, as well as the continuing development, coherence, and influence of the California empowerment project, not only beyond LA's Eastside but also regionally, beyond the state.[viii] With the crucial flipping of Arizona in 2020, we saw what we call a "California corner," including Nevada, come together in presidential politics—an emergent bloc potentially as significant as the famous "blue wall" of Great Lakes states.[ix] The roles of Latina/o leadership, organization, and voter mobilization were defining strategic features of this incipient bloc.

As this second book was nearly finished, however, Trump was elected again, this time to greater effect, flipping both Nevada and Arizona back to red, and for the first time winning the national popular vote, but shy of a majority. As a result, we have come to see the Latino-empowerment experience as a continuously evolving political project that, in addition to transformations already mentioned, in its most recent ten years came into conflict with a uniquely strong and protracted, if segmented, *national* backlash—sure to be branded in retrospect as the "Trump Revolution," as the Reagan presidency is also recalled.[x]

As we recount in chapter 13 and the epilogue of this book, in the weeks and months that followed the election, resistance to the new Trump administration—from Latinos and non-Latinos, in California and beyond—emerged more slowly than in 2016–17, but began gathering force. The historic cycle of progress, backlash, and resistance in Latino empowerment, born in the mid-twentieth century, could be seen persisting into the second quarter of the twenty-first, with the expectation in California of further progress to be earnestly resumed by 2026. But the main Latino political project was not simply regrouping to carry on as before. That Trump—running, among other things, on a harshly anti-immigrant agenda—won growing shares of the Latino vote across three consecutive national elections indicates that the Latino-empowerment experience is again in some sort of transition, as is the complicated environment in which it continues to evolve. A key question is how best to understand and explain it.

First, however, we should recognize in basic terms what Trump's reelection, as a high-consequence historical event, both was and was not, in order to have a balanced sense of its significance. It was the fifth successful Republican presidential *reelection* since World War II, each of which was, in its time, considered a definitive win and historic Democratic defeat. Indeed, the first three Republican presidents reelected in this period—Eisenhower in 1956, Nixon in 1972, and Reagan in 1984—won in genuine electoral landslides. Even in 2004—the closest of the first four reelections—George W. Bush won with an absolute majority of the popular vote.[xi]

The dimensions of Trump's 2024 reelection were widely misrepresented and misunderstood, primarily due to his sweep—by narrow margins—of battleground states.[xii] He was, in fact, the first of the five Republicans reelected since World War II to not reach 50 percent of the national popular vote, which is relevant for the immediate future. Trump outdid his predecessors among Latino voters, garnering perhaps as much as a 46 percent share, according to a major exit poll.[xiii] Nixon, Reagan, and Bush each won over a third of the Latino vote, from 35 to 44 percent, in their reelections; but none of the Republican presidential candidates that followed them four years later, running in open races, was able to reach a third of the Latino vote, receiving just 24 to 31 percent. Only one of those successors, George H. W. Bush in 1988, was elected at all, and he was then ousted after a single term.[xiv]

Second, we must take the still-longer view of Latina/o political empowerment that both this and our previous book provide. We argue that the recently much-discussed shift to the right of Latino votes since 2016, most of all in 2024, cannot be fully understood without taking into account how and why Latino politics had a progressive character in the first place, and that its dominant policy priorities have significantly evolved several times.[xv] In our first book we called this a distinctly *progressive Latino political tradition*, born of particular experiences and conditions in a historically specific setting.[xvi] That progressivism was both paradoxical, given the rural Latin American origins of most US Latinos, and comprehensible, in light of their US urban experience in and since the Great Depression and World War II.

California Latino political power was literally "born in the barrio," taking shape in the late 1940s in Eastside LA's storied and diverse Boyle Heights neighborhood. Initial failure there, followed by breakthrough electoral success, forged a strategic political model that was intentionally scaled into a movement, which in the span of a dozen years spread outward to create a *statewide* Latino electorate. Another dozen years later, Eastside LA political leaders began institutionalizing networks of Latino elected officials and, working with allies and in coalitions stretching across the country, started to advance major policy-reform priorities that strategically furthered Latino empowerment nationally. These efforts—which not only accelerated the development of a Latino professional political class but also involved many other activists, organizations, institutions, and sectors—retained and built upon key elements of the LA model. All along the way, progressive Latino politics had to compete with both the community's inherited cultural conservatism and intermittent right-wing efforts to exploit traditional values to sow political division and win Latino votes.

What can be called *barrioization* has been central to the development and influence of the LA empowerment model.[xvii] Eastside natives had moved away and later returned—*rebarrioized* themselves—to become part, and eventually major leaders, of the movement.[xviii] Most Latinos, however, have no personal connection to the particular big-city barrios where the California Latina/o-empowerment project got started. Many activists and future leaders from communities starkly unlike Boyle Heights or East LA effectively *self-barrioized* to also join the movement. Many were from beyond Los Angeles altogether but had ties to networks rooted in LA and developed within the Democratic Party framework. Eventually, leaders inevitably arose entirely outside of metropolitan LA and reached prominent positions in state and national politics, primarily on their own, without passing through or being indebted to Latino LA. Given their differing personal experiences, local circumstances, and bases of support, they brought their own perspectives and strengths to bear on both Democratic Party politics and the Latino policy agenda.

It is in these circumstances, and partially due to them, that a significant and growing minority of Latino voters—many first-timers—have shifted the *aggregate* Latino vote to the right.[xix] Other factors, as well, played major roles in changing the makeup of the aggregate vote. Latinos were particularly impacted by the financial crisis of 2008–09, which began as a home mortgage crisis that wiped out the life savings of many.[xx] President Barack Obama critically boosted his Latino approval ratings and support for reelection in 2012 by providing protection to undocumented-immigrant "Dreamers" with his Deferred Action for Childhood Arrivals (DACA) executive action. An unanticipated consequence of that wildly successful program, however, was that the Dreamer movement faded from public view, and the face of the immigration issue changed in ways that, with each passing year, eroded many Latino voters' identification with waves of new undocumented arrivals.[xxi]

Trump both helped create, and took advantage of, a widespread public sense of crisis on the border, while he personally connected more directly with first-time, infrequent, and low-information voters, and vigorously stoked contempt for professional politicians of both parties. He did the same with public discontent with the wars in Iraq and Afghanistan. The COVID-19 pandemic, and especially official responses to it, hit working-class Latinos—many deemed "essential workers," and most of whom were far less able than the college educated to shift to remote work and schooling—particularly hard. They did, however, begin receiving emergency stimulus checks, ostentatiously bearing Trump's signature.[xxii] An astounding economic recovery under a new administration then followed, but was disconcertingly accompanied by two years of price inflation at levels not seen since the 1970s, which had outsized effects on Latino families' budgets. Approval of the incumbent Biden administration fell to and remained at record national lows, and once-notable Latino trust in government virtually collapsed.[xxiii]

A relatively new and growing factor is the emergence of a separate, Republican-funded *conservative* Latino political project—a countermovement to Latino progressivism that is pointedly hostile to the Democratic Party, and government generally, more than it is to Latino Democrats per se.[xxiv] Overall, this countermovement was certainly boosted by the result of the 2024 election, but its emergent base of support suffered considerable erosion and even partial collapse over the course of the Trump regime's first 100 days in power. We return in the epilogue to early data on Latino public opinion regarding the first quarter of the second Trump administration—as it frantically tried to mount its promised mass deportations; chaotically decreed budget cutbacks and mass firings of government workers; bullied allies and neighbors; and abruptly threatened, imposed, and withdrew tariffs on imports from the whole world.

Most Latino political leaders remain fundamentally progressive and overwhelmingly Democratic—hardly any have changed party affiliation—but progressive Latino politics generally can be seen as transitioning to a *post-barrio era,* one that more reflects suburban, small-town, and rural Latino interests, values, and perspectives, and is challenged by an increasingly divided electorate. From the start, the pioneers featured in *Power Shift*—wherever each was from—all showed a commitment to the historic barrios of greater Eastside and Central LA. But today, the most prominent Latino leaders produced by California and featured in this book include those never tied to Los Angeles at all—such as current Speaker of the state Assembly Robert Rivas of Salinas and House Democratic Caucus Chair Pete Aguilar of Redlands—or those who had been based in LA but transcended it since taking statewide or federal positions, and even diplomatic appointments abroad.[xxv] The historic barrios of Boyle Heights and East LA, for all their decades of influence, have not produced a new leader of comparable stature since the 1990s.

For the rest of the 2020s and into the decade that follows, we will all get to see in real time the increasingly visible competition between, on one hand, the historic progressive Latina/o-empowerment project and, on the other, enhanced right-wing efforts to win a growing share of Latino votes. The former has transitioned to new generations of leadership no longer attached to LA's Eastside, but it retains a belief in an indispensable role for activist government in advancing progress and social justice. The latter promotes a frankly cynical attitude toward government, politicians, and mainstream news media. This book provides the background, context, and insight into the rise of Latino political power and its ongoing evolution, without which it is impossible to understand the role of Latinos in today's ongoing struggle over the country's political direction.

Introduction:
Worlds in Collision
Prelude

Madam Clerk, a Latino is nominating for leader of this chamber a Black man for the first time in our history.
—Rep. Pete Aguilar
Democratic Caucus Chair
US House of Representatives
January 3, 2023

SOUTHERN CALIFORNIA REPRESENTATIVE PETE AGUILAR, forty-two, rose to nominate his colleague, Hakeem Jeffries of Brooklyn, fifty-three, as Speaker of the House, to succeed Northern Californian Nancy Pelosi, eighty-three, who had led her party in that chamber for sixteen years. This moment in Washington, DC, in 2023, as Aguilar said, was historic, but it resonated with the whole journey of California Latina/o political empowerment, reaching back over seventy-five years to the Eastside of Los Angeles. The old saying "History might not repeat itself but sometimes rhymes" applied well. Eight years before, Aguilar had boldly leapt from a city council seat to Congress, much like the first California Latino elected to significant office in 1949.[1] And also like that predecessor, Pete Aguilar acquired the coveted status of "appropriator," having landed a seat on the powerful Appropriations Committee.[2]

Rep. Pete Aguilar nominates Rep. Hakeem Jeffries for Speaker of the House. Copyright C-Span.

Also like another Southern California Latino political pioneer in 1980, Aguilar allied with a talented African American colleague from a different city, in the latter's bid to become the first Black Speaker (albeit of the state Assembly in 1980).[3] But the contrasts were also notable, and bound up with how the California Latina/o-empowerment project has expanded and diversified, transcending its LA origins and overcoming backlashes to achieve national recognition and influence. The leaders of these efforts rarely found themselves to be the only Latina or Latino in the room or on the committee anymore. For the most part, they no longer had to assume their non-Latino colleagues had no idea what they were, although the two parties differed substantially in that regard. Most of the country was quite unlike California, but there was now a visible and growing Latino presence in nearly every state.

Aguilar and Jeffries's party did not control the House in 2023, but the chaotically divided Republican majority could not muster more votes for its leader—who also happened to be from California—than the Democratic minority united behind Jeffries.[4] Consequently, after his first historic nomination speech, Aguilar repeated it another fourteen times over several days, until the majority finally elected its Speaker. The exercise was repeated the following fall, when that Speaker was recalled by his own colleagues, forcing more votes in the same session, which prompted Aguilar to nominate Jeffries yet again, and again. After the

2024 elections—in which Aguilar further narrowed the House majority's margin of control by helping flip three Republican seats in California—he once again nominated Jeffries. But even if they would now contend with an even-weaker majority in the House, Jeffries and Aguilar would have to resist and sometimes deal with a federal "trifecta"—a Republican Party led by their old nemesis Donald Trump, now in control of the White House and both chambers of Congress.

The two young—by Washington standards, certainly—legislators seemed to have burst onto the national scene with the leadership dramas in the House, but they had, in fact, been introduced to the nation in the years prior. The first step in their ascent came courtesy of a rising Latina superstar—Alexandria Ocasio-Cortez—who upset a previous Democratic Caucus chair, a white male New Yorker who was thought to be next in line for the speakership after Pelosi.[5] "AOC" thus opened the space for Jeffries to ascend to caucus chair and Aguilar to vice chair. Jeffries went on to serve as one of the managers of Trump's first impeachment trial before the Senate in 2020. Aguilar made his national debut on the "Select Committee on the January 6 Attack," leading the third of the committee's nationally televised hearings in June 2022.

During Trump's 2024 campaign, he and congressional Republicans threatened to criminally investigate and prosecute January 6 Committee members if Trump was reelected and regained control of the Department of Justice.[6] Aguilar, the highest-ranking Latino in the House and leading member of the Congressional Hispanic Caucus, was now a protagonist at the highest level that Democratic Latino politics had ever reached. This development was made possible by a lifetime of growth of the Latino vote, the formation and weight of a Latino professional political class, and the clout of megastate California and its congressional delegation.[7]

Trump Shock II: Latino Realignment, Continuing Paradox, or New Era?

The Latina/o political-empowerment project we trace in this book collided with a massive and protracted national backlash in the US presidential elections of 2016, 2020, and 2024, when the country swerved right, then left, then right again.[8] In each case, *most* Latino leaders and voters—especially in California—expressed continuing support of their transgenerational quest, primarily channeled through the Democratic Party, for political inclusion, representation, and progressive policy reform.[9] In 2016, however, and even more in 2024, they suffered severe setbacks in the results and in the new administrations that followed.

Over the last decade, this movement has resisted the latest backlash, led by Trump, to the rise and development of the Latino community and other changes in American society.[10] But the resisting majority of Latina/o voters—the movement's base that showed up at the polls—did, in fact, proportionately shrink over this period.[11] By 2024, this political project appeared to many to be in retreat. The very idea of a "Latino vote" in national politics was seriously questioned.[12] As the country's ideological and partisan polarization persisted and deepened, Latinos have become increasingly divided, as well, and are even said to be realigning as part of a national shift to the right. But as we show in this book, the project of Latina/o political empowerment has deep roots, has achieved great progress in representation and policy impact, and has repeatedly come back from stunning losses. In a Trump-dominated era—widely taken as indicating the exhaustion or failure of a brand of Democratic politics—considered together with shifts in both Latino voting and leadership, we can see a transition to a new period in, and a modified form of, Latino-empowerment politics.

To grasp this transition and its significance, we must not only fully appreciate the long progressive era that preceded it, but we must also put that era in context and recognize its paradoxical nature, how it came about, and how it not only persisted but dramatically expanded across the country. For a lifetime now, the fundamental question about Latina/o political empowerment and its national impact has been a paradox: why this people, predominantly with origins in conservative, rural, and small-town Catholic Latin America, ever became a key part of the progressive, big-city-dominated Democratic coalition in the US. In the 1980s, Ronald Reagan famously said "Hispanics are Republicans, they just don't know it yet."[13] He urged the preeminent Latino political leader of his time, Henry Cisneros of San Antonio, to join the Republican Party.[14] This book shows, among much else, how wrong Reagan was—especially as far as his own state was concerned. We take a mainly California point of view. Since California suddenly became a new and fast-developing US state over 150 years ago, Latinos have struggled to improve their working and living conditions here.

Another key to understanding progressive Latino-empowerment politics and its apparent recent decline and transition to, for the moment, something somewhat different, is to recognize the importance of *place*. Waves of migration from Mexico, from the onset of the Revolution of 1910–20 and continuing until the mass repatriations of the Great Depression of the 1930s, was overwhelmingly from the conservative Mexican countryside.[15] That is one large category of places of origin or ancestry of the Mexican American population of the US.[16] In California during that time, however, Mexican immigrants and migrants settled in a variety of communities, not simply in LA barrios.[17] In chapter 1, we examine less known but historically important alternative places in California where some of the predominantly Mexican American Latina/o leaders featured in this book settled or originated from. There, we look especially at two forms of community: the primarily residential Mexican agricultural labor *colonias* of California, and the company/mining towns of the Southwest.[18]

But there is no doubt that Latina/o political empowerment as a successful and persisting movement in California was indeed born in an urban barrio on the Eastside of Los Angeles.[19] That origin, and its export to other communities, has had enormous but largely unrecognized influence on Democratic Latino politics to this day.[20] We may now, after a full lifetime of consequential history, be seeing that precise LA-barrio brand of Latino politics to some extent passing into history. But that does not mean the end of California Latino political leadership, either in the state or nationally, as this empowerment project has both evolved and extended well beyond its urban LA origins. Significant new leaders have arisen outside of LA who may prove to be better suited than their forebears for navigating the political turbulence of today.

Forging Latino Power, as the title suggests, however, is not simply, or even primarily, about Latino and California resistance to Trump, soldiering on a decade after he launched his movement and first campaign;

more significantly, we show how California Latino political power spread from LA and diversified to have an impact on Latinos everywhere, as well as on the country's politics as a whole. After a lifetime of progress, this movement's continuing capacity to defy the power of the two Trumpian backlash presidencies, defend the most vulnerable members of the Latino community, and continue to develop and effect further policy reforms and innovations are among its signal ongoing achievements.

The Latino Landscape and Expanding Empowerment

Contrary to the stereotypical "up from the barrio" narrative, the leaders featured in this book came from highly dissimilar communities, even within the LA metropolis, and especially from elsewhere in California, across the Southwest, and outside the US. Besides the urban American barrio, two other kinds of communities—farmworker colonias and company towns—stand out in this experience, even if most of them have disappeared. To appreciate how far Latina/o political empowerment and its leadership have come, we must know their distinctive origins. Chapter 1 provides key examples, including California's first company town, which was also its first mining town, as well as the site of the state's first Mexican labor colonia dating to before the Gold Rush. In such settings, we see early examples of critical issues like racism, unequal education, and labor abuse, which would inform and galvanize future leaders who were raised there. Those include Dean Florez, born and raised in a Central Valley farmworker colonia, who embarked on a political career that took him to the leadership of the state legislature. They also include the legendary Dolores Huerta, originally from a company mining town in far-off New Mexico, who in California became best known as a leader of the farmworkers' movement.

It is no accident that a stable base for Latino political development in California was not built until a century later, in the Eastside LA neighborhood of Boyle Heights. People of Mexican origin—whether from elsewhere in California, the Southwest, or Mexico—found allies there, mainly Jewish, who were experienced in urban and labor politics. From there, as we trace in chapter 2, the young Latino-empowerment movement intentionally expanded to other LA neighborhoods, and most consequentially

Dolores Huerta, atop a car, calling on farmworkers to leave the fields and join the strike in 1965. Photo by Harvey Wilson Richards. Courtesy of Paul Richards.

ventured well north, first to San Jose and then throughout California's Central Valley. This chapter centers on how Dolores Huerta, along with Cesar Chavez, was "discovered" and made into a statewide community organizer and policy lobbyist by a historic, yet still little known, Mexican American civil rights organization founded in Boyle Heights in 1947. Eventually both Huerta and Chavez moved to LA, where they became prominent leaders of the Community Service Organization (CSO). There, they and the organization won recognition from both John and Robert Kennedy for mobilizing the California Latino electorate for the 1960 presidential election, well before they returned to the Central Valley to establish the United Farm Workers (UFW) union.

Chavez, with critical support from Huerta and others, split with CSO in 1962 and left LA to organize farmworkers in his own way in the San Joaquin Valley, as we recount in chapter 3. They set out with an astonishingly bold plan that remains little known or understood: to devote five to six years to quietly organizing farmworker communities in CSO fashion, while denying any intent to establish a union. Their strategic objective was to delay challenging the state's powerful growers until they were in a position to stage a valley-wide general strike that would force the state government to intervene. But they abandoned that plan in 1965, when Filipino farmworkers organized by the AFL-CIO asked them to support their strike against table-grape growers. The UFW emerged from that combined action and went on to become for a time the dominant Latino political force in California. The union effectively superseded its CSO forebear, maintaining critical ties to Los Angeles through its consumer-boycott infrastructure and deep involvement in several election campaign efforts in the city. The union reached the height of its national political influence and visibility in mid-1976, when it organized then-Governor Jerry Brown's field effort in Democratic presidential primaries across the country, and Chavez gave the speech placing Brown's name in nomination at the Democratic National Convention. But the UFW then experienced a crushing defeat on a California ballot initiative in the fall election. For the subsequent decade, further development of Latina/o political empowerment took a different course, with a focus on key national policy reforms followed by a new era in urban electoral mobilization.

Pivot to Immigrant Rights and the Rise of the Latino Lobby

Years of intense Latino political effort in Washington, DC in the 1970s–'80s helped erect three pillars of the community's empowerment: Census reform, immigration reform, and the enhanced protection of Latinos in the 1982 extension of the Voting Rights Act. Those reforms laid the foundation for nearly all subsequent Latino political development across the country to this day.[21] Chapter 4 examines the turn to this policy agenda and the roles of Latino leaders and organizations in it. Before the '70s, the closest thing to a Latino position on immigration had been opposition to the World War II–era guest-worker "Bracero Program," which was repeatedly extended all the way to 1964.[22] The labor movement, including the UFW, and most Latino leaders and organizations tended to not distinguish between braceros and undocumented migrant workers, wanting both kept out of the country. Early in the '70s, however, with the Bracero Program long gone, solidarity with the undocumented began developing in LA. By the late '70s, provoked by a proposed national immigration crackdown advanced by the Jimmy Carter administration, mainstream Mexican American organizations and Chicano-movement activists united in opposition. A consensus among the Latino political class in defense of undocumented immigrants became a prominent cause that significantly modified the empowerment movement born in LA. The demand for immigration reform to legalize the undocumented was consolidated as one of the trio of issues on the emergent Latino national policy agenda.

If, on one hand, the Carter administration inadvertently provoked a Latino political pivot on immigration, on the other it also helped enhance California Latino participation on both the census and voting rights fronts. Having Los Angeles Latinos in the administration led to the recruitment of perhaps the most impactful lawyer to emerge from East LA. Antonia Hernández joined the staff of the Senate Judiciary Committee, newly chaired in 1979 by Edward Kennedy. Then, after working in Kennedy's presidential primary campaign the following year, Hernández stayed in Washington to head the DC office of the Mexican American Legal Defense and Educational Fund (MALDEF). Antonia was thus established in the national policy arena in time to play a key role in strengthening the Voting Rights Act for Latinos, as it was due for renewal in 1982. Hernández subsequently became president of MALDEF and moved its headquarters to Los Angeles.

A decade of resistance to a national immigration crackdown, from the mid-1970s to mid-1980s, served as the crucible to forge a permanent Latino policy lobby in Washington. As recounted in chapter 5, another Latina activist lawyer from East LA, Martha Escutia, became a central part of this effort. Escutia made her way to Washington, where she interned as an undergraduate and attended law school. There she helped set up the congressional office of a new representative she had campaigned for back in Eastside LA. Escutia wound up staying in DC when she became the legislative director for a leading Latino advocacy organization, just as a protracted policy debate over immigration reform was again heating up. Between Martha's LA political relationships, her contacts on Capitol Hill, and deep personal knowledge of the processes of Mexican migration to the US, she had much to contribute to the Latino effort to effect an acceptable reform of immigration policy. After her years in DC, Escutia returned home, where she eventually launched her own political career in LA County's "Southeast Cities."

Legalizing Millions, Ensuing Backlash

Getting a complete count of the Latino population in the US Census for the first time in 1980 was a "big bang" for the community's national empowerment. A comparable historic leap came in 1987, when millions of undocumented workers and their families were mobilized to apply for legalization, as we recount in chapter 6. Hidden within this story is the critically important role Dolores Huerta played in making possible the 1986 law known as the Immigration Reform and Control Act (IRCA), and in particular the provision that allowed for the legalization of well over a million undocumented farmworkers. But even before IRCA went into effect, a campaign was launched in LA to urge undocumented immigrants to come out of the shadows and legalize their status, with Latino media playing a leading role, along with the Catholic Church, Latino and immigrant-rights organizations, and elected officials.

Spanish-language news media leaders in LA—Monica Lozano, of the daily *La Opinión*, and Jorge Ramos, initially of the TV station KMEX—are featured players in our telling of this historic effort. Their platforms were both the largest of their kind in the country and the fastest growing in their industries, which attracted corporate America's interest. But their personal origin and development stories are critical for understanding the social commitment they brought to their respective mass-media corporations. Growing advertising revenue allowed these platforms' operations to expand and further professionalize while Lozano and Ramos developed more activist leadership roles in the community. The action networks they helped convene in the legalization campaign would be reactivated and emulated time and again to advance collective community goals around the same three pillars noted above: in 1990, to again mobilize Latino participation in the Census; in 1992, to participate in the first elections following that decade's redistricting, which coincided with another pivotal presidential contest; and in 1994, to resist Governor Pete

Wilson and his Proposition 187, which targeted undocumented immigrants and their children.

The legalization of millions of undocumented residents in the late 1980s accelerated urban Latino population growth nationally, which in metropolitan LA allowed new, predominantly Latino electoral districts to be created at all levels of government. Influential elements of the majority community, however, repeatedly showed their dissatisfaction with the increasing visibility and empowerment of minorities, as expressed in the "English Only" movement of the 1980s–'90s and the passage of state legislative term limits in this period. Nevertheless, in the early 1990s, newly drawn Latino districts propelled the political careers of Xavier Becerra, Hilda Solis, and Martha Escutia. Reapportionment and redistricting based on the 1990 census allowed Becerra to leap from just his first term as a member of the state Assembly to Congress, where he served a quarter century before becoming California attorney general, and then the first Latino to head the Department of Health and Human Services in the Biden–Harris administration.

However, as chapter 7 illustrates, the combined effects of just the initial inclusionary Latino political advances of the 1980s and early 1990s motivated a culminating and historic backlash symbolized by the "Save Our State" ballot initiative, better known simply as "187." Proposition 187 would have barred millions of California residents from public services based on federal immigration status and expelled hundreds of thousands of students from public schools at every grade level throughout the state. That threat, combined with then-Governor Pete Wilson's embrace of 187 in his 1994 reelection campaign, gave rise to the first instance of mass, organized resistance to repatriation pressures in US history. The Latino-empowerment movement in California suffered severe losses in 1994, but Latino resistance powered a historic comeback almost immediately thereafter, with breakthrough advances in politics and policy. A new generation of LA-based Latino leaders came forward to resist Wilson and 187, including Kevin de León, who decades later would become the first Latino to lead the state Senate, and Alex Padilla, who went on to a series of "firsts" at both the city and state levels, and eventually became the first Latino to represent California in the US Senate.

Expansion, Diversification, Comeback . . . and More Resistance

The historic electoral setbacks of 1994 were followed by a statewide Latino-led comeback in 1996, made possible by developing leadership networks and the power of community resistance. As chapter 8 recounts, Latina/o political empowerment expanded and diversified beyond Eastside LA and Mexican American men, with figures such as Hilda Solis, Tony Cárdenas, and Dean Florez of the San Gabriel, San Fernando, and Central Valleys, and Liz Figueroa and Deborah Ortiz in Northern California, all elected first to the state Assembly and then to the Senate. This networked spread of Latina/o electoral representation built an infrastructure that continuously recruited and developed new talent and tapped new resources. Its significance in state politics as a whole was underscored by the 1996 election of the first Latino Speaker of the California Assembly, followed by the second in 1998, along with the first Speaker's subsequent election as lieutenant governor, and the new governor's decision to drop the state's legal defense of Proposition 187.

The country's most prominent Latino political leader at the time, Henry Cisneros—the former four-term mayor of San Antonio and President Bill Clinton's first-term secretary of Housing and Urban Development—moved to Los Angeles in 1997 to become president of the Univision TV network, which *The Wall Street Journal* described as unique in the history of corporate America in its commitment to the political empowerment of its audience.[23] The famous Cisneros was not the only Texas Latino of note who was pulled to LA in the late 1990s. The still-unknown Eva Longoria also made her way to Los Angeles, where in the next century she not only became the biggest Latina TV star ever, but an activist of national renown. Longoria's rise as a political leader was crowned by her cofounding the premier Latina/o campaign fundraising operation in the country, known as the Latino Victory Fund (LVF), and her increasingly prominent role in Democratic National Conventions from 2012–20.[24]

In the pivotal stretch of 1999–2000, Latino leadership in the top power positions of organized labor in LA County once again flexed their recently developed muscles. The Latino-led County Federation of

Labor ("the Fed") hosted the AFL-CIO's 1999 national convention and pushed it to finally accept the need to organize the new US proletariat of undocumented-immigrant workers. Months later, the Fed backed state Senator Hilda Solis's challenge to a sitting Latino member of Congress in the San Gabriel Valley. By taking out the centrist incumbent and sending "labor warrior" Solis to Washington instead, the Fed positioned her to be tapped eight years later, by President-elect Barack Obama, to be nominated the first Latina or Latino secretary of labor—still the highest-ranking Latina to serve in US government.

Eva Longoria's first time addressing the Democratic National Convention, on its last day in Charlotte, North Carolina in 2012, prior to President Barack Obama's acceptance speech. Photo by Tom Pennington/Getty Images.

For a few years, at least, the new century seemed to have left behind the progress-backlash-resistance cycle in the Latino political experience. Latino-friendly Republican George W. Bush became president in 2001, and the next year California Governor Gray Davis, also Latino friendly, was reelected. Nevertheless, as recounted in chapter 9, Assembly Member Dean Florez, chair of the legislature's Joint Oversight Committee, defied and embarrassed his governor in 2002 by probing a no-bid state contract with software giant Oracle. Florez's high-profile hearings in an election year alarmed the governor, but Davis was nonetheless handily reelected. However, when popular discontent with a budget crisis and other issues arose, Davis was recalled from office before he could complete the first year of his second term.

The new backlash in California was embodied by a cartoonish strongman, Arnold Schwarzenegger, who led the recall of Governor Davis in 2003 and succeeded him in office.[25] But the "Terminator" was soon tamed by a Latino leader with big institutional muscle, Fabián Núñez, who began his career as an immigrant-rights activist and a leader of the 1994 resistance to Proposition 187. Graduating to labor leader, Núñez used his union base to win election to the state Assembly in 2002, representing LA, and in a meteoric rise ascended to the post of Speaker in his first term, just months after Schwarzenegger had taken over as governor. As we recounted in *Power Shift*, Speaker Núñez, with the clout of the state's organized labor behind him, led the campaigns that in 2005 derailed Schwarzenegger's project of governing by ballot initiative, rather than by working with the state legislature.[26] This historically pivotal, yet underappreciated, turn of events marked the rise of Latina/o political empowerment to de facto statewide leadership status in California, and it both consolidated and made plain a historic shift in the center of gravity of Latino power in the state—from activism on the outside to governing from the inside.

By the end of that year, however, House Republicans passed a sweeping bill to crack down on undocumented immigrants and criminalize any assistance to them.[27] The threat of this bill, in turn, precipitated in 2006 the greatest concentrated series of street protest marches in US history up to then, involving millions of Latino demonstrators across the country. The march and rally leading to LA City Hall was the biggest by far, attracting an estimated half million participants—at least five to six times as many as the previous record march against Proposition 187 in 1994.[28] The new backlash was thus met with a vengeance by unprecedented Latino resistance, which helped kill the nativist bill in the Senate.

Mobilize to Naturalize—*¡Ya Es Hora!*

As stunning and impactful as the immigrant "mega marches" of 2006 were, this national mobilization nevertheless highlighted a continuing and disconcerting reality. In spite of the catchy and oft-repeated slogan

Culmination of the nationally record-breaking immigrants' rights march to LA City Hall on March 25, 2006. Photo by J. Emilio Flores.

Hoy Marchamos, Mañana Votamos ("Today We March, Tomorrow We Vote"), there was no appreciable increase in the Latino vote in that year's midterm elections. Chapter 10 tells the story of how a coalition of LA institutions came together to remedy the fact that so many of the immigrants eligible to become citizens and voters chronically failed to do so. The National Association of Latino Elected and Appointed Officials (NALEO), the Univision flagship TV station KMEX, *La Opinión*/ImpreMedia, and the regional office of the Service Employees International Union, together with the Washington-based National Council of La Raza (now UnidosUS) and each of these national institutions' affiliates and offices in cities across the country, devised a multifaceted and multistage campaign to first promote mass, mobilized naturalization (*¡Ya Es Hora: Ciudadanía!*), to be followed by a registration campaign and, finally, a campaign to promote voting in the next presidential election. Citizenship applications soared during this campaign in 2007, and the number of Latino votes increased by two million in the 2008 general election—contributing to the Obama breakthrough and approaching the long-sought goal of ten million voters nationally.

The LA Latino ascent to, and continuity in, key leadership positions became a hallmark of this decade and into the next, as we show in chapter 11, but it was also marked by these leaders' policy advances. After losing in his first attempt, Antonio Villaraigosa was elected and reelected mayor of Los Angeles, and in a major flex of his continuing clout in Sacramento, managed to assert an unprecedented measure of influence over the LA Unified School District. In 2008, fellow labor leader John Pérez, from the same LA district as Núñez, succeeded him in the state Assembly and, like Núñez, became Speaker in his first term. Eric Garcetti first succeeded Alex Padilla as president of the LA City Council in 2006, and then he succeeded Antonio Villaraigosa as mayor in 2013. In 2012, Padilla became only the second Latino to win statewide office since the 1800s, with his election (and later reelection) as secretary of state. Latina/o leadership of the mighty LA County Federation of Labor continued after the untimely death of Miguel Contreras in 2005, when his pioneering labor-activist widow, María Elena Durazo, was elected to succeed him.

Kevin de León, assisted in his rise to the Assembly by his longtime San Diego friend and ally Núñez, lost to Pérez in his bid for the speakership, but persisted in a remarkable policy-development effort that he took with him to the state Senate, where he became the first Latino Senate president pro tempore.[29] Although in terms of policy achievements he became best known for—in direct response to Donald Trump's first presidential win—establishing California as a "sanctuary state," that was not his proudest accomplishment in Sacramento. As also told in this chapter, through years of work, de León fashioned a national breakthrough retirement instrument, which did not become available until he was termed out and had moved on to the LA City Council.

Overall, the consolidation of this Latino power base in California, and especially in LA, became a model for Latinos elsewhere to follow. It also enabled these leaders and their institutions to boost empowerment efforts beyond the state's borders, in particular the neighboring states of Nevada and Arizona. Chapter 11 goes on to track the complicated politics of immigration reform in Obama's first term. The congressional Republicans' blocking of both comprehensive reform and the far more limited DREAM Act led Obama in 2012 to authorize executive action, known as DACA, to protect undocumented immigrants brought into the country as children. This program helped Obama's approval rating among Latino voters bounce back from its lowest point, in time for his reelection. None of these recurring instances of progress, backlash, and resistance, however, prepared anyone for the rise of Trump in 2015–16.

Jorge and the "Build That Wall"-Breathing Dragon

Despite having lost control of the Senate in the 2014 midterms, President Obama's reelection in 2012—with a majority of the popular vote for the second time—had many Democrats more than optimistic about their coalition's prospects for 2016. Chapter 12 covers how as the cycle got underway at the start of the year before, Democrats looked more united behind the expected candidacy of Hillary Clinton than Republicans behind their putative front-runner, Jeb Bush, ex-governor of Florida. But there were clear indications on both sides of serious discontent with returning to a choice between a Clinton and a Bush. The country had twenty years of Bush–Clinton–Bush Jr. presidencies from 1988 to 2008, which were marked by severe recessions, scandals, hurricanes, terrorism, and seemingly endless wars. The political moment was inviting for an insurgent outsider candidate on either side. Two men were eager to step in—Vermont Senator Bernie Sanders on the left, and "reality TV" personality Donald Trump on the right.

As this chapter shows, Trump struggled to win attention as a potential candidate until he latched on to the issues of the Mexican border and immigrants—provided to him by extremist columnist Ann Coulter. Ironically, in retrospect, Univision nightly news coanchor Jorge Ramos was the conduit that brought Coulter's anti-Mexican diatribe to Trump's attention. Ramos and Univision then clashed with Trump and sounded the alarm that an aspiring US presidential candidate was stoking hostility toward Mexico and Mexican immigrants for political gain. Ramos and Univision were the first to forcefully respond to Donald Trump as he began his march to the Republican nomination in the summer of 2015. Univision answered Trump's ad-libbed campaign announcement, in which he called Mexican immigrants "drug smugglers" and "rapists," by canceling its planned broadcast of his beauty pageant. Then Ramos flew to a Trump campaign presser in Iowa to confront him on camera and got himself ejected from the press conference.

Jorge Ramos confronts Donald Trump at an Iowa press conference on August 25, 2015. Photo by Scott Olson/Getty Images.

This episode marked the beginning of the specifically Latino resistance to the backlash engineered by Trump and his team to propel his presidential campaign. Most Latino leaders and organizations, however, could not bring themselves to believe that such a figure could win the presidency. But he did. Once the incredible result was in, California Latino leaders flew into resistance mode. They had seen this sort of threat to their community before, and they knew what they had to do. Chapter 12 goes on to trace the manifold ways in which Latinos and California worked to resist Trump at every turn. Congressman Becerra returned to his hometown to become the state's attorney general, and from that post led the nation in filing or joining a record number of policy lawsuits against the Trump administration. Secretary of State Alex Padilla took the lead among his counterparts across the country in helping Democrats win elections to the same office in other states, and redoubled efforts to increase voter registration in California. A record seven Latino Democrats appeared on the 2018 statewide primary ballot—five of whom had represented metropolitan LA in Sacramento or Washington.

The first national resistance climax was reached in that year's midterm elections, with California Latinos substantially contributing to Democrats' recovery of a majority in the House of Representatives—stunningly underscored by a clean sweep of congressional seats in traditionally "red" Orange County. Four of the seven Latino candidates running for statewide offices prevailed. Padilla was reelected, and Becerra won his first election to retain the office of attorney general to which he had been appointed. State Senator Ricardo Lara, basing his campaign almost entirely on opposition to Trump, won his historic bid for insurance commissioner in a cliff-hanger. And Tony Thurmond, of Panamanian descent, was elected state superintendent of public instruction. The Latino politics of resistance was already producing empowerment breakthroughs in California.

Despite the year being dominated by three crises at once—the COVID-19 pandemic, the Black Lives Matter national movement against racist police killings, and a growing sense of a threat to American democracy from a president and his supporters who refused to accept the outcome of the 2020 election—Latinos in California continued to make advances in key areas, such as higher education. Former Assembly Speaker John Pérez, now as chair of the University of California system Board of Regents, led that world-class institution into a new era of administrative diversification and record Latino enrollment; a Latino was appointed to head the California State University (CSU) system—the country's largest—for the first time in history, and both the CSU and the massive California Community Colleges system moved to adopt ethnic studies requirements in their curricula. But as fall approached, uncertainty regarding the November election and the ravages of the pandemic seemed to crowd all other issues out of public consciousness. The rapid spread of COVID-19, increasingly fierce disputes over how to respond to it, and the president's months-long effort to skew and delegitimate his coming defeat in advance combined to distress and divide the nation beyond living memory.

Election officials across the country took special measures to promote safe voting, which yielded historic results. The Latino community suffered the worst rates of infection, illness, death, and economic pain in the country—most of all in Los Angeles. But California's governor, Secretary of State Padilla, and county authorities acted to ensure that all registered voters were mailed ballots that required neither postage nor even leaving one's home to vote. With votes soaring to more than twenty million ballots over the 2016 national total, one unexpected result was that the news media refrained from declaring a winner for four days while the counting continued, with most of the country in pandemic lockdown mode throughout. The occupant of the White House kept aggressively, and alarmingly, rejecting the result.

We Had Next

Chapter 13 grapples with the harsh reality that the 2024 election inescapably cast the success of the resistance in 2020 in a different and unwelcome light, extending to the ways in which 2020 had advanced Latino empowerment. The challenge, however, is to neither lose sight of how five and a half years of Latino resistance produced major breakthroughs in the makeup of a new national administration, and a new period of Latino inclusion and progress, nor to deny the severity of the reversal of 2024. Even if every passing day and week of the second Trump presidency reveals itself to be something considerably worse than how the first one started out, it is nonetheless *not* the case that all Latino political progress of the years from 2021 to 2024 has been nullified—certainly not from a California point of view.

This final chapter notes the lasting breakthrough of California finally being represented by a Latino in the US Senate. Furthermore, the state Assembly elected its sixth Latino Speaker during the Biden–Harris years, and the first Latina appointed to the state Court of Appeals became in short order not only the first named to the state Supreme Court, but in fact the chief justice. These are major, enduring advances indeed, and there is more besides. When Xavier Becerra returned to California to become the state's first Latino attorney general, he left behind his position of chair of the Democratic Caucus in the US House of Representatives.

Becerra had been only the second Latino to rise so high in House leadership, but six years later another Southern California Latino—Representative Pete Aguilar of Redlands—became the third.

That Northern Californian Robert Rivas of Salinas now heads the Assembly marks both continuity and change. He represents a largely rural district south of San Jose, stretched among four counties. Anthony Rendon, whom Rivas succeeded, had been the tenth consecutive Assembly Speaker from Southern California and the second-longest-serving in state history. That the transition to Rivas took place simultaneously with the rise of Pete Aguilar in the Democratic House leadership underscored a striking new reality: The highest-ranking Latino leaders in both the California Assembly and the US House of Representatives were suddenly not from Los Angeles anymore, nor did they owe their positions to the many LA Latina/o members of their respective chambers. By contrast, when Trump was first elected in 2016, Latinos from metropolitan LA led the House Democratic Caucus and both chambers of the California legislature.

Institutionally, California brings both strengths and limitations to meeting the challenge of defending its people and values from the hostile designs of the second Trump presidency. Governor Gavin Newsom and Attorney General Rob Bonta were quick to show a readiness to resist the new regime. Their approach appeared to reflect—especially with Bonta—the influence of the standard set by the state's Latino leaders in dealing with Trump's first term. But the governor in particular had to balance a range of considerations and contingencies, including both the leadership style of Speaker Rivas, the devastating firestorms that ravaged Los Angeles in January 2025, and the state's consequent need to obtain federal support for recovery from a nationally unprecedented degree of destruction due to a natural disaster.

We see significant and potentially great meaning in the aforementioned Latino advances achieved during the Biden–Harris years, taken together with the advent of enhanced competition for Latino votes and changing Latino voting patterns. Here, the challenge is to make out the factors involved in these changes and what they amount to. Latino politics is in transition, with new leaders dealing with grave new threats of mass deportations, the wholesale dismantling of programs established to advance historically marginalized communities, and growing divisions among Latino voters. The California Latina/o-empowerment project has indeed moved on to some extent in a new direction, but California Latinos, as well as Latinas and Latinos from other states, are very much in the struggle to define the nation's future.

History had already shown us that a next backlash should always be expected. The cycles of Latino empowerment continue, and in retrospect it appears that with every new turn, the community and its leaders have continued to press forward and labored to advance to a stronger position. Now, however, they find themselves contending with what could be called the mother of all backlashes, in the form of a national regime containing openly authoritarian elements that see retaining power as an existential imperative. The value of a deep dive into the Latino-empowerment experience as traced in this book depends on whether it can, in its own small way, contribute to furthering constructive resistance that results in greater inclusion and progress.

Part I

Worlds of Invisibility and Erasure

To be seen, heard, and taken into account in society or politics takes much more work for some than others. Some communities are rendered invisible and disregarded in countless ways. Urban barrios have often been disguised or hidden from general view—the proverbial "other side of the tracks (or river)"—and isolation has been a common experience for many Latinas and Latinos in these communities. It is no wonder, then, that the rise from a marginalized barrio, to college and on to a successful career, is a central and inspiring narrative of overcoming this social and political invisibility, subordination, and marginalization.

In that story of uplift, the barrio can, in fact, be seen as the penultimate step of Latino urbanization and integration. It is much better known and more visible than an *ejido* or a *ranchería* in Mexico, a *colonia* beyond city limits, a circuit of migrant labor camps, a segregated company town, or a remote mining or railway-station town. But these other, sometimes earlier, paths and settings of exclusion, struggle, and transcendence shaped future Latino leaders. They have also shaped currents within emergent Latina/o political-empowerment culture, in lasting ways distinct from the experience of a typical urban barrio.

Apart from various forms of residential and educational segregation, millions of Latinos have been made invisible by their immigration status, their role in the division of labor and working hours, or archaic and prejudicial terminology. Misleading or misapplied labels like "Golden State" and "Silicon Valley," or misidentifications—like of the Garcettis of Los Angeles, the Roybals of New Mexico, or the Ronstadts of Arizona—can submerge, exclude, or erase people from maps and rip them from the fabric of shared history and culture. Language policies and practices, as well as selective attention or inattention by media, authorities, teachers, scholars, and public institutions can silence "other" voices and experiences.

To assess progress made in Latino political development, we must take into account diversity of origins and journeys, and degrees of difficulty in overcoming powerlessness. These histories are necessary to call attention to continuing forms of social invisibility, isolation, and exploitation, and to find and share solutions to them.

Chapter 1

Where to Begin: Decentering the Barrio

FROM MANHATTAN'S WESTSIDE TO LA'S EASTSIDE, from Washington Heights to Boyle Heights, the big-city Latino barrio in recent years has had a great run in American culture. From an acclaimed musical to a masterful history, the arts and academia have offered lovingly drawn insider looks at the urban barrio experience on opposite coasts.[1] That an authentic Latino narrative must begin with either immigration or in the barrio, or one followed by the other, is well established in the public mind. But while sustained Latina/o political empowerment in California did indeed begin in fabled Boyle Heights, the barrio experience is far from a universal point of departure for understanding the long, broad, and multifaceted journey of Latino political development as a whole.

Tracing that journey necessarily leads us out of the barrios of LA to communities of other sorts, to learn of the particular challenges Latinas and Latinos faced there and the struggles they undertook. How might they have been influenced by, or connected to, better-known barrio-based empowerment efforts and advances? Did they exert their own influence, for good or ill, beyond their confines? Even if sooner or later they wound up in LA, many key Latino leaders did not originate in an urban barrio at all. They came from mining towns, company towns, and railway-station towns. But the most prevalent and historically consequential form of Mexican American community in twentieth-century California, *besides the barrio*, was the *colonia*—and there were other significant forms, as well, in the state and across the Southwest. Starting in the 1920s, from the Sacramento Valley in the north to the Mexican border in the south, Mexican American farmworker colonias sprang up, initially as shantytowns, throughout the state's rich agricultural regions, typically just outside a town's city limits. Unlike established urban neighborhoods such as Boyle Heights, which became barrios only when Mexicans and Mexican Americans moved into them, the classic colonia is a cluster of shelters that farmworker families themselves, and sometimes nonfarmworker Mexican-origin families, individually cobbled together on unoccupied land.[2]

Awareness of the significance of the colonia in the Mexican American experience in California has largely vanished among Latinos and non-Latinos alike, despite the excellent work of some prominent scholars, journalists, and organizers.[3] Besides the intentional hiddenness of most colonias, many people don't know about them because urban renewal and freeway construction projects demolished many of them. Colonias housed people who worked in the citrus belt ringing Los Angeles, but the belt's ongoing conversion from orchards into suburbs made those communities magically disappear. The discarding of historical evidence, the evolution of some colonias into urban barrios, and even the loss of the colonia concept soon followed.[4]

When all Latino communities, whatever their structural and historical differences, are lumped together as barrios, other experiences and places are erased from memory and understanding. Furthermore, awareness matters because what Carey McWilliams dubbed the "colonia complex" persists in some areas, as the affluent seaside town of Half Moon Bay discovered only due to a mass shooting in 2023 that took the lives of seven farmworkers on two mushroom ranches.[5] Without awareness, there can be no understanding that the affluence of the citrus-belt towns, with their elite colleges, is intrinsically related to the poverty of the farmworker labor colonias. Awareness and understanding are essential to appreciating the systemic barriers that long delayed sustained empowerment. But by the same token, only through awareness can we ever know how colonia residents also found ways to act on their own behalf.

"Spanishtown"

Long a major locus of Mexican communities of the US Southwest from Colorado to the coast, the remote mining settlement has receded from popular memory and consideration, even among Latino historians. We associate pioneering Latina/o leaders such as Dolores Huerta with California's agricultural Central Valley, Herman Gallegos with the San Francisco Bay Area, and the late Esteban Torres with East LA, where they and their families landed. But these luminaries were born in mining towns in Colorado, New Mexico, and Arizona, where their parents and earliest neighbors mined copper and coal—more *Salt of the Earth* than *West Side Story*.[6]

The mining experience, as work and as community, dates to the earliest years of Mexican-origin Latinos in the United States—not to mention centuries of Spanish colonialism in Mexico and beyond in what became Latin America. The start of such communities in California is the state's most astonishing and neglected example. Its first commercial mine was initially developed before the immensely more famous discovery of gold, before statehood, before the US war with Mexico ended, before peace negotiations began, and before US annexation of the northern half of Mexico's territory, but just months after the Mexican resistance to US conquest in California ended in January 1847.[7]

The great significance of what was dubbed the "New Almaden" mine and settlement lies in its combination of further "firsts." It almost instantly became the site of the state's first Mexican labor colonia and developed into not only California's first mining town but a full-fledged company town. This, then, became the starting point of residential segregation of Mexicans and Mexican Americans in the state—when it was still legally part of Mexico—as well as of segregated schooling, employment discrimination, and even what we now know as environmental racism. Remarkably, much of the Latino political and policy agenda in California is rooted in conditions dating back over 175 years.

How did this come to be? When US forces invaded Mexico from multiple directions in the "Mexican War" of 1846–48, a pair of British entrepreneurs based there acquired rights to the Santa Clara mine, sight unseen. What was initially just a cave would eventually grow into a sprawling industrial operation within the present-day boundaries of the city of San Jose. Few Bay Area residents have ever wondered how its biggest city's newspaper came to be named *The San Jose Mercury News.*[8] The masthead refers to what the Brits made of this mine, which they renamed after the world's richest mercury mine, *Almadén,* in the storied Spanish region of Castile–La Mancha, south of Madrid. Successive owner-operators made good on borrowing that brand for *Nueva Almadén*/New Almaden, which became the world's *second*-richest mercury mine, more valuable than any gold mine in California.[9]

The two British principals, Eustace Barron and Alexander Forbes, had mining, textile, and trading operations in Mexico. But it appears Forbes alone had colonial designs on that most removed part of the country known as Alta California. Although Forbes had never been to the territory, he dreamt—and wrote, in the first book about California published in English—of not just establishing a company town there, but indeed fashioning all Alta California as a *company colony,* modeled on the British East India Company's colonization of the Indian subcontinent.[10] His book was published in London in 1835, on the eve of the Anglo settler uprising in Texas. Forbes needed the support of the British Navy for his scheme, which meant seizing Alta California before either the new Texas republic or the US took it first. The Texans' immediate request to join the Union strengthened the US position, but Congress was deadlocked on the issue of slavery, which delayed annexation.[11] Nearly a decade passed before Texas was admitted as a slave state in 1845. Mexico, however, was constitutionally opposed to slavery, had never recognized the breakaway territory, and again tried to reestablish its control. What the US called the Mexican War soon broke out.[12]

A Mexican Army captain had acquired rights to an area in California where he planned to develop a mine out of a cave he determined to be rich in mercury ore. The "vermillion cave," as Carey McWilliams memorably dubbed it, was in the hills near the Santa Clara Mission and the Pueblo of San José, near the southern tip of the San Francisco Bay Area.[13] But the US invasion of Mexico doomed the officer's project. Barron and Forbes first leased and then bought the captain's rights to the Santa Clara mine, and in 1847, with the war over in California but still raging to the south, took possession with an expedition of one hundred experienced Mexican hard-rock metal miners.[14] Barron and Forbes had epic good fortune. They now had an especially rich source of what was commonly called "quicksilver," essential for the process of *extracting* gold and silver from their ores.[15] New Almaden started supplying the toxic and volatile element to silver mining operations in Mexico. And then came the discovery of gold nearby, soon enough followed by silver in Nevada.[16] Thus, Scottish businessman Alexander Forbes practically realized the Spanish conquistadors' dream of El Dorado in Northern California, made possible by Mexican miners who would labor underground to produce for him unsung mercury, midwife to silver and gold.[17] But as we will also see, the day would come when the miners would assert themselves and make history of their own.

Brought from one part of Mexico to what was still at that time another part, the miners and their families put up their camp on what came to be known as "Mine Hill," proximate to the cave entrance of the first New Almaden mine. The company euphemistically called the Mexicans' camp "Spanishtown," perhaps to complement the cachet of the original Almadén. This residential cluster did, in fact, become more than Mexican, as Chileans drawn to the region by the Gold Rush had to find other means of survival when California effectively barred foreigners from either prospecting for or mining gold.[18] Over a mile away on the valley floor, the miners also began developing the compound for the owners and management, unironically dubbed "La Hacienda," at the only source of drinkable water on the property. In his groundbreaking *Mercury and the Making of California*, architect and historian Andrew Scott Johnston assesses in detail and at length how New Almaden "was at its core a Spanish/Mexican hacienda, or estate, on the California frontier, and it was through the hacienda model that mercury wealth was created and controlled," a "Spanish Empire plantation-like system." Mexicans built the mining structures, dug shafts as deep as two thousand feet, and over time painstakingly carved out a network of over a hundred miles of tunnels under the hills.[19] This was the first, biggest, and richest such operation in California, but far from the only one. Johnston charts "dozens" of lesser mines and camps up and down the state's coastal range that, following New Almaden's lead, were built as "planned communities on the hacienda model."[20]

That imported model, combined with ensuing waves of Anglo-American settlers and the imposition of the US legal system, resulted in a massive transfer of the Californios' land and their "systematic disfranchisement at the hands of squatters, lawyers and surveyors," reinforced with "violent assaults by Northern California vigilantes."[21] Beyond New Almaden, these developments over time transformed "ethnic Mexicans," as historian Stephen Pitti puts it, "into a low wage labor force, absorbed and discarded by white farmers as seasonal needs dictated." A new racial order was established in which "ethnic Mexicans became a veritable 'internal colony' in Northern California."[22]

Spanishtown settlement at the New Almaden mine complex in 1863, the year it was acquired by the Quicksilver Mining Company, and by which time the miners had long built themselves sturdy houses. Photo by Carleton Watkins, Huntington Library.

The Valley's First Revolt

After a decade and a half of rich years producing tons of mercury shipped around the world, even Brits Barron and Forbes fell victim to the new legal system's usurpation of land grants and rights. The owners were forced to sell their New Almaden operation to the Quicksilver Mining Company of the US.[23] The new management doubled down on the company-town concept, enclosing its nearly nine thousand acres of property, charging an entrance and exit fee, and banning peddlers that had supplied Spanishtown residents for years. Quicksilver furthermore banned any sale or use of alcohol other than by the company's canteens, changed how the underground miners' pay was calculated, and switched paydays to monthly instead of twice monthly. All these measures were aimed at not only squeezing the miners but indebting them to the company store.[24]

The new American owners now also favored recruiting Cornish miners, for which a separate "Englishtown" was built, closer to the "Hacienda," where amenities were concentrated. Spanishtown and Englishtown formed the basis of separate and unequal schooling. A one-room school with a single teacher in Spanishtown went up to only the fourth grade.[25] The Mexican boys were not valued for what they might contribute, if educated, to the developing state, but for the endless chore of retrieving firewood from the surrounding hills and hauling it back on pack burros.[26] The multiroom English school near the Hacienda had several teachers and went up to eighth grade. We do not know how many Mexican children transferred to the English school to continue their education, or how they fared there, but records indicate that half a century passed before any Spanishtown student went on to enroll at the nearest high school, in San Jose, for which they would have had to complete eighth grade in the Englishtown school.[27]

Environmental damage wrought by the mining of notoriously toxic mercury still lingers: The expansive New Almaden property—although for decades now a county park of wooded hills and streams—remains the Bay's main source of mercury pollution.[28] Our knowledge of the impact of mercury poisoning on generations of miners and their families in California is woefully scarce, and the evidence lies buried at dozens of remote locations. But we know that hundreds of miners perished and thousands were injured at New Almaden alone in the first half of the 1850s, the majority of deaths attributed to exposure to mercurial, sulfurous, and other gases, the rest due to work-related accidents.[29] The fatally poisonous effects of this industrial operation on workers and their families, however, does not appear to have sparked labor action. It was instead the mining company's greed, in combination with dramatic historical events unfolding thousands of miles away, that led to a series of other firsts: independent worker organization, mutual-aid projects, the first labor strikes in Santa Clara Valley history, and even the emergence of a proto-Latino identity and politics.

Quicksilver Mining Company acquired New Almaden in 1863, in the midst of not only the US Civil War but also the French invasion and occupation of Mexico. Mexican immigrants in California for the first time banded together politically in response to the attack on their homeland. With encouragement from the Mexican government, they formed over a hundred organizations, *juntas patrióticas*, throughout the state in support of the beleaguered republic headed by President Benito Juárez. The Mexican Army's celebrated victory over advancing French forces in the Battle of Puebla—on May 5, 1862—electrified Mexicans all the way to the mining camps in the hills of California.[30] Before the year was out, the first of three New Almaden juntas patrióticas announced its formation in a San Francisco weekly: *Los mexicanos, que actualmente vivimos aquí, somos pobres, que ganamos la subsistencia con el sudor de nuestro trabajo; pero nos hemos organizado en Sociedades Patrióticas* ("We Mexicans, who now live here, are poor, we earn our subsistence with the sweat of our labor; but we have organized ourselves into patriotic associations").[31] These juntas were no mere committees organizing Cinco de Mayo fiestas and issuing declarations of moral support. Although the cause was Mexican, they brought immigrants, native Californios, and Chileans together to raise funds for the Juárez government's resistance to a new conquest. The New Almaden juntas published lists of over 1,200 dues-paying members in the local Spanish-language papers. The scattered local associations in Northern California sent the funds they raised to a *junta central directiva* in San Francisco, which in turn remitted them to Mexico, "approximately $1,000 every two weeks."[32]

Pitti argues that the French invasion, President Juárez's determined resistance to the great power's aggression, and Mexico's victory at Puebla, combined with the juntas' astonishing success in mobilizing support, emboldened the miners to resist exploitative policy changes that

Quicksilver implemented beginning in 1863—the same year the first anniversary of the Battle of Puebla was celebrated. It is not hard to see how one set of developments would lead to the other. Newspapers and pamphlets arrived regularly at New Almaden. Spanishtown residents gathered to hear news from Mexico read aloud, as well as of the progress of their own supportive patriotic efforts, detailed in letters and reports by correspondents. Spanishtowners also congregated for fundraising events and Mexican national holidays, marked by stirring speeches. The US Civil War added motivating talking points, as the juntas embraced the Union cause as a moral crusade against slavery, which Mexico had abolished decades before. Tensions built in 1864: French forces reached Sonora, the home state of many miners; Democrats opposed Lincoln's reelection by calling for appeasement of the South's treason; and Quicksilver management kept finding new ways to exploit its workforce.[33]

The papers and activists supported Lincoln's reelection in 1864, comparing the president with Juárez, and his opponents with traitors in Mexico who supported the French occupation. Complaints about the mining company were spiced with comparisons of its treatment of miners to slavery. When, on the heels of Lincoln's reelection that November, the company's hired security evicted some complaining workers, "outright protests" began. And yet, the following January, management went further, declaring the miners' self-built Spanishtown homes to be company property, for which it would begin charging rent. Hundreds of miners stopped work, and as many as a thousand confronted the management with a list of demands. The company retreated and signed an agreement, but it soon reneged. Another worker walkout ensued, followed by management promising some concessions before again striking back with more firings, evictions, and renewed exploitative measures. Workers apparently planned to go on an indefinite strike at the end of month, leading the company to appeal for intervention by the county sheriff, state militia, and the Northern California regiment of the Union army, which set up camp nearby for a week. The threat of overwhelming force—which US mining companies would, in fact, use against their workers on both sides of the border in the early twentieth century—quelled the 1865 Spanishtown revolt. More conflict and strikes broke out in 1866. Some concessions were won, but lacking a real union organization and any recognized labor rights, New Almaden's Latino labor force began to dwindle, increasingly replaced by white workers recruited by the company. There would never again be another strike. Both the mainly Mexican, foundational era of mercury mining in California, and the revolt that erupted there in the 1860s, faded with the passing of the century.[34]

Thus, before California became world famous as the Golden State, it could well have become known as the mercury state, or the Mexican labor-colonia state.[35] The Mexican American experience across the Southwest did not begin in either urban barrios or seasonal, migratory farmwork. Mining companies and the railroads drove the initial demand for Mexican-immigrant labor toward the end of the nineteenth and early twentieth centuries.[36] In the twentieth, Mexican farmworker colonias proliferated far more than all of California's mining towns, company towns, and railway-station towns combined, but mercury mining played the pioneering role in an emerging new era of exploiting Mexican labor at scale, and in its segregation into virtually hidden, self-built shelter communities.

After the creation of the first Spanishtown, a century would pass before sustained and effective efforts were mounted to organize those communities—California's "colonia complex"—to reform their work, their living conditions, and the opportunities available to their children.[37] In the post–World War II era, a new history would begin to unfold nearby, when an organizer from a breakthrough Los Angeles Mexican American community organization began working the agricultural colonias just east of San Jose and was taken to meet a young man named Cesar Chavez. After succeeding there, the organizer ventured not far afield to Stockton, where he encountered a promising young woman, born in another far-off corporate mining town in another state, who after a name-changing marriage became known as Dolores Huerta.

The Coal Miner's Daughter

Dawson, in northeast New Mexico, where Dolores Huerta came into the world in 1930, was once a booming, coal-mining, Phelps Dodge company town on the Vermejo River, at the southern, open end of a canyon of the Sangre de Cristo Mountains.[38] A horrific mine explosion in 1913—the second-deadliest in US history—killed 263 miners, including Huerta's uncle Marcial, before Dolores was born.[39] Marcial's remains were buried in the cemetery among the fallen miners' graves, sectioned off and marked by distinctive black iron crosses.[40] "You will never forget it," says a popular guide to New Mexico ghost towns about the forlorn cemetery. "It is a hard person who is not deeply moved by the sight."[41]

As a company town, Dawson had no government—it was run by the mining corporation. The town's local elections were for the company's "Welfare Committee," organized in the early 1920s. By then, women had won the right to vote throughout the country, and in New Mexico they had been voting in school-board elections since the previous century, before it became a state. But only men could vote for representatives on the Phelps Dodge Welfare Committee, and they were divided by "nationality" for voting purposes. The men voted for a representative of the mining district they lived in, and for a representative of their "nationality," which appeared on the ballot in a revealing order: "American, Italian, Slav, Greek, Spanish-American, Old Mex. Mexican, Negro."[42] Dawson's few Black families lived at the end of a Dawson back road, in a tiny clump of homes known as "Coontown." Dolores's father was classed as "Old Mexico Mexican." According to what her aunts told her, their family at one time also lived among the "Negros" of Coontown.

Dolores's parents, Alicia Chávez and Juán Fernández, were born, met, and married in Dawson when Alicia was seventeen and Juán was twenty. He lost a brother-in-law in the same mine accident that killed one of Alicia's brothers. But for all they had in common, Juán and Alicia were different from the start, and they soon grew more so. Alicia was from an old Hispano family with generations in New Mexico.[43] For a time, she was registered as a Republican; later, in California, she would become an independent business owner, and there she organized a local Hispano small-business association. Juán was the son of a Mexican immigrant, a coal miner, a committed labor organizer with the United Mine Workers of America (UMWA), and a Democratic Party activist. Their upbringing in a paternalistic, authoritarian, and racially stratified company town such as Dawson makes it all the more remarkable that Alicia had the courage to leave Juán, who abused her, and take their children to nearby Las Vegas, New Mexico.

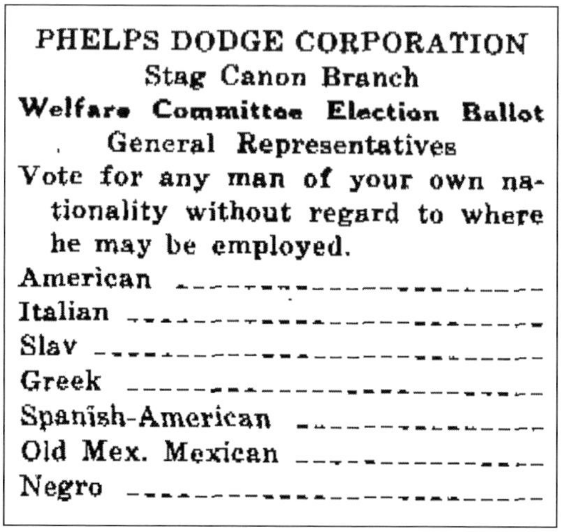

PHELPS DODGE CORPORATION
Stag Canon Branch
Welfare Committee Election Ballot
General Representatives
Vote for any man of your own nationality without regard to where he may be employed.

American ____________________
Italian ____________________
Slav ____________________
Greek ____________________
Spanish-American ____________________
Old Mex. Mexican ____________________
Negro ____________________

Welfare Committee Election Ballot, published in the town paper, The Dawson News, *on December 22, 1921. The order of the "nationalities" is not alphabetical, nor does it correspond to the relative size of each group; rather, it appears to be a ranking of ethno-racial status. Dawson News Archives, Volume 1, No.47, December 22, 1921, p. 257.*

Eventually, Alicia and the children headed west to Stockton, where, after spending years working several jobs at once, she managed to become a small-business owner and community leader. After Alicia left, Juán didn't last long in Dawson, and he may even have been forced to leave the company town. The Great Depression led Phelps Dodge to close all but one of its mines in the canyon, dismiss the single men, and reduce the family men to working three days per week. The company was also notorious for firing union activists and banishing them.[44] Juán ended up following Alicia to the Las Vegas area, where he continued his UMWA activism with greater success at the hard-metal mining camp at Tererro, around a couple of mountain ridges toward the old state capital of Santa Fe. Juán came to head the Tererro union local, and in 1938, at the age of thirty, was elected to the New Mexico House of Representatives. Fernández formed part of a new "labor bloc" in the state's lower house.[45]

As for Dawson, by 1950 it was but one of hundreds of Southwestern ghost towns, many of them abandoned mining settlements. Nearly every structure had been razed or rolled out. Dawson's mines were not closed for workers' safety, but because Phelps Dodge no longer wanted to pay them to extract coal from deep within the hills.[46] The site's most visible remaining feature is the cemetery, a thicket of mainly white crosses staked into a lonely meadow.

Dawson Cemetery, where hundreds of miners killed in explosions were buried, including an uncle of Dolores Huerta's before she was born. Photo by Geraint Smith.

The company town is not a US invention, but in establishing thousands of them, across two centuries from coast to coast, American business leaders perfected its several incarnations—from mining towns to railway stations to brickyards and other factory towns.[47] Eighteen years after Dolores Huerta was born, Gloria Molina, whose story is featured in our first book, also started life in a company town just outside Los

Angeles city limits, in Simons Brick Yard Number 2, known to Eastsiders as *El Pueblo de Simons*.[48] Both Simons Brick in California and the Phelps Dodge copper mining company, which built Dawson in New Mexico, held their towns up as model communities, business-designed utopias. But the company towns shared a fundamental purpose with what would seem to be their opposite, the Bracero Program—the agricultural guest-worker arrangement with Mexico started during World War II—and its camps. Both were designed to extract labor from controlled workforces, albeit controlled in different ways, and thereby avoid any possibility of workers organizing themselves autonomously—that is, unionizing.

Farmworker Colonias and Resistance

California farms began employing Mexicans on a large scale early in the twentieth century, as Asian immigrant workers were violently driven out and increasingly restrictive immigration policies choked off new arrivals from across the Pacific.[49] In Southern California, especially, the border's proximity had the benefit—for the growers—that Mexican migrant workers initially did not settle like the Chinese and Japanese. As one grower, in testimony to a congressional committee in 1911, said of the Mexicans he hired, "I don't know where they come from. They just keep coming, year after year. When the work is finished, I do not know where they go."[50]

Labor migration from Mexico accelerated during World War I and grew into the next decade, as immigration policies became ever more restrictive for southern and eastern Europeans as well as for Asians. Filipino immigrants were an exception to these policies because the US had colonized their homeland; the colonial relationship meant they could not be deported. "Time and again," activist writer Carey McWilliams observed, "the growers have emphasized the fact that the Mexican, unlike the Filipino, can be deported."[51] And yet, the migratory Mexican farmworkers began to settle.

Ernesto Galarza—scholar, author, labor organizer, and union leader who, as a child in the 1910s, had been a farmworker with his family—wrote probingly about domestic farmworkers, corporate agribusiness, and braceros.[52] Galarza devoted years to trying to organize both the domestics and the braceros, and ultimately concluded that the availability of either braceros, or "wets" (as he, too, often referred to the undocumented), made unionizing farmworkers impossible. He depicted the formation of colonias as a form of migratory worker resistance to the "continuous turmoil" of imposed and enforced mobility.

> I didn't have an appreciation of what mobility does to people—to families and to individuals—until I came back to California to work with the National Farm Labor Union. And then I saw at first hand how people, farmworkers especially, strive for stability. The Mexican families particularly sought out a place where they could have steady work and where they could establish community, kinship of some sort. So I began to see up and down the state of California these little clusters of communities—"colonias," they were called. Some were very small, not more than twenty-five or thirty people; others were quite large, as the Bakersfield or the Imperial Valley colonias. This is where people began to drift and settle down out of this continuous turmoil of mobility. They came back and spent the winter season living a community life that sort of recharged them and gave them the comfort of kinship and of family connections and of communities and of neighborhoods.[53]

Mexican colonia settlements, depending on the definition used, could have a variety of origins. In some cases, such as with *La Colonia Mexicana* of Shafter, near Bakersfield, farmers encouraged their creation outside city limits—whether to stabilize their workforce, or to deftly lodge it away from the towns, neighborhoods, and schools they kept to themselves, or both. McWilliams highlighted the segregationist motive, archly observing that the location of the colonias was neither accidental nor natural. "On the contrary," he continued, "location of the colonias has been carefully planned." He argued that they were placed just far enough away to make separate schools necessary and "to minimize civic conveniences in the satellite colonia."[54]

According to Galarza, as California agriculture became increasingly corporatized and "family farms" receded into myth, what came to be known as agribusiness favored a mobile field-worker labor force with high turnover. This contributed to a wholesale transition from Asians from across the vast ocean to migrant Mexican farmworkers from across the nearby border. Under these circumstances, the formation and growth of colonias, however substandard the shelter they provided, were acts of resistance to the human and economic costs of constant mobility. This aspect of the colonia phenomenon became vividly apparent in two oft-repeated developments: first, when settlements were razed and the residents who were forced out reconstituted their communities elsewhere; and second, when residents resisted redevelopment plans that would destroy the homes they had built for themselves.[55]

Getting Organized

Dolores Huerta is so identified with California farmworkers, Cesar Chavez, and their historic Mexican American labor union that she was often mistaken as having been a farmworker herself. But she could hardly have been more unlike Cesar, who *had* been a migrant farmworker, was from a farmworker family, and was still living in a farmworker colonia just outside of San Jose when they eventually met through their involvement with LA's expanding CSO.

Fred Ross, the organizing guru who had devoted his previous five years to helping build CSO in Los Angeles, was conducting his trademark "house meetings" to set up a CSO chapter among the colonias of East San Jose when he was taken to meet Chavez.[56] That the colonia matters in understanding the California Latino-empowerment experience is due in no small measure to the emergence of the house-meeting community-organizing strategy in Ross's prior work among colonias of the citrus belt surrounding LA. This strategy was adapted to the particular conditions of Mexican American communities in Southern California, starting with their relative lack of organization.[57] Herman Gallegos—originally from a mining town in Colorado—was another discovery of the San Jose CSO organizing drive. Gallegos did not live in the Eastside colonias, but he worked at a gas station among them while attending

San Jose State College. He and Chavez, already friends, teamed up to help start the CSO chapter and worked the intense voter-registration drive that was every new chapter's first project. After outperforming all others in the campaign that registered four thousand new voters among the colonias hugging the east side of San Jose, Gallegos and Chavez were elected the chapter's first president and vice president.[58]

The fast CSO startup in San Jose and its successful voter drive owed much to 1952's open presidential election—the first without an incumbent running since 1928. It provided both a prominent focal point for collective action and a sense of urgency.[59] If there was any prospect that voting could benefit the community, the chance to give it a try came with an absolute and imminent deadline—not unlike the ticking clock in that year's iconic movie, *High Noon*. Harry Truman, who had the US military bogged down in a stalemate in Korea, was retiring, and both Democrats and Republicans tried to recruit World War II–hero Dwight Eisenhower to be their candidate. Eisenhower, a political centrist, tapped red-baiting California Senator Richard Nixon to be his attack-dog running mate on the Republican ticket.[60]

That same year, Congress revised naturalization policy. The "McCarran–Walter Act," as it was called, is generally known for its restrictionist immigration provisions. But in one key respect, it gave ethnic organizations like CSO, which was Mexican American in all but name, a new way to organize and promote civic engagement between elections. Henceforth, immigrants over fifty who had lived in the country for at least twenty years were exempted from the English-language requirement and could take the citizenship test in their native language.[61] CSO got into the naturalization business, organizing citizenship classes and mobilizing immigrant seniors to enroll. After the McCarran–Walter Act eased naturalization for older long-term immigrants, CSO launched its citizenship program in LA with four classes in 1953. By November 1954, the program had grown to thirty-five classes offered across the metropolis. Some three thousand enrollees completed the process in a mass swearing-in ceremony that month at the Hollywood Bowl.[62]

New US citizens take the Oath of Allegiance in a mass ceremony at the Hollywood Bowl on November 12, 1954. Los Angeles Daily News *Negatives Collection, Library Special Collections, Charles E. Young Research Library, UCLA.*

Success in San Jose was pivotal on several levels to exporting the LA model of Latino empowerment to the rest of the state and beyond. It brought in Chavez, turning him into an organizer and CSO's star workhorse. According to Ross, Chavez registered voters for a biblical forty straight nights before taking an ordered night off.[63] It put Ross back onto the payroll of Saul Alinsky's Industrial Areas Foundation, which had funded his organizing in LA. He soon got Alinsky to also hire Chavez, and together they plunged into organizing new CSO chapters full-time, all over the state and into Arizona.[64] The San Jose experience furthermore fatefully connected CSO with Bay Area activist priests. It also reconnected Ross with Mexican American colonias of farmworkers. That, in turn, led to the organization's first beachhead in the San Joaquin Valley, where it discovered Dolores.

La Colonia Mexicana of Shafter, California

The rise of Dean Florez from *La Colonia Mexicana,* just outside the Central Valley farm town of Shafter, near Bakersfield, to a leadership position in the California State Senate, captures several themes of this book: the expansion and diversification of the California Latino-empowerment project, which was born in and was long dominated by Eastside LA; the incorporation of new talent into that quest and their acquisition of transformative political skills; the role of mentors in the advent of a new generation of leaders; the effects of growing internal competition among Latino leaders and their networks; the tapping of new resources to advance the empowerment cause; and more.[65] Florez presaged a trend that would take a couple of decades to become apparent. On one hand, Latino LA made Florez into a political professional, but unlike many other Latinos who came to LA from somewhere else and made their career there, Dean chose to return to the rural town of Shafter to run for office. His success suggested that LA Latinos, and in particular those from the Eastside, would not forever dominate California Latino politics.

Florez was part of the third generation of his family to live in what they simply referred to as *La Colonia*. Dean grew up there until his immediate family moved into Shafter, but he continued to take the school bus back to the colonia daily to his grandmother's home, where the family had dinner with her every evening. As an unincorporated community within Kern County, Dean's colonia had no government of its own, nor paved streets, sewer system, or trash pickup. At least a school bus rumbled through its dirt roads to pick up the kids every day—early and all at one spot—to take them into Shafter and back. Dean became a record-setting track star at Shafter High, and like his dad before him, played varsity football—until he badly broke a leg during the first game of his senior year. His parents, in the stands, heard his leg snap in two.

Florez had been scouted and was looking to score a football scholarship to Arizona State as his ticket out of Shafter when he suffered what, in retrospect, he came to call his "lucky break." Forced to completely change his plans and dreams, Dean focused intently on healing and running again. When a physically restored Florez arrived at UCLA in 1982 on a track scholarship, as a transfer from Bakersfield College, he did not know what East LA was. A fourth-generation Californian—with ancestors before that from New Mexico and Texas—he spoke no Spanish, and the local Chicano students branded him a *pocho* (i.e., assimilated). There, Dean began what he calls his "East LA training," his process of learning about what was to him another world, both culturally and politically—the LA-barrio-based world. In a couple of years, he learned enough to be swept into office as the first Latino to be elected UCLA student body president.[66] And he did not stop there.

Dean Florez with campaign supporters in 1986, celebrating their victory in making him the first Chicano elected UCLA student body president. Courtesy of Dean Florez.

Dean Florez eventually returned to Shafter—armed with his UCLA degree, an MBA from Harvard, and expertise in municipal finance—to employ political skills he had learned from Eastside LA politicians. He led a campaign that registered seventeen thousand new voters, got his mother elected to the Shafter City Council, and went on to challenge and unseat an incumbent Republican state assembly member. From there, Florez was elected to the state Senate, rose to the position of majority leader, and openly explored a run for statewide office—with Gavin Newsom as his campaign chair.

In his political career, Florez played a key role in expanding Latino empowerment from LA to the state's Central Valley—which could only have happened by combining his colonia origins with his LA education and connections. In the end, he passed on a statewide run and talked his friend Gavin into running for lieutenant governor instead. Termed out of legislative office, Florez returned to LA, the city that had transformed him years before, and started his own business—without ever having lived in an urban Latino barrio. Back in the colonia, his secret asset had been Nana, his politics- and sports-obsessed grandmother, in a home without indoor plumbing, built on a dirt street by her farmworker family a century before, when the community was founded.

The Long Arc of California Latino Empowerment

The previous episodes, stretching in time from the mid-nineteenth century to the early twenty-first, illustrate a good part of the diverse settings and conditions in which California Latinos have labored to fashion an effective politics of inclusion, in a state they helped make perhaps the most highly developed part of the world.[67] While understanding this diversity of origins helps decenter the singular "up from the (big-city) barrio" narrative of Latino progress, for California it also affirms how LA's Eastside interacted with those different communities and drew human capital from them. This would eventually radiate back out and expand the project of Latina/o political empowerment well beyond the metropolis. Openness to outsiders has long been recognized as essential for centers of innovation across history and around the world, and especially as a source of urban American and Californian dynamism. This applied as well to the late-twentieth-century world of Los Angeles Latino activism, from the Eastside to Westwood, UCLA's tony urban village.

A compendium of varied narratives helps us see the role of other key factors, like that of strategic allies and alliances between the Mexicans, Californios, and Chileans in nineteenth-century mining towns; and the Mexican American and Filipino farmworkers in twentieth-century San Joaquin Valley. We showed in our first book how interethnic allies of LA Latinos such as Jewish activists in city and labor politics, as well as Black, Italian, and Armenian Americans in state politics, were critical to California Latino political development. As we shall see in the next chapter, a transcontinental, interethnic, but deeply Catholic alliance of the 1960s would boost and poignantly mark the journey of Latino political inclusion and empowerment.

Chapter 2

Building an Electorate and the Dream of Empowerment

History had a way of freezing Huerta in its bright strobe.[1]

The first and last steps the coal miner's daughter took toward the rich ambassador's son came eight years apart in California. Of the times that history brought Dolores and Bobby together, the world most remembers the last, when they stood side by side as he made his final, tragically hopeful remarks to the world. Photo by Frank Carroll/NBC Newswire via Getty Images.

Dolores Huerta's encounters with Robert F. Kennedy are landmarks in the story of California Latino political development. That story includes the Latina/o-empowerment project's expansion beyond Los Angeles, as well as its persistent rootedness in LA. Huerta and Kennedy first met in 1960 near San Diego, where Dolores was directing an election-year voter-registration drive for Community Service Organization (CSO), the legendary founding effort of Mexican American political empowerment in the state.[2] The visiting Kennedy was managing his surviving older brother John's presidential campaign. Dolores had a gripe to air about that campaign and was fearlessly taking it to the top. Cesar Chavez was then living in LA, where he was in charge of CSO's efforts throughout California and Arizona.

By the next time Kennedy and Huerta met, several years later, Dolores had left CSO to help Chavez build the United Farm Workers (UFW) union in the San Joaquin Valley, well to the north. Kennedy, having resigned as attorney general in the Lyndon Johnson administration, was now a first-term US senator from New York, participating in a hearing in Delano on agricultural labor. This was the epicenter of the farmworkers' movement, where the UFW was headquartered; the grape pickers were on strike, and they were about to march three hundred miles up the valley to the state capitol in Sacramento. The senator famously humiliated the county sheriff in that hearing, and the next day cheered the farmworkers as they set off on their march. Two years later, Kennedy was back in Delano to be with Chavez when he broke his first public fast.

The final occasion that brought Dolores and Bobby together was back in LA, where the UFW had just wrapped up its biggest effort to date: mobilizing the Eastside vote in the pivotal California Democratic primary. That last time, as well as the first, Dolores approached Kennedy determined to overcome invisibility, and she succeeded.[3] By that day, June 5, 1968, CSO and UFW had built and mobilized a California Latino electorate capable of deciding a statewide race, a presidential nomination, and just possibly a transformative national election. That effort ended tragically in LA, but within a decade the union would try again, from coast to coast, all the way to the Democratic National Convention in New York City.

Mexican American civil rights activism is often taken to mean the farmworkers movement that Huerta helped lead in the 1960s and '70s.

But even just in California, the wider Mexican American/Latino–empowerment cause well predated the UFW.[4] Both Dolores and Cesar Chavez were already prominent leaders of the LA-based empowerment movement years before they left to organize the UFW in San Joaquin Valley.[5] The road to Latina/o political empowerment in California, so to speak, was laid down in layers. The 1930s saw Huerta's family settle in urban Stockton, which would become a key point on that road, while Cesar's family came later from Arizona to join the migrant farmworker trail. In the 1950s, CSO recruited, politicized, and developed Cesar and Dolores into organizers and leaders, ultimately bringing them to Boyle Heights, where the organization was headquartered. First Cesar and then Dolores moved on in the 1960s to build the new UFW layer atop the one they helped develop during their years in CSO.[6]

New Start in Stockton

Dolores and her brothers started school in New Mexico, but by Christmas 1936, Alicia again moved her children, this time to Stockton, California, where her sister lived. Even in the depths of the Great Depression, Stockton had work. As an inland seaport on the San Joaquin River, in the midst of the great California Delta, Stockton connected the vast agricultural San Joaquin Valley to San Francisco Bay and the world, attracting migrants from across the Pacific, as well as from across the country. Alicia found work as a waitress by day, at a cannery by night, and within a few years was able to open an inner-city lunch-counter eatery. Her widowed father, Herculano Chávez, soon also left Dawson and moved in, helping with the children. What developed into Alicia's little restaurant—the Delta Cafe—was not in a barrio but in the downtown area, at the edge of skid row, among Stockton's intermingled Chinatown, Little Manila, and Japantown communities.[7]

Dolores describes her mother as having been shy but highly active and competitive. She pushed her also-shy daughter to be active as well. But the muggy port town made Dolores sickly, until 1941, when she spent a summer back in New Mexico with her father. By then a traveling salesman based in Albuquerque, Juán hawked cookware far and wide on credit, and collected payments. Accompanying her father not only let

Dolores see much of her enchanted homeland within a day's road trip, she also observed a line of work that involved making pitches to strangers door to door and later following up with them—much like community organizing, which requires the same skills, energy, and dedication.

Alicia Chávez with her children, Marshall Fernández, Dolores C. Fernández, and John X. Fernández. Courtesy of Huerta Family.

That fall, her health restored, Dolores was back in Stockton and in grade school, along with her extraordinarily diverse friends and classmates, as World War II began to rage in Europe and across the Pacific in Asia. The US was far along in preparing to enter the war and had relaunched the military draft. Across the country, registration and enlistments surged—with Juán in Albuquerque among them. The December 7 bombing of Pearl Harbor by Japanese forces drew the US directly into the war and especially rocked California. The following February, Southern Californians were panicked by misplaced fear of an aerial attack on the mainland by Japan.[8] The spring brought the sudden forced removal and incarceration of Japanese Americans all along the West Coast, including schoolmate friends of Dolores. The following year brought race riots in LA, with off-duty servicemen attacking Mexican American "zoot suiters."[9] Amid this upheaval, Alicia remarried in 1942, and with her new husband, James Richards, took over the Mikado Hotel, which was on the same block as her cafe. The new couple acquired the hotel from Alicia's friend and business neighbor, Micky Kamachi—as a result of the evacuation of the entire Japanese American community—and they renamed it the Hotel Richards.[10] The family moved into the hotel as the war intensified on three fronts.

Seasonal agricultural workers favored the low-rent Hotel Richards, by skid row, where during harvests some growers mustered transient field workers and loaded them onto buses.[11] This gave Alicia and Dolores contact with braceros—or rather, *ex*-bracero contract farm laborers from Mexico.[12] The very first five hundred braceros admitted under the new program had arrived in Stockton that September for the sugar-beet harvest. The young men who ended up at the hotel had been unhappy with their assigned field jobs and bracero camp life. So they skipped their contracts and looked elsewhere for housing and work, although they were now undocumented. Alicia bugged those hotel guests to continue sending money home to their families in Mexico, and she helped them with their remittances.

The imported-labor arrangement went on throughout the war, which Congress then extended repeatedly until 1964. The initial phase of the Bracero Program as a whole was not limited to agriculture. In fact, during the war, more braceros—the so-called *traqueros*—were employed by US railroads rather than in farmwork, but the program's image was indelibly stamped by those first five hundred men, housed at a government-run camp, for the sugar-beet harvest.[13] And yet, from even the most local point of view, the Bracero Program was at most a minor detail amid the whirlwind of wartime mobilization. At first tens and then hundreds of thousands of recruits, troops, and officers poured into California to report for duty or training. Even Dolores's father, Juán, having registered for the draft but then wisely enlisted in the US Navy, was assigned to a supply depot in Stockton. Within a couple of years, California's and the country's wartime landscape and atmosphere would be further augmented by hundreds of thousands of mainly German army prisoners of war—a widely unknown home-front experience—who would also be housed in camps and used as "guest workers."[14]

Alicia's business success in wartime California gave Dolores a middle-class upbringing in ethnically diverse Stockton. Her shyness banished, Dolores became active in her church, Girl Scouts, music lessons, and dance, and eventually even became a Stockton High majorette. Dolores picked up an Anglo boyfriend, Ralph Head, whom she married two years after she graduated and with whom she had her first two children, but they soon divorced.[15] When Dolores came of age, her mother took her to register to vote as a Republican. Not yet political, Dolores did not understand what that meant or, perhaps, what it would mean to her soon.[16]

As Dolores recalls, the Stockton of the 1930s and '40s was such a mélange of ethnicities that it hardly had distinct racial or ethnic neighborhoods. But in time she learned of the nearby colonia known as *El Barrio del Chivo*, or "Goat Valley," with its unpaved streets and lack of drainage, indoor plumbing, power, or sidewalks.[17] Later, at Stockton College, on the north side, Dolores learned that out-of-town white students were advised not to venture south of Harding Way—meaning the southern two-thirds of the city, including the downtown area and Asian American communities she lived among. In 1945, Dolores's younger brother was beaten up by white boys for wearing a zoot suit to a party celebrating the end of the war. She would later recount that the issue of police abuse of Mexican Americans played a key role in her decision to dedicate herself to social activism.[18]

Dolores worked secretarial jobs until she earned her credential to teach grade school. Meanwhile, the top organizer of LA's CSO, Fred Ross, a native San Franciscan, had moved back to the Bay Area in 1952 to take another job. In his spare time, Ross started the new CSO chapter in San Jose, seventy-five miles southwest of Stockton. There, he met promising recruits: activist public nurse Alicia Hernandez, freshly minted college grad Herman Gallegos, and twenty-five-year-old former farmworker Cesar Chavez, and his wife, Helen.[19]

Colonias Matter

The San Jose CSO chapter had a weekend radio program on KLOK, which is how Dolores and Stockton's Mexican American community first heard about the organization and the services it offered.[20] Fred Ross's arrival in 1955 to set up a Stockton chapter was thus heralded in advance, and not everyone in the community welcomed the news. A former college teacher invited Dolores to one of Ross's house meetings, but she heard from her cousins that a businessman she knew was urging people to stay away. The man, a family friend, had a drugstore on the same block as her mother's hotel, which Dolores and her children had moved back into after her divorce. The druggist claimed Ross and his associate were communists.

Although Joe McCarthy had been formally censured by the Senate at the end of the year before, the "era" that bore his name was not over—certainly not in California. Nixon, the state's top anti-communist, was in his first term as vice president, and first in line to succeed Eisenhower. One of Huerta's jobs had been at the Sheriff's Department, where she had contact with FBI agents. An agent looked into the matter for her and assured Dolores that CSO was a legit community organization, free of communist influence. Huerta's politicization may have started when she confronted her businessman neighbor over the lies he was spreading about Ross, and thus figured out what she believed to be his motive. Like her mother, the druggist was a Mexican American business owner and a Republican. Apparently, he did not want CSO registering fellow Mexican Americans, who would likely vote Democrat. Having heard that CSO was coming over from San Jose, he would certainly have known how alarmed his fellow Republicans there had become over the historic registration drive of three years before. It had become a front-page scandal when the party had its poll watchers act aggressively to intimidate first-time Mexican American voters on Election Day.[21]

As for Ross, despite his years organizing Mexican Americans, he still spoke no Spanish. In East San Jose he had the help of Alicia Hernandez, who set up meetings and served as a translator, but in Stockton he had to manage without her. That was how he first impressed Dolores. Ross had his house-meeting script carefully written out in Spanish, and he read it aloud phonetically. "The guy was so courageous!" Dolores exclaimed. And that was not all. Huerta's own accounts have varied on how persuasive she found Ross on that first encounter. In more than one, she said she was skeptical that these little, homey gatherings could lead to a general meeting with enough attendees to start a new organization. Dolores said she had never heard of such a thing and called Ross's claim—or Ross himself in making it—"slightly *loco*."[22]

What Dolores has more often recalled is that she was most impressed by hearing and seeing that CSO in LA had successfully fought police abuse of Mexican Americans, and that several cops had even been convicted and jailed for it. Ross brought receipts—newspaper clippings that backed him up. Separate incidents of LA police beatings of Mexican Americans in December 1951 and January 1952 were widely exposed by a CSO campaign. This effort involved Councilman Roybal, whom the organization had helped elect and reelect; an initially reluctant American Civil Liberties Union; and an array of savvy media tactics. In the end, attempts by the LAPD and prosecutors to frame the victims, among them the CSO president at the time, for assaulting the cops failed spectacularly. Police officers were indicted and tried, five were sentenced to jail, others were fired, and dozens received official reprimands for their abuses.[23] LA had never seen anything like it, and neither had Dolores. She agreed to host a house meeting, but she was not yet an organizer, and it showed. Only two friends attended her meeting; neither of them joined.

Expanding CSO into Northern California positioned it strategically closer to Sacramento, the state capital, where Huerta would become the first-ever dedicated Latina/o policy lobbyist, working for the organization.[24] These steps would not only be transformative for Dolores, they led to establishing CSO in state and even national politics, and soon connected it to organized labor at the national level, with consequences for the rest of the century. And furthermore, they allowed Dolores to acquire the skills that decades later would let her play a critical, but largely unknown, role in the national battle over immigration reform.

Registering Voters, Making Citizens, Organizing Farmworkers

In spite of her initial skepticism, the first Stockton CSO general meeting in 1955 was well attended and fully won Dolores over. She dove into building the new chapter, volunteering to serve as its secretary and registering voters. Soon, her two nights a week of door-to-door voter registration grew to six. And while she was at it, Dolores reregistered herself as a Democrat. She got her mother and younger brother involved in growing the chapter and its work. Alicia applied her competitive drive to registering the most voters every week. Dolores met a recruit named Ventura Huerta and married him later that year, taking the surname under which she would become famous. Not only did Dolores change her party registration and devote her evenings to the organization, but soon she quit her job and abandoned her fledgling teaching career altogether. In time, her dedication to the CSO cause would hasten the end of her second marriage as well.

That same year, Dolores met the highly touted Cesar Chavez at a CSO dinner in Oakland, and she was famously underwhelmed. Both their families had come to California from dry Southwestern states during the Depression, but they had landed in very different places and had starkly differing experiences. The state's agricultural economy—now the most robust in the country—underlay both their families' livelihoods, but they saw and lived completely different dimensions of it. Besides, Dolores had developed into a confident, outgoing, college-trained educator accustomed to performing in public. She had lived most of her life since adolescence in a downtown hotel run by her mother in a gritty but bustling and highly diverse city. At both Stockton High and Stockton College, she was a contemporary of the young woman, only three years her elder, who went on to become the movie star Janet Leigh. Future jazz legend Dave Brubeck graduated from the college music department a few years before Dolores enrolled, and he played gigs around the town before the war. Born in the Jazz Age, Dolores loved the music, learned to play more than one instrument herself, and aspired to be a professional dancer. Jazz could well have been the soundtrack of her life to that point, but she would turn her talents to performing in ways and arenas far afield from music and dance.

Quick and articulate—dubbed *Siete Lenguas* ("Seven Tongues") by her grandfather—Dolores may have come on too strong for the still painfully shy Cesar, who slipped away after a polite hello.[25] It would take years of them both working for CSO, but mainly not together, to get to know each other. It was *that* shared experience that gave them big things in common. First Cesar in 1952, and then Dolores in 1955, had the novel and life-changing experience of being politically awakened and recruited by Fred Ross, whose message was powered by what Mexican Americans in an LA barrio had been able to accomplish in a handful of years. From then on, Dolores and Cesar devoted themselves to acquiring and growing their ability and means to organize and improve whole communities and, by extension, the world.

By fateful coincidence, Cesar and Dolores, independently of each other, were drawn into organizing farmworkers in 1958. Cesar in Oxnard and Dolores in Stockton found that—contrary to opinions otherwise—it could be done, that *they* could do it. But at the same time, they discovered that the federal Bracero Program was the greatest impediment to developing a union that could reform the travesty of farm labor in California. They saw firsthand not only that the growers were organized against their efforts, but also that law, policy, and government at every level were stacked against local, residential farmworkers—their fellow Mexican American Californians.

Prior to those organizing experiences, however, Dolores and Cesar had been more concerned *for* the braceros than *about* the program that had brought them to California, or its effects on local farmworkers. Chavez had assisted Father Donald McDonnell's ministering in bracero camps. Dolores described her mother, Alicia, as acting as surrogate mom to the young ex-braceros staying at her hotel, whom she even took to dances to meet local girls. In fact, after her second divorce, Alicia married an ex-bracero named Juan Silva.[26] Dolores had even secreted injured men out of the bracero camp to get them needed medical attention.[27] But organizing local community farmworkers to register to vote, bring them into her CSO chapter, and later get them to join a workers' association exposed Dolores to the impact the Bracero Program was having on them, just as Cesar experienced in Oxnard.

The Evil Genius of the Bracero Program, 1942–1964

The New Deal, with its limited and contested reformism, had already codified in federal law what would much later be understood as a dual labor-market system.[28] As a matter of national policy, this emergent system at first only split agricultural and nonagricultural work and workers but eventually bifurcated urban labor and job markets as well. There was no New Deal for farmworkers: Rural labor was denied unions, work protections, and participation in Social Security. As labor historian Cletus Daniel put it, agricultural and industrial workers long shared a "community of powerlessness," but the National Labor Relations Act (NLRA) of 1935 marked their "point of abrupt divergence."[29] The exclusion of agriculture—the economic sector that still had the most workers in 1930—from New Deal reforms "transformed farmworkers in California . . . into what was for all practical purposes a rural caste." [30] Worse was to come with the advent of World War II.

The US national commitment to a second and much more far-reaching "total war" mobilization provided the pretext and cover for officially deepening the bifurcation of its job and labor markets by reintroducing imported contract workers.[31] After World War II, the ideal imported-labor force could only be workable in large-scale, seasonal agriculture.[32] This is where, decades later, the repeated extension of the Bracero Program came in. At its height, well over four hundred thousand braceros were admitted annually from 1956 to 1959. Prudent, sustainable exploitation at such a scale required that workers be interim, transient, and regularly rotated in and out. Such conditions would be unviable with citizens or even just resident immigrants, given their families, social relations, and legal rights. The perfect proletarians should be imported without family, preferably unable to communicate in English, ideally racially and religiously distinct from both US elites and most Americans. Perhaps best of all, the imported could be easily deported: "a labor force," as Ernesto Galarza put it, "that could be expanded or contracted at will," without social or political consequence.[33] Relative social invisibility and isolation were key to this highly exploitative government-sanctioned program. Such workers, and their work, were cut off from social contact, especially from those most likely to be interested in their well-being: idealistic religious activists, labor organizers, reporters, reformers, progressive prosecutors, and perhaps concerned politicians.

Both the new law of 1951 and contracts between growers and workers barred braceros from anything other than strictly seasonal farmwork and from handling any machinery. It also required they return to Mexico every year. Thus, the division of labor within seasonal agriculture alone consigned Mexicans to the most difficult, worst paid, and least visible work. It also prevented workers from establishing any stability, home life, or community in the US. Ronald Mize argues that the Bracero Program was a "total institution," which, much like prisons and mental hospitals, dehumanized workers and made collective resistance nearly impossible.[34]

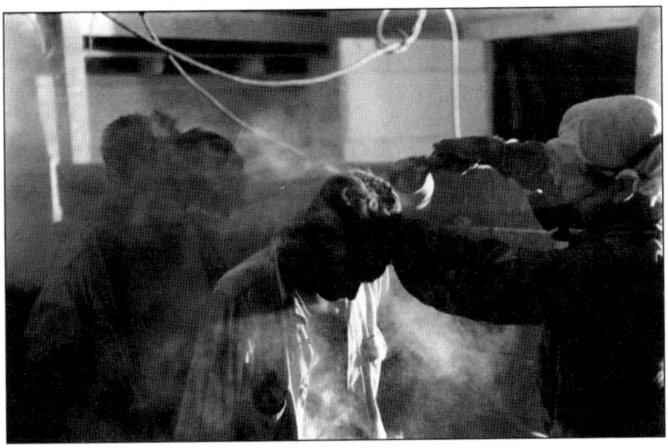

A bracero gets fumigated with DDT upon entry to the United States in July 1959. Photo by Michael Rougier/The LIFE Picture Collection/Shutterstock.

Among the program's aggravating factors was that the ongoing recruitment and mobilization of prospective braceros in Mexico served to stimulate, rather than substitute for, undocumented immigration, leading to the national campaign of mass apprehensions and deportations officially dubbed "Operation Wetback" in 1954.[35] At the same time, concern was rising within the Church about the needs of the growing, overwhelmingly Catholic Latino population. The Black civil rights movement was fostering a deepening awareness of intolerable racial inequities in American life, and this "American dilemma" was not just black and white.[36] And then there were dramatically tragic accidents that took the lives of both braceros and undocumented workers in transit, as well as the increasing political isolation of the specialty-crop growers in California, as harvesting cotton in Texas became mechanized.[37]

During most of the 1950s, criticism of the endlessly renewed program steadily mounted. Legislative design built a prizefight structure into the policy debate. Starting with the new Public Law 78 (PL 78) of 1951, each Congress reauthorized the program for another two years. Throughout the decade and into the next, the fight would resume every two years between opposing sides on the issue, the growers would win, and the opponents would regroup for the next round. But opponents, at times supported by the US Labor Department, won a few adjustments of their own. The Catholic Church, organized labor, Mexican American organizations, and others stepped up pressure on policymakers to end the program.[38] This was a growing national campaign of resistance to a corrupt and immoral national policy.

California produced several activist priests who played historic roles in focusing attention on Mexican Americans, farmworkers, and braceros, starting with Robert Lucey of Los Angeles, who went on to become archbishop of San Antonio in Texas and wielded great influence across the Southwest. Lucey became a friend and advocate of Saul Alinsky and organized his fellow clergy to recognize that the Church had a particular responsibility to address the needs of "the Spanish-speaking."[39] Similarly, a pair of passionate young Bay Area priests succeeded in leading San Francisco's archdiocese to engage Mexican Americans, with an emphasis on both community and labor organizing. These efforts had influenced the founders of CSO in LA—and later both Cesar and Dolores in Northern California, before they had met Fred Ross or heard of CSO.[40] In the late 1940s, the Bay Area duo won their archbishop's support to form a roving apostolate—dubbed the "Spanish Mission Band"—in his sprawling domain.

The Mission Band ministered to Mexicans and Mexican Americans wherever they could be found, from the colonias near the Bay to the bracero camps around Stockton. One of them, Father Donald McDonnell, set up shop just east of the San Jose city limits, where Cesar and Helen Chavez lived, and got Cesar deeply involved in his work.[41] The other priest, Father Thomas McCullough, happened to be assigned to the Stockton parish Dolores was active in. Together, the two "Macs" spent years urging labor unions to organize farmworkers. Fed up with the AFL-CIO's chronic reluctance and delays, in 1958 McCullough took matters into his own hands and set out to organize what he named the

Agricultural Workers Association, which he recruited Dolores to help develop.[42]

Father Thomas McCullough arrives at a Bracero Program labor camp to hold outdoor mass. Photo by Michael Rougier/The LIFE Picture Collection/ Shutterstock.

Cesar, meanwhile, had become a full-time traveling CSO organizer, but actually worked for Saul Alinsky's Industrial Areas Foundation. Between them, Chavez and Ross set up dozens of new chapters.[43] Back in Chicago, Alinsky's closest friend headed the United Packinghouse Workers of America (UPWA), which had organized packing sheds in Oxnard, on the coast between Los Angeles and Santa Barbara, but had had no success with the field workers and had been unable to win contracts.[44] Chavez was reassigned to organize the local Oxnard field workers into a CSO chapter and then hand them over to the union as something of an incipient bargaining unit, or at least a community-support base for the union's efforts.[45] The union funded the project through CSO, which put Cesar on CSO's staff and payroll—and moved him strategically closer to the organization's LA headquarters.

Cesar's Year in Oxnard

Toward the end of the Great Depression, after they lost their farm in Arizona, the Chavez family lived and worked for a time—miserably, by Cesar's account—in the Oxnard colonia, twenty years before he came back in 1958 to organize the community for CSO.[46] On his return, Cesar had trouble grasping that the majority of men there, who knew nothing but farmwork, could not get hired at the county's many citrus ranches. He put the issue off for weeks while he mobilized the colonia, with great success, to register and vote in that fall's elections.[47] The residents opened Cesar's eyes to what they considered their big problem, one that, once he realized it, welded together his assignment to organize farmworkers with organizing their community. The issue was the Bracero Program, whose apotheosis haunts immigration-policy debates to this day in the form of proposed new agricultural guest-worker programs. The first braceros from Mexico had arrived in Stockton in 1942, following the forced removal of Japanese Americans from the West Coast. For most of the public, "interning" the Japanese and importing braceros was overshadowed, and justified, by the ongoing World War II military mobilization, which that year turned California, in historian Kevin Starr's words, into a "garrison state."[48]

There was no Bracero Program in 1938, when Cesar lived in the Oxnard colonia with his farmworker family, first in a small tent and then a shack.[49] But when he returned in 1958 to organize farmworkers, the US was importing nearly a half million braceros a year, and the largest complex of the program's labor camps was right there, in Ventura County, near Oxnard. He had long said he wanted to organize farmworkers and had never lost touch with the farmworker life, yet he had no idea how much the Bracero Program had grown in the postwar period, nor the impact it had on the locals.[50] Now in its seventeenth year and just past its peak, the program was functioning as the perfect, near-invisible match for the growers' demand for submissive, unorganizable, seasonal labor without a community, homes, family, transportation, or freedom—other than the freedom to be shipped back to Mexico if they had a complaint, or to "skip" their contract and join the ranks of "wets," whom nobody at the time more respectfully called "undocumented workers."

Chavez was aware of the program before Fred Ross came looking for him in 1952, and had even visited bracero camps near San Jose, helping Father McDonnell set up to hear confessions and celebrate mass.[51] But as he informed Ross, he had no idea of its scale or impact. On his first day back in Oxnard, Cesar noted a curious sight he later described to his mentor in chilling terms: "Then I saw them, Fred, sort of a two-way trickle along the edge of town. Like ants, only they were men, farm workers imported from Mexico: braceros." Chavez followed the trickle returning to the "Buena Vista Camp" of the Ventura County Farm Labor Association. They passed through "a high steel fence," where he could peer inside, through the gate. "I never dreamed it would be so big!" he exclaimed to Ross. "This huge mess-hall, and behind that... rows and rows of barracks as far as you could see, that housed over four thousand workers."[52]

From Civic Inclusion to Worker Resistance

Chavez had the benefit of great timing to start his year in Oxnard. He got there not knowing the colonia's main problem, took a while to learn it, and did not know how to address it. But landing there in September 1958, in the midst of a historic state election cycle, was for him another perfect opportunity to fire up a new CSO chapter. With six weeks to go to Election Day, Chavez knew *exactly* what to do. He put off dealing with the jobs problem, which allowed him to focus on transforming the economically defeated colonia into a roaring political power machine. This was an especially good cycle, with Latino candidates on both the local and statewide ballots, and a prominent Democratic candidate for governor who earlier that year made a direct appeal for the Latino vote, running radio ads in Spanish during the primary.[53]

Fred Ross kept meticulous daily records and notes on his work and that of the people who reported to him. According to his account, Chavez blitzed Oxnard with seventy-five house meetings, pitching CSO to over three hundred residents, and called everyone twice to get them to the first general meeting. The new chapter then launched two campaigns: setting up citizenship classes (and getting hundreds of immigrant residents to enroll) and registering those who were already citizens to vote. The classes could not produce new voters in time for the election, but they contributed to a sense of community-wide civic engagement. A third campaign, to get out the vote, culminated on Election Day. Each of the colonia's fifty blocks had an organizer who contacted every registered voter in four ways—with a visit, leaflet, letter, and phone call. Radio spots and a roving car with a mounted "squawk box" resounded throughout the colonia, providing the "air war." The colonia's five precincts each had a CSO captain to monitor polling places every hour and report to the block organizers on who had already voted. As the day wore on, backup squads visited lagging voters and follow-up phone calls went out.

The front page of the Oxnard daily paper reported that well over a thousand voters went to the polls, over twice as many as in the previous election. Later, the paper published a lengthy editorial that both congratulated CSO on its successful efforts in the colonia and expressed concern. With a meticulous precinct analysis of returns befitting a crack political consultant or an academic, the newspaper asked, "But if political power is being concentrated in Colonia, who will control it and what will be its goals? . . . Good citizenship consists of more than voting for candidates with Mexican names. . . . Perhaps the Community Service Organization could tell these new voters that . . . a good citizen resists efforts of others to use him for their own purposes."[54] CSO civic-engagement efforts up and down the state both contributed to and benefited from that year's Democratic Party landslide. And they nearly elected the first Latino statewide official of the century, Hank Lopez of LA, who lost in a cliff-hanger. But the fact that Lopez was the only Democratic candidate to lose among the statewide races—despite a surge in Latino votes—indicated a lack of support for a Latino candidate from party leadership and among the party's majority of voters.[55]

Having proved himself and CSO to the colonia, and the colonia to the city and county—and perhaps to the growers as well—Chavez turned to the jobs problem, which, as far as residents were concerned, was entirely about the growers' association's complete control over farm labor, their unlimited and preferential use of braceros, and the federal, state, and local government agencies involved. Over the course of the decade, the growers had systematically driven most locals out of farmwork, even though the law stipulated that braceros could be used only when local farmworkers were not available. Chavez had trouble understanding the elaborate farm-labor system until he repeatedly went through it himself and found it impossible to get work. What the locals had been telling him became clear, so he started organizing the unemployed to go through the referral system over and over again. Cesar worked up a report on each futile attempt to be hired, compiling a mountainous evidentiary record.[56]

Cesar came to the same conclusion that legendary activists like Galarza and the two priestly Macs before him had reached separately: The bracero policy caused crippling harm. What came up during his first meeting with Oxnard colonia residents, and repeatedly afterward, was that their greatest need was to find work that they knew how to do: the field and orchard work they used to have before expansion of the Bracero Program. Chavez freely shared with Ross that he had no answer for that; when people brought it up, he had to stall. But it finally hit him: He had to make *jobs* the top priority of the Oxnard colonia CSO. He had arrived searching for "the key" to carrying out his charge of organizing local farmworkers. It was obvious, but not within the CSO repertoire. No chapter had ever had an employment committee before.[57]

Chavez was fashioning, on his own, the two major tracks of resistance to the system that immiserated domestic farmworkers and deprived them of work: bringing that system to the attention of both authorities and the public, as well as organizing those affected by it. These two dimensions basically defined the work of Ernesto Galarza, perhaps the premier activist fighting to end the Bracero Program. Galarza had worked the fields in his youth with his family, but he had managed to win a scholarship to Occidental College in LA. At the 1957 CSO board meeting in LA, the year before Chavez went to Oxnard, Galarza headed a panel on the Bracero Program and became chair of a new committee to work on the issue. Thus, with whatever level of serious commitment, the CSO board seemed to put the organization squarely on the side of the mounting resistance to the program—the side of the Mexican American farmworkers affected by it.[58]

The employment committee of Cesar's new Oxnard CSO chapter succeeded in winning support for its jobs campaign from every family in the colonia and every farmworker family in Oxnard.[59] Chavez flooded the Farm Placement Services office with increasing numbers of applicants, lodged a cascade of formal complaints, resorted to pickets and several protest marches, and scored some interim wins. He succeeded in turning the CSO office into what Marshall Ganz called "a de facto hiring hall," which some small growers started coming to daily to make hires.[60] But he had a deadline, or rather, CSO had a deal for a single year of funding from the UPWA for Cesar's organizing work. Chavez wanted another year in Oxnard, to turn the chapter he had organized into a union, stage strikes, and win contracts. But he had a bitter disagreement with CSO president Tony Rios, who made Cesar stop what he was doing, hand over his dynamic, fighting chapter—itself an incipient community-based farmworker union—to the United Packinghouse Workers, and leave. As Cesar later recounted to Jacques Levy, he shouted to Rios, "You don't stop me, I quit!" But Rios spent hours arguing with him, until Cesar gave in and agreed to move to LA and become the national director of CSO. He went on to spend two years in that position, trying to convince the CSO board to back his approach to organizing farmworkers.

Decades later, in an extended interview she gave in Santa Barbara, Dolores looked back on Cesar's experience in nearby Oxnard. Deeply involved at the time in the fight against new guest-worker legislation in DC, she characterized Cesar's year in Oxnard as a "big campaign . . . to get rid of the bracero program."[61] Although that was not how his assignment was negotiated and defined in advance, it is fair to say that he turned it into precisely that. Another time, in speaking about CSO's achievements, Huerta claimed, "And, of course, we were the ones that ended the bracero program."[62] Dolores's main contribution came on the legislative front, first as CSO's advocate in the state capitol and then later in the same role for the National Farm Workers Association—eventually renamed the United Farm Workers (UFW). In 1963, she lobbied in Washington against the program's extension. By then, however, the Kennedy administration expected that if Congress again extended PL 78, it would only be for a final year. In 1964, when the California legislature nevertheless considered a resolution calling on Congress to extend the Bracero Program yet again, Dolores wrote to Chavez that she would do her "damndest to kill it."[63] Indeed, the program died after that year's harvests.

The Organizer-Lobbyist

Dolores Huerta's CSO experience was, if anything, more complicated at the end of the 1950s and early 1960s. She had first glimpsed how local Stockton-area farmworkers and their families lived when she was registering voters, and the sight of their poverty—dirt floors and hungry, barefoot children—disturbed her. So she was ready when one opportunity to try to organize farmworkers came along, and then another. There were some striking parallels with Cesar's Oxnard experience, but soon an unexpected turn sent Dolores in a new direction that would put her in another genuinely pioneering role. The first opportunity came as part of the farm-labor initiative the CSO board adopted in 1957. Ernesto Galarza obtained support from the Meatcutters Union to organize Stockton-area farmworkers.[64] Huerta's CSO chapter established a farm-labor committee, with Dolores heading it, which took on the new challenge. This was on a smaller scale and shorter timeline than Chavez was working on in Oxnard, so the end came sooner. She, too, had to hand her group of about 150 farmworkers over to an established union, only to see her work fall apart.[65]

Then came a historic but short-lived effort initiated by Father Thomas McCullough, which he named the Agricultural Workers Association—whose acronym, AWA, is pronounced like the Spanish word for water, *agua*. McCullough's approach to organizing was remarkably like the community-based house-meeting method Fred Ross brought to building CSO in LA, San Jose, and Stockton. The priest referred to the little groups that met in private homes as "cells," and he called the procedure of using each meeting to generate two or more new meetings "cellular division."[66] It was now late 1958, and by then Dolores, one of McCullough's parishioners, had years of experience with house meetings and, more recently, organizing farmworkers. She was naturally drawn into this new effort as part of its core steering group, which launched a vigorous organizing campaign. By November, AWA was conducting nightly house meetings, focusing on the "home guard" residential farmworkers, most of whom lived in El Barrio del Chivo and other pocket colonias in unincorporated areas around Stockton. The campaign aimed to take full advantage of the farmworkers' time off following the fall harvests.[67]

The AWA effort succeeded in mobilizing a highly diverse group of hundreds of farmworkers and their families. Within the first winter months of 1959, AWA had formed an interim board of directors, adopted a constitution, and made plans for a number of mutual-aid programs. McCullough intended from the start for this campaign to prod the AFL-CIO to act, and it did. The labor federation had long sought an end to the Bracero Program and could see it coming—and was also aware of the progress AWA was making. In competition with the Teamsters, the AFL-CIO finally decided to both hasten and position itself for the post-bracero era by setting up an incipient farmworkers union.[68] The new Agricultural Workers Organizing Committee, or AWOC, would also be based in Stockton and expected to incorporate the workers already organized by AWA. At their monthly general meeting in June, AWA members voted to fold their organization into AWOC.[69]

McCullough thus achieved his goal. Dolores became AWOC's executive secretary and joined its board. Even though Galarza had his own National Farm Workers Union, he, too, helped AWOC get started but resisted merging his organization with it. Both Dolores and Galarza, however, soon had big differences with the man appointed by the AFL-CIO to head the new effort, and his whole approach. The Federation knew the worlds of the AFL's craft guilds and the CIO's industrial unions—that is, the work and workers on the primary side of the dual labor and job-markets system institutionalized by the New Deal's NLRA. But it knew nothing of modern agriculture, and especially not the large-scale, row-crop agribusiness of California. The only experience that the Federation's choice to lead AWOC had was organizing auto workers back East in the 1930s. Norman Smith would spend years in California's agricultural valleys looking for the equivalent of a factory gate, with shifts of industrial workers streaming out at specific times whom he could draw together with a shouted speech. He wound up settling for the small fraction of transient farmworkers who were picked up before dawn for day labor on skid-row streets like Stockton's. He never focused on the residential home guard, never held a single house meeting, and had no success developing AWOC into a union.[70]

From her board seat and staff position, Dolores tried to push AWOC to organize in the way that was working for Cesar in Oxnard and that she and McCullough had had success with through AWA, but to no avail. When Smith turned from first trying to organize the transients to then dealing with the labor contractors that rounded them up on skid row, Huerta had enough. She resigned herself to an early exit, to leaving behind the farmworkers that she, her husband, and her brother had organized.[71] But before she left, Dolores found herself cast in a transformative instance of high-impact political theater, one that pointed the way to the next stage of her social justice career. Stockton's proximity to Sacramento was a strategic plus; in fact, it opened a whole new world of activism to Dolores. In his second term in the state Assembly, legendary San Francisco legislator Phil Burton took charge of an interim committee on farm labor. Emboldened by the Democratic near sweep of the 1958 elections and having figured out how he could use hearings aggressively to advance his agenda, Burton undertook a lifelong campaign of civil rights and social justice reform. His biographer, the late John Jacobs of *The Sacramento Bee*, vividly described the legislator's staging of a field hearing of his farm-labor committee in Stockton's Civic Auditorium in 1959, before an audience of hundreds of growers. Both growers and Huerta testified.[72]

Like Cesar was doing in Oxnard, Dolores had organized local unemployed farmworkers to go through the job-referral process. She took with her to the hearing six of those who had been denied jobs that very morning. The workers described their experience, which enraged Chair Burton. He declared he would charge straight to a work camp to see for himself what was going on and how much the braceros—who had been hired instead of the locals—were being paid. Burton discovered that a grower had lied to him at the hearing about their wages, and he was in violation of the law that required braceros to be paid the locally prevailing rate. According to his biographer, "on the spot, Burton ordered the growers to fork over full wages with back pay, and insisted that the growers in the region hire local workers from then on. . . . Farm workers all over the San Joaquin Valley got pay raises that day."[73]

Burton was the first of an all-star quartet of elected officials Dolores became close to. The impact of the Stockton hearing led to the idea that

CSO should have a legislative director, its own lobbyist in Sacramento. When Cesar left Oxnard for Boyle Heights to become CSO staff director, he made Dolores his lobbyist. There had never before been a professional advocate for Mexican Americans at the state capitol, no fellow Latina or Latino mentor to tap, nor any Latino legislator in either chamber. Dolores invented her role. Her Stockton home was less than an hour from Sacramento, and by virtue of her link to Phil Burton, she now possessed a golden key to the legislative process. As Jacobs put it, "Burton transformed her. He taught her to write letters, whom to send them to, and how to organize the constituencies of the legislators she wanted to persuade."[74] Dolores could not have had a better guide and tutor, one memorably characterized as a unique and "absolute political genius."[75] The statewide network of CSO chapters would serve as her ground troops with which to move legislators.

The legislature had traditionally been "totally dominated by business, commercial and conservative labor interests," as John Jacobs put it. Public-interest advocacy had just started to emerge with the arrival of the first lobbyist for the American Friends Service Committee (AFSC) in 1957. When Dolores arrived in 1960, she became part of the emergent public-interest "Raggedy Ass" lobby, as it was known, which was led by the AFSC and included the American Federation of Teachers and American Civil Liberties Union.[76] She had an ample agenda to advance in Sacramento, in particular on voting rights. It took new legislation to mandate that all counties deputize citizens to register voters door to door, and a separate bill prohibiting racial or ethnic discrimination in authorizing deputy registrars. Private vigilante-style challenges to the right to vote at polling places were also banned.

But the biggest challenge Dolores had to take on was a bill that would allow for noncitizen immigrants to qualify to receive state assistance for seniors who lacked access to Social Security—such as farmworkers, who were excluded from New Deal programs. Organized labor supported the bill, which had been introduced, and failed, at least four times since 1953. CSO had used the issue in its organizing for years, but it had no advocate in Sacramento before Dolores.[77] Having connected with Burton the previous year in Stockton, she was able to prevail upon him to carry the "old-age assistance to noncitizens" bill in the next session, in 1961. CSO and its allies went all-out with massive letter-writing campaigns and bringing constituents to the capitol for committee hearings, where letters were presented in a heaping wheelbarrow. That summer, hundreds of CSO members thronged the capitol to see their bill signed into law by Governor Pat Brown.[78]

1960: Passing the Torch

Let the word go forth, from this time and place,
the torch has been passed to a new generation of Americans.
—John F. Kennedy
Inaugural Address, January 20, 1961

Decades are artificial markers, but there is no denying the historic differences between the 1950s and the 1960s—no less for Latinos than for the country and the world. The dawn of the new decade saw Dolores Huerta pioneering advocacy for Mexican American policy in Sacramento. There, she began advancing a state agenda that CSO, despite years spent organizing communities, had yet to achieve. Cesar Chavez was CSO's new executive director, reunited with his original San Jose partner, Herman Gallegos, who was elected national president. Cesar had put Dolores in the lobbying role and was proceeding to mobilize the whole organization for its biggest-ever push on voter registration, to coincide with the open presidential election that fall. In 1959, he met Senator John Kennedy, whose campaign went on to make an unprecedented bid for Latino votes in 1960. That effort would not succeed in winning California for JFK, but Dolores, and then Cesar, began building a close, historic, and ultimately tragic bond with Bobby, the candidate's younger brother and campaign manager.

The Black civil rights movement in the South was developing into a generational social and political crisis for the country—and a national opportunity for progress. CSO had shown in LA and Oxnard that Mexican American communities in California could be similarly mobilized in defiance of an oppressive, exploitative, and even brutal white power structure. Both Cesar and Dolores were committed to organizing farmworkers and wanted every CSO chapter to establish a farm-labor committee. The new decade seemed charged with energy and pregnant with possibility. For all that CSO had accomplished, however, the organization was approaching the end of its peak effectiveness. Signs were mounting. Founder Ed Roybal, entering his twelfth year on the LA City Council, had twice been frustrated seeking higher office, in bids for lieutenant governor in 1954 and LA county supervisor in 1958. Although CSO had worked wonders advancing Mexican American civic engagement—and made Roybal's political career possible—as a nonprofit organization it could neither endorse candidates nor raise campaign funds. Roybal felt compelled to establish a new organization and network, the Mexican American Political Association, known as MAPA, to independently endorse and support selected Democratic candidates. By the fall of 1960, Roybal was openly criticizing CSO, the organization he had founded and that launched his political career, for refusing to endorse Kennedy for president.[79]

Although CSO was capable of drawing public attention in its nonelectoral campaigns—from combating police abuse in LA to sustained mobilization in Oxnard against the Bracero Program—it otherwise had a nondescript name and relatively low profile. Saul Alinsky rued CSO's "drab and non-distinctive name," and hoped that a book by Ross telling the story of the organization could raise its profile.[80] It is not surprising that in 1960, when Roybal's MAPA became the California vehicle of the historic "Viva Kennedy" campaign, it got credit in a *Time* magazine cover story for registering 140,000 new Mexican American voters—voters that CSO had actually registered.[81] That was when, and why, Dolores first connected with Robert Kennedy in his capacity as JFK's campaign manager. Dolores was leading CSO's voter registration in San Diego when she got a call from Cesar, telling her about the misrepresentation in *Time*, which the Kennedy campaign was responsible for. He told her RFK was headed for the famed Hotel del Coronado, and she should go there and tell him to set the record straight. Dolores found a copy of the magazine—Bobby's first cover—and took the ferry to Coronado Island.[82]

Robert F. Kennedy on the cover of Time *magazine. From* TIME. *©1960 TIME USA LLC. All Rights Reserved. Used under license.*

As Dolores recalls, RFK must have been alerted to the matter and was prepared to douse the fire that a subordinate had caused. As she approached, magazine in hand, he started exclaiming "I know, I know!" Bobby apologized for the error and promised to write to *Time* to give CSO its due. It took until the last issue before the November 8 election—then featuring John Kennedy on the cover—for letters from JFK, Herman Gallegos, and RFK to appear, one neatly stacked upon the other.[83] The struggle to overcome Latino invisibility, mistaken identity, or erasure scored a win, but it would have to continue. More than pride was at stake in this particular case. The historic 1960 CSO registration drive had been financed by the California Federation of Labor, to which the organization had to report.[84] CSO could not afford to have its work or role overlooked or misrepresented by either a presidential campaign or the country's most prestigious national publication.

Leaving CSO—and LA

With Kennedy elected in 1960 and all the Mexican American voters CSO had registered that year—plus the eight new congressional seats California gained from the census and reapportionment—the 1962 midterm elections seemed fated to finally send a California Latino to Congress for the first time, which they did. That election year was pivotal—but in opposite directions—for California Latina/o political empowerment and its main organizational vehicle, CSO. After thirteen years on the LA City Council and two frustrated attempts at higher office, Ed Roybal still wanted more. After ten years with CSO, Cesar Chavez wanted more. Dolores wanted more after her seven, and Fred Ross wanted more after his fifteen. In 1962, with a stunning public resignation at the CSO convention in Calexico, Cesar led the way out.[85] He soon moved his family to Delano to start over and build a new organization, one personal visit and house meeting at a time. Roybal seized an opportunity to announce his run for Congress, where he would start again at the bottom and work his way up to a national Latino policy agenda, along with new, national organizations to advance it.[86] Dolores remained the best that CSO still had going for it, pushing for long-sought legislation in Sacramento and achieving multiple policy wins. Cesar told her to continue there for CSO until he had built a base that could support both their families in Delano, however modestly.[87]

CSO's contributions to Latina/o political empowerment, and its legacy, can be assessed and appreciated in several ways. Data on Latino voter registration going that far back is lacking, but it appears the majority of those on the rolls in California by late 1960 must have been registered in CSO campaigns. That would mean that more than one generation of California Latinos whose families date back to that era were first brought into civic life by that one historic organization—the statewide electorate CSO had set out to create. Added to that was the breakthrough achievement of representation on the LA City Council, the additional thousands of immigrants mobilized and led to become US citizens, and the start of Latino policy advocacy in the state legislature, which produced important reforms.

Furthermore, the 1962 midterms saw the first Latino "wave" election in California history. Not only was Roybal elected to Congress by a landslide majority, two Mexican Americans from LA's Greater Eastside were elected to the state Assembly. Roybal's MAPA endorsed Governor Brown for reelection, and he then came to East Los Angeles to headline the annual 16th of September parade there. Brown succeeded in beating back a challenge by former Vice President Richard Nixon.[88] Thus, by

January 1963, Latino LA had achieved unprecedented representation in both Washington and Sacramento, allowing both Dolores and Cesar latitude to move on from their roles in CSO.

Another way of assessing CSO's legacy is to focus on what derived from it—in particular, Roybal's thirty-year congressional career, the national organizations he went on to found, and the critical policy advances he achieved—and not least of all, the farmworker movement Cesar and Dolores built and led. That movement would go on to create a whole new level of Mexican American/Chicano empowerment, far beyond the fields and well beyond California. And yet another way is to consider the *vision* of empowerment that Chavez and Huerta left LA's Eastside with, when they undertook a new stage of struggle. They had first discussed it, modestly enough, on a Sunday morning at the kitchen table in Cesar and Helen Chavez's home in Boyle Heights, where they lived while he ran CSO. As we will see, however, the vision, the dream, the plan that Cesar and Dolores took with them from his kitchen in LA to the colonias of the San Joaquin Valley, while little known or appreciated, was nothing short of breathtaking.[89]

Chapter 3

Plotting *La Causa*: The Farmworker Revolution

I wish I had time to tell you my latest dreams.
—Chavez to Ross, January 1962

All the way to the final showdown at the 1962 convention, Cesar and Dolores pushed for CSO to not only *support* the farmworker cause but to *lead* it, using its signature approach to organizing, combined with its now proven clout for getting bills passed and signed into law. But the Bracero Program was still in operation, and no effort to unionize farmworkers had ever managed to win official recognition from growers and negotiate a contract.[1] Chavez and Huerta nonetheless felt sure it could be done with a different strategy: They believed they could build an effective union by organizing farmworker *communities*, not workplaces, involving whole families, not just workers, as Cesar had substantially achieved in Oxnard.[2] And they were determined to not leave this historic imperative to anyone else. Building on CSO's momentum, Dolores would spearhead the first stage of advancing legislation in Sacramento, enlisting all chapters in a drive to extend the state minimum wage to agriculture. This would be a "recognition" effort of a different kind. With veiled reference to the AFL-CIO's Agricultural Workers Organizing Committee (AWOC), this campaign would be a "crusade" that Cesar believed would get CSO "indisputably recognized as THE organization for the farm workers."[3]

The plan called for all chapters to establish farm-labor committees, which would undertake new organizing in support of the bill.[4] Given his enthusiasm and choice of words, we can assume that Cesar envisioned a drive surpassing both the organization's record 1960 voter-registration campaign and its breakthrough legislative effort for noncitizen seniors. Winning this new lobbying battle would set the stage to organize as-yet-unorganized farmworker communities. And that next step would be transformative. It would in part turn CSO into a league of farmworker colonias—a union of a new type—in addition to its urban barrio chapters with their farm-labor support committees.[5] Getting CSO to take on another legislative campaign seemed viable, but the idea of organizing farmworker communities as Chavez had done in Oxnard was another matter. Cesar had experienced painfully how CSO National President Tony Rios's commitment to farmworkers seemed to go only so far, as long as there was a sponsor channeling money to the organization's financially strapped main office. Once the money ran out, Rios pulled Cesar out of Oxnard. "If I had had the support of CSO," Cesar later recalled to Jacques Levy, "I would have built a union there."[6]

The immediate step Chavez proposed seemed uncontroversial, as it would follow the historic success Dolores and CSO had in 1961 by winning financial support for needy immigrant seniors who were not citizens. But Cesar had much more in mind beyond just a new lobbying effort, and both Rios and the board were wary. They were concerned, among other things, about their relations with the AFL-CIO, whose California Federation had financed the 1960 voter-registration drive, and still had its own AWOC effort in the field.[7] At the 1962 board meeting prior to the convention, Rios surprised Chavez with an alternative plan—along with a new patron to finance it—which the board approved, leaving Cesar's proposal to the convention itself. Chavez informed the board he would resign if the convention failed to adopt his proposal, but it seems he was not taken seriously, especially given the money backing up the new Rios plan. Would the national director walk away from a wealthy patron's $50,000 for three years to organize farmworkers? His closest allies and supporters did not believe it.[8] But the answer was yes, he would, and he did. Early on the sidelines of the convention, Chavez had another blowup with Rios over the issue of raising CSO membership dues. It seems evident that Cesar had no intention of pursuing his dream of organizing farmworkers if he had to answer to Rios and the CSO board. This was compounded by their commitment to external financing over making CSO self-supporting by increasing dues, and their deference to the AFL-CIO to boot. He later recounted to Jacques Levy that while the convention was still going on, the head of AFL-CIO's AWOC offered Cesar a job, which he immediately rejected, saying "I can't organize with you guys. You're not going to give me the freedom I need."[9]

Cesar's Astonishing Vision

The general belief, echoed in many published accounts, is that Cesar left CSO, and Dolores followed, because the organization refused to organize farmworkers. But that's a distortion. Chavez could have proceeded to organize farmworkers in at least three different ways. He could have stuck with CSO, remaining in charge of the whole operation, with fresh funds to hire new organizers, Dolores handling the legislative agenda, and farm-labor committees in all chapters. Alternatively, he could have joined AWOC and taken it to a new level, as only he knew how. Or he could finally strike out on his own.

Profile of Cesar and Dolores, 1966. Jon Lewis Photographs, Beinecke Rare Book & Manuscript Library. Copyright Yale University.

The astonishing vision Dolores says Cesar shared with her, but perhaps not even with his mentor, Ross, makes his choice comprehensible. That vision was to organize farmworker communities throughout the San Joaquin Valley for five to six years, until a valley-wide *general strike* could be called. It would be one great strike, resembling a revolutionary uprising, that would require years of stealth and great discipline to prepare. Chavez had long criticized traditional unions for prematurely calling strikes. He believed that they should not be used for organizing and the strike weapon was "a gun with one bullet."[10] Preparation and timing were everything, and the timing might only be right with the whole valley already organized. He trusted his judgment alone on when to pull the trigger. The basic idea of a general strike is that the workers who lead it call on all other workers to join in, thereby overcoming the disadvantage of acting in isolation. Chavez and Huerta believed that by organizing communities, not just a sector of workers and workplaces, working people in general could be persuaded to rise up against the grape growers—but they were still years away from reaching that extent of organization. And yet even this audacious plan was not the whole of the vision.

From its earliest years in LA, the founders and leaders of CSO intended to grow it into a national organization. Thus, they had their founding "national convention" in the Monterey Bay area in 1954, with Cesar as one of the founders.[11] And when he was persuaded to leave Oxnard in 1959 for "National CSO" in LA, he assumed the role of national executive director. His vision for a farmworker union would be even more ambitious, and the scale of the ambition was not his alone. If a strong union was consolidated in California, it could expand in stages to encompass all the two to three million farmworkers across the country—which would make it "substantially the largest bona fide union in the world."[12] Even if AFL-CIO with its AWOC plan had no general-strike fantasies in mind, it nevertheless dreamt of one great union. This vision was widely shared all the way into the mid-1970s; as economist Phil Martin put it, "the UFW was expected to organize most of the 2.5 million hired farm workers across the US."[13]

The target of his organizing vision shifted from the citrus belt surrounding LA to the table-grape industry and its Mexican American farmworker colonias prevalent throughout the San Joaquin Valley. That Cesar and Helen had family in Delano, where they would start, was of immediate practical importance. But the valley also had multiple strategic advantages. Unlike Oxnard, grape country lacked a major Bracero Program presence. Grape harvesting, furthermore, was spread over much more of the year than other crops, which meant that domestic, residential farmworkers lived in stable, if marginalized, communities up and down the valley. The relative scarcity of braceros would allow for years of organizing along mutual-aid lines without falling into a premature conflict or job action.[14] Organizing would proceed, not as if to build a union or toward a strike, but as a mutual-aid society, to address community needs. Cesar wrote to Ross that this was the first point he was making in his house-meeting pitch, that the goal was neither to create a union nor to ever go on strike.[15] The reason for this, however, was both to avoid arousing fears among the farmworkers and their families, and especially to not tip off either the growers or the authorities that did their bidding. The Delano-based National Farm Workers Association (NFWA) developed much like CSO but without an emphasis on voting. In place of an initial voter-registration drive, Chavez began by conducting a one-man farmworker census, by which he spoke with and "registered" thousands during his endless car trips around the region. He held house meetings, as well, to set up local committees throughout the valley.

In Delano, the emergent organization established a service center, a thrift shop, a life-insurance plan, a newspaper, and a credit union. Apparently, neither Dolores nor Cesar let on about the general-strike goal during the first three years of organizing, but once the Filipino AWOC strike came along, time had run out. Cesar urgently called the top NFWA leadership together, saying "the world is coming to an end." [16] They had to face what he regarded as an existential choice: somehow stick with the plan that they could not fully reveal, or declare their support for the strike. If they chose to join the Filipinos, there would be no turning back—they would de facto become a union on strike, firing their one bullet, and would need to merge with what remained of AWOC: Larry Itliong's locals. The situation he and his striking workers created called for a general NFWA meeting, discussion, and vote. Cesar scheduled the pivotal gathering for September 16, the day commemorating the start of Mexico's revolutionary war of independence.

The vote to strike was by boisterous, overwhelming acclamation, accompanied by chants of *Huelga! Huelga! Huelga!* They began picketing the fields with great enthusiasm that fall, but as the months wore on, fall turned to winter, harvesting wound to its annual halt, and morale sagged. That's when the precocious union/movement turned to the idea of a march to Sacramento. This was designed to recharge the spirits, take the strike and union message on a winding route through the San Joaquin Valley, and rally at the capitol to demand that the governor intervene to bring the growers into negotiations. Fortunately for the incipient union/movement, the Senate subcommittee on farm labor had come to California to conduct a series of hearings, and Senator Bobby Kennedy showed up for the final hearing on March 16 in Delano, where he played a starring role. Kennedy spoke to throngs of farmworkers outside the hearing and even joined them on a picket line, turning the movement into a national issue overnight. The march to Sacramento started the next morning, with morale at an all-time high.[17]

Cesar signals start and end points of 1966 march to Sacramento on hand-drawn route, with daily goals. Above the farmworker eagle symbol appear the words Peregrinación, Penitencia, Revolución *(Pilgrimage, Penance, Revolution). Jon Lewis Photographs, Beinecke Rare Book & Manuscript Library. Copyright Yale University.*

More good fortune was to come on the way north. When it got to Stockton, the march was met with its biggest reception before Sacramento—a cheering crowd of thousands—and a phone call for Chavez. The boycott had started prior to the holiday season the year before, targeting just two big companies. One of them, Schenley Industries, suddenly wanted to negotiate immediately, in the run-up to Easter, when the march would cross the river into Sacramento. Schenley was especially vulnerable as a national liquor distributor, not just a grape-growing company in Delano. Picket lines outside retail outlets got the corporation's products pulled off shelves. Schenley executives could see the media coverage the march was getting and opted to negotiate with the proto-union before it reached the state capitol. The head of the company talked Cesar into driving down to Beverly Hills late that night, and after some acrimony, they agreed on a simple contract. Chavez had negotiated the first "real union contract in California farm labor history," as Marshall Ganz described it, and drove back north to rejoin the march. It was a historic victory for both the boycott and the march, validating the momentous choice the NFWA leadership and members had made the previous September.[18]

March from Delano to Sacramento led by the NFWA banner of the Virgin Mary, Our Lady of Guadalupe, Patron Saint of the Americas. Photo by Harvey Richards. Courtesy of Paul Richards.

Had historical time allowed for the dreamt-of general strike, it is easy to imagine that a similar march from Delano to Sacramento would have been a key part. The 1966 march drew in multiple ways on the iconography of revolutionary movements in Mexican history. There was the procession led by a banner with the image of the *Virgen de Guadalupe*, gathering strength as it passed through dozens of rural towns and colonias; and the movement's repeated chant and slogan, both hiding and suggesting the word *revolución* with the fig leaf of *Viva La Causa*, common to both the Mexican and US wars of independence.[19] And there was the nightly reading of the "Plan of Delano," modeled after the manifesto issued at the outset of the Mexican Revolution led by Emiliano Zapata, who became an icon of the urban Chicano movement.[20] The text of the *Plan de Delano*, recited by the baritone-voiced activist and Chicano playwright Luis Valdez, who had developed it in close consultation with Chavez, invokes "revolution" five times.[21] Besides that, someone, most likely Cesar, must have shared with Valdez the idea of a general strike, at least as an original vision of the movement. Valdez wrote the lyrics of one of its most popular songs, "Huelga en General," by which he meant *general strike*. The song proclaims both "¡Viva la revolución!" and "¡Viva huelga en general!"[22]

Dolores addresses the rally at the culmination of the farmworkers march to the California capitol, Easter morning 1966, demanding an agricultural collective-bargaining law. Photo by John Kouns. Courtesy of the Tom & Ethel Bradley Center at California State University, Northridge.

The march from Delano, after covering over three hundred miles in twenty-five days, massed at the state capitol building, joined by thousands of supporters. That is where, on the morning of Easter Sunday 1966, Dolores proclaimed the movement's central demand, as well as the weapon she said they were prepared to use to back it up:

> On behalf of all of the farmworkers of this state, we unconditionally demand that the governor of this state, Edmund Brown, call a special session of the legislature, to enact a collective-bargaining law for the farmworkers of the state of California. We will be satisfied with nothing less....
>
> We are citizens, and we are residents of the state of California, and we want the rules set up to protect us in this state, right here.
>
> If the rules to settle our economic problems are not forthcoming, we will call a general strike to paralyze the state's agricultural economy....
>
> The social and economic revolution of the farmworkers is well underway, and it will not be stopped until we receive equality.

Dolores gave voice that Easter morning to a vision and a dream that grew out of the years she and Cesar spent in CSO, becoming organizers and leaders, overcoming more than a century of displacement, marginalization, exploitation, invisibility, and erasure that had marked the Mexican American experience in California. But that was the dream, not the current reality or revised strategy. Governor Brown was not in Sacramento that Sunday. He offered to meet the next day, but Chavez turned him down.[23] There would be no discussion of the movement's demand, no special session of the legislature, no farm-labor-law reform—not for another decade—and no general strike. But in the span of less than a month's time, what was soon to be rebranded as the United Farm Workers (UFW) of America had garnered far more attention than CSO had in its first fifteen years combined.

The still-not-chartered union thus was committed to sustaining an unplanned and unforeseen local strike, knowing it could not be won locally. They were deprived of the unfinished secret weapon that, in Cesar and Dolores's plans, would have made the difference—the dreamt-of general strike that would sweep the whole valley and force state government to act. Lacking that strategic weapon, the movement turned to multiple other means to widen the scope of the conflict beyond its local beginnings: the march, boycotts, fasts, and other tactics borrowed from Gandhi and the civil rights movement, including using national leaders to draw national media attention. There were dramatic occasions when different means combined, to historic effect. When Cesar's first public fast approached its end in early March 1968, his inner circle had a choice of national leaders to invite to Delano for the ceremonial mass. Dr. Martin Luther King had just sent Chavez a long and touching telegram, his second. As a fellow student of Gandhi and the country's premier civil rights leader, Dr. King would have made a logical choice. But Senator Robert Kennedy was the UFW's ace national supporter, and he had been in touch throughout the fast. Furthermore, the news media's eyes were fixed on RFK, who seemed likely to soon declare his bid for the presidency. So they invited Kennedy. The Chavez–Kennedy reunion for the breaking of Cesar's fast—as an act of communion between fellow Catholics—was a proverbial moment for the ages.[24]

Triumph and Tragedy in LA

Though it did not make development of Mexican American electoral power its top priority, as CSO had, the UFW proved itself at least equally adept at registering voters and getting them to the polls. On the return flight from Los Angeles, RFK reportedly made his decision to run, and he declared his candidacy days later. The union knew it could make the difference in the country's biggest primary and immediately swung into action, with a particular focus on LA's Eastside. Strike-related duties were suspended: The California Latino-empowerment movement, now in its UFW-led phase, again had a president to elect—its greatest champion yet.

With high-profile tactics, and especially the development of the consumer boycott of table grapes, the farmworker movement had already had an impact on urban Mexican Americans, other Latinos, and the wider public. Boycott organizers were sent to major markets across the country and into Canada to connect with progressive organizations and church groups to mobilize them in support of the boycott and strike. The California farmworker rebellion in the San Joaquin Valley seemed to stimulate the emergence of the Chicano student movement in the cities. Thousands of LA high school students walked out of their classes near the end of Cesar's twenty-five-day fast. The same Episcopal Church of the Epiphany in Lincoln Heights that, just weeks earlier, had been the base for organizing the student walkouts now became the UFW's primary election campaign HQ.[25] As soon as he was physically able, Chavez set out to speak at universities in support of the Kennedy campaign, as well as in churches and at outdoor rallies. On April 4, RFK was about to address a campaign rally in the Midwest, and Chavez was preparing to speak at a church in Sacramento, when they got word of Dr. King's assassination in Memphis.[26]

Primary elections, as a rule, are far less salient, draw far fewer voters, and involve a fraction of the effort and resources of general elections. But in growing and mobilizing the California Latino electorate, the 1968 RFK campaign led by UFW—in spite of its tragic end on the night of the primary—appears to have surpassed CSO's historic effort in the 1960 general election. Both JFK in his 1960 fall campaign and RFK in the 1968 primary conducted whistle-stop train swings through the San Joaquin Valley, attracting heavily Mexican American crowds. But while JFK reportedly drew out hundreds at each stop, RFK drew thousands.[27] Bobby won all the counties the train passed through, and more, but LA was the county he needed most, and he won it by the widest margin.[28] Cesar directed both the CSO and UFW efforts, and at least one source claims the UFW registered more voters in the abbreviated 1968 primary campaign than CSO did for the fall 1960 general.[29] In an oral-history interview just a couple of years later, Cesar himself claimed to have deployed fifty times the number of people to campaign for Bobby as he had for John eight years before.[30] Some part of this was due to the operation Fred Ross put together, paying registrars a quarter per signature gathered, plus bonuses for the most productive. But Cesar principally had the Eastside organized down to the block level, and more resources than ever before.[31] Several precincts—Dolores told Kennedy it was four—maxed out at 100 percent voter turnout well before the polls closed. In multiple precincts, the vote for RFK soared past 90 percent, and in one of them hit 100 percent. According to biographer Jean Stein, Dolores told Kennedy of this as she escorted him from his hotel room to the victory party in the Ambassador's ballroom, prompting the senator to hug her.[32]

More Battles to Win . . . and Lose

With race riots sweeping the country, the Vietnam War intensifying, and antiwar protests gaining strength, LBJ withdrawing from the election, civil rights morphing into Black Power, and the women's and Chicano movements taking off, historical time accelerated to a breakneck pace—and a national backlash in the 1968 election took the form of the return of Richard Nixon.[33] The subsequent Nixon administration tried to help the California grape industry with massive Defense Department purchases for the military, but the growers opted to negotiate with the UFW—with negotiating teams headed by Dolores Huerta—and nearly all signed contracts with the union in 1970.[34] Just two years later, however, the California farm lobby attempted to weaken the union with a ballot initiative that would deprive it of a secondary boycott weapon—the tactic of picketing grocery stores that carried nonunion produce. When the Arizona legislature passed a law that year with the same effect, the UFW found itself fighting a two-front war. Chavez decided to lead a special effort himself in his native state and relocated to Phoenix to attempt to recall the governor, who had immediately signed the openly anti-UFW bill into law. The union mobilized and expanded its network in Arizona to gather recall signatures and register voters, and Cesar undertook another extended public fast. It was in this struggle that the union adopted the slogan *Sí Se Puede*. The recall qualified for the primary ballot, but the attempt to oust the governor failed. The UFW's focus on Arizona did, however, propel the state's Mexican American community to a new level of political development, and critically boosted Raúl Castro's campaign for governor in 1974. Arizona thus elected a Mexican American governor five decades before California even had a serious candidate for that office on a general-election ballot. Although Castro's performance was troubled, and he resigned to become US ambassador to Argentina during the Carter administration, the seeds of Arizona's historic role in the 2020 presidential election were sown, resown, and cultivated decades in advance.

Following its 1972 loss in the Arizona primary, the union had to turn its full attention back to California and the farm lobby's ballot initiative, known as Proposition 22. The initiative's presence on the fall ballot made this existential test of the UFW's electoral capabilities both more direct and more consequential than the 1968 presidential primary had been—and despite Nixon's landslide reelection, the union won with an astounding repudiation of the growers. The UFW was now confirmed as a major player in California politics and policy—the most formidable Latino political force in US history. It furthermore had a new champion in the state Assembly with the election of Richard Alatorre from LA, who immediately founded the Chicano Legislative Caucus. The union's unambiguous defeat of Proposition 22 gave it new clout in its dealings with the AFL-CIO and established a personal bond between Chavez and then–Secretary of State Jerry Brown. The next step in the UFW's political ascent was the end of Ronald Reagan's governorship and Brown's election as his successor in 1974, which was followed by perhaps the most extraordinary inaugural address in California history. Jerry Brown had, of course, witnessed the rise of the UFW from the start, in particular its challenge to his father in 1966 with the march to the capitol and demand for a special session of the legislature to address farmworkers' collective-bargaining rights. At some point, perhaps after his father's defeat to Ronald Reagan for reelection that fall, Jerry seems to have concluded that he had erred in his handling of the farm-labor question and the UFW.

Precisely eight years after Reagan ended his father's political career, Jerry Brown was sworn in as governor of California before a joint session of the state legislature, which he proceeded to address. Thus, in January 1975, the new Governor Brown declared he would summon a special session of the legislature for the sole purpose of considering and voting on a bill governing agricultural labor relations, the first law of its kind in the country, to establish collective-bargaining rights for farmworkers—precisely what Dolores Huerta had demanded from the steps outside the capitol in 1966. And so it came to pass.

Enactment of the California Agricultural Labor Relations Act (ALRA) in 1975 further confirmed the UFW's extraordinary clout in the state—now in both the electoral and policy spheres—and radically transformed its fundamental work of union building and maintenance that year. But it meant that suddenly, within months, the UFW had to compete with the Teamsters—the biggest union not in the AFL-CIO—in hundreds of recognition elections at farm operations all over the state, to determine which of the two, or neither, would represent the workers. The UFW performed impressively well in those contests, timed per the ALRA to coincide with harvests at each location, when the most farmworkers would be present. The days of house meetings and community organizing were well behind it now. The struggle had shifted decisively to the workplace, and to competing for the approval of whoever was employed at each location—independent of the community they lived in, or whether they lived in California year round at all.

There was little respite following that year's harvests, as a new presidential election loomed in 1976—effectively an open race. Nixon had been forced out—and the incumbent-but-unelected president, Gerald Ford of Grand Rapids, Michigan, was in his first contest beyond his own congressional district. Not long into the caucuses and primaries, the previously unknown governor of Georgia emerged as the front-runner for the Democratic nomination. Brown had been California's governor for just over a year when the election cycle started, and Carter began his ascent from nowhere. Under the circumstances, it would be only natural for Brown to at least consider and likely opt to get his name on the state ballot as a "favorite son" candidate—as his father had done three times—and thereby enhance California Democrats' influence at the convention.[35] After letting some sixteen contests pass and finding the Democratic field—Carter, in particular—uninspiring, Brown casually strolled into the last stretch of the race and quickly managed a stunning upset with a decisive win, clear across the country in Maryland.[36]

Brown had already been riding high in the polls in California, and his greatest achievement by far was securing the first farm-labor law in US history. In a span of five months, starting at the end of August 1975, over four hundred local union-recognition elections were held throughout the state, with the UFW winning nearly half and receiving twice the total votes as the rival Teamsters.[37] But by February 1976, the new Agricultural Labor Relations Board (ALRB) had exhausted its budget, putting on hold any more elections until sometime the next fiscal year. The UFW found itself with full-time volunteers and seasoned organizers with little to nothing to do, just as the country's attention was turning to the presidential primaries.[38] After abruptly entering the race and proving his national appeal in Maryland, Brown called on the UFW to conduct his field efforts in the remaining states. Eight years after answering the call from its last great champion, Bobby, the UFW again took on a presidential primary campaign—but this time not only in California. There was little prospect that Brown could amass enough delegates in the remaining states to stop Carter, but he could get to the convention in New York City that summer as a major player.

With just a few days' notice, the union's talented organizers helped Brown nearly beat Carter again in neighboring Oregon, and they then went on to pull off new upsets in Rhode Island, Nevada, and New Jersey. And of course, to nobody's surprise, Brown blew away the presumptive nominee in California, the most delegate-rich state, by a three-to-one margin.[39] California Latinos attended the nominating convention in New York as Brown delegates, with Cesar Chavez as their moral leader. Another of Brown's historic moves was to have Chavez, the former farmworker with an eighth-grade education, give the big speech placing Brown's name in nomination, before a television audience of some fifty million Americans, and more abroad.

This moment certainly appears to have been the apex of the UFW's political ascent, unsurpassed in the Latino experience before or since. What followed in the coming months and years has served to confirm such a take. Immediately after the convention, the UFW got to work on another big lift—its own initiative on the fall ballot, designed to strengthen and protect the gains of the ALRA. Among its various provisions, the new Proposition 14 would have required the legislature to adequately fund the ALRB and mandated that union organizers have access to meet with farmworkers on the growers' property. The union mobilized all its resources behind this initiative of its own creation, but this time lost decisively, humiliatingly, to the growers' lobby.[40] Whereas in 1968, 1970, 1972, 1975, and in the last primaries of 1976, the UFW had shown that farmworkers could win, that November showed they could also lose in a landslide.

According to longtime close aide and confidant LeRoy Chatfield, an "embarrassed and hurt" Cesar Chavez disallowed any public discussion or internal critique by the union's hundreds of volunteers and staff of the "devastating" electoral loss. "Chavez simply expected the movement to ignore the reality of this defeat and the public rebuke that came with it, pick up the pieces, pull itself together, and carry on as if nothing had happened," Chatfield wrote decades later.[41] The growers' extraordinarily successful mobilization and margin of victory appear to have hurt Democrats on the California ballot, including Carter and incumbent US Senator John Tunney, who was ousted by aggressively right-wing academic S. I. Hayakawa.[42] Both Carter and Tunney had endorsed the UFW's proposition, and Tunney was closely associated with the Kennedys—often compared to Robert Kennedy in particular.[43]

Between backing Brown in the primaries and investing so heavily in the proposition battle in the general election, the union effectively dealt itself out of the transition to the first wholly new national Democratic administration since 1960. It had furthermore either dismantled or deactivated much of its boycott machinery over the previous years. For the Latino-empowerment agenda, on the other hand, the 1976–77 political conjuncture was of transcendent importance: Three immense national issues had been gestating for years, decisively shifting attention to Washington, DC. Two of the three issues were closely related: the next decennial census and voting rights. Latino advocates, among whom Representative Roybal played a principal role, had for decades been pressing for legislative redistricting that would allow Latino voters to elect representatives of their own choosing. They, and he, saw a complete and accurate census count, as well as further reform of the Voting Rights Act, as a fundamental prerequisite to such redistricting.

But besides those issues, increasing undocumented migration across the border from Mexico was a growing national concern throughout the 1970s, significantly bolstered by a series of congressional hearings. Immigration reform was now the proverbial third leg of the stool of a national Latino policy agenda. But other Latino activists, leaders, and organizations did not see the UFW and farmworker movement as being on board with their emerging immigrant-rights consensus. Developments in 1977 would drive national Latino policy, politics, and advocacy for the rest of the century and into the next. Although the UFW was never part of the emergent Latino lobby on immigration, as we will see, the union—and Dolores Huerta in particular—would eventually play a critical but little-known role in the ultimate outcome of the immigration-policy battles of the 1970s and '80s.

Part II

Going National: From LA to DC and Back

LATINOS AS A GROUP DID NOT so much opt to be involved in national policy as they had national policy thrust on them, forcing a choice between silence, accommodation, or resistance. That was the case with the 1930 census, which for "the first and only time" counted "Mexican" as a "race or color," along with the alternatives of White, Negro, Indian, and several Asian and Pacific Islander categories. There was no Latino in Congress at that time to question the Census Bureau about this novel classification, but a long and vigorous campaign to drop the "Mexican" race category—with the support of by-then-Senator Dennis Chávez of New Mexico—succeeded just in time for the next census in 1940.[1] The first Latino mobilization on a national policy issue was in the record books—and it was a successful case of the *politics of resistance*, but one with virtually no input by Californians.[2]

Resistance to the Bracero Program set up during World War II became the second Latino effort in national policy when Congress repeatedly extended it, two years at a time, in the 1950s. As legislative director of LA's CSO, Dolores Huerta lobbied in both Sacramento and Washington against renewal of this contract-labor program, while Cesar Chavez, also working for CSO, mobilized domestic farmworkers in opposition to it in Southern California. These efforts succeeded when the program was shut down in late 1964.[3]

Over the course of the 1970s, the Mexican American Legal Defense and Educational Fund (MALDEF), the National Council of La Raza (NCLR), and the League of United Latin American Citizens (LULAC) opened offices in Washington. They became the initial core of a national Latino lobby that first came together to resist immigration-policy proposals that threatened to worsen discrimination against Latinos in employment and create a massive new bracero program.[4] These organizations were bolstered by the founding of the Congressional Hispanic Caucus (CHC) and the National Association of Latino Elected and Appointed Officials (NALEO) in the mid-1970s. All these entities successfully mobilized in support of a key Census reform and for enhanced protection of Latino voting through the 1982 extension of the Voting Rights Act (VRA). The most intense and sustained Latino policy effort culminated with the passage of an expanded version of the Immigration Reform and Control Act (IRCA) of 1986, which resulted in the legalization of some 2.7 million undocumented immigrants and seasonal farmworkers. This experience proved to be the crucible for the making of an impactful and coalitional Latino lobbying capability. Thus, by the mid-1980s, a permanent Latino lobby had been consolidated and institutionalized in the nation's capital, and it had proven its capabilities in both the politics of resistance and the politics of inclusion.

Chapter 4

Representation in DC and Pivot to Immigrant Rights

"Crushing defeat" of UFW's Proposition 14 in November 1976 could have been a stunning blow to Latino aspirations for full empowerment in California, as it was to the farmworker movement.[1] Just months after reaching peak visibility and influence at the Democratic National Convention in New York, the most potent Latino political force to that point in US history saw its hard-won clout collapse on Election Day. But news of the farmworkers' landslide loss drew relatively little notice and was soon forgotten—even by Latinos who were deeply involved in California politics that year but were not part of the union's all-out "Yes on 14" campaign. On election night, the country, and most politically minded Latinos, were instead gripped by Jimmy Carter's unexpectedly narrow win over Gerald Ford, which put an end to more than just two terms of Republican control of the White House.[2] By electing another white Southern Democrat, the country appeared to be putting behind it both the revolutionary 1960s and the Republican backlash to those countercultural years—at least for the next four. The first full transition to national Democratic governance since 1960 was underway.[3] If for California Latinos the 1960s and early '70s were marked by *movement politics* and protest in the streets, the 1976–77 transition signaled a turn to an era of political professionalism. At that time, several national policy reforms were needed to enable further big strides in Latino empowerment. A rush was on to advance Latinas and Latinos to significant positions in the new administration, which would lay the foundation for expanding and elevating Latino political development across the country for decades.

What no one could foresee, however, was that Carter's election and presidency would be a one-term parenthesis between two landslides led by right-wing Californians—Nixon in 1972 and Reagan in 1980. In California, the backlash against the 1960s had actually begun earlier, with Reagan's 1966 election as governor, which ended the progressive governorship of Jerry Brown's father, Pat Brown. Nixon, who had lost his own challenge to Brown in 1962, headed the national backlash with a narrow win in riotous 1968. Despite his criminal offenses against US democracy, Nixon did not govern as an ideologue.[4] By the 1980s, however, President Reagan would try to go much further than merely undoing changes wrought by the '60s. He aspired to dismantle the New Deal and the coalition that had made it possible.[5] Nevertheless, even under Reagan, Latinos would be able to build on both the inclusionary advances and the major resistance effort they undertook during the Carter interlude—in particular, reform of the coming 1980 census, preparation for the 1982 extension of the Voting Rights Act (VRA), and an effective Latino role in the extended battle over immigration reform, which would stretch all the way to 1986.

After the 1976 Democratic presidential nominating convention—and irrespective of any personal take on its nominee Carter—Latino leaders and activists worked hard to be included in the Carter general-election campaign, and then again in the transition. Up to that point, Latinos active in Democratic politics had no reason to be attracted to this obscure former governor (and peanut farmer) with a soft-spoken Georgia drawl. Once the convention was over and Carter had won, they had to start from scratch to secure roles in his general-election campaign. By devoting all its resources to its ill-fated Proposition 14 effort, the UFW had dealt itself out of this next phase of California Latino engagement with national politics. But Latinos who were focused on the presidential contest had other assets on their side. That LA's Henry "Hank" Lacayo had risen to national political director of the colossal United Auto Workers (UAW) union was key, given the UAW's heavyweight role in Democratic politics.[6] His sister, Carmela Lacayo, served with the Carter campaign on both the California and national steering committees.[7] George Pla, then at TELACU, became deputy manager of Carter's California campaign.[8] Gloria Molina took a leave as chief of staff to State Assembly Member Art Torres to head the Carter campaign's Latino outreach in the state.

The election gave way to an equally intense transition effort: the struggle for Latino representation in the new administration. Key appointments started coming: Richard Alatorre's chief of staff, Lou Moret, to the Commerce Department, which houses the Census Bureau; pioneer Latino demographer and UCLA professor Leo Estrada to a key advisory committee to the bureau; Gloria Molina to the White House Personnel Office.[9] The day after his inauguration, President Carter promoted Carmela Lacayo to vice chair of the Democratic National Committee. But, as in 1960, California Latino efforts were still at a disadvantage relative to Texas. Carter won Texas, as JFK had sixteen years earlier, but both lost in California. Back then, Edward Roybal had angled for the State Department position Esteban Torres now sought in 1976–77, but neither reached it. Under Kennedy, key diplomatic appointments had gone instead to Latinos from Texas, Arizona, and Puerto Rico.[10] Late in Carter's single term—in an apparent catch-up gesture prior to the 1980 elections—Los Angeles educator and breakthrough school-board member Julian Nava was appointed as the first Latino ambassador to Mexico.[11] Esteban Torres was named US representative to UNESCO, with the rank of ambassador. George Pla's assignment was over, so he passed on the Carter inauguration festivities and left frigid DC for LA. But critical work remained to be done. In a move pregnant with political meaning, Carter named Leonel Castillo of Houston to be commissioner of the Immigration and Naturalization Service (INS), which under Republicans had been a position held by a former general with a militaristic approach to border control and immigration enforcement. Castillo's appointment not only showed the relative advantage Texans enjoyed, it signaled that the Carter team intended to act on undocumented immigration and that Latinos would have an outsized role in the policy debate to come.

The other big recurring issue for Latinos concerned the next renewal of the Voting Rights Act (VRA). The original VRA of 1965 was explicitly designed to address discrimination against African Americans in the Old

South. It was first renewed in 1975 and, with considerable difficulty, expanded to include protections for "language minorities"—meaning Latinos, Asians, and Native Americans. But even after the 1975 amendments to the VRA, it remained a weak tool for increasing Latino representation in elected office, most of all in California, which had the largest Latino population of any state. One of the compromises that allowed for that expansion was limiting the 1975 extension to just seven years, as opposed to the original law's authorization of ten.[12] Thus, by the time Carter took office, the VRA had only five years left to go before it had to be renewed again, which would be a precious opportunity to make the voting law more useful to Latinos.[13]

For some, the great inclusionary goal, and imperative, would be to crown this presidential term with a 1980 census that attempted the first complete count of the Latino population in US history. Groups officially considered "races"—whites, Blacks, Native Americans, and Asians—had always been counted by the Census through its question on race. Only Latinos, not considered a race but an ethnic group, were left out. By 1977, reform of the decennial census to advance Latina/o political empowerment was on a much shorter timeline than the next renewal of the VRA. Mountains of census forms had to be printed by 1979 and distributed well ahead of time, not only across the country—to both states and territories, from the US Virgin Islands and Puerto Rico, in the eastern Caribbean, to Guam, halfway across the Pacific—but around the world, to reach military, diplomatic, and other personnel stationed overseas. Thus, there were only two years to resolve difficult questions affecting the census instruments. Of the big-three issues, Latinos would achieve only the reform of the Census during Carter's term in office, as we tracked in our first book.[14] The process of doing so, however, was itself of incalculable importance. Latinos of disparate national origins had to come together to institutionalize a highly visible and consequential change in national policy—the addition of a four-word item to the universal census questionnaire: "Is this person Hispanic?" That little question would put Latinos on par with African Americans in the gathering of official data by the government, but it was explicitly *not* the addition of a new "race question." It was a new *ethnic* question that preceded the one on race. A "yes" answer was followed by a new set of alternative responses. This change led to the first "big bang" census count of the Latino/Hispanic population, with major implications for government and policy at every level, as well as for politics, business, culture, education, and scholarship.

The immigration issue differed qualitatively from representation and voting rights, which were all about Latino inclusion, and of the big three, immigration took the longest to resolve legislatively. Latinos had been increasingly compelled to respond to immigration-enforcement policies and practices since the Nixon administration. The issue was highlighted nationally by a series of hearings and a labor-influenced bill offered by Peter Rodino, a Democrat and chair of the House Judiciary Committee, and Edward Kennedy in the Senate.[15] Latino leaders and advocacy organizations increasingly saw the Rodino bill as something that could lead to employment discrimination against their communities, in the guise of cracking down on employers who hired undocumented workers.[16] A latent potential politics of resistance was taking form in Latino, and especially Mexican American, activist circles, out of public view. That potential would become reality and succeed for two consecutive presidential terms—not in bringing about a long-sought reform but in blocking an undesirable one. In this case, a long and historically unprecedented Latino-resistance struggle would win repeatedly before an inclusionary alternative could emerge.

The Carter Plan and Latino Immigration Pivot

The first Latino issue Carter tackled, or *tried* to tackle, was "illegal immigration." Alarmism over unauthorized Mexican migration had been building since the first Nixon term. But on this issue, not even the Carter team's top Latino and border-state appointee, Commissioner of INS Leonel Castillo, had a finger on the pulse of the organized Latino community, particularly Mexican Americans/Chicanos. By Carter's first year, as he painfully discovered, the views on immigration—especially undocumented migration—held by most Mexican American leaders, activists, and organizations had evolved beyond recognition since the defeat of the Bracero Program in 1964. This transformation would be made clear by the community's vociferous response to the "Carter Plan"—the new administration's ill-fated attempt at comprehensive immigration reform.[17]

Latino activists and organizations had long opposed seasonal labor from Mexico and supported immigration-law enforcement, but now the politically organized Mexican American community—with the exception of the UFW—united in opposition to INS raids, roundups, and mass deportations, especially in urban areas.[18] Several key trends contributed to the reversal of Mexican Americans' historically restrictionist position on immigration. The long struggle against the Bracero Program was concerned with government and grower-controlled importation of Mexican men for farm labor, seasonally housed in camps during harvest periods.[19] Years before the program ended, however, some growers began sponsoring some of their workers for immigrant visas (a.k.a. "green cards"). This was not so much to enable selected workers to settle legally in the US, although that would be their right, but to allow them to freely come and go from Mexico, whatever the fate of the bracero policy.[20] Having this perk to dangle over workers gave foremen and supervisors added leverage. Many other Mexican migrants either skipped their bracero contracts or came looking for employment outside of the official program, as undocumented workers. Together, these developments spurred the rise of undocumented families settling in urban areas, along with the continuing circulatory migration of single men in seasonal farmwork.

By 1960, it was clear that the Bracero Program would not be extended much further.[21] The number of temporary work permits granted started dropping significantly and steadily, while apprehensions of undocumented Mexican migrants and the issuing of green cards—while still at a low level—began rising every year. Thus, when the Bracero Program shut down at the end of 1964, US agriculture, primarily in California, had already cut its reliance on the program's imported workers by about half since its peak years in the 1950s.[22] The following year, a major reform of the Immigration and Nationality Act (INA) tightened the previously loose requirements for employers to sponsor a worker for an immigrant visa.[23] But the law didn't take effect until mid-1966, giving growers and workers more time to arrange for employer-sponsored green cards. After that, however, new, unsponsored migrant farmworkers from Mexico would be predominantly undocumented.[24] Twenty-three years of bracero schemes had shown as many as two million men from all over Mexico what farmwork in the US entailed, and exactly how and where to find it.

Throughout the 1960s, both the "green carders," as the UFW called them, and undocumented farmworkers took over the roles previously filled by braceros; in fact, for the most part, they were ex-braceros.[25] No longer tied to farm labor by the bracero system and its camps for single men, increasing numbers started fanning out away from their old employers, finding work in cities and towns. They also started bringing over family members and having US-born children. The growers were already using labor contractors, who had no trouble replacing those who left farmwork with new undocumented migrants.[26] Thus, for many Mexicans, seasonal farmwork was becoming precisely what the Bracero Program had been designed to avoid—a stage or step in ultimately migrating permanently.[27] This process would both grow the overall undocumented population and significantly change its composition. At some point, undocumented immigrants in the cities would come to outnumber those in the farm-labor force and include increasing numbers of women and children.[28] This broad transition proceeded apace as the farmworker movement in California advanced and catalyzed the supportive Chicano movement in urban areas.

The California farmworker movement of the 1960s saw migratory agricultural workers from Mexico—who were not residents of the communities it organized—as an endless supply of outsider "scabs" and strikebreakers who undercut the movement's organizing efforts.[29] This was exactly how CSO, other Mexican American organizations, and the AFL-CIO had seen the Bracero Program years before. But a starkly different experience was unfolding in the cities. As far back as the early 1950s, a group of Mexican American labor activists in San Diego started *Hermandad Mexicana* ("Mexican Brotherhood"), a mutual-aid organization to assist and organize Mexicans who crossed the border daily—holders of green cards as well as what were known as "border crossing cards"—to work menial jobs in San Diego.[30] In the late 1960s, legendary labor and political activist Bert Corona and Soledad "Chole" Alatorre emulated the San Diego Hermandad initiative, but specifically for resident undocumented-immigrant workers in the LA area. Soon they set up mutual-aid service centers called "Casas" in several localities, including well beyond the state.[31] The Casas attracted young, idealistic Chicano-movement volunteers interested in directly serving and helping organize undocumented Mexican immigrants in the cities where they both lived. Among them were future Latina/o labor activists and leaders profiled in our first book—María Elena Durazo in Oakland and Antonio Villaraigosa and Gilbert Cedillo in LA.[32] By contrast, the only opportunity UFW offered in the cities was to support their consumer boycotts, together with, and sometimes organized by, white activists.

The new Chicana/o volunteers in the Casas, many of whom were or had been MEChA (Movimiento Estudiantil Chicano de Aztlán) activists in college—like Durazo, Villaraigosa, and Cedillo—actively recruited more Chicano students on campuses with a new message of Mexican working-class solidarity and a critique of capitalism. Part of that message—demands for an immediate end to deportations, unconditional amnesty for the undocumented, and outright elimination of the border between the US and Mexico—departed from what they heard from or associated with either MEChA or the UFW. A political divergence developed between some of the Casas and Corona's Hermandad Mexicana Nacional, the umbrella organization. Led by the big Casa on Pico Boulevard in LA, several of the Casas separated from Hermandad and formed an independent organization primarily known simply as CASA.[33] At the core of the CASA belief system was the slogan *Un Pueblo Sin Fronteras*—"One People Without Borders"—and the organization's newspaper was titled *Sin Fronteras*.[34] A basic CASA organizing tactic was to hawk the newspaper at events and on campuses. That called for a level of ideological coherence and discipline, both in terms of the paper's editorial content and its members' ability to hawk it to strangers, alien to Hermandad Mexicana, which was almost entirely service oriented. CASA recruits were organized into earnest study groups.[35]

Sin Fronteras and the study groups were key differences between CASA's and Hermandad's basic practices, and they contributed to what became a critical divergence between the organizations: whether to conceive of themselves as a revolutionary movement and actively build a revolutionary organization to lead it. That was the path CASA took, while Hermandad did not. Although Corona considered himself a socialist and was something of a self-made intellectual, he was highly pragmatic and had long been involved in electoral politics. CASA and Hermandad Mexicana shared a commitment to aiding and defending undocumented immigrants. They also shared an emphasis on unity between Mexicans and Mexican Americans/Chicanos, a growing sentiment among the urban Chicano movement and, increasingly, traditional Mexican American organizations as well. What was developing here was a sense of linked fate—that whatever was done or could be done to the undocumented could and would threaten Mexican Americans in general, as had happened in the past.[36] Former Chicano-movement activists already saw—as did the student movement and the emerging academic field of Chicano studies—the repatriation pressures, mass detentions, and deportations of the early 1930s and 1950s as grievous assaults on the whole community of Mexican origin, irrespective of their legal status.

The idea of a shared political identity among all people of Mexican origin on either side of the border, regardless of birthplace, citizenship, or immigration status, acquired a currency thanks to the various movements of the 1960s; this was unheard of in what had been previously considered the "postwar era" in the US. The dominant Mexican American organizations of the 1950s—LULAC and the American GI Forum in Texas, and CSO in California—fervently promoted US citizenship, registration, and voting. Their male leadership, furthermore, was dominated by military veterans of World War II and the Korean War.[37] Among these men, a record of military service carried unquestioned prestige. Many Chicano-movement activists, however, showed little or no interest in citizenship, registration, or voting drives, unless channeled into the separatist political project of the La Raza Unida Party. Conventional electoral politics was a tough sell in the era of assassinations, riots, and a series of failed presidencies. Furthermore, in the context of the bitterly controversial Vietnam War and antiwar movement, many Chicano activists freely expressed contempt for military service. This new attitude was dramatized by the rise of the Chicano Moratorium Against the War movement in 1969–70 and the personal evolution of its most visible leader,

Rosalio Muñoz. Muñoz went from high school class president, to the first Mexican American UCLA student body president, to card-burning draft resister and full-time antiwar activist. The Chicano Moratorium march and rally in East LA on August 29, 1970—which devolved into a riot when LA County Sheriff's deputies attacked—became enshrined as the climax of the 1960s Chicano movement's character as a resistance struggle.[38]

*Sheriff's deputies descend on Chicano Moratorium demonstrators on Whittier Boulevard near Indiana Street as the march erupts into chaos on August 29, 1970. Photo by Boris Yaro/*Los Angeles Times.

Uniting to Resist

Undocumented immigration happened to rise as a salient issue during Republican administrations in both Washington (under Nixon) and Sacramento (under Reagan). While in the early 1970s, prominent Democrats and organized labor shared the same concerns and supported similar responses to "illegal aliens" as did Republicans, the first legislative response came at the state level in 1971, when a California Republican assembly member introduced a bill that would sanction employers for hiring such workers. Advocates of solidarity between Mexican Americans and Mexican immigrants were quick to respond. As "illegal immigration" was not an issue in urban barrios, critics of the bill were able to cast draconian immigration enforcement as the real threat to the community.

Step by step, the "Mexican American perspective" on undocumented immigrants took form. A US House subcommittee controlled by Democrats held hearings on "illegal aliens" in Los Angeles and other cities, but the federal bill that emerged from them did not reach the House floor until late 1972 and had no prospect of passing the Senate. Nixon–Ford administration officials then began promising a new campaign of mass deportations. The will to resist these measures steadily spread, from Corona's Hermandad and its Casas to CASA and the Chicano generation, and increasingly to mainline Mexican American organizations struggling to remain "relevant" to the Chicano generation. Historian David Gutiérrez describes how at state legislative hearings and the congressional hearings on "illegal aliens" in 1971, Latino organizations such as LULAC, the Mexican American Political Association (MAPA), and the American GI Forum publicly testified to and explained how they had changed their position on undocumented immigrants—which at that time they mainly referred to as "undocumented workers." Nevertheless, the California "employer-sanctions bill" passed with the support of organized labor, including, "quietly," that of the UFW, and was signed into law by Governor Ronald Reagan that year.[39] Set to go into effect in 1972, the law was met with protests and court challenges.

On the federal level, the Rodino subcommittee hearings led to the Rodino bill, which would have enacted employer sanctions nationwide. Although it failed in 1972, the bill was promptly reintroduced in 1973. To fight this renewed threat, CASA, Hermandad, and other organizations formed their National Coalition for Fair Immigration Laws that year.[40] Both Corona and his Hermandad Mexicana, as well as its more leftist CASA spin-off, publicly criticized and protested the UFW and Cesar Chavez personally for having supported the California employer-sanctions bill. A lasting and often bitter dispute developed between the farmworker movement and urban-based Mexican American and Chicano activists who were leading the transformation of the community's political stance on immigration.[41]

The two camps were each pursuing different forms of both politics of inclusion and politics of resistance. The farmworker movement sought inclusion in organized labor, the inclusion of agricultural work in labor-law protections, and the power to compel agribusiness to recognize and negotiate terms with its union. This agenda could not advance if growers were free to recruit and hire workers outside the movement and who were not part of the communities the incipient union had been organizing since 1962. The union could do nothing to stop legal migrant workers from coming into California from other states to harvest crops, and it tried but failed to pressure authorities to stop "green carders" crossing legally from Mexico for temporary farmwork.[42] But it could, and did, support the bill to sanction the employers of undocumented migrants, and that meant de facto supporting the accompanying detention and deportation of their workers. Furthermore, when the union initiated or supported a strike, and a grower hired undocumented workers to maintain production, the union protested and called on authorities to enforce immigration laws. From the union's point of view, what it saw as collusion between growers, the INS, and Border Patrol amounted to the same corrupt system of the days of the Bracero Program, which it was compelled to *resist*.

Urban Mexican American organizations and activists, on the other hand, sought inclusion in and equal treatment by *all* public and publicly chartered institutions and their decision-making processes, including the political system, schools, higher education, housing, the professions, and public facilities—ultimately, the *equitable* incorporation of Latinos into every sphere and level of American life. A fast-growing population—regardless of immigration status—bolstered these organizations' and leaders' critiques, agendas, and demands. In agriculture, *seasonal* undocumented migrants—not the undocumented who resided in the same communities as legal residents and US-citizen farmworkers—presented the same problem for organizing a farmworker union that the Bracero Program had. In urban areas, however, the growing undocumented-immigrant population was *not seasonal*. To urban Mexican Americans in some parts of California, undocumented immigrants were increasingly their neighbors, coworkers, and fellow students—and in many cases, family members or other relatives. Mexican Americans' politics of inclusion included the undocumented residents of their cities and neighborhoods, and they became particularly supportive of undocumented students in public schools.[43]

Thus, the farmworker movement and urban Mexican Americans were responding politically to different parts of the growing undocumented population, as would become clear by the end of the ten-year national battle over immigration policy. In California, those sympathetic to undocumented immigrants mobilized in 1971–72 to protest the state's employer-sanctions law, which "vanished" due to the state's inability to enforce it and especially when state courts ruled it unconstitutional.[44] They mobilized again in 1973 along the same lines to oppose the Rodino bill, which was passed by the House but ignored by the Senate. By then, even the UFW had broken with the AFL-CIO and announced its opposition to the federal bill.[45] The union's change of position, however, did not eliminate the rancor and mistrust that had developed between it and the growing immigrant-rights sentiment and movement, nor did it even last. Years later, the union would return to the AFL-CIO position in favor of sanctions on employers for employing undocumented workers.[46]

The Vietnam War was another critical factor at this time. A character-defining turning point for the Chicano movement was its head-on collision with the forces of the state, in Los Angeles in August 1970, over the war. For many, the violent suppression of the Chicano Moratorium march and rally against the war that year in East LA sealed a permanent enmity between their community and the state—especially regarding its law enforcement and war-making machine, which at that time seemed inextricably intertwined. This understanding and sensibility were reinforced by having a Republican administration in charge that was simultaneously expanding the war in Vietnam and making an issue of "illegal aliens" at home, while at the same time locked in battle with the antiwar movement. Months earlier that year, National Guard troops had opened fire on a student protest at Kent State University in Ohio, precipitating a sense of national crisis over the continuing war. The suppression of the Chicano Moratorium in East LA was the Mexican American Kent State. In his second term, Nixon underscored the link between his national-security state at war in Vietnam and the threat of mass deportations at home when he appointed the just-retired commandant of the Marine Corps, General Leonard Chapman, to take charge of the INS.[47]

After Nixon resigned in disgrace in 1974 and Ford assumed the presidency, continuing Attorney General William Saxbe announced that the administration would undertake to round up and deport "a million illegal aliens." Saxbe went further to claim that this plan was supported by the UFW, which Cesar Chavez emphatically denied.[48] But for many activists, the union would not be able to shake the impression that it was anti-immigrant. When the Carter administration unveiled its plan to combat undocumented immigration, the whole gamut of Mexican American and Chicano organizations, minus the UFW, vowed to resist it. A historic Chicano-movement leader in Texas, José Angel Gutiérrez, called for a "First National Chicano/Latino Conference on Immigration" for the express purpose of formulating a united front against the Carter Plan and a strategy to resist it.

The conference was an astonishing display of how the immigration issue could now bring together Mexican American and Chicano-movement activists and organizations that had been hostile to each other for years. The fiery Gutiérrez, founder of the politically separatist La Raza Unida Party in South Texas, opened the conference by caustically denouncing the "*Democ-atrás*"—a double entendre that insulted Democrats as politically backward on immigrant rights and as anatomical rear ends. He was soon followed at the podium by Vilma Martínez, head of the Mexican American Legal Defense and Educational Fund (MALDEF), who vehemently denounced Gutiérrez's rhetoric. Nevertheless, she and MALDEF, Gutiérrez and Raza Unida, the head of LULAC, and the head of CASA all united in their opposition to the Carter immigration proposal.[49]

This turn of events was, in a very real sense, a final victory for what remained of the Chicano movement, as well as for the Mexican nationalist movement led by CASA and Hermandad Mexicana. There could be no question that the "Chicano generation" would forcefully reject the very idea of supporting immigration-law enforcement against Mexican undocumented workers and their families.[50] That the "Mexican American generation" had opposed the Bracero Program was fine, albeit not well known. *That* had been resistance to a corrupt and exploitative state policy. *That* was punching up at the racist state and the growers it served. But once that program was gone, to turn on undocumented workers themselves would be to punch down, to be complicit with repressive agencies of the state and right-wing nativists. The Chicano movement was above all a resistance movement—resistance to assimilation, inferior education, police abuse, economic exploitation, white standards of beauty, and success. Chicanos could not abide calling the *migra* on Mexicans—*even if they were being used as strikebreakers.* Bert Corona's message to Cesar Chavez was—however unrealistic in practice for farm labor—*organize* the undocumented, do not deport them.[51] That message resonated with Chicanos; for many of them, the message to boycott grapes, lettuce, and Gallo wine was supplanted by the slogan *Raza Sí. Migra No!*[52] This was not, by any means, a decision to turn away from the farmworkers. It was a stand against immigration authorities and their raids, roundups, and detentions—a stand that would eventually see those authorities as an immigration *gestapo* and give rise to the twenty-first-century demand to "abolish ICE."[53] Even the older Mexican American generation of organizations and activists, who would not go so far as to agree with open borders, could not help but associate themselves with the *Migra No!* sentiment.

Ironically, the farmworker movement had inspired and propelled the Chicano movement in the cities. The unprecedented visibility of the farmworker cause, boosted by its ties to Robert Kennedy, its mediagenic tactics, the iconic flag, its cultural guru Luis Valdez and his Teatro Campesino, its open conflicts with Reagan and Nixon, and more, was transformative for urban Chicanos. The UFW consumer boycotts in US cities directly mobilized Chicanos, along with white liberals. The UFW even more directly mobilized Mexican American/Chicano volunteers and voters in numerous election field efforts. But in the 1970s, when "illegal aliens" and immigration policy came back to the fore, the Chicano generation's countercultural stance of unyielding resistance fueled a steady and consequential shift in perspective: Whereas the Chicano movement's moral poster child had for years been the farmworker, it was slowly being replaced by the image of the undocumented immigrant.[54]

Decades later, this shift would be complete with the consolidation of the image of the "Dreamer"—the undocumented immigrant brought to the US as a minor—as the moral poster child of the Latino struggle for inclusion and empowerment in the twenty-first century.[55]

The Carter administration withdrew its 1977 plan and instead supported legislation establishing a "Select Commission on Immigration" made up of both congressional and White House appointees.[56] With the commission's final report not due until fall 1980, no new immigration bill would emerge during Carter's single term. Immigration policy would continue to be a hotly contested issue, but the national Latino policy agenda would be dominated by the other two national challenges—the Census and the Voting Rights Act—for at least a couple of years into the Reagan Revolution of the 1980s. The reprieve on immigration would prove to be strategically formative for the development of Latino clout in Washington, focused in particular on the House of Representatives, which would remain under Democratic control until the mid-1990s.

Ms. Hernández Goes to Washington

> *. . . the work goes on, the cause endures,*
> *the hope still lives, and the dream shall never die.*
> —Edward M. Kennedy
> August 12, 1980

Gloria Molina's appointment to the Carter White House personnel office was consequential for California Latina/o political development and its impact on the country. From that empowerment perspective, Molina's hire had its big payoff when she pulled a reluctant Antonia Hernández—her East LA lawyer friend and Chicana comrade in arms—into the policy battles developing on the DC front. Hernández and Molina had bonded when they first came together for a historic class-action lawsuit against the huge Los Angeles County General Hospital, which loomed over LA's Eastside like a forbidding fortress. For many women of color, it was indeed forbidding—a place where doctors were eager to sterilize them, with or without their permission, and were rewarded for doing so.[57] As recounted in our previous book, in late 1973, Hernández, a public-interest lawyer fresh out of UCLA, approached community leader Molina and her young Chicana feminist organization, *Comisión Femenil Mexicana de Los Angeles*, about Latinas who had been sterilized under pressure or without signed consent after giving birth at the hospital. Although the lawsuit did not prevail in court, it was a turning point for the Eastside, and for Chicanas and Latinas far beyond LA.[58] Antonia and Gloria established themselves as fierce fighters for their community and women of color.

They were continuing to serve, Antonia with her legal work and Gloria as district director to first-term State Assembly Member Art Torres, when the 1976 presidential election came around. Taking a White House personnel job in the new Carter administration, Gloria began recruiting Latinas and Latinos to serve in DC, and she was naturally on the lookout for a position she might be able to sell Antonia on. Every opportunity Gloria pitched to Antonia for the first two years met with the same answer: "No." Then, after the 1978 midterms and with the new Congress coming in 1979, Gloria caught wind of an opportunity for Antonia to serve as a staff counsel to the powerhouse Senate Judiciary Committee, which none other than Ted Kennedy was taking over as chair. But her friend still had no interest. It took the combined efforts of Gloria, a brilliant aide to Kennedy, and Antonia's lawyer husband to persuade her to take a job that would change her life and help usher in a new era of Latina/o empowerment.[59] In the twentieth century, generations of Latinos—Mexican Americans in particular—famously revered the Kennedys. President Kennedy, who in 1960 memorably campaigned in East LA, addressed a Latino gathering one 1963 night in Houston, when Antonia was in high school. The next day he was assassinated in Dallas, and the students were sent home.[60] Gloria Molina was a campaign volunteer headed for the victory party at LA's Ambassador Hotel in 1968 when Robert Kennedy was fatally shot, and her car was turned back at the gate.[61] The moments and experiences that bound so many to the Kennedy brothers remained vivid.

Though moving to Washington would separate Antonia from her close family, she was motivated to become involved in making federal law, especially when such huge issues for Latinos as immigration policy and voting rights would be rising to the top of the agenda following the next presidential election. She was herself an immigrant, but only because her US-born father's family had been pressured to return to Mexico during the 1930s. Antonia, the eldest of seven children, had grown up in East LA, and her family had spent summers in the fields as migrant farmworkers. Antonia's outlook was shaped by the movements and upheaval of the 1960s, and she identified as a Chicana.[62] After graduating from Garfield High, Hernández attended East LA College and then was able to transfer to UCLA, where she stayed for law school. As a student, Antonia worked in the university's Upward Bound program, where she had a major influence on Chicano high school students, including Gilbert Cedillo, who found the experience life-changing and went on to a historic career in labor and politics.[63] In her first job as a public-service lawyer, Antonia had almost immediate impact and became famous, along with Gloria Molina, for leading a groundbreaking lawsuit against LA County's General Hospital.

Hernández took the Senate staff job in 1979 and got to work when a core civil rights question was reaching maturity on more than one front, and others were brewing. The Supreme Court had ruled on a Fair Housing Act case in 1977. To win, plaintiffs had to prove that a local law, policy, or procedure was intended to discriminate by race—not just that it had racially discriminatory results.[64] Kennedy was already a cosponsor on the Senate side of a bill fashioned by the House Judiciary Committee that would salvage the act by replacing the "intent test" for proving discrimination with an "effects test."[65] That was also the year, however, that revolutions toppled US-supported governments in Iran and Nicaragua. Before the year was out, a mob stormed the US embassy in Tehran and took fifty-two Americans hostage, and then the Soviet Union invaded Afghanistan. With President Carter wounded, Antonia's boss, Senator Kennedy, rose to challenge him in the 1980 primaries. The effort to fix the fair-housing law would have to wait until a lame-duck session following the November elections. But right in January of that year, the Supreme Court made any fix on the housing-rights front a heavier lift. This time it dealt a blow to the Voting Rights Act (VRA) by requiring the same sort of discriminatory intent in legal challenges to electoral procedures. Because "racial purpose" or intent is so much harder to prove than racially unequal effects or results, this ruling in the VRA case rendered practically useless the section of the act that was applicable not just to the Old South, but to the whole country.[66]

Thus, Antonia faced a new fork in the road: between the law and policy track she had just joined the year before, and the electoral-political track her boss was leaping to. She lacked experience in electoral politics but was from a loyal Democratic family. Antonia took a leave from the Judiciary Committee staff to volunteer for Ted Kennedy's presidential campaign. The climax of that effort came on the June night when the senator—like his brother Bobby before him—won the California primary. Walter Cronkite, in a live interview, slipped and greeted the incandescently beaming candidate as "President Kennedy." The dream had not died.

Antonia Takes Over MALDEF-DC

The Mexican American Legal Defense and Educational Fund (MALDEF), a creation of LULAC and a major grant from the Ford Foundation, was founded in 1968 in San Antonio. It was explicitly modeled after the NAACP Legal Defense Fund (LDF), previously led by Thurgood Marshall—famous for the 1954 *Brown v. Board* case, which banned segregated public schools—who became the first Black Supreme Court justice. MALDEF, however, got off to a rocky start. It lost a major case at the court and was compelled by the Ford Foundation to change leadership and move out of San Antonio. After MALDEF moved to San Francisco, lawyer Vilma Martínez, who had been on the LDF staff, took over as president and general counsel, and methodically transformed the organization into a prestigious and effective agent of change.[67]

For all her early success as a Los Angeles Latina public-interest lawyer, Antonia's work as counsel to the Senate Judiciary Committee, enriched by her part in the third Kennedy presidential campaign in twenty years, prepared her for new challenges in ways she could never have experienced had she stayed in LA. But with the senator's failed campaign over in mid-August 1980 and the chairmanship of the Judiciary

Committee now belonging to his colleague Joe Biden, Antonia was looking to head back home. Significantly foreshadowing battles to come, however, a new obstacle to progress on civil rights was developing in the Senate, specifically in response to the bill that would fix the Fair Housing Act, which had been put off until after the November elections. At the same time, Antonia was being recruited to take over MALDEF's Washington office—a request she was fending off, as she had with the Senate job two years before.[68]

Then came November's stunning news that not only had Ronald Reagan—long an opponent of civil rights laws—been elected president, but his party was also taking over the Senate. Antonia would have to make a quick choice. MALDEF President Vilma Martínez called the next morning. Martínez knew that Antonia would soon be out of a job, and she and her husband had not yet had a chance to plan their next move. There was nobody better than a superbly connected former counsel to the Senate Judiciary Committee to advocate at the Capitol for Mexican Americans and other Latinos on the pressing issues of voting rights and immigration. Vilma prevailed upon Antonia to stay in DC—to fight the good fights to come in the Reagan era.[69] Skies had darkened for further progress on civil rights, and in the short time left that year, they darkened further still. The previous January, the Supreme Court ruled that Voting Rights Act challenges to electoral procedures had to prove that policies they sought to overturn not only had discriminatory effects but were intended to discriminate by race.[70] Then came the elections. But even before control of the presidency and Senate changed hands, there came another setback during the lame-duck session—the years-long effort to strengthen the Fair Housing Act by explicitly adding the effects test in its implementation was filibustered and died.

In 1981, Antonia Hernández took on the job of chief advocate for Latino interests within the civil rights establishment in Washington. That community, however, remained divided over whether Latinos as a "class," and their priority issues, belonged in civil rights law at all.[71] This was in spite of court rulings that had struck down segregation of Mexican Americans in public schools, as well as their exclusion from juries, and in spite of the inclusion of "language minorities" in the 1975 renewal of the VRA. In fact, that renewal was the cause of bitter division between Blacks and Latinos within that policy community's institutionalized hub, the Leadership Conference on Civil Rights (LCCR). There had been controversy within this indispensable coalition over whether Latino organizations and other non-Black minority groups legitimately belonged in LCCR.[72]

Voting Rights Act: Black and Latino Priorities

The 1965 Voting Rights Act (VRA) was propelled by perhaps the most dramatic battle of the Black civil rights movement. Peaceful African American marches in Alabama demanding voting rights created a political crisis that moved the Lyndon Johnson administration to shepherd a bill through Congress, signed into law late that summer. The first of the marches, from Selma to the state capital in Montgomery, was violently blocked by Alabama state troopers at the Edmund Pettus Bridge. This historic "police riot," dubbed "Bloody Sunday," became the most commemorated episode of the movement.

The centerpiece of the VRA was its Section 5—the "preclearance" provision that placed electoral procedures throughout the Old South under the supervision of the Department of Justice. That measure was to be in effect for five years, which meant the pro-civil rights lobby in Washington made renewing Section 5 its top priority in 1970 and again in 1975. The federal policy area of civil rights is dominated by the coalition known as the Leadership Conference on Civil Rights (LCCR), founded in 1950 by thirty organizations, which have since grown to over two hundred.

Until the 1970s, civil rights law was understood to address racial discrimination against Blacks. By the time of the 1975 VRA renewal, however, Latino, Native American, and Asian American organizations had joined LCCR and were pushing for the act's protections to be extended to them as "language minorities." Some African American leaders and organizations feared that expanding VRA's scope risked renewal of the act as a whole, creating a persistent tension between them and Latino groups in particular.

Thus, going into the effort to again reauthorize the VRA in 1982, the top priority of Black groups remained to preserve the Section 5 preclearance authority over the South, while that of Latinos and other language minorities was to preserve the bilingual voting-rights provisions, which had only been in effect since 1975. Furthermore, Latino advocates wanted to strengthen another provision of the act, Section 2, to outlaw electoral procedures anywhere in the country that had the effect of disadvantaging electoral participation or representation of a "protected class," without having to prove discriminatory intent *in court.*

In 2013, the Supreme Court rendered the act's Section 5 unenforceable by finding its coverage formula unconstitutional, but in 2023, it affirmed the continuing enforceability of Section 2.[73] *Also in June 2023, the court rejected a lawsuit that would have made state legislatures the sole authority over federal electoral procedures in their states, unreviewable by either state or federal courts.*[74]

Hernández took over MALDEF's Washington office just as LCCR was gearing up for the next VRA renewal. The House Judiciary Subcommittee on Civil Rights had been working on the issues involved since 1979.[75] Focusing specifically on the need to extend the act before its Section 5 expired in August 1982, the coalition was in the midst of bolstering itself by hiring its first full-time director while also hammering out its VRA-extension priorities. New LCCR Executive Director Ralph Neas took office on March 31, 1981. Judiciary Chair Peter Rodino introduced the first version of the extension bill on April 7. Neas's first move was to pull together a VRA-extension steering committee of twenty-five from the 165 member organizations. As expert insider Michael Pertschuk later wrote, the committee "was to meet almost every Friday for the following sixteen months; during the heat of the campaign, it would meet four or five times a week. Its deliberations, sometimes rancorous, would often last several hours."[76] Thus, just as the immigration-reform debate was picking up with the release of the final report of the Select Commission on Immigration set up by Congress and the Carter administration, Antonia found herself having to focus "like a laser beam" on the voting-rights bill.[77]

The LCCR steering committee, working closely with the House Subcommittee on Civil Rights, embarked on a prodigious amount of work for a combination of reasons. LCCR, Subcommittee Chair Don Edwards of California, and full Judiciary Committee Chair Rodino were determined to lead in the face of the turn against civil rights by other branches of government. As historian John Hebert Roper put it, "The judiciary, through the Mobile case, and the executive branch, through the announced policies of Reynolds, made it obvious to Edwards that congressmen must fill the vacuum created by the other two branches."[78] Roper might have noted that the House would have to lead the whole Congress as well. As a consequence of the election, Senator Orrin Hatch, who led the filibuster that killed the Fair Housing amendments, became the new chair of the Constitutional Rights Subcommittee of the Judiciary. As Pertschuk observes, Hatch and company drew "strength and legitimacy from the Court's decision in their single-minded crusade to eliminate effects tests in all civil rights laws—and to prevent an effects test from being applied to voting rights."[79] On the other side of the Capitol, the Edwards subcommittee launched eighteen days of hearings, conducted both in Washington and in locations in the South and Southwest. Over two hundred witnesses testified, the majority mobilized by LCCR.[80]

At the same time, the Immigration Subcommittee of the House Judiciary, which had been developing a big bill after years-long preparation by the Select Commission on Immigration, withdrew its own proposal under withering fire from Latinos and others. Having the VRA extension and the immigration-reform bill—then by far the two preeminent Latino policy priorities—hammered out at the same time in the House Judiciary Committee controlled by Democrats complicated life for Latino advocates. On the Senate side, the Republicans made extreme conservative Strom Thurmond chair of that chamber's Judiciary Committee. As a practical matter, advocacy organizations would have to decide how to allocate their severely limited resources between the issues of voting rights and immigration reform, calibrate and time their demands, and use their access to negotiate with and influence members of the House committee and its all-important chair, Peter Rodino of New Jersey.

Latino Republicans willing to work on either issue seemed to have a better shot at influencing the Reagan White House than the Senate Republican majority or its Judiciary Committee. The Reagan team and that of Vice President George H. W. Bush were dominated by Californians and Texans and were thus considered more aware of and sensitive to the rapidly growing Hispanic population—as just established by the 1980 census. That, combined with the need to look ahead to the 1984 reelection contest, made the necessary 1982 VRA renewal a politically "critical conjuncture" for the White House, which was literally weighing the desirable optics of a VRA-extension White House signing ceremony, with prominent Hispanic Republican leaders invited and seen on the national stage.[81] Having Antonia Hernández heading its Washington office, however, gave MALDEF a special angle. As a former counsel to the Senate Judiciary Committee when Kennedy was chair, Antonia had, in fact, served Democratic and Republican senators alike. The atmosphere was cordial and relaxed, and Antonia found the elderly Senator Thurmond—once a segregationist "Dixiecrat" firebrand—a courtly Southern gentleman. Hernández herself was extraordinarily practiced in speaking calmly and softly—even sweetly—in presenting policy options and concerns.[82]

The negotiated voting-rights bill, containing most of what the Latino lobby considered its top priorities, passed the Senate committee almost unanimously—Senator Thurmond was among those voting yes. Final passage by both houses of Congress, and Ronald Reagan's signing, followed in short order. This June 1982 extension of the VRA, with amendments, banned procedures that had the effect of giving legally "protected classes" of ethnic and racial groups less than equal opportunities to elect representatives of their own choosing. MALDEF could proceed to sue states and local jurisdictions across the country on behalf of under- and unrepresented Latino communities—as could the Justice Department itself. That same month, the Supreme Court ruled on a MALDEF case of immense historical and political weight for Mexican Americans. In its decision on *Plyler v. Doe*, a case that had been making its way up from Texas since 1977, the court ruled that the state had an overriding public interest in the education of undocumented schoolchildren. Public schools were henceforth barred from even asking about their students' (or their parents') immigration status, as had been mandated by a Texas law, which was then rendered constitutionally null and void. MALDEF had achieved its greatest victory, unsurpassed to this day.[83]

Establishing in effect the right of resident school-age children to attend public school, and consequently establishing public schools as sensitive protected zones free of immigration-law enforcement, was an essential step toward a larger, more fundamental Latino national policy goal—what would come to be known as comprehensive immigration reform or "CIR." It would take several more years of strenuous efforts to reach this objective, and in the process fashion Latino policy clout in Washington.

Chapter 5
Forging the Latino Lobby

California Latina and Latino professionals had long been less likely to serve in Washington than their Texas counterparts.[1] Consequently, Latino efforts to influence national policy were light on California talent before the one-term Carter presidency at the end of the 1970s.[2] Like her fellow East LA Latina Antonia Hernández, Martha Escutia took a path to DC that illuminates how that continental divide began to erode, and how California Latinos—especially from greater Los Angeles—eventually came to have an outsized presence in the twenty-first century at the highest levels of national leadership. Their Washington experience would prove formative for Hernández and Escutia, both of whom returned to LA in the mid-1980s and became top leaders in advancing Latino representation in government, law, higher education, philanthropy, and more.

Martha Goes to Washington

Antonia Hernández was still working on Capitol Hill in 1979 when Martha Escutia started law school walking distance away, at Georgetown Law Center, in the Judiciary Square area of Northwest Washington. They had not yet met, but Martha and Antonia were homies from East LA. Martha, however, had just graduated from USC, the crosstown rival of Antonia's UCLA. And although several years younger, Martha got to DC first, for a semester as an intern for her undergrad major in public administration. That was Martha's first US trip east of LA. On her introductory tour of the Capitol, she was intrigued by the sight of what seemed like platoons of busy people in suits, armed with briefcases, buzzing through corridors. They were lobbyists, there to advocate for their "special interest" clients. None looked like her; they were all white.[3] Told that one could become that sort of policy advocate by going to law school, Martha decided *that* was what she wanted to do, but to advocate for her community. She was glimpsing her own future, one that would make her much like Antonia—whom in a few years she would approach for a job.

Martha's journey to a career that took her from East LA to USC, then to Washington to study law, then to Europe for more international law, and finally back to California to serve in the state legislature as one of its leaders, is a monumental story of transcendence over devastating experiences and disordered circumstances. In 1963, when she was six, the eldest of four children, Martha woke to her baby brother's cry and found their parents had abandoned them. Life-altering transitions rarely come so early, but in the binational Escutia-Sandoval family experience, they went back generations, on both sides of the border. This background primed Martha to eventually play a perceptive and empathetic role in the immigration-policy battles of the 1980s. But her complicated backstory may also have destined Martha to again move on before the immigration reform's fate was secured by a final vote in Congress and Ronald Reagan's signature in the fall of 1986.

Not unlike the migratory butterflies of her father's home state of Michoacán, Martha's family story includes virtually every form of migration back and forth across the border. Her mother, Marina, was from mining country in the northwestern state of Sinaloa. Marina's family made their way to East LA, where she attended a year of high school and soon married. She was raising her children there when her husband's abuse made Marina flee back to Mexico, leaving their four kids behind. From then on, Martha's maternal grandparents raised her. Her step-grandfather, the most loving person in her life, had come to California as a bracero, all the way from Mexico's southernmost state of Chiapas. A picker in the citrus belt surrounding LA, he was able to stay legally when his employer sponsored him for a green card. Martha's grandmother did not want to raise all the children, so her father returned to take Martha's younger sister and two brothers—still preschoolers—to his native Michoacán and left them there to be raised by his parents.

Martha was already about as Mexican as a native Californian can be—but would become even more so. While she was still in grade school, Martha's grandparents took her with them to live in Guadalajara for two years. When they returned to East LA, Martha's classmates mocked her for being a greenhorn immigrant, a *tijuanera*.[4] Her grandmother, who disapproved of Marina's divorce, resented having to raise even just Martha, spoke hurtfully of and to her, and could turn violent. It all made Martha want to hide. Her grandfather, whom she and her cousins called Papú, gave Martha an out.[5] She used to get up in the middle of the night to make his lunch before he left on his long commute to Pacoima, in a far-off corner of the San Fernando Valley. He would get back early enough to pick her up and take her to the local library. Martha spent hours there every day, finding solace in books her grandparents could not afford. After doing her homework, she read her way through her beloved encyclopedias, "from A to Z," as she would recall. Martha longed for her own set of encyclopedias, works that since their invention had imposed order on a confusing and chaotic world.

A young Martha smiles as she holds a balloon in one hand and her grandfather Papú's in the other. Courtesy of Martha Escutia.

Martha's grandparents lived on a two-house lot, along with her aunts, uncles, and their children. Her cousins took the place of the younger siblings that her father had spirited away. This gave Martha a chance to develop skills that would serve her repeatedly over decades—from organizing her cousins in a runaway scheme to forming a bug club with monthly dues. With bundled-up handkerchiefs tied to sticks, Martha led them down the sidewalk. They got as far as the church two blocks away, where they encountered a priest who led them back home. Her "East LA Insect Club" marked another level of organization. The cousins worked the neighborhood for empty bottles they could cash in for nickel deposits. Each contributed a quarter monthly to buy insect-mounting kits. Then they spread out to catch specimens of all the bugs in the neighborhood and stick them to boards for display. Their growing collection was Martha's Enlightenment encyclopedism come to life with dead bugs—pinning order out of nature's buzzing anarchy. The club died when one of the cousins made off with the treasury.

Apart from adventures with her *primos*, the circumstances of her upbringing made Martha shy and studious. But few, if any, people who have known Martha the professional can imagine her shrinking from a fight, much less being shy and quiet. Nonetheless, both sides of Martha's brain drove her to seek safe spaces away from home, and finding them took initiative. She had the library, the encyclopedias, and her insects to mount and classify. But around the corner was also a music and art school, where she wanted to learn to paint and play piano. Students had to have a piano at home to enroll in music lessons, so that was out. But two blocks away was the neighborhood church compound, complete with a school and convent. The sisters let Martha use their piano, but that was not good enough for the Los Angeles Music and Art School. So, she turned to painting and struck a deal to trade work for lessons. She cleaned up the art room after every lesson, once the other children had left. And the convent still served as a place to hide.

Finding Mom

Experiences widely spaced apart in time drew Martha out of her shell and pointed her toward a public political life. Years passed before Martha's grandparents tracked down her mother in Mexico City. They took Martha to stand outside the phone company where Marina worked, and they all waited for her to come out. Once they finally reconnected, Martha began spending summers with her mother, who had never gotten her US citizenship. Marina was a "green carder," so to keep her immigrant visa current, even though she didn't live in the US anymore, she had Martha send in the annual resident-alien registration card for her. In time, that arrangement would lead to a confrontation with lasting consequences.

Although not a citizen, either, Martha's Papú was strongly pro-US and pro-Democrat. His stepdaughter Marina, however, veered off in a radically different direction, remarrying a Communist Party activist and college professor in Mexico City who was imprisoned in the aftermath of the 1968 student movement there. That movement, against repression and demanding democratization of Mexico's one-party state, was itself notoriously suppressed by army troops who massacred protesters and incarcerated survivors. After her new husband, Fabio, was released in a general amnesty, Marina and Fabio lived together in the Tlatelolco public housing complex—the very site of the 1968 massacre. The couple regularly hosted what seem to have been Mexican Communist Party cell meetings in their apartment. The now-teenage Martha would hide in a bedroom, put off by the harsh anti-US rhetoric that dominated discussion. During one meeting, the guests wanted to know why Martha avoided them. When they insulted her as a *yanqui* imperialist, Marina failed to defend her daughter. So Martha pushed back for herself. Turning to her mother, Martha asked why, if she hated the US, she had her daughter maintain her green-card status? Was it in case her new marriage failed, so she could return to the imperialist United States? Marina answered with a slap. While they personally put the incident behind them, Martha was henceforth allergic to radicalism and self-identified as anti-communist.

One late-summer Saturday morning in 1970, Martha was pushing a lawn mower in front of her grandparents' house when helicopters appeared overhead. Police sirens wailed from every direction, and she could see smoke rising from the park and Whittier Boulevard a few blocks away. Papú burst out of the house, shouting to her and her cousins to rush inside. It was August 29, and several law-enforcement agencies, led by LA County Sheriffs, were attacking the rally gathered for the Chicano Moratorium Against the War, tear-gassing and charging into the park, swinging batons, and striking everyone they could reach to disperse the crowd. Papú was watching live TV coverage as the protest rally was driven from the park into the boulevard, which precipitated a riot and fires that spread for several blocks.[6] That glimpse of "East Los" Chicano-movement history may or may not have had anything to do with Martha's never identifying as Chicana—she was strictly and proudly Mexicana.

The Education of Martha Escutia

Aware of Martha's academic promise, Papú decided to pay for her to attend a small Catholic high school instead of Garfield, where Antonia and many other future Latina/o leaders went. But she would have to take the bus, dressed in her school uniform—and find ways to avoid the Chicana gang girls on her final walk home. Martha would have more walking in store. The Eastside had become highly politicized over the years. Her civics teacher had students walk precincts for an election campaign, and then Martha volunteered for another. Her childhood experience collecting bottles was refreshed with a new pitch.

Her school was too small to have a college counselor, so without guidance, in the fall of 1974, Martha fixed on USC after seeing its dramatic come-from-behind win over Notre Dame on TV. Besides managing to be a disciplined, straight-A student, Martha's addiction to encyclopedias made standardized tests a breeze. Urged by a Chicano student recruiter from Yale who visited her school, Martha applied there, too, and got in. But Yale's generous financial aid offer still required a $1,000 contribution from her family, so that was out. Martha would spend the next four years taking two buses every day to USC, while also working evenings at a downtown bank.

Due to a potentially damaging experience that instead turned out well, Martha improvised her own college orientation late in her senior year in high school. As the top student in her class, she prepared to deliver her valedictorian address in both English and Spanish, but the nuns objected. She was thinking of her grandparents, with whom she had only ever spoken in Spanish, and estimated that the majority of her classmates did the same with their parents. By telling Martha she could not give her speech in both languages, the nuns struck a nerve that may have been touched only once before. When Martha replied that they could not stop her, the sisters stripped her of the title of valedictorian and suspended her for the last two weeks of school. Afraid to tell her grandparents about the suspension, Martha left as though she was going to school, but instead she took the buses to USC, which she had never visited before. She explored one department after another, was welcomed as an incoming student, and began meeting professors. When high school graduation day arrived, the girl who had earned the salutatorian title, but who was now listed in the program as valedictorian, implored Martha to give the speech she alone should give. When the other girl's name was called, Martha shocked the small audience when she stood, strode to the podium, and gave her speech, which she had memorized in both languages.

At USC, Martha found more than a safe space—it was an immense new home. The university's culture promotes the "Trojan family" idea at every turn. Not coincidentally, the school's Latino Alumni Association is the most successful of its kind in the country. Two professors became father figures to Martha, employed her as a research assistant in her final college years, and prepared her for doctoral studies in public policy. Her major took Martha to DC to spend a semester interning at the US Capitol. This made her change direction, away from doctoral studies and an academic life to law school and policy lobbying. News of Martha's new career objective came much to the chagrin of her USC professors. After getting over their disappointment that Martha was choosing advocacy over academia, the professors surprised her with a going-away reception and a check for $3,000. They had taken up a collection to cover her first year's rent in Washington so she could focus on her studies without having to work at the same time, as she had while at USC. Papú had the same idea and took a second job so he could also help her. Law school would be tough enough.

Her final college experience set up a culminating challenge at home that would provide the closest Martha would come to closure in her often-painful family life. Martha wrote her senior thesis on domestic violence, taking her father's abuse of her mother as her eyewitness case study. She had found another, more sophisticated way to try to make sense out of chaos, but her grandmother denounced the account as a vile fabrication and called Martha's mother in Mexico City to press Martha to disavow it. Marina flew to LA, read the thesis, and corroborated what Martha had written. But the next time Martha reached out to her mother, she got no response. She found Fabio, who told her that Marina had divorced him and left with their son for the Soviet Union. Disbelieving Fabio's story, Martha spent years trying to track her mother down and even hired a private investigator, to no avail. Martha finally accepted that her mother had once again disappeared from her life.

Mock Court, Supreme Justice

New tests awaited at Georgetown Law, in the midst of Martha's second, dazzling introduction to a wider world. For the first time in her education, Martha found she could do no better than average. Her hardest class was tax law with Martin Ginsburg, whose wife, Ruth Bader Ginsburg, sat on the Washington, DC, Circuit Court of Appeals. A particular challenge loomed ahead. All law students were required to participate in mock court to argue an assigned case before a volunteer panel of real federal judges. In the drawing, Martha got the losing widow's side in a case over a drug manufacturer's failure to recall a faulty drug that contributed to her husband's demise. She also happened to draw the three-judge panel presided over by Ruth Bader Ginsburg. Martha's shyness remained strong enough for her to plead to her professor and the dean to excuse her from the competition. Her professor came to her meeting with the dean and chimed in that Martha would need extra time just to complete the legal brief required before the mock trial—an extension she had not asked for. That demeaning ad lib provoked Martha to object, guarantee that she would submit her brief on time, and withdraw her request to sit out the mock trial.

She dove into the task of writing a brief on behalf of the plaintiff, who had lost in district court. The loss hinged on both fact and law: A pharmaceutical company is liable if it ignores findings published in a scientific or medical journal that one of its products is flawed. But in this case, the findings regarding the product in question had appeared only in newspapers, not yet in a professional journal, when it had cost a life. Perhaps because Martha was from LA and one of the papers that reported on the product was the *Los Angeles Times*, it occurred to her to call and ask if it had won any awards for science or medical reporting—which it had. All three papers she called had won such awards and happily faxed her detailed letters to that effect. Martha attached the letters to her brief as exhibits.

The stakes got higher still. Judge Ginsburg canceled at the last minute, but none other than Justice—and future Chief Justice—of the Supreme Court William Rehnquist was persuaded to fill in. Nevertheless, Martha's scoop gave her confidence she had not felt since delivering her valedictorian speech in high school. While they waited for the panel's verdict, Martha's professor apologized for having underestimated her and said she was "lyrical" in oral argument. Two of the judges split, leaving the decision to Rehnquist, who ruled in Martha's favor. Rehnquist then addressed Martha directly, adding that he was impressed with her resourcefulness, and he expected to see her argue a real case in his courtroom—the Supreme Court—within ten years.

Martha and the Killer Instinct

Mock court nearly capped Martha Escutia's makeover, from the shy girl she had been while growing up to the forceful advocate she was becoming, but real-world hurdles remained ahead. After graduating in 1982, she returned home to study for the bar exam and arrived just as LA's Latino Eastside was gearing up for another historic electoral cycle. The first elections following the 1980 census were at hand, in districts redrawn by the Assembly committee that Richard Alatorre chaired. Ten years after being elected in his own breakthrough, Alatorre had recently been catapulted into the leadership commanded by Speaker Willie Brown.[7] Reagan's 1980 election sent Latinos in the Carter administration back to LA, so the 1982 midterms were the first chance for some to reassert themselves on the local scene. Suddenly there were two new congressional districts to run in, a staggered pair of opportunities to expand Latino-empowerment efforts into the San Gabriel Valley, east of East LA.[8] Martha volunteered for both, first in the midsummer special election in a district that included East LA, and then in the general election in a new district created by reapportionment and redistricting. TELACU had its candidates to run, and George Pla managed both efforts.

Martha had just joined the first campaign when Pla announced he needed a volunteer to take on the task of opposition research, usually farmed out to a well-paid consultant. The campaign could not afford to hire one, so it needed a volunteer with research skills and a "killer instinct," as Pla put it to the group. Martha tentatively raised her hand. To overcome the campaign manager's disbelief, she explained that she could at least do the research. Martha had to produce the "oppo book" by the end of the week. That sent her back to the familiar stacks of the USC library, where she worked assiduously around the clock. The book Martha produced on the opponent's missed votes, bad votes, and bad positions, as well as fundraising events and campaign contributions that either pointed to corruption or betrayal of community interests, caused a minor sensation in political circles all the way to the Westside. It seemed impossible a rookie volunteer could produce such a thorough, superbly organized, and documented volume of "oppo." Martha vowed she would never do such work again without compensation.

Both campaigns Martha worked on were winners. The first of them, in the special election, sent Matthew "Marty" Martínez to Washington early, to complete the former incumbent's unexpired term in the 97th Congress. After the November election, Martha joined his staff to help organize Martínez's office for his full term to come in the 98th Congress, in the town she knew well. But once his DC operation was fully staffed and up and running in 1983, Martínez laid Martha off to make room on the payroll for his girlfriend. Having moved back to Washington, Martha suddenly needed a job. She headed for the MALDEF field office, now run by Antonia Hernández. Since Martha had passed the California bar exam, she expected to be hired as an attorney, but she couldn't find any takers. Law firms, including MALDEF, hired men who had yet to pass a bar exam, but none would make Martha an offer. She had to settle for an embarrassing temp position as a receptionist at a law firm that hired classmates of hers as associates. She finally got picked up by what would soon become the dominant Latino advocacy organization in Washington, the National Council of La Raza (NCLR), which needed a legislative director—a position in which she could quickly have an impact.

Immigration Policy War Resumed

Government agencies and legislators had a big head start advancing restrictionist views on immigration over advocates for immigrants, the Latino community, and civil libertarians. The Nixon administration had long before declared a "War on Drugs," and in its first year effectively closed the US-Mexico border with its "Operation Intercept" policy.[9] That crackdown proved far too costly to the whole border region to be sustainable, but the shift to a crackdown on unauthorized migration then came as a matter of course. The AFL-CIO had long opposed continuing immigration and saw new immigrant workers as at best "unorganizable," giving Democratic legislators license to advance restrictionist proposals.[10] As noted in the previous chapter, Democrats Peter Rodino, of the House, and Senator Edward Kennedy joined forces in the early 1970s behind the first federal bill intended to eliminate the "jobs magnet" for immigration by sanctioning employers with fines and the threat of imprisonment for hiring undocumented workers.[11] The Rodino bill passed the House twice but never got a hearing in the Senate. The Carter administration took the issue on and developed a revised bill, again sponsored by Rodino, which also passed the House. The organized Latino community, particularly Mexican Americans, as well as others, opposed it so vehemently that both the administration and the legislators were forced to back off and resort to the old formula of creating a commission to study the issue.

At long last, the bipartisan Select Commission on Immigration and Refugee Policy released its voluminous report early in 1981, which reopened intense national debate on what has since come to be known as "comprehensive immigration reform." But back then, and since the early '70s, it was known as the problems of "illegal aliens" and "illegal immigration." The commission was months late with its massive, encyclopedic, and highly anticipated opus, but the delay may have been deliberate. The nature and makeup of the commission itself, in combination with a transformational new presidency, invested this trans-administration initiative with enormous momentum. The eminent President of Notre Dame Father Theodore Hesburgh headed the commission; it had heavyweight and diverse representation on its board; they had guided years of work by a large and top-flight research staff; and they had conducted extensive hearings across the country. Surely a new bill with such an effort behind it would emerge and pass both houses this time.[12]

Opponents of the threatened national crackdown on undocumented immigrants had, since the early 1970s, formed a series of publicly announced coalitions and networks of resistance. Just weeks before the commission's report, also in February 1981, the National Immigration, Refugee, and Citizenship Forum was launched. It was explicitly conceived of as a coalition of resistance to both the commission's anticipated recommendations and the legislation expected to follow. But the commission was composed of members of both houses of Congress from both parties, executive agencies, leaders of affected communities of interest, and others. This meant it already had done extensive prelobbying for the broad outlines of a bill and could count on widespread support from legislators, the administration, elite media, and organizations from the AFL-CIO to the NAACP. The resistance Forum on immigrant rights, on the other hand, was just getting started—a far cry from the way the Leadership Conference on Civil Rights reigned over its issue domain.[13]

A year later, Wyoming Senator Alan Simpson introduced his long-awaited bill, which closely resembled both the previously failed Rodino bill and the DOA Carter Plan. Before the end of summer 1982, Simpson's version, combining the familiar elements of employer sanctions, guest workers, a secure form of identification, and legalization of certain long-settled undocumented immigrants, passed overwhelmingly in the Senate. The politics of immigration reform had clearly changed in the Senate since the mid-1970s—but also in the House. That fall, the resistance employed all tactics at its disposal to prevent the twin bill that Representative Romano Mazzoli introduced from coming to a final vote in the House. This time the resistance Forum and other opponents had the ear of both Judiciary Committee Chair Rodino and Speaker Tip O'Neill, which allowed for deft use of timing and procedures to push the floor vote on the bill into a lame-duck session of the 97th Congress, following the 1982 midterm elections, where they could smother it with amendments and run out the legislative clock.

As Kamasaki recounted in his insider blow-by-blow account of these legislative battles, *Immigration Reform: The Corpse That Will Not Die*, the resistance strategy of "filibuster by amendment" was anything but "mindless work." To be accepted for debate and discussion, amendments had to be distinct and germane. Producing and filing them in such numbers required massive expert and coalition work. Talking points on each had to be drafted for multiple speakers. The emergent Latino lobby on immigration reform reached one of its high points of coordinated action in the 1982 lame-duck congressional session, with MALDEF and LULAC working around the clock to draft amendments that Congressional Hispanic Caucus (CHC) members filed, some two hundred in total, in addition to nearly one hundred filed by others.[14] Killing Simpson–Mazzoli was an astonishing win, seen by some as a "Hispanic veto." But the bill was certain to be reintroduced in the next Congress, the 98th, and Speaker O'Neill had to promise that it would not get blocked again from going to the floor and getting a vote.[15]

"The Group" and the Rookies

Besides her wide and deep personal experience with and understanding of Mexican migration, Martha brought key assets with her to NCLR. Among them were the many contacts and relationships she had both in California and DC. Her work on the two new Eastside LA Latino congressional campaigns in 1982 served Martha—and NCLR—well in Washington in 1983. Even though she had parted ways with Marty Martínez after helping set up his office, her production of the "oppo book" established Martha as a rising whiz kid within powerful Westside LA political circles. Key among those was what was known as the "Waxman–Berman machine," led by LA Congressman Henry Waxman, political consultant Michael Berman, and his freshly elected brother, Congressman Howard Berman, former majority leader of the California State Assembly. The Waxman–Berman operation provided critical support for the election of both Martínez and Esteban Torres on the Eastside, which Martha was in the middle of.[16]

The NCLR staff was dominated by men from Texas, although the state received a small fraction of the immigration from Mexico that California did. Furthermore, in working for Martínez, Martha had connected with a range of women staffers on the Hill. Legions of rising and aspiring male executives used golf to network and build relationships—to the detriment of many women. But Martha and women in Capitol circles had their own networking means, one of which was Jazzercise classes. Martha worked that resource relentlessly and threw in Mexican ballet folklórico for good measure.[17] The payoff was critical in her work at NCLR. That Martínez had let her go mattered not, as she had a strong relationship with Esteban Torres ("ET"), the other freshman congressman she had volunteered for, and especially with one of his staffers. While Martínez would be a virtual nonentity in Congress, Esteban Torres and his office were singularly important for Latino advocates on the immigration issue.[18]

Martha Escutia testifying at Civil Rights Commissioners Confirmation Hearing on July 13, 1983. Copyright C-SPAN.[19]

Martha's personal ties to Representative Torres and to one of his principal aides complemented the relationship between Torres and the head of NCLR, Raul Yzaguirre, which dated to perhaps the late-1960s.[20] From 1983 to 1986, Martha could march her NCLR colleagues and their allies into ET's House office unannounced and use it as a "hub" of their operations—whether the congressman's chief of staff liked it or not.[21] The value of this resource, as Kamasaki later described, included "favors only a congressional office could deliver quickly" to advocates working the Hill in an era before cell phones, email, and internet: "copies of hearings, reports from the General Accounting Office and Congressional Research Service, the latest 'Dear Colleague' letters lawmakers use to stake out positions, and key passages from the Congressional Record."[22] Furthermore, Martha could drop into Berman's office to type up talking points for the congressman to deliver that day in a floor debate on an immigration bill amendment. But not even Martha knew the secret role Berman, who was close to Dolores Huerta, would come to play in the ultimate disposition of the bill.

When Martha joined the fight over immigration policy as NCLR's new legislative director in 1983, the main vehicle she had to work with was the small, informal, and unannounced alliance of insiders known simply as "the Group." This was an unofficial subset of the larger National Immigration, Refugee, and Citizenship Forum and included that coalition's president and vice president, along with representatives of the ACLU, the Immigration Lawyers Association, MALDEF, and LULAC, who had first brought them together.[23] The Group was more agile and like-minded than the sprawling Forum but still contained a variety of concerns and priorities. This would complicate the inevitable switch to negotiating an acceptable comprehensive reform, after years of emphatic opposition to policy packages like the old Rodino bill, the Carter Plan, and recommendations of the Select Commission. Most organizations participating in the Forum as well as the Group opposed the centerpiece of those proposals—employer sanctions. Others—especially the ACLU—would never accept anything like a national ID card, which was a corollary to sanctions. And yet others considered unacceptable any major new guest-worker program, as demanded by employers if they were to be barred from hiring undocumented workers. All immigrant-rights advocates demanded an ampler legalization component than any proposed bill had yet offered.

The sustained resistance to immigration-policy reform initiatives dating to the early 1970s resembled the extended struggle to end the Bracero Program a generation earlier. But those efforts were driven by moral outrage over an existing situation. They had a single, simple goal—end the program now!—and were encouraged by the seeming inevitability of success. Opposition to immigration reform in the 1980s, however, was based on resistance to the hypothetical future consequences of a complex bill that increasingly seemed sure to pass, in one form or another. That meant the resistance would lose—unless it decided to make a deal. But the resistance was a thing with many heads, responding to a package bill with many provisions.

Most participants in both levels of resistance—the big Forum and the compact Group—understood that flat-out rejection, which had worked to kill the Carter Plan in 1977, would not work for long in the 1980s. The strategy of "filibuster by amendment" that had worked to kill Simpson–Mazzoli in 1982 would not even be an option again in the House, at least not in the same way. But changing circumstances allowed other ways to resist. For the 98th Congress (1983–84), both the CHC and the emergent Latino lobby had fresh blood—new members with different thinking, strategic relationships, and new energy. The calendar was different too. The delay game in 1983 could push any new attempt to take Simpson–Mazzoli to the House floor to the next year, where it could be entangled with the politics of the Democratic presidential primaries and nominating convention. And from the hundreds of amendments filed the year before, an alternative bill altogether could be forged and deployed to siphon off congressional sponsors and votes, and to animate new talking points. The Group invested months in developing a Latino immigration-reform bill that Representative Roybal would sponsor, but not until early 1984, so the push had to rely on Speaker O'Neill's own decision to put off scheduling Simpson–Mazzoli to go to the floor until then.

NCLR's new policy analysis director, Charles Kamasaki, took his DC position just before Martha came on board. He also inherited the organization's immigration-specialist portfolio, which made him NCLR's primary representative in the Group, which had no titles, procedures, or rules. The opportunity to be heard in the Group's discussions—and even just informed that it was to meet—was iffy for these rookies. By virtue of having arrived at the scene a little after Charles, Martha's role in the Group remained secondary to his. But her contributions helped tip the balance of the whole effort in the direction of ultimately securing an immigration-reform compromise that could legalize untold numbers of settled but unauthorized immigrants, and perhaps some circulatory migrants as well.

At that moment in 1983, NCLR was not yet seen as the leading Latino advocacy organization in Washington. That distinction belonged to the much older LULAC, which had a hard-charging executive director known as Arnold, or Arnoldo, Torres. He had first convened the Group, and dominated it. Among those in the know, MALDEF—which LULAC had helped create in the late 1960s—had more prestige, especially due to the wins it had obtained the year before at the Supreme Court on equal access to public education for undocumented children, and the reinforced and extended Voting Rights Act. The three organizations developed a de facto division of labor in Washington, but they were involved in a curious dance fueled by their differing strengths, a convoluted tension between the Mexican American power poles of Texas and California, and what might be called a professional conflict between full-time lobbyists and those who were primarily litigators.[24] MALDEF was at its core a public-service firm of litigators, while in Washington, LULAC was all about lobbying. NCLR, while relying on its policy-research strength to provide expert testimony and reports, was fundamentally on the lobbyist side of this divide. Litigators wanted the most explicit and precise laws possible to argue in court, and they were loath to compromise with legislators or their staffs for the sake of a few more votes. The lobbyists wanted to make winning deals, with the most votes possible in the House—especially at a time when the Senate and the administration were not seen as friendly.

The DC "Latino Lobby"

LULAC, founded in Texas in 1929, got the national Latino lobby started. With Ford Foundation support, LULAC helped create MALDEF in 1968, which soon moved to San Francisco.[25] NCLR, also created in 1968, but primarily by Californians, was headquartered in Phoenix to avoid an image of control by California. In the early 1970s, NCLR moved to Washington and came to be dominated by Texans there. All three opened DC offices, but the organizations differ in structure. Membership-based LULAC is organized into local chapters (called "councils") and has an elected president. The entirely professional, board-driven MALDEF has no members, but elite networks of supporters concentrated in big cities, where it holds annual benefit galas. NCLR (now known as UnidosUS) is a hybrid professional organization, the only one of these three headquartered in DC, and with a national network of hundreds of diverse, independent, community-based affiliates. LULAC and NCLR/UnidosUS hold big national conferences in a different city every year.

These organizations developed an informal division of labor in their DC work based on their respective strengths: In the 1970s and early '80s, LULAC was best known on the Hill and regarded as the largest and oldest Latino organization; MALDEF became respected for its legal expertise; and NCLR carved out a niche as a policy-research outfit. This trio, founded and led in the twentieth century by Mexican Americans in the Southwest, initially seemed isolated in their efforts in Washington, far from the communities they sought to represent. But they all came to redefine themselves as pan-Latino, and with every passing year, an increasingly dense national meta-network of Latino leaders and communities developed, dissipating the sense of isolation and distance.

This process was accelerated in the mid-1970s by the creation of two pan-Latino organizations founded in Washington, the Congressional Hispanic Caucus (CHC) and the National Association of Latino Elected and Appointed Officials (NALEO).[26] *The rise of the Spanish-language Univision television network, later joined by Telemundo, strongly complemented the process as well, especially with their nightly national news programs. Soon, robust national Latino professional associations and chambers of commerce also reinforced this trend, filling out a year-round calendar of national conferences, conventions, and benefit galas taking place across the country. Members of Congress and administration officials increasingly took note.*

Two other actors without a continuous presence in Washington still appeared repeatedly at the Capitol during the immigration battles, adding a split-screen grassroots dimension to perceptions of the Latino lobby in

Congress. The United Farm Workers (UFW)—and Dolores Huerta most of all—were well known in DC, where Dolores had been lobbying since the early 1960s, but the UFW did not participate in or coordinate with either the Group or the Forum.[27] *Dolores and the UFW stood for a single issue: no new bracero program. The other actor, discussed in chapter 4, was Bert Corona's Hermandad Mexicana, known for its differences with Cesar Chavez and the UFW on the issue of undocumented workers and immigration enforcement. Corona coordinated with the Group, most of all NCLR, and Congress members such as Representative Roybal, bringing scores of urban undocumented workers for "Lobby Days" on Capitol Hill.*[28]

MALDEF also had a fresh face in Washington representing it in the Group in 1983, attorney Richard Fajardo. Frustrated because Arnoldo Torres did not fully accept them in the Group, which he had originally convened and continued to informally lead, the rookies—Kamasaki, Escutia, immigration-policy fellow Dan Purtell of NCLR, and Fajardo of MALDEF—decided, in Kamasaki's words, on a "huge undertaking" that summer. They would arrange as many meetings of their own with members of Congress and staff as they could. Martha, especially, went to work on her array of Capitol Hill contacts.[29]

The rookies, hungrier than the Group's veterans, managed to schedule over a hundred congressional meetings to lobby members on specifically Latino concerns and priorities in immigration reform. They were a sort of mod squad of advocates from Latino organizations—a Latina (Escutia), a Latino (Fajardo), an Asian American (Kamasaki), and an Anglo (Purtell). Between them, they knew all there was to know about immigration and Latinos, and they lobbied many members and staff who had never heard of their organizations, nor ever met with Latino advocates or anyone else on the immigration issue. That summer, this squad rushed between as many as four congressional meetings a day. Martha Escutia had become the very sort of business-clad lobbyist buzzing through Capitol corridors that had caught her eye on her first visit as a college student years before.

Such intense efforts continued throughout the succeeding years—from 1983, when Martha entered the fray, to 1986, when she left. So, following the summer of the hundred meetings on the Hill, and through the years that ensued, both the rookies and the Group as a whole needed close allies in the House—and Martha had them. Each of these factors contributed to the Group's transition from an unflagging public stance of rejection of Simpson–Mazzoli to de facto engagement in compromise. Amendments, negotiated delays, and scores of meetings drove steadily toward conditions and concessions that would make a bill acceptable—or at least not absolutely unacceptable. Furthermore, with each passing year, session of Congress, and reintroduced bill, the potential number of settled undocumented residents who would qualify for legalization steadily grew, making the proposed bill increasingly inclusive. The attraction of this potential inclusion of a large mass of immigrants into legal and eventually civic life increasingly counterbalanced the imperative to resist the exclusionary intent and effects of employer sanctions.

What did the resistance—and the Latino lobby in particular—want, besides to delay the immigration bill? At the most interpretive level, it would be fair to say that Latino advocates objected to the very premise of an "illegal alien" problem. At issue was the storied immigrant nature of the US versus the same old recurring nativism. But this time, it was a prejudiced reaction to the growth, rise, and visibility of Latinos in general. Such arguments, however, would cut no ice in the legislative process. Even if mainstream Latino activists, leaders, and organizations opposed, or simply could not support, discrimination or "removal" based solely on immigration status, neither could they, at that time, effectively call for a moratorium on deportations, or total nondiscrimination against undocumented workers, much less "open borders." Instead, they had to argue for what later became known not as an "amnesty" for settled undocumented residents, but "earned legalization" with conditions attached. They had to, in effect, offer support for enhanced border enforcement in exchange for lessened internal enforcement.

They also had to argue that employer sanctions would cause discrimination against Latino US citizens and legal immigrants—in other words, voters and future voters. These political considerations would become clearer in the fall of 1983, when the Group graduated from working up amendments in order to delay a bill they opposed, to drafting their own bill as an alternative, but even then with delay still in mind. Instead of employer sanctions, the Latino bill called for enhanced enforcement of labor laws, which were regularly flouted by employers of undocumented workers, and for a much bigger program of legalization.

This was a studied game of sly moves, countermoves, and fine tuning, at times like trying to crack a safe. In the process, however, MALDEF half retreated, was half relegated to the margins, as the organization remained adamant in rejecting any package that included employer sanctions in any form, however modified or balanced by other provisions or expansive legalization. MALDEF differed not only in being an organization of litigators, rather than lobbyists; its decision-makers were less directly engaged with the development of and battles over immigration reform. MALDEF's head and headquarters in San Francisco were the furthest removed from the Washington day-to-day. The organization's immigration-policy director, Linda Wong, was equally removed in Los Angeles. And MALDEF's Washington office director, Antonia Hernández, was first focused on the VRA in 1982 and then went on extended maternity leave in 1983. Her representative that year in the Group and the Immigration Forum, Richard Fajardo, was constrained to articulating MALDEF's standing position, to show no willingness to consider negotiating in any way on employer sanctions—the centerpiece of every immigration-reform bill since 1972—whether on antidiscrimination mechanisms or sunset provisions.[30] Ultimately, as the other Latino actors grew to accept the inevitability of employer sanctions, a different issue remained as the last holdup to allowing the painfully modified bill to be put to a vote on the floor of the House. Another Latina actor, with a different proposal, emerged to tip the balance.

Enter Dolores—and Howard

Dolores Huerta had lobbied for UFW against Simpson–Mazzoli since 1982, but ultimately, she worked most of all with close friend and ally Howard Berman, who did not get to Congress until 1983. Before that, Dolores worked with Florida Representative Claude Pepper, a senior member of the House Rules Committee, which set the rule that allowed for the hundreds of amendments that sank the bill in the 1982 lame-duck session.[31] Huerta, Cesar Chavez, and UFW had labored furiously to get Howard Berman elected Speaker of the California Assembly in 1980, when he was deadlocked in battle with then-Speaker Leo McCarthy. As traced in our previous book, Berman lost that contest when Willie Brown entered the competition.[32] He then ran for Congress to join his ally, Henry Waxman. Dolores supported Berman for Congress and urged him to become involved in the immigration-reform issue, which, according to some accounts, he did somewhat reluctantly. He joined the Judiciary Committee chaired by Rodino, but not its Immigration Subcommittee headed by Mazzoli.[33] This positioning would become perhaps curiously significant.

After Simpson–Mazzoli barely passed the House again in June 1984, Huerta focused on the effort to get the Democratic National Convention and its presumptive nominee, Walter Mondale, on record against the bill. Latino delegates threatened a walkout on the first ballot for the nomination if Mondale failed to take a stand. The pressure campaign worked. Mondale issued a statement opposing the bill, and the threatened walkout was averted.[34]

The action shifted to the conference committee that was convened to reconcile House and Senate versions of the bill, which had arrived with divergent amendments. House Judiciary Chair Rodino presided over the conference, and he appeared to have developed a particular antipathy to an amendment introduced by Representative Leon Panetta that would have vastly expanded the guest-worker provisions of the bill and had by itself passed by a large margin on the floor of the House.[35] Rodino met with Berman and, knowing he unswervingly represented the UFW position on guest workers, secretly pledged to not let a bill unacceptable to him pass the conference committee. Even though Berman was not on the Immigration Subcommittee, Rodino tasked him with trying to find a point of compromise for both growers and farmworkers—cutting out Immigration Subcommittee Chair Mazzoli. So empowered, Berman presented a long series of amendments to kill the bill in its form at that time, and push it yet again to the next Congress altogether, the 99th, to be seated in January 1985. This was neither the Group's nor the Latino lobby's filibuster by amendment—this was Berman alone, acting on behalf of UFW. After a vote on another issue pitted the Senate and House conferees against each other, Rodino abruptly adjourned the meeting, killing the bill for the final session of the 98th.[36]

Nonetheless, amid the frustrations of 1984, the shape of a possible resolution had subtly emerged. The most difficult remaining problem was what was known as the "farm-labor issue"—a quintessential California dispute. Berman of LA, who was the primary author of the state's historic Agricultural Labor Relations Act (ALRA) of 1975, which also bore Richard Alatorre's name, was the farmworkers' designated representative and in constant touch with Dolores. Panetta, of Northern California's agriculturally prodigious Salinas Valley, emerged as representative of the growers on the issue of guest workers. Repeatedly in that year's long conference committee deliberations, then-Representative Chuck Schumer of New York tried to save the bill by privately negotiating with key members on particularly difficult points.

It seems fateful that Schumer—whose talent for quietly orchestrating deals that saved major-but-troubled bills would reach new heights decades later, in 2022—would bring Berman and Panetta together in a sustained effort to resuscitate Simpson–Mazzoli. That is exactly what Schumer did in 1985, as the House yet again grappled with the challenge of immigration reform. The three—Schumer, Berman, and Panetta—began a series of secret meetings late that year, which stretched into 1986. It is in this context that during one of her stays in Washington, Dolores pitched to Berman, in his office, an alternative to guest workers that growers had used decades before.[37]

Instead of creating a new bracero program to officially import workers from Mexico again, Dolores said, why not just legalize the undocumented farmworkers already here? "How would that work?" Berman asked. Dolores explained that when the Bracero Program ended in 1964, many braceros were administratively legalized and given green cards, without any new law or program.[38] What she was referring to is borne out in the historical record. As discussed in the last chapter, prior to the 1965 revision of the Immigration and Nationality Act (which did not take effect until mid-1966), employers could easily sponsor immigrant employees for "green card" visas. To do so again, however, would take a new provision in the immigration-reform law.

Berman appears to not have brought this idea up in his meetings with Schumer and Panetta until early 1986, but when he did, they readily agreed to explore it. The members' staffs took on the complicated work. Huerta's proposal, despite its difficulties, gained momentum. Soon the details were being discussed and negotiated in formal committee hearings. By then, the Simpson–Mazzoli framework was being significantly altered and left behind, which moved Chair Rodino to become the primary House sponsor of the bill, now and evermore known as Simpson–Rodino.

The option Huerta introduced—to the right person at the right time—was not original to her. However, Howard Berman, as well as the most meticulous and accomplished students of the politics of the Immigration Reform and Control Act (IRCA) agree that it was this proposal that saved the bill in the fall of 1986. It appeared that the bill would die for a third time when, in late September, a procedural House vote to advance it failed. This was partly due to continued wrangling between those still demanding a big guest-worker program and those who supported the new farmworker legalization plan. Schumer again went to work to revive the bill, insisting that Senator Pete Wilson's guest-worker proposal would doom it. Two weeks after the failed rules vote in the House, the chamber took it up again, bringing Simpson–Rodino back from the dead. More votes remained in both chambers, on a limited number of amendments and on the bill, and then more in the conference committee, before the bill went back to the two chambers. The last of all the votes was taken in the Senate on October 17, and the final bill was sent to Reagan for a White House signing, which he delayed until two days after the November midterm elections.

Dolores herself does not publicly emphasize her critical role in passing IRCA, which contrasts so sharply with all that UFW and Cesar Chavez have been and continue to be criticized for regarding undocumented migrant farmworkers and immigration enforcement. But no other Latino actor in the decade-long immigration-reform struggle can claim a greater role in politically making possible the legalization of millions of undocumented immigrants. The idea to adjust the legal status of undocumented farmworkers became the Special Agricultural Workers program (SAW) of IRCA, which added over a million to the total of nearly 2.7 million legalized.[39] Unlike the main "amnesty" program, farmworkers would not need to show continuous residence, just a history of seasonal work in US agriculture.[40] The potentially enormous, two-track legalization process shifted the center of the Latino-empowerment story back to LA.

Chapter 6

Inclusion Unbound: Legalizing Millions

Year after year, while Latino advocates in Washington kept fighting what they saw as a bad immigration bill, the LA community's capacity to support their efforts and subsequently take on a large-scale program to legalize the undocumented kept growing. In some instances, advances in the politics of inclusion in LA directly enhanced the strength of Latino resistance and ability to hold out for better policies in DC. In others, activist Eastside political clout was enhanced in Sacramento, where state resources could be tapped. And yet others brought advances at City Hall and in news media, the Catholic Church, labor unions, the public school system, advocacy organizations, and the demographics of the community as a whole—all of which contributed to eventually achieving a massively inclusionary and empowering result.

Had the Carter Plan become law right away in the mid-1970s, only a small fraction of the immigrants processed under IRCA a decade later would have been legalized. The long delay in finally passing a better bill meant that millions of new immigrants became eligible, and many would be better informed, prepared, and assisted in applying for legalization, known formally as an "adjustment of status." At the start of the policy debate in 1977, initially modest proposals for legalization (or "amnesty") of the undocumented required evidence of a person's continuous residence since at least January 1, 1972, to be eligible. Because of the holdup, however, the cutoff date to qualify for IRCA's main legalization program ended up being moved a whole decade, to January 1, 1982, the year

Simpson–Mazzoli was first introduced in Congress. Furthermore, the much more lenient SAW program for farmworkers did not require residence at all. IRCA's ultimate implementation in 1987–88 was not ideal by any means, but had it occurred in the 1970s, it would have been worse in every way.

Ronald Reagan's defeat of Jimmy Carter in 1980, as we noted in the last chapter, had the silver lining of returning experienced Latino political talent to LA, such as Esteban Torres and Gloria Molina. Just a year before what would later become the new legalization eligibility cutoff date, Latino influence in Sacramento catapulted to a historic new level with the rise of Willie Brown to Speaker of the Assembly, strategically assisted by Eastside members Richard Alatorre and Art Torres. Alatorre—one of Brown's three lieutenants—then took the reins of the Assembly's Reapportionment and Redistricting Committee, and by the end of 1982 the Eastside's (and California's) Latino representation in Congress tripled, from one to three.[1] As also described in the last chapter, the election of Esteban Torres—dubbed the "unsung hero" of IRCA by Kamasaki—especially bolstered the work of immigrant advocates on Capitol Hill, both to delay and improve the bill. Although the ranks of Latinos in the state legislature did not grow in the 1982 cycle, their visibility and vigor were greatly enhanced, with Art Torres toppling an ineffectual Eastside old-timer to advance to the Senate, while the feisty and telegenic Molina succeeded him in the Assembly and became the first Latina ever elected to the legislature

The repeated postponements of IRCA included instances when its passage seemed imminent, which set off furious spurts of planning for implementation involving dozens of nongovernmental and community-based organizations (NGOs and CBOs). Those planning efforts won foundation backing and, according to Kamasaki, developed "both a strategy and a division of labor" through a series of meetings in 1983 and 1984.[2] These mobilizations were somewhat akin to war games and mock trials—exercises that prepare participants for a real battle to come.

A tragic feature of the Reagan Revolution was its fueling of internal conflicts in Central America, which ultimately pushed hundreds of thousands of refugees north.[3] Civil war in El Salvador, especially, precipitated a heavy flow of new immigrants, with Los Angeles as their primary destination. Significant numbers also came from Guatemala and Honduras, and somewhat fewer from Nicaragua. The Pico-Union area west of downtown LA began an epic transformation, diversifying the community from almost all Mexican origin to, increasingly, truly Latin American. And with these new subcommunities came new activism, organizations, coalitions, and institutional responses.[4]

Transforming the Church

Just as the long Reagan–Bush decade got underway, a passionately activist Mexican American priest, Father Luis Olivares—Padre Luis—became pastor of the historic Catholic Church known as La Placita, on the plaza of the original Pueblo of Los Angeles, wedged amid downtown, Chinatown, and Union Station.[5] Seeing in real time the ongoing refugee influx into his parish, Olivares evolved from a champion of the farmworker movement to LA's prophetic leader of the city-based sanctuary movement. A dramatic change at the top of the Archdiocese of Los Angeles in 1985, in the form of a new archbishop with historic ties to California Latino social causes, gave Olivares the opening to take his own dramatic action. He timed a key public move to coincide with the feast of the Virgin of Guadalupe, the brown patron saint of Mexico and the Americas. The specter of death squads, army massacres, and even genocide taking place in Central America weighed over the solemn gathering. Olivares challenged his still predominantly Mexican-origin congregation to embrace the arriving Central Americans. Joined by high clerics of a range of faiths in a deeply moving procession and ceremonial mass, Padre Luis took to the pulpit to boldly—even fiercely—declare the church to be a sanctuary, where first scores and then hundreds of undocumented refugees could sleep at night, protected from immigration authorities by his and the Church's moral authority.[6] Olivares would himself become the target of death threats, and his friend Cesar Chavez, who had repeatedly been threatened himself, urged the priest to hire personal security.[7]

Roger Mahony, only the fourth archbishop and the first native Angeleno to head the LA Archdiocese, was still introducing himself to his new domain when Olivares made his move. Activist priests and bishops in the Southwest had been pushing the Church to focus on the Mexican and Mexican American community since at least the 1940s, as recounted in chapter 2. After the experiences of fighting to end the Bracero Program in the 1950s and support the farmworker movement in the 1960s—in which Mahony played a major role—the Church in the 1970s began taking steps at the national level to bolster its "Hispanic Ministry" with a series of pastoral summit conferences, called Encuentros, that gathered strength with each new convening.[8] In 1985 Mahony was strategically placed in LA as part of this process, which would culminate on June 1, 1986, with a spectacular assembly of some fifty thousand Latino Catholics in Dodger Stadium. There, Mahony would announce, in Spanish, the Los Angeles component of the Church's National Pastoral Plan for Hispanic Ministry, then still under development.[9] *Los Angeles Times* columnist Frank del Olmo wrote that this was "almost certainly the largest gathering of Latinos that this nation has ever seen. . . . [T]here is no turning back. After Celebración '86, the local Latino community will never be the same."[10]

This context provided cover for Olivares to defy the law by protecting refugees in his church, four months after Mahony's arrival in LA and three months into the Church's national consultation to develop its pastoral plan. Mahony, focused on organizing the historic stadium event and his plan for LA, needed the full support of the most heavily Latino parishes in particular. Padre Luis's congregation was virtually all Latino and among the nearest to the stadium. As the archbishop with the most Latino parishioners in the country, Mahony had by far the biggest stake among all his fellow bishops in the success of the ambitious pastoral plan that was coming together. As the finished national plan itself would read:

> The Church has historically been the strongest advocate for immigrants and has actively advocated for just and humane laws and policies. The prophetic voice of the Church is needed more than ever as we live through a time of renewed xenophobia, racism, and discrimination. The work of missionary disciples is urgently needed amid the inhumane

> and immoral treatment of asylum seekers, families, and unaccompanied minors, particularly at the US southern border. The Church's long-standing support for immigration reform is not merely a humanitarian gesture or a struggle to achieve a justice unfulfilled. Rather, our support signifies our efforts to accompany communities that too often remain at the margins and demonstrates our solidarity with them.[11]

Neither Mahony nor anyone else could have known that the IRCA immigration reform would finally pass Congress and become law that fall, and that the window for millions of undocumented immigrants to apply for legalization would open six months after that. But the plan of action he rolled out for his new archdiocese at Celebración '86 could hardly have been better preparation for the role his parishes would play in encouraging and helping the undocumented to "come out of the shadows." In addition to providing a range of new services, the plan called for church volunteers to visit every Latino home in the archdiocese, which spans three counties. Four hundred trained volunteers were ready to start and able to devote their summer to this mission. Mahony was mobilizing Latinos en masse to transform the Church in Greater LA, and their role in it, ahead of mobilizing the undocumented among them to apply for *amnistía*.

*The scene at Los Angeles Memorial Coliseum before Pope John Paul II celebrated mass there on September 15, 1987. Photo by Patrick Downs/*Los Angeles Times.

This effort reached a climax for the ages the following year, in the midst of the legalization campaign, when Pope John Paul II visited Los Angeles, led a seven-mile parade in his Popemobile, and conducted open-air masses in both Dodger Stadium and Los Angeles Memorial Coliseum—drawing hundreds of thousands and calling attention in his homilies to the Church's role in the legalization effort.[12]

At the same time, turning-point changes were also afoot on other fronts. Antonia Hernández took over the now-powerhouse legal advocacy organization MALDEF and moved its headquarters to her native LA. With Alatorre's key empowerment work done in the state Assembly, he returned to restore Latino representation—which had been missing since Roybal left for Congress in 1962—to the LA City Council. The next year, Alatorre was joined on the council by none other than Gloria Molina, in another historic, inclusionary breakthrough for the community's representation. As Molina mobilized voters from Northeast LA to Pico-Union to score her second historic electoral first, María Elena Durazo initiated a revolution in labor in the same area by organizing Latina immigrant workers to unseat the out-of-touch white leadership of a key hospitality union local.[13] Perhaps the most impactful developments involved LA's leading Latino news organizations: the daily *La Opinión*, as well as TV station KMEX and the national network it was part of. All these elements of a dynamic Latino LA in transition were lined up before the IRCA legalization program went into effect on Cinco de Mayo 1987.

Inventing Latino News

Diversification and growth of the Latino population, combined with the legacy of the Chicano and early immigrant-rights movements in California, contributed to the rise of a unique force in US ethnic history: the multimedia Spanish-language news industry.[14] The astonishing results of the 1980 census reported a near-doubling of the state's Latinos over the preceding decade and caught the attention of corporate America. National advertisers came knocking at the doors of a handful of Spanish-language media outlets, prime among them LA's *La Opinión* daily paper, along with the city's KMEX Channel 34 TV station and the Spanish International Network (SIN) it belonged to. Rising ad revenue, in turn, allowed these outlets to grow and further professionalize their staff, expand their outreach, develop their products, and play increasingly activist roles in the metropolis. By the end of the 1980s, corporate America went considerably further than advertising in this burgeoning and evolving market; Hallmark Cards acquired SIN, which was rebranded as Univision, and the Times Mirror Company purchased a 50 percent stake in *La Opinión*. How these lofty corporate moves related to the legalization of millions of undocumented immigrants must be understood, however, at a more human level, including the transformations and transformative roles of Latina/o news leaders such as Monica Lozano and Jorge Ramos.

The years-long struggle to reform the Census and have the "Hispanic" category included in the short-form questionnaire sent to all homes institutionalized but could hardly consolidate a "pan-ethnic" Hispanic/Latino identity among a diverse population dispersed across the country.[15] The extended wrangling and negotiations over what term to use marked the beginning of a national effort to cultivate a strategic sense of common interest among leaders and organizations of different origins, generations, and politics. The campaign to promote participation in the Census was an immensely important step. But the most consequential efforts of all would continue within Spanish-language media and the messages it conveyed daily via every channel—in print as well as on TV and radio—to their various audiences. The original goal of this media industry, however, was not to inculcate their audiences with a sense of common interest on a national scale. Their own sense of mission would evolve with the times.

In the case of the newspaper-publishing Lozano family, the evolution from an identity that was conservative and purely Mexican to a progressive US Latino outlook stretched across three generations and two countries. In Jorge Ramos's case, the transition would be a personal one, contained within a part of his professional life in the US. For both, throughout their transformations, Los Angeles and their corresponding Spanish-language news organizations in the 1980s served as indispensable anchors to relevance and reality.

Ramos arrived in LA on January 2, 1983, after giving up on pursuing his career as a journalist in his native Mexico City. His work there was censored by the broadcast network that employed him, which was allied with the one-party authoritarian state that had ruled his country since decades before he was born.[16] Exactly a year after touching down at LAX, carrying all his possessions in a bag and a guitar case, Jorge began working for the news department at LA's KMEX Channel 34. This started him on his path to becoming such a dominant TV newsman that he would eventually top polls taken among Latinos as the first, second, or third most recognized national Latino leader.[17] Although on arrival he considered himself purely Mexican, with no intention of staying or becoming a US citizen, his new network, like its LA flagship station, would become an unprecedented advocate for immigrant rights and Latino empowerment. Ramos would rise to become the face of the network—at least of its news department—and eventually raise his hand to take the US oath of citizenship.

Monica Lozano, after living away from Southern California for a dozen years, returned in the fall of 1985 to start work at the paper her Mexican-immigrant grandfather had launched nearly sixty years earlier. *La Opinión* was already growing fast when Monica assumed the position of managing editor. It took her leadership, however, to reinvent the paper's content and editorial staff and, through them, its relationship to the community and role in Los Angeles and California. Like Jorge, Monica became the public face of her news organization, which she set out to refashion into a bold instrument of Latina/o empowerment.

Monica Lozano in the La Opinión *newsroom in 2009. Photo by Mandalit del Barco/NPR.*

Choosing Between LA and Mexico

As a young man, Monica Lozano's grandfather Ignacio became a central figure in the recently arrived expatriate component of San Antonio's Mexican community, which grew as a refuge from the Revolution of 1910–20. He came from the neighboring state of Nuevo León in 1908, as violence was on the rise and Mexico's dictatorship drifted toward crisis. After finding an acceptable job with a Spanish-language weekly, Lozano brought up his mother and sisters to join him. San Antonio had long boasted the largest Mexican-origin population of any US city when Lozano founded his own weekly, *La Prensa,* in 1913. Soon expanded to a daily, Lozano's paper eventually became the largest in the country in Spanish. His sisters ran the Librería Lozano bookstore next door to the paper, which itself published original books of literary merit. But Don Ignacio and his elite San Antonio circle—who saw their exile from revolutionary Mexico as temporary—were anything but "Latino" in the current sense. They had no interest in becoming US citizens or in US politics. His paper was focused on their homeland, to which it advocated an eventual mass return.[18]

Thirteen years later, on Mexico's Independence Day, September 16, 1926, Don Ignacio launched a second daily paper, *La Opinión,* in Los Angeles. He continued to profess belief in maintaining a pristine Mexican identity and in collective repatriation. But like it or not, large forces were moving him and his business in another direction. *La Prensa* in San Antonio hit its peak circulation in 1930—just prior to the mass repatriations of Mexicans and their US-born children under the Hoover administration.[19] As a result, both *La Prensa* and *La Opinión* suffered severe losses of circulation, but *La Prensa* more so—such that it could never fully recover.[20] Nevertheless, Don Ignacio did not move back to Mexico.

True to its origins as a relatively elite weekly forum for mostly conservative Mexican refugees with high cultural and intellectual tastes, as a daily *La Prensa* had a much larger circulation on Sunday than on weekdays. The fatter Sunday edition featured long, literary essays by some of Mexico's most prominent intellectuals. That was true, as well, of *La Opinión*—which also had a Librería Lozano next door—for decades, but by 1940 that paper's weekday circulation in LA surpassed *La Prensa*'s.

As the venerable San Antonio paper dwindled, while *La Opinión* slowly but steadily recovered from the 1930s Depression and repatriations, the Lozanos increasingly lived at their LA home. Once Don Ignacio's son, Nacho—Monica's father—graduated from Notre Dame, he became assistant publisher of *La Opinión* and never lived in San Antonio again.

Don Ignacio passed away in LA in 1953, which elevated Nacho to publisher. Don Ignacio's widow, Alicia, returned to San Antonio with the family patriarch's ashes, where she oversaw *La Prensa* for several years before selling it. True to her late husband's attachment to their homeland, she moved to Mexico City, where she had cousins. Accompanied by her daughter, Mary Alice—Nacho's older sister—Doña Alicia had Ignacio's ashes moved and interred at the famed Basílica de La Virgen Guadalupe. Like many of his compatriots in the US, in life Don Ignacio wanted at the very least to symbolically return to Mexico in death, if need be.[21] In Los Angeles, Nacho met and married Marta Navarro, who was a rare Mexican American student at UCLA at that time. The couple had three children in LA: Leticia, Jose, and Monica. No Lozanos remained in San Antonio; the family was now divided between Los Angeles and Mexico City.

It took until the signal year of 1965 for *La Opinión* to fully recover its pre-Depression circulation, and the paper continued to change as the community grew and developed. By 1970, weekday circulation surpassed that of the Sunday edition, and by 1975 it reached that of *La Prensa* at its old 1930 height—as its readership became predominantly working class. Then came the 1980s, and the pace of business accelerated in multiple ways. Circulation had more than doubled, from just over 22,000 daily in 1975 to nearly 58,000 in 1985, making *La Opinión* one of the fastest growing papers in the country. Those relatively low figures do not reveal the publication's reach, however, which must be multiplied by each copy's average "pass-around rate." Not surprisingly, the paper's Spanish-dominant (and monolingual-Spanish) readership, concentrated in large households and mostly working among fellow Spanish speakers, meant its pass-around rate was much higher than that of the *Los Angeles Times*. And while the *Times* was overwhelmingly sold through home-delivered subscription, *La Opinión* had to be intentionally purchased every day, whether at a shop or from a coin-operated street rack. Daily buyers were more consciously invested in the paper and far more likely to carry it around with them all day. With each copy's average readership estimated at between 5 and 6, *La Opinión* was reaching well over 100,000 readers in 1975 and over 300,000 by 1985—the year Monica returned from Northern California to start work at the paper.[22]

Although they never knew their grandfather, Monica and her siblings were raised in one sense just like their dad, Nacho, had been; at home, they spoke to their parents exclusively in Spanish. Although born in LA, Monica even had an experience that many immigrant children share. When her first-grade teacher, a Catholic nun, ordered Monica to answer a direct question in English, she could not find the words, panicked, and burst into tears. Repeatedly in life, Monica would feel like an outsider. During regular summers with her grandmother, aunt, and cousins in Mexico City, Monica longed to be accepted as truly Mexican. Years in Northern California and Oregon, however, transformed her into an increasingly activist-minded Chicana.[23] Her sojourn began with her final years of high school at Santa Catalina, on the Monterey Peninsula, followed by college at the University of Oregon in Eugene. At the latter, she, like many Chicana/o students in those years, became passionately involved in supporting the UFW, and deeply interested in Latin America beyond Mexico. But Monica was connected to Latin America, on both sides of her family, in ways her fellow students and friends were not.

Monica's mother, Marta Lozano, née Navarro, was originally from the Texas border town of El Paso, born to a Mexican family of some social stature on both sides of the border, with property in Mexico. Marta's aunt Delfina married a rising local politician, Raymond Telles, who in 1957 was elected El Paso's mayor, making him the first Mexican American to lead a medium-sized city in the US.[24] Being a suddenly prominent Mexican American Democrat, Telles was drawn into the "Viva Kennedy" presidential campaign in 1960, co-chaired nationally by US Senator Dennis Chávez of New Mexico, LA City Council Member Edward Roybal, and Texas state Senator Henry P. Gonzalez. Telles campaigned extensively for Kennedy alongside Senator Chávez, as the Viva Kennedy effort catalyzed an unprecedented mobilization of Latino voters.[25] After

Kennedy won, Vice President Lyndon Johnson—former Senate majority leader from Texas—called Marta and Monica's uncle Raymond to follow up on President Kennedy's offer to nominate him as US ambassador to Costa Rica.[26] That would make Telles the first Latino US ambassador in history. Johnson forcefully made clear to the young mayor that, whatever his own political plans might be, he had no choice but to accept the honor.

At that time, the height of the Cold War, Latin America was a growing concern—bordering on panic—for US foreign policy, due mostly to the Cuban Revolution led by Fidel Castro, who took power in 1959.[27] JFK had used the Cuban Revolution to pillory Nixon on the Eisenhower administration's foreign policy failures. Kennedy was the first presidential candidate to ever devote a major campaign address to US policy in Latin America, during which he proposed a signature initiative he called a hemispheric "Alliance for Progress."[28] Costa Rica, then, would be no diplomatic backwater for Ambassador Telles—it would be the showcase of the foreign aid program and its support for democratic development. Next door in Nicaragua, the brutal, dynastic Somoza dictatorship was both a key worry and useful contrast. That previous US administrations had installed and maintained dictatorial regimes in Nicaragua, Guatemala, and other countries was common knowledge in Latin America.[29] The Kennedy administration was eager to change the reputation of the United States in the region and mobilize it in the name of democracy against Cuban and Soviet influence. It fell to Telles to work full-time to dispel the image and memory of the "ugly American," and he was given an unusual amount of time, serving well into the Lyndon Johnson administration.[30]

Thus, throughout her upbringing, Monica had not only traveled to Mexico regularly and visited for extended lengths of time, but she also had an uncle who had been a historic US ambassador in Central America.[31] Raymond and Delfina Telles's daughter, Cynthia, partially grew up in Costa Rica and later became close to her Lozano family cousins, Leticia, Jose, and Monica. Besides that, Monica's publisher father was active in the Inter-American Press Association, traveled throughout the region, became close to his counterpart Latin American newspaper-owning families, and was even elected president of the association.[32] That activism and prominence led to Nacho being named US ambassador to El Salvador when Monica was still in her sophomore year at the University of Oregon.

Monica became so interested in Latin America that she and a college girlfriend decided to explore as much of the region as they could by bus, working their way down through Mexico, Central America, and into South America. They started out in the summer of 1976, when Mexico was hit by unrest in the countryside, financial crisis, and a severe monetary devaluation. They made it to San Salvador to visit Monica's parents (and their toddler son Pancho) at the US ambassador's residence, and pressed on as far as Peru, which was then under military rule. Nearing six months on the road and out of money, the college women flew home.

From Latino San Francisco Back to LA

Impatient with college in Oregon after months of exploring Latin America, Monica eagerly moved on at the first opportunity to live and work in San Francisco—a little over halfway to her family home in Orange County. "The City" was regarded as the most progressive in the country, and it was the cradle of an emergent multinational Latino identity that went back decades, even over a century. In the early Gold Rush days, this part of California had attracted Latin Americans from as far away as Argentina, and Chilean miners especially.[33] The farmworker movement enjoyed strong support in the Bay Area, but as the 1970s gave way to the 1980s, the Latino vibe in San Francisco resonated with the sounds of political and cultural resistance to the military dictatorships that ruled South America, and to the growing threat of direct US military intervention in Central America.[34]

From the viewpoint of progressive and activist Latino San Francisco, Ronald Reagan seemed to personify all that was wrong with the country. He combined, from his years as governor, a history of hostility to the farmworkers, peace, and the student and women's movements with his newfound bellicosity in Central America and disregard for the refugees that US policy had created in that region. On top of this came his indifferent and irresponsible attitude toward the new horror of the HIV virus epidemic and its death sentence at the time, AIDS. Monica's years in San Francisco—living in the vibrant Mission District—became filled with both celebration of Latino and Latin American culture, and a regular diet of political protest and agitation. It was a life in and of "the movement."

Monica found work in a chain copy shop—a gig relevant to her past, present, and future. Rising to manager of a succession of shops in the chain, she learned how to take command of an operation, identify its problems, and resolve or mitigate them. Furthermore, Monica was to a significant extent in the business of meeting the print needs of the movement and the City's counterculture—its flyers, posters, newsletters, and screeds. An accomplished amateur photographer, and having worked one summer during high school as a photographer at *La Opinión*, Monica also honed her eye for graphics, visual storytelling, and layout.

Unsurprisingly, and in spite of the manifold ways her family personally and professionally connected with Latin America, and especially Central America, Monica was alienated from their lifestyle, priorities, and the conservatism of the family business. Like almost everyone she knew in the City, Monica also came to believe she hated Los Angeles, where she had been born. But when her father had a serious health scare in 1985 and decided to retire the following year, by the newspaper's sixtieth anniversary, he prevailed upon Monica to return to the family fold and take a novel executive position in the editorial department of *La Opinión*—a role she would largely get to fashion for herself.[35]

La Opinión's newsroom had never experienced a significant Lozano presence.[36] The paper was the family business, but its editorial content was not a regular topic of discussion or interest in the Lozano home, which for decades had been in far-off Newport Beach.[37] Monica—a young, US-born and -educated Chicana, albeit from an affluent family—abruptly entered a newsroom that had been dominated by traditional Mexican men for six decades. She was the publisher-owner's younger daughter and had the new title of "managing editor," but no formal authority over "executive editor" Sergio Muñoz, who excluded her from the daily front-page meeting held in his glass-walled office, a slight the whole newsroom could see.

Muñoz was something of a Mexico City intellectual who had come to LA to pursue a PhD in philosophy at USC. His position at the leading Spanish-language paper in the US, with a history stretching to the Mexican Revolution, greatly enhanced his standing in Mexico City and with the political and cultural elites he was still connected to there. He oversaw high-level Sunday cultural supplements, commissioning articles by Mexican luminaries and paying them in dollars. Under Muñoz, *La Opinión* recaptured the spirit, content, and type of Mexican collaborators that *La Prensa* had enjoyed in its glory days before the Great Depression.

Monica's dad, Nacho, liked to say that his father had founded Mexican newspapers in the US, but under his own direction, *La Opinión* became an American paper that happened to be published in Spanish. In many ways, however, the publication's content did not reflect that aspiration. It still focused largely on Mexico and had few reporters to cover US stories, either national or local. Other than in sports, in which the Mexican passion for boxing ruled, the paper's few reporters had no regular "beats." It relied heavily on translating wire-service stories for its US and local content—to the extent that the copy editor even translated and transliterated proper collective and place names. As was the norm in Mexico, New York was "Nueva York" in *La Opinión*, as it had been in *La Prensa* before it. Missouri and Mississippi appeared as "Misuri" and "Misisipi." The LA Dodgers and Lakers became "Los Esquivadores" and "Los Laguneros."

In Monica's view, the paper had to embrace its actual role and reality as a "major US metropolitan daily" in the country's second-largest city, with an overwhelmingly working-class immigrant readership that had great needs. Those included learning about the city and country they lived and worked in, and where their children would make their whole lives. She went to war over translating proper names, as if the paper were published in another country. As managing editor, it was her job to make new hires in the editorial department, and she began bringing in younger journalists with more diverse national origins. Monica figured out that she could change both the structure of news gathering and the paper's content by hiring journalists and editors for specific new beats. She started with health and healthcare access for low-income immigrants, especially women. And her main daily work was to lead the production, entirely under her own direction, of new content in "special projects" for tabloid supplements; physically, they were like Muñoz's cultural supplements, but otherwise they were completely different.

Promoting Amnistía

When Monica started at *La Opinión*, the IRCA immigration bill was mired in its final ten months of agonizing negotiations. Then it suddenly and surprisingly passed Congress and was signed by Reagan—the nemesis of California and Latino progressives. A year-long window during which undocumented immigrants could apply for legalization was set to open precisely six months after the signing. A number of institutions would have to gear up to meet the challenge of mobilizing those who might qualify. Effective promotion of the unprecedented process—especially to immigrants who lived in fear of authorities—first of all required "trusted messengers." This was a quality enjoyed, to a greater or lesser extent, in the Latin American immigrant community by the newspaper they knew and paid to read, broadcast media like KMEX, the Catholic Church, and Spanish-speaking leaders, both political and nonpolitical. But the first step was to make the opportunity known, explain it, and keep it on people's minds throughout the year during which applications would be received—all of which privileged the role of news media.

Another critical consideration was that the process was document heavy. It required evidence of continuous residence for at least the previous six years at the start, and up to seven years or more by the end of the legalization period. Promoting and guiding applicants through the process amounted to a challenge that seemed tailor-made for the sort of special supplement a major newspaper could produce. Long before the internet, when this type of information was provided via a broadcast, it was nearly impossible to study, share, and reference. The print supplements came illustrated and had no distracting advertisements. *La Opinión* could print over a million copies, supply them to churches and community organizations, and distribute them at public events.

Producing the content itself required collaboration, most of all with MALDEF, headed by Antonia Hernández, for its legal expertise. Somewhat ironically, as we saw in the previous chapter, Antonia and MALDEF had opposed every incarnation of the bill to the very end. But she and her organization immediately joined the implementation coalition convened in Washington by LA congressional representatives Torres and Roybal—who had themselves split over the final vote—the very day of Reagan's signing ceremony.[38] Ultimately, everyone was on board with the legalization program, commonly referred to as amnistía by Spanish speakers, even if MALDEF abhorred that term.[39]

Armed with as many copies as she could carry, Monica flew to San Francisco with her latest special project in hand to work the contacts with organizational and community leaders and activists she had built in her years there. And then the *Los Angeles Times* wanted in on the act—or at least its highest-ranking Latino journalist, reporter, and columnist, Frank del Olmo, did. Recognizing that the *La Opinión* brand had credibility among Spanish-speaking immigrants that the *Times* did not, the two papers, in an arrangement that Monica and Frank worked out, jointly produced another supplement, eight pages in English and eight in Spanish, with each paper printing hundreds of thousands of copies as needed over the time that remained of the legalization window.

Over the Air

A year before Monica returned to join her family newspaper, and just six months into Jorge Ramos's first US job, his new employer, KMEX TV, and its network, SIN, took a stand on behalf of Latino immigrants by staging a national conference in LA on the long-debated Simpson–Mazzoli bill. The network's underdeveloped news department in Miami had a noticeably Cuban-exile point of view, and to Ramos the local LA newscast, which he watched every night on his little black-and-white portable TV during his year at UCLA, looked technically primitive—he called it "very basic." Station and network management were aware of weaknesses in their news products and decided to make a statement by taking action on a major issue. The conference was a landmark event in multiple ways. Seven years had passed since the Carter administration had unveiled its short-lived plan, which had catalyzed opposition from a remarkably united Mexican American front. Since then, however, much had changed in the community's activist sector, and the LA conference reflected that, starting with its name and sponsors. The 1984 "Hispanic Conference on Immigration Reform" in LA retained no trace of either the Chicano movement or associated leftist currents that had converged in San Antonio for the "Chicano-Latino Conference on Immigration" in 1977—forces and history that had no relevance to an aspiring middle-class journalist from Mexico City who was looking for a way to equip himself in LA to again challenge his country's stifling, authoritarian system.[40] His new employer was signaling a different and more viable path for a journalist to have a consequential social and political impact.

This was now heralded as the "Decade of the Hispanic"—even though that label was contested and destined to be eclipsed by the term "Latino," especially in California—following the lead of the 1980 census and the campaign to mobilize community participation.[41] This time, the conference location was the uncontested capital of the undocumented population, and the White House was occupied by the state's former governor, Ronald Reagan, himself a longtime resident of the city-region. And this time, the focus of attention was not an administration's half-baked proposal but a fastidiously negotiated, bipartisan bill. Although many of the same Mexican American forces were arrayed against it, this time the fight was not with the administration, and this conference included the Republican National Hispanic Assembly, chaired by an Angeleno.

KMEX, a.k.a. Channel 34, was headed by another Mexican American Republican who nonetheless embraced his station's need to serve the community with an "advocacy type of journalism."[42] Danny Villanueva had been trying to take the station in this direction since at least the tumult of the late 1960s, when he hired the famous *Los Angeles Times* journalist Ruben Salazar to direct the news department. With the emergent Latino lobby on immigration in DC still fighting the proposed reform more than trying to improve it, the strong statements against the Simpson–Mazzoli bill emanating from the conference and the coverage that local Spanish-language TV was giving to the issue across the country significantly "validated" the lobby's resistance efforts in Washington.[43] Jorge was thus plunged into a Latino LA that had left the Chicano and farmworker movements behind before he got there, and was starting to engage in national and transnational policy issues concerning not only his native Mexico but Central America as well. His whole journalistic experience once again seemed tied to presidential politics and power on both sides of the border.

Ramos, Rebellion, and Reagan

As a writer of many books and columns, and a stellar TV news personality who has given almost as many interviews as he has conducted with others, Jorge Ramos has had many occasions to publicly reflect on the forces and experiences that shaped him. Three factors stand out. He has always been something of a rebel. For nearly his whole professional life, he has felt, and been treated as, an outsider. And perhaps the most prominent experiences of his career have involved presidents of both Mexico and the United States, and their power, from Ronald Reagan to Miguel de la Madrid to Barack Obama to Donald Trump.[44]

Born and raised in Mexico City, Ramos chafed at the authoritarianism of both his father and the Catholic Church. He studied communications in college and was not drawn to any particular career. But while he was still a student, Ramos got a job writing copy at the country's most prominent news radio station. It was 1981, and Ronald Reagan had just started his presidency when he was shot in the chest at close range. Ramos was the only staffer at XEW with a passport and who spoke a smidgen of English. That sent him to Washington to do his first story as an on-air correspondent. The experience sold the young Jorge on broadcast journalism. But he was told he did not have the voice for radio. Instead, he was able to move to the TV news department within the same media company—Mexico's virtual monopoly named Televisa. Ramos knew well that the network worked hand in glove with Mexico's one-party government and that censorship prevailed throughout the country's news media. But the rebel in him had to test the limits. On just his third report, he included an observation critical of the country's authoritarian practice known as the *dedazo*—meaning the "big finger"—by which the incumbent president named his successor. He was ordered to rewrite it.

Ramos knew it would come to this. He had researched a way out and found a certificate course in journalism at UCLA that would arrange for a year-long student visa. He knew his English was not good enough, so he did a tutorial. While in Tijuana, still working on the report he had been ordered to change, and change again, Jorge crossed the border and headed for Westwood to begin a new life. A friend and colleague who had worked at KMEX in LA gave Ramos the name and number of the station's news director. By now it was 1983, and the station was growing as advertisers were increasingly attracted to the Spanish-language market. The news director and the station's president heard Jorge's story and offered him a job, which allowed him to apply for a work visa. Ramos started at Channel 34 the first day he could legally do so—January 2, 1984. The US president who survived the assassination attempt he had been sent to cover three years earlier was now running for reelection, but for the next couple of years, Jorge would develop his craft reporting local news stories in LA.

The network eventually plucked Ramos out of daily reporting and first tried him out as the cohost of a newsy morning program. Then came a big change in ownership and a corporate-level decision that the nightly network news needed both an upgrade and a shift in tone and perspective. The national market was overwhelmingly of Mexican origin, but the national news broadcast based in Miami failed to reflect that. The network was rebranded as Univision and moved its news department to Southern California. Its new nightly news anchors would be an attractive young Mexican man, Ramos, and a beautiful young Mexican American woman from Los Angeles, María Elena Salinas, both formed as TV journalists at the flagship LA station, KMEX.

Ramos and Salinas had not only honed their skills at the local station's news department, they had also helped develop its activist approach to covering the Latino community and its concerns, progress, and need for empowerment—an approach they then took with them to the revamped and renamed network. As Ramos put it to us, "The kind of journalism that we were doing, and that we are doing right now... is journalism with a point of view. Sometimes we have to take a stand. This concept of journalism that is not neutral is something we developed at Channel 34, and that we continue doing now at many of our stations." Ramos and Salinas debuted as coanchors of their nightly network news program in 1986, the tenth and climactic year of the US national debate over undocumented immigration that had begun with the Carter Plan. Their *Noticiero Nacional Univisión* reported on every twist and turn in the politicking on Capitol Hill. The bill's repeated deaths and resurrections, passage, and signing into law made for dramatic TV. And next up was the implementation.

In six months, millions of undocumented residents and migrant farmworkers could begin to apply for their "adjustment of status," which, if approved, a year later would earn them a green card, just like the one Jorge had in his pocket. They heard the news over and over again from Ramos—by then the best-known Mexican immigrant in the country. By Cinco de Mayo 1988, when the window for the main legalization program closed, hundreds of thousands of immigrants in the LA market alone had handed over all the information they could scrape together to document their "undocumented" presence in the country since at least 1982. They had applied for amnistía and now were hoping for the best.

The Mexican "Diaspora"

Extended national policy debate since the 1970s–'80s over Mexican immigration and control of the southern US border, combined with growing international migration and refugee flows around the world, stimulated new waves of studies and forms of analysis. Intensified and sustained communications and financial flows between emigrants and their homelands, which came to be called a new form of "transnationalism from below," was one feature of this phenomenon. Another was a new focus by homeland governments on their nationals abroad and their homeland relations. A third was an expansion of the term "diaspora," applied ultimately to all communities and networks of migrants outside their countries of origin—even if those emigre populations had rarely, if ever, used the concept themselves. Such was the case with Mexican immigrants in the US, as memorably captured by a Mexican diplomat who defined them as "an unconscious diaspora."[45]

Growing urban concentrations of recent Mexican immigrants became increasingly organized in the late 1980s, a trend explicitly encouraged by Mexican government policy in the 1990s and 2000s.[46] *The mass legalization of undocumented immigrants wrought by IRCA in 1987–88 contributed to this policy change and even political change within Mexico itself. In many ways, Jorge Ramos became a dominant face in Mexico of the country's diaspora in the US, as his broadcasts, podcasts, columns, and books became readily available. The emigre journalist's stature in the US elevated him in his home country to a prominence he believes he could never have reached had he remained there, and he became famous for his aggressive interviews with presidents of Mexico and other Latin American countries, as well as of the US.*

Impact

The mobilized legalization of over two million immigrants from Mexico and Central America in a concentrated period was certain to have a series of major consequences for years, at various levels, both north and south of the border.[47] Undocumented workers who had felt bound to their employers could begin looking for better jobs, in many cases abandoning farmwork and settling in cities. With or without getting new jobs or moving, they could be more assertive, whether in the workplace, in accessing public services, in dealing with greedy and negligent landlords, or in otherwise demanding that their rights be respected the same as for any other legal resident. While it would be years before any of those whose status had been adjusted by IRCA could seek to become citizens and voters, legalization relieved them of an often-paralyzing vulnerability, fundamentally improving their lives and that of their families both back home and in the US.[48]

In 1986, the LA Archdiocese undertook to mobilize Latinos not only irrespective of their immigration status but, in fact, with a particular interest in helping the undocumented. In 1987, government, the Church, Spanish-language media, and a range of nongovernmental organizations campaigned to specifically mobilize the undocumented to seek their legalization. That mobilization was not a one-off, as those whose status was adjusted needed to take classes in English and civics to graduate to the next stage of acquiring lawful permanent residence. These efforts were soon followed by another specifically Latino mobilization—national in scope and led by MALDEF's LA office—to encourage full participation in the 1990 census. That count revealed the fast pace of Latino population growth in the city and county of Los Angeles. This growth was the result of two factors, but we do not know which was greater: the immigrants legalized by IRCA who either were already in LA or settled there after leaving farmwork elsewhere in the state, or their family members who had recently come to join them. But we do know that the 1990 census counted over half a million more Latinos in the city, raising their share of the population from 25 percent to over 34 percent—closely matching the increase in the city's foreign-born residents.[49]

What was, in turn, entirely predictable was that this burgeoning population would lead to another consequential round of reapportionment and redistricting based on the census, which would create new opportunities to win increased Latino representation in government—pushed for by a lobbying campaign that MALDEF also led. At stake was the rare opportunity of the 1992 electoral cycle, a presidential election year, which would doubly enhance voter turnout. What was not anticipated—but perhaps should have been—was that the inescapably visible growth and political progress of the Latino community would soon fuel a historic sociopolitical backlash among the declining majority population in the 1990s.

Part III

After IRCA: New Advances, Backlash, Resistance, and Breakthroughs

In spite of divisions among Latina and Latino leaders, organizations, and activists, the trio of big national policy reforms of the 1980s proved to be triumphs of both inclusion and resistance for Latino politics. Criticism and misunderstanding of the pan-ethnic "Hispanic" category adopted by the Census lingers to this day among activists and some Latina/o scholars, even though virtually all those involved in electoral politics and organizations representing the community strongly supported and defended this reform. Groups as different as MALDEF and Hermandad Mexicana never relented in their opposition to IRCA, and most of the Congressional Hispanic Caucus voted against it, but their years of resistance contributed to constructively delaying and improving the bill. Unity came with the campaign to legalize the undocumented, and organizations like Hermandad richly benefited from public funds provided for the English and civic-education provisions of the law that followed the mass "adjustment of status."

Only in the 1982 renewal of the Voting Rights Act, which strengthened its enforcement and preserved its language-rights provisions, were Latinos undivided. Taken together, the results of the policy battles over the Census, voting rights, and immigration boosted empowerment efforts across the country, and in 1991–92 made possible big Latino electoral advances in metropolitan LA. Not surprisingly, however, a fierce statewide backlash followed, in the form of ballot initiatives targeting undocumented immigrants, bilingual education, and affirmative action. Latino resistance to the backlash built on key advances in organized labor to yield a historic political breakthrough in 1996: the first Latino Speaker of the California Assembly, the state's second-most-powerful office. A new generation of leaders emerged steeled by the experience of backlash and resistance. The policy setbacks in education and affirmative action in the public sector, however, lasted into the next century.

The 1990s also saw Latina/o political empowerment expand beyond the Eastside in Greater LA, and its leadership diversified by gender and class. The great comeback of 1996 dispelled the notion that the officeholding lead that Texas Latinos had in state politics would continue. LA's ability to attract and develop fresh leadership talent, as well as draw a top national leader like Henry Cisneros away from Texas, confirmed the unique vitality and influence of the West Coast Latino metropolis. Nevertheless, in spite of epochal developments that, by the turn of the century, appeared to have changed the world—from the geopolitical balance of power to the impact of high tech on work, the economy, and communications—the new millennium would not herald the global consensus and "end of history" that some wishfully proclaimed. For its part, the late-twentieth-century Latino political-development cycle of progress, backlash, resistance, and hard-fought renewed progress would persist decades into the twenty-first. Donald Trump's return to power in 2024–25 made sure of that.

Chapter 7

Democratizing LA and Facing the Backlash of the '90s

Even as Latina/o political empowerment scored major advances in the 1980s, there were signs of what was in store for LA and California Latinos on a bigger scale in the '90s. On the backlash side, reactionary midterm-election ballot propositions emerged first in San Francisco in 1986 and then in Los Angeles in 1990. The earlier initiative amended California's Constitution, making English the official language.[1] The '86 cycle had other backlash elements besides, spearheaded by the then–Republican governor's reelection campaign. George Deukmejian branded both his elections, in '82 and '86, as repudiations of his predecessor Jerry Brown's two terms as governor.

Jerry Brown had a particular impact on California's judiciary during his first governorship (1975–83), appointing five of the seven justices on the state Supreme Court, including the first woman chief justice, Rose Bird, and the first Latino associate justice, Cruz Reynoso. Reynoso, born and raised in citrus-belt farmworker colonias south of LA, had been a leader of the Community Service Organization and head of California Rural Legal Assistance, a federally funded public agency that Ronald Reagan, when governor, fought with and tried to shut down. Brown made Reynoso the first Latino ever appointed to the state Court of Appeals, and then again to the state Supreme Court. As the Republican candidate for governor in 1982, George Deukmejian campaigned to recall three of Brown's Supreme Court appointees, including Reynoso. Deukmejian narrowly beat LA Mayor Tom Bradley in 1982, but his recall effort on the same ballot failed. In 1986, a well-funded movement again targeted three Supreme Court justices. Reynoso was among them, but the other two were different from those in 1982. Deukmejian again faced Bradley but won this time in a landslide, and all three justices were recalled. That allowed Deukmejian to appoint three justices of his own all at once—including a new chief justice—abruptly flipping the court majority from liberal to conservative.[2]

The 1990 ballot measure, which imposed severe term limits on state legislators, was a reaction to the long tenure of Speaker Willie Brown and his Assembly coalition. But there were inclusionary advances in the 1980s as well. Since Republicans in Congress had supported, and President Reagan signed, the 1982 extension of the Voting Rights Act, it was not a complete surprise when Reagan's Department of Justice (DOJ) announced in early 1985 that it was investigating a possible violation of the VRA by the LA City Council's 1982 redistricting.[3] This was an opportunity to embarrass the Democratic Party–controlled city, call attention to the fact that the council had not had a Latino member for over twenty years, and deliver for the healthy percentage of Latino voters that Reagan had managed to attract a few months before, in his 1984 reelection. What is more, the DOJ's investigation was launched just before Antonia Hernández had taken over and moved MALDEF headquarters to LA. In 1986, MALDEF had to follow the DOJ's lead and join its lawsuit against the city. Gloria Molina won the special election early in 1987, doubling Latino representation on the council. The new electoral plan also fashioned an aspirational third district in the San Fernando Valley, one that in the '90s would both further grow Latino representation and expand it beyond the Eastside.[4]

Just as Molina's city council campaign was shifting into high gear in January 1987, her *comadre* Antonia and MALDEF were rocked by a sudden split on its board, when men in control of its executive committee moved to dismiss Hernández and replace her with a former governor of New Mexico—who happened to be a man. Hernández sued to retain her post and won, but the fight unsettled the organization until it was resolved in March with a vote by the full board. A year would pass before MALDEF was ready to build on the experience of suing the city and take the next logical step for the community, for the organization, and for Antonia personally: once again taking on LA County, run by a board of five white men, as it had always been since the 1800s.[5]

The 1990 term-limits proposition was a project of longtime Reagan ally and hard-right chair of the LA County Board of Supervisors, Pete Schabarum, who, after a football career, was elected to the state Assembly during Reagan's governorship. Indeed, then-Governor Reagan also appointed Schabarum to the LA board in 1972, when an incumbent died. After winning a special election to serve out his predecessor's term, Schabarum was reelected four times to full four-year terms. Nevertheless, his ballot initiative would limit state legislators to three two-year Assembly terms and two four-year terms in the Senate. In a grudging concession to limit accusations of hypocrisy, in 1990 Schabarum chose to not run for a sixth time, which could hurt his pet term-limits initiative. Instead, he devoted his considerable fundraising to getting the statewide ballot measure passed.

The Schabarum proposition had populist appeal across party lines, moving California's legislature in a direction opposite to where legendary Assembly Speaker Jesse Unruh had taken it in 1966—even while using some of the same arguments. At that time, right-wing populist Reagan ran as an outsider, pledging to be a "citizen governor," against professional politician Pat Brown, who was seeking his third term. Unruh managed to get both Reagan and Brown to endorse his proposition to "professionalize" the state legislature—make it full-time with more pay, staff, and budget, and thus more powerful. Reagan was persuaded that corruption could be contained by making it possible for legislators to forgo outside income, at a time when literal bags of unreported cash commonly fueled election campaigns and legislative leadership contests.[6] Now, in 1990, the argument was that to contain corruption, it was the professional legislators who had to be termed out and their staffs and budgets cut. The proposition, which Pete Wilson supported, passed on the same ballot that elected Wilson governor for the first time.[7] The next time Wilson would be on the ballot, he would be paired with a more notorious proposition.

Fighting County Hall

Although MALDEF could only join as a follower in the 1986 suit against the city, led by the DOJ's Civil Rights Division, the experience served as rehearsal for the bigger lift of suing the county, on the same grounds, over its board districting plan. While the city council has fifteen members, the much larger county is divided into just five huge supervisorial districts. One challenge was that unlike the Democrat-led city, which opted for a negotiated settlement, the conservative majority of three on the county board, led by Schabarum, would steadfastly fight any lawsuit to the end. Reagan's DOJ hesitated to sue the board chaired by the supervisor that Reagan himself had appointed when he was the governor. This time MALDEF took the lead in early 1988, filing suit against the county, which DOJ then joined. Another key challenge was to devise a district shaped to contain a Latino majority, while still equal in total population to the other four, and acceptable to a federal judge—who also happened to be a Republican first appointed to the state bench by Reagan, the same year Reagan had appointed Schabarum to the county board.[8]

Antonia Hernández, President and General Counsel of MALDEF, at a press conference on August 25, 1988, announcing federal voting rights lawsuit to order redrawn supervisorial districts for Los Angeles County. Photo by Steve Grayson. Los Angeles Herald Examiner *Collection/Los Angeles Public Library.*

By the time the LA County voting-rights trial began in January 1990, MALDEF's national campaign was underway to urge Latino participation in that year's decennial census. The coincidence was electrifying. There could be no more vivid, ongoing example than this historic case of the stakes involved in achieving the fullest possible count of the Latino population: to win, at long last, representation on the most powerful county board in the country. As MALDEF's census campaign director, Arturo Vargas, recalled decades later, the lawsuit against LA County "gave us all wind to our wings. We were eager for a good count so that we could really make an impact in 1991 redistricting. And we did. Still my most impactful career moment."[9] But the regular 1990 electoral cycle was also underway, and a curious dance of ethnic politics and civil rights law played out.

Schabarum's chief of staff, Sarah Flores, was a Latina Republican. She had served the district since before Schabarum was appointed to the board as an interim supervisor. Flores had risen to executive secretary for the previous officeholder, and she told the *Los Angeles Times* that in the 1970s she had trained Schabarum in his new job, which combined executive and legislative functions.[10] Schabarum, who had promoted Flores to deputy supervisor, held his decision not to run for reelection "secret until the last minute"—even from Flores.[11] She was the logical candidate to succeed him, but he refused to support her, endorsing a white male judge instead. The other two right-wing supervisors saw electing Flores as a way to fend off the voting-rights lawsuit. She came in first in the primary election, but just days later MALDEF won its suit in federal district court. The appeals court upheld the decision, canceling the result of the primary and putting off another election until the following year, when a new, court-ordered district plan would be in place.

Schabarum's strategy of keeping secret his decision not to run again for reelection worked insofar as it was meant to keep Congressman Esteban Torres out of the supervisor's race. But MALDEF's victory in district court reset the clock, inviting other major Latino pols to make a run. Once again, Gloria Molina answered the call, but this time she would have to face her former boss, state Senator Art Torres. Never before had the Latino community in California seen an internal contest at this level and on this scale. Although again on the ballot, Sarah Flores was no longer a factor. Molina had beaten well-connected Latino men in 1982 to become the first Latina in the state Assembly, and in 1987 to become the first Latina on the LA City Council. Now in 1991, she beat the most well-connected Latino of the three to become the first Latina or Latino on the county board in over a century, and by succeeding Schabarum, she flipped control of the nonpartisan board from hard-right Republican to liberal Democrat. Policy changes started on Molina's first day in the supervisor's chair.[12]

Redistricting Redux: Southeast Side Story

The success of the IRCA legalization campaign did not become fully known until 1990—at the same time as the new mass mobilization for the census count, and as MALDEF's VRA lawsuit against the county was driving toward its historic win. Gloria Molina was then elected and took office as LA county supervisor in early 1991. Shortly thereafter, the census results showed the Latino community's surprisingly sustained, robust growth since 1980 in the city, county, and state.[13] Reapportionment and redistricting came next, in advance of the rare, and perhaps historically unique, simultaneous opportunities of the 1992 elections: a presidential year, a reapportionment cycle with seven new seats for California in Congress, and redistricting expected to expand opportunities for Latina and Latino candidates in the state legislature.[14]

As we have seen, however, there was also a contrary trend that had been repeatedly signaled throughout the preceding decade. Besides George Deukmejian's two elections as governor over LA Mayor Tom Bradley—the second time by a wide margin, coupled with the recall of the three State Supreme Court justices—in 1990, Republican Senator Pete Wilson defeated San Francisco Mayor Dianne Feinstein to become the next governor. Furthermore, the 1986 "English Only" ballot initiative was followed, also in 1990, by the term-limits initiative. Straight, white conservative California had shown a capacity to mobilize, undiminished since the glory days of Ronald Reagan, and had its own favorable demographic trends. Conservative inland Southern California had also been steadily growing and stood to gain from redistricting perhaps as much as, or more than, Latinos in metropolitan LA. These two dimensions of late-twentieth-century California were on a political collision course.

Los Angeles County contains eighty-eight mainly small incorporated cities, about a fourth of which form a sort of buffer zone between big-city LA and suburban Orange County, but which are contrarily known as the "Gateway Cities" between those two dissimilar areas.[15] Some of the Gateways that are closest to LA and East LA came to be known after 1992 as the "Southeast Cities," as a result of an effort to pull them together into a single California assembly district for the decennial redistricting process required following the 1990 census. Census results were released in phases, starting in December 1990, with consequences for the apportionment of congressional districts among the states. Detailed data by race and "Hispanic origin" down to the block level in urban areas—used in the actual drawing of legislative districts—became available later in 1991. Such finely detailed data, available to download for state and local governments and organizations such as MALDEF, was political-empowerment currency to be eagerly calculated and carefully allocated to advance priority Latino representation goals.

MALDEF encouraged lawyers and organizations in different Latino areas to advocate for their local communities in the redistricting process. The still unnamed Southeast Cities, which had come to be overwhelmingly populated by Mexican immigrants and Mexican Americans, were of particular interest. Martha Escutia, then running governmental affairs and public policy for United Way of Los Angeles, happened to have moved back home to East LA, just a few blocks away from the nearest of these little cities. Antonia Hernández called to ask her to help organize these municipalities to advocate for their shared interests in redistricting. After some initial reluctance, Martha took Antonia's urging and ran with it—beyond the point Antonia had in mind.

True to form, Martha threw herself into this challenge. She saw how those cities bordering on and closest to her native East LA, which she had returned to after years in Washington and Europe, were divided among four state assembly districts. The division of these small, overwhelmingly Mexican and Mexican American communities much resembled that of East LA up to just a decade before, until Richard Alatorre became chair of the Assembly Reapportionment Committee at the end of 1980.[16] After a MALDEF training session in using census data to draw district lines, Martha brought together her area contacts for a series of breakfast meetings at a Mexican restaurant in Huntington Park, owned by the family of a college friend from her years at USC. To invest the meetings with credibility, she brought in elected officials, Assembly Member and Latino Caucus Chair Richard Polanco and state Senator Art Torres, as well as UCLA demographer Leo Estrada, to serve as a technical advisor. Her contacts included city council members and other representatives of the local communities. What emerged from these meetings was the newly formed "Southeast Coalition" and a district plan to press upon the Assembly Reapportionment Committee.[17]

Escutia then took her district plan back to MALDEF to present to Antonia Hernández and staff attorney Richard Fajardo, who were left unexpectedly aghast. Martha did not know that MALDEF had its own carefully designed plan, and hers did not match theirs. Martha's plan took from the districts of several incumbents, including those of Latinos Xavier Becerra, then a first-term assembly member, and Lucille Roybal-Allard, to fashion a new district. By then, Martha considered the newly branded Southeast Cities her pro bono clients, and she respectfully declined to defer to the MALDEF plan. When the Assembly Reapportionment Committee met in Los Angeles, Martha was scheduled to testify, but Chair Peter Chacon gaveled the session to a close before she could complete her presentation. The *Los Angeles Times* cast doubt on the prospects for a unified Southeast Cities assembly district, and in fact, the redistricted map produced by the committee passed the Assembly without regard for the Southeast Coalition's cause. Martha thought her efforts had come to naught.

Willie Brown appeared to be approaching the second redistricting of his Assembly speakership as if the conditions of the previous ten years had not fundamentally changed. This time, Brown had put San Diego Assembly Member Chacon in charge of redistricting and expected him to deliver results similar to those produced by Richard Alatorre a decade before.[18] The Chacon map, however, was not negotiated with the Republican opposition, and they had no illusions that the Speaker they had helped elect in 1980 would protect their incumbents. The biggest difference, however, was that this time the governor was not Democrat Jerry Brown, but Republican Pete Wilson, who vetoed the Democrats' redistricting bill. With no realistic prospect that the legislature would produce a bill he could sign by the legal deadline in advance of the 1992 primary elections, Wilson turned to the state Supreme Court, which appointed a panel of "special masters" to produce the redistricted maps.[19] By that time, the California court was made up of six Republican appointees and only one Democratic holdover from the 1960s. The retired judges the court named as special masters were widely expected to imperil the Democrats' legislative majorities, and they indeed redistricted without regard for protecting incumbents of either party. Longtime political analyst Sherry Bebitch-Jeffe averred that in failing to anticipate the governor's veto, Willie Brown, "the consummate politician," may have made "the consummate political blunder. In trying to protect his incumbents, Brown may have doomed them. In trying to salvage his speakership, he may have destroyed it."[20]

The masters nonetheless sought to heed the mandate of the VRA, and so they respected the right of racial and language minorities to elect representatives of their choosing. One of the masters' clerks surprised Martha Escutia with a phone call, asking her to testify in another public hearing, this time for the benefit of the masters' redistricting assignment. Once again true to form, Martha submitted a formal legal brief to the retired judges and was able to make her full oral presentation. As she left the hearing, an unknown man approached her, offered his card, and asked if Martha had ever thought of running for office. She laughed the question off but noted that this man, Henry Lozano, a longtime political operative, was chief deputy to Congressman Edward Roybal, who was nearing his final term in office.

The special masters, apparently persuaded by Martha's and the Southeast Coalition's argument that their "pint-sized cities" formed a community of interest that merited representation in the state Assembly, adopted their proposed district virtually unaltered, as well as several other majority-Latino legislative districts. Now it only remained for the coalition network to recruit a candidate or candidates to organize a campaign and get elected to represent them in the Assembly. But the most viable candidate to come forward was a local leader who had never supported creating a new, combined district. At that point, the coalition turned to Martha, asking her to run. Again she resisted, pointing out that she did not live in the new district and considered herself a behind-the-scenes activist lawyer. Richard Polanco, however, as chair of the recently renamed Latino Legislative Caucus, prevailed with his pledges to support her campaign.

Escutia relented and moved into Huntington Park, where her district-creating effort had begun at Avila's El Ranchito restaurant. When she was growing up in East LA, Huntington Park was where her family had gone Christmas shopping but could not live, due to illegal yet lingering racist real-estate practices. Since then, however, immigration had made "HP" the most heavily Mexican and Mexican American town of its size in the country.[21] She began raising money, recruiting volunteers, and working the new district she knew better than anyone—and she won the election in a landslide.[22] Martha had created her own opportunity and set off on her new career.

The new maps, in tandem with Polanco's extraordinary electoral efforts, produced startling results: The first Latina from California elected to Congress, Lucille Roybal-Allard, grew the state's Latina/o congressional delegation from three to four; and Latina/o representation in the state Assembly *doubled*, from four to eight, while representation from LA County also doubled, from three to six. In another major breakthrough, the county as a whole elected its first Latino and Mexican American district attorney, Gil Garcetti, by an overwhelming margin. To top it all off, for the first time since 1964, California flipped from red to blue in the presidential election, going with challenger Bill Clinton over incumbent George H. W. Bush.[23] Within the doubling of assembly members in the California Latino Legislative Caucus, women *quadrupled* in strength, from one to four. National media dubbed 1992 the "Year of the Woman," which it certainly proved to be in California, where two women—Barbara Boxer and Dianne Feinstein—were elected to the US Senate on a single day. For the state's Latinas, the trend did not end with that cycle. In a special election held just over halfway through the new Assembly term, a fifth Latina was elected, making women the majority of the now-record nine Latinas/os of the chamber.[24]

New Era?

In multiple ways, 1993 appeared to be the dawn of a new political era. January 20 saw the first inauguration of a Democratic president since 1977. Latinos, and especially Latinas, emerged as a significantly enhanced force in the state legislature. After the required five years of legal residency, hundreds of thousands of formerly undocumented immigrants in Southern California were becoming eligible to apply for citizenship. The Latino electorate appeared on the verge of unprecedented and accelerated growth. And yet, new storm clouds were again gathering on the horizon.

Since 1987, attending to the needs of the newly legalized and those entering the legalization pipeline had become a growth industry. After first acquiring a one-year "adjustment of status," the formerly undocumented immigrants were required to complete forty hours of classes in English, US history, and civics to qualify to become lawful permanent residents (LPRs), which would grant them the official immigrant visa known as a "green card." Such federally funded classes could be offered by community colleges and high schools with adult-education programs, and by qualified community-based organizations that had assisted with the first phase of legalization. This provided consequential opportunities for Latino organizations in LA, such as Hermandad Mexicana and One Stop Immigration, and activists like Nativo Lopez, Fabián Núñez, and Kevin de León.

This opportunity was life altering for de León, who after his first year at UC Santa Barbara had flunked out and was jobless, homeless, couch surfing, and sleeping in his car. Kevin did not want to return to San Diego and tell his single mother about the dismal situation he found himself in. Salvation came in a phone call with Fabián, his closest friend since before high school, who was running a branch in Pomona of One Stop's growing program. Núñez told de León he, too, could teach English-language, history, and civics classes for immigrants in Santa Barbara. Nobody could have imagined that this program, a consequence of the IRCA immigration reform of 1986, would provide the first step on a journey that would culminate in the next century, first with Núñez becoming Speaker of the California Assembly, and then de León president pro tempore of the state Senate.

Kevin de León's first try at college in idyllic Santa Barbara in 1986 had been his ticket out of his miserable home life in the San Diego barrio of Logan Heights, but it also plunged him into an identity crisis. The future state senator grew up in poverty that haunts him still. His mother and one of his uncles rented rooms secured by padlocks in a house in Logan Heights.[25] Kevin's most vivid memory of that home is the constant, disgusting presence of roaches in the space beneath the house that he called his room.[26] San Diego Police were also regular visitors because, as de León put it, his uncle was "always getting in trouble." Kevin learned his mother had divorced a man who was not his father, with whom she had two daughters, all living in Tijuana. He visited them often, which made the border something of a fiction to him. De León doesn't remember hearing about his own father until he was five, and it was only in grade school that he learned his mother was originally from Guatemala. He would also visit and stay over with his aunt's family in El Monte, just east of LA. Since his relations at each home spoke Spanish and were either fully or partially Mexican, he says he was "hardwired" to think of himself as Mexican as well.[27]

As a child, Kevin often accompanied his mother to the houses she cleaned in white, middle-class neighborhoods. He learned English from watching TV in those homes, and picked up enough to be an average student in school. A particular teacher he had for both fifth and sixth grade provided him with two years of training in a simple form of analytical reading and public speaking.[28] Miss Juanita Wright, an African American woman from Texas, had her students go through newspapers, choose and clip an article, and then talk to the class about it. Each week, speaking without notes, they had to identify the standard "who, what, when, where, and why" of their chosen article. This introduced Kevin to the *Los Angeles Times*, and he came to see the difference between it and *The San Diego Union-Tribune*. He was engaging with newspapers, reading with purpose, and, most importantly, speaking to the whole class about what he had read. Over the course of those years, this regular exercise made him a confident speaker—a skill that would serve him well the rest of his life.

Nevertheless, by his own account, de León continued to be an undistinguished student, even at what he called the worst or second-worst high school in town. The most lasting benefits of his years at San Diego High were running on the school's cross-country team and the opportunity to cement what became a lifelong friendship and political partnership with Fabián Núñez. The two became close enough for Kevin to let Fabián see how he lived. "I had never met anyone more broke than I was," Núñez told *Pacific Standard* magazine in 2018, when his accomplished friend, then-president pro tem of the state Senate, was also the Democratic Party–endorsed challenger to Senator Dianne Feinstein in that fall's elections.[29] Another high school friend took Kevin with her to the Upward Bound college preparatory program at UC San Diego, which he was attracted to, but he did not have the grades to be admitted. It took recourse to a policy called "Special Action/Exception" to allow Kevin to participate in Upward Bound and for that program to help him be admitted to UC Santa Barbara.[30]

His exception admission did not work out for either the policy or Kevin, as he was placed on academic probation each quarter of his freshman year, and then suspended. But suspension from UC Santa Barbara, despite rendering him homeless for a year, made him available, hungry, and eager for the surprise lifesaver his best friend, Fabián, tossed him in 1988—to become a teacher and counselor to immigrants in the legalization pipeline. Kevin would be paid based on the number of students he could recruit and enroll. His first tasks, then, were those of an organizer, and something of an entrepreneur.

With Núñez guiding him, de León first secured the regular use of an enclosed courtyard in the predominantly student community of Isla Vista, neighboring UC Santa Barbara. He then had hundreds of flyers made and studied the curriculum he would teach. At that point, Santa Barbara High was the main provider of these classes, so Kevin went there to distribute his flyers one evening. The parking lot was full of hundreds of cars, and Kevin methodically placed a flyer on each windshield.

He stood outside the front entrance, where he began delivering his pitch in Spanish as the immigrants came strolling out at 9:00 p.m. He held his first class with just four students, but soon he needed to find an indoor space, get it set up, and recruit friends he could train and hire to teach. The recently homeless college dropout was growing his skills rapidly.

De León negotiated a lease for a roughly five-thousand-square-foot upper floor of a building in nearby Montecito and hired a carpenter to put in dividing walls and chalkboards. His adult instructional became something of a community center. Eventually, after local demand peaked, Kevin decided to move out to Claremont, far to the east of LA, where he could team up again with Núñez. He replicated there what he had learned to do in Santa Barbara, set up a string of teaching centers around the region, and settled into the role of an adult-education administrator. Unlike Kevin, Fabián had completed years of college at UC San Diego before he married, left school to work, and moved to Claremont. With his many credits, Núñez completed relatively quickly a double-major BA at nearby Pitzer College. De León, following his friend's lead, was admitted to Pitzer but would take until 2003 to complete his degree.

Here It Comes

As positive as the start of the decade had been for Latina/o empowerment in California—with the results of the census, redistricting, and 1992 elections—an ominous factoid appeared halfway through 1990: the longest economic expansion in US history, associated with the presidency of Ronald Reagan, stalled. Economic downturns had long been accompanied by the stirring of anti-immigration sentiment, especially in the case of the Great Depression. Now California, which had more immigrants than any other state and was particularly impacted by defense cutbacks, could be especially susceptible to the allure and exploitation of nativism. The joyous fall of the Berlin Wall in 1989 heralded the end of the Cold War, but it also froze the development of a generation of advanced weapons systems and raised the likely prospect of base closures. No state would lose more jobs in defense and aerospace than California. This was a structural economic change that would not be ameliorated by a cyclical recovery. Already, in his first State of the State address in January 1991, new governor Pete Wilson had outlined a series of budget cuts deemed necessary due to both his inherited deficit and the continued projected fall of tax revenues. He made no mention of immigration or "illegal aliens" at this time, but by especially targeting the Aid to Families with Dependent Children (AFDC) welfare program for the severest cut, Wilson laid a predicate for what was to come.[31]

At that time, recently legalized immigrant farmworkers had begun drifting into urban areas, seeking better work and lives. Resentment started brewing at the sight of immigrant brown men using Home Depot parking lots as impromptu day-labor pickup sites in areas such as Orange County and LA's San Fernando Valley. Before the year ended, Wilson began beating the drum that the AFDC program in California was a "magnet" for immigrants across the country, but he was not yet making claims about "illegals," who were ineligible for welfare benefits. Wilson then began a campaign demanding that the federal government reimburse California for the cost of welfare payments to immigrants in the state.[32]

Having lost the governor's race in 1990 to Wilson, San Francisco Mayor Dianne Feinstein was on the ballot again in 1992 in a bid to take Wilson's old Senate seat, but as that was a special election to complete Wilson's final term, she would have to run again in 1994 to retain it. Perhaps not surprisingly, Feinstein was particularly attuned to rumblings about immigrants and how they were allegedly straining the state's coffers, through the public schools and hospitals and especially through law enforcement and the prison system. By 1993, in these matters Senator Feinstein, the San Francisco Democrat, seemed to increasingly echo Governor Wilson, the San Diego Republican.[33] Her more liberal colleague, Senator Barbara Boxer, who would not face voters for another five years and did not have to handle the state's budget woes, was nevertheless not far behind, calling for the state's National Guard to be deployed at the border.[34] At the grassroots, an organization had emerged in Orange County to apply pressure for a crackdown on undocumented immigration in particular. Citizens for Action Now went on to form a larger coalition that began gathering signatures for what it originally dubbed the "Save Our State" (SOS) ballot initiative, ultimately known as Proposition 187.[35]

For Kevin de León and Fabián Núñez, as experienced activists and advocates for Latino immigrants, all these developments were concerning, but nothing appalled and offended them more than the position taken by one of the new Latina/o assembly members from LA elected in the breakthrough cycle of 1992. In just his first year in the Assembly, Louis Caldera joined in a bill that would strip undocumented residents of the state of their driver's licenses. Similarly appalled was another member of that 1992 Assembly class, Martha Escutia, whose self-designed district bordered Caldera's. Caldera claimed he only supported the anti-immigrant bill for the purpose of "improving it" with amendments, but Escutia, de León, and Núñez did not buy such reasoning. They saw his support of the bill as caving to anti-immigrant hysteria and betraying his constituents.[36] That, along with the drive to put a more sweeping anti-immigrant proposition on the 1994 ballot, when Wilson would be up for reelection, compelled the Núñez–de León duo to move to LA and enter the political fight. Even more, the Caldera betrayal convinced them that they would eventually have to run for office themselves. For the next year, at least, they would be working out of One Stop Immigration's home office in Boyle Heights, where the California Latina/o-empowerment movement had begun. In this phase, the neighborhood was now cementing its commitment to immigrant rights and refusal to compromise with the new nativism that it equated with anti-Latino racism, and it was demanding its leaders in California do the same.

The Battle of 187

De León and Núñez were newbies in the LA world of immigrant-rights activism in 1994, and One Stop gave them free rein to try anything to mobilize the community to battle the state's governor and fight the new nativist wave. While they had spent the preceding half decade plying a practical dimension of the politics of inclusion by helping bring undocumented immigrants into legal and eventually civic life, they were now effectively about to orchestrate what sociologists call a *countermovement*, a movement of resistance to renewed anti-Latino nativism. In many ways, they were starting from scratch. De León, at least, had already learned how to write a press release. Back when he was setting up his first immigrant learning center in the Santa Barbara area, he called an elected official's office to ask if they issued press releases and could send him one. The staffer he spoke with answered cheerily, "Sure! Which one?" Kevin replied that just any would do. After studying the release closely, he called the office back to ask what the three pound signs (# # #) at the end meant.

Now, de León and Núñez were free to organize press conferences, rallies, marches, creative protests, and more, but with severely limited resources. They needed to make the most of all the ways they could to convey a message to the community and help mobilize it—a plethora of Spanish-language radio, TV, and print outlets; weekly English-language, Latino-themed television chat programs; a range of public-access programs on cable; an array of Latino and other ethnic organizations with regular meetings, newsletters, and in-house bulletins; Latino and other ethnic officeholders, some with multiple field offices; and more. Social media did not yet exist, so it took more work to communicate either broadly or narrowly to separate publics and communities.

A condition of their staged media availabilities was that One Stop Immigration's director, Juan José Gutiérrez, would always have the option of speaking first, with Fabián following, most times leaving Kevin third. Therein came another recurring exercise in thinking and talking on his feet. De León compares this to the experience he read about in his youth in a biography of Malcolm X. Like so many in Harlem before him, Malcolm's public-speaking skills were forged in the tradition of the Black street orators, going back to at least Marcus Garvey.[37] Such speakers competed with each other in what was known as "soapbox speechifying," quite like the even more demanding freestyle rap contests of our time. In the treacherous practice of One Stop press avails and presentations to groups, Kevin applied a technique he developed in speaking to an array of people more knowledgeable than he in a particular area: He listened for someone else to say a key term and quickly figured out how to riff on it.

To the Big March

Pete Wilson had already targeted immigrants in his first State of the State address in January 1991, signaling he would demand the federal government reimburse California for the amount he said the state paid for public services for recent immigrants, drawn to California from other states. The new governor referred only to legal immigrants, which suggested a throwback nativist mindset that provoked strong and widespread criticism. Seemingly chastened, he made no mention of the issue again in his 1992, '93, or '94 State of the State addresses.[38] But by January 1994, still struggling with a budget deficit while running for reelection with record-low approval ratings, Wilson included in projected state revenues $2.3 billion he claimed the federal government would owe California in the coming fiscal year for the cost of services provided to immigrants, this time both legal and undocumented.[39] Age-old nativist politics and sentiment in the US were once again focused on the most vulnerable among us—the undocumented immigrant—as they had in the 1930s, '50s, and '70s.

On its face, Wilson's combining the alleged cost of services provided to documented and undocumented immigrants alike seems puzzling, but it was a clever strategic move for a couple of reasons. First, it allowed him to raise the amount he was demanding, so as to cover more of the $3 billion deficit in his proposed budget. Second, this feint was akin to what is known in graphic design and moviemaking as the "hairy arms" tactic.[40] Assembly Member Louis Caldera had already shown that if a proposed policy could be construed to apply to both categories, even Democrats and liberal media would leap at the chance to make the distinction, insist legal immigrants be protected, and, as the cliché goes, throw the undocumented under the bus. Caldera did that with driver's licenses. Wilson could again expect widespread pushback against scapegoating legal immigrants for California's continuing budget crisis, with the result that nativist ire was concentrated on the undocumented.

Ten days after submitting his budget to the legislature, an unprecedented natural disaster hit Los Angeles, which agitated nativist sentiments even more. At 4:30 a.m. on Monday, January 17—Martin Luther King Jr. Day—a magnitude 6.7 earthquake centered in the San Fernando

Valley shook the whole region. It was the worst quake ever recorded with its epicenter in a major urban area in North America.[41] Beyond the scores of deaths and thousands injured, structural damage and fear of aftershocks—especially among Mexican and Central American immigrant families—sent many more thousands to camp overnight in public parks. The Clinton administration had Department of Housing and Urban Development (HUD) Secretary Henry Cisneros, the country's most prominent Latino leader, on the scene for weeks, coordinating the emergency response. A controversy erupted when Cisneros moved to address the shelter issue—beyond the six tent cities the National Guard had erected for fourteen thousand people—by providing eighteen-month housing vouchers to move displaced families into longer-term arrangements. Responding to criticism of public benefits for "illegals," congressional Democrats limited undocumented residents, including those with US-born children, to ninety-day vouchers.

We had already seen, going into 1994, that top California Democratic leaders were not inclined to help Latinos fight Wilson on immigration. Feinstein had begun echoing the governor on the issue, and Boxer had chimed in, as well, on toughening the border. Caldera had demonstrated that the growing nativist wave was reaching into the ranks of Democratic officeholders. Leaders were becoming aware of a grassroots effort in Orange County that had developed into a broader coalition working to put a draconian measure on the November ballot to deny undocumented residents nearly all other public services. The strategy of specifically targeting the undocumented was catching on.

State Treasurer Kathleen Brown, Jerry Brown's younger sister and Wilson's heavily favored Democratic challenger in that year's governor's race, invited Latino leaders to a backyard gathering at her impressive LA home. There, Brown warned them that she and the Democratic Party could not take the risk of branding their campaigns as being about fighting Wilson on immigration.[42] Gutiérrez, Núñez, and de León were there; the One Stop trio reportedly huddled and decided to take all the time they had remaining to enlist powerful collaborators to mount—in the final two to three weeks before the election, when voter attention would peak—an all-out protest march against Wilson and any nativist measure that might be on the November ballot.[43] They would be taking a page from the historic and pivotal Chicano Moratorium Against the Vietnam War march and rally of 1970, and, deliberately or not, trying to improve on it.[44]

As in the case of the moratorium, One Stop would stage a couple of smaller marches to build a movement and call attention to the date of its grand finale, the mid-October climax of its resistance campaign.[45] This strategy was working well enough that Assembly Speaker Willie Brown summoned Gutiérrez, Núñez, and de León to meet with him in Sacramento. The already-legendary Speaker feared that a big march defending undocumented immigrants could tip the coming election and even cost him his majority. Brown beseeched the trio to call their resistance movement off, but they refused. By then, they had brought in the powerful collaborator they needed to have a chance of matching, and even surpassing, the Chicano Moratorium's twenty to thirty thousand participants in 1970. Their new partner, Gilbert Cedillo, general manager of the largest and most politically active union in town, Local 660 of the Service Employees International Union (SEIU), had shown up to the second of their preparatory marches in May. That contact was developing into as fateful a connection for de León and Núñez as any they would ever make in their lives.

As we recounted in *Power Shift*, Cedillo shook his head at the sight of the meager resources he saw One Stop bringing to bear for a major public event.[46] He was nevertheless impressed with the thousands of people the One Stoppers succeeded in drawing to their second protest in May. He invited Gutiérrez, de León, and Núñez to his union headquarters to discuss how to pull off a bigger and higher-impact march and rally. Gilbert gave his guests a tour of his big labor domain, including the print shop with multiple presses, the coffee room with a platter piled high with muffins, and his own GM's office with its big bowl of fruit on a sidebar, which Núñez and de León eyed hungrily. He urged them to help themselves and take all they wanted, which they happily did. The GM said he would get his board's approval to go big on an October march. His print shop would handle all the paper—flyers, posters, and mailers. The union would set up a stage and bring its big PA system on a flatbed truck. He could also rent fleets of buses to shuttle legions of students and alumni of One Stop's far-flung English and civics classes to the march's starting point at *Los Cinco Puntos*—the famed crossroads between Boyle Heights and East LA.

Bringing labor into the resistance to 187 and Wilson's increasingly harsh anti-immigrant campaign may have indirectly had another benefit. Labor was strongly supporting Democratic candidate Kathleen Brown, and she, of course, highly valued the support. In Los Angeles, the most politically active labor leaders and entities were Cedillo and his Local 660; the political director of the County Federation of Labor, Miguel Contreras; and President María Elena Durazo of the hospitality union HERE Local 11. The state treasurer may have been discouraging to Latino leaders on the immigration issue early on, but she seemed to grasp a key distinction for both the Latino community and Latino labor that Wilson was oblivious to: the difference between enforcement at the border and "interior enforcement." Proposition 187 was all about the latter—turning all state and local agencies and all their staffs, including public schools, into enforcers of immigration laws. Its harshest consequence would be the expulsion of three to four hundred thousand undocumented children from the state's schools.[47] The harshest measure Brown advocated, on the other hand, was to use the military for "border support functions."[48] After 187 qualified for the ballot in July, Brown began to criticize it and, with her brother's encouragement, increasingly made the proposition the leading distinction between herself and the governor.[49] Despite polls in September that showed 187 "winning overwhelmingly," Brown rejected efforts by her staff to moderate her opposition to the proposition. "If I go down because of this, so be it," Brown declared in a speech, doubling down on her emphasis on border rather than interior enforcement.[50]

In spite of his by-then-lengthy history of anti-immigrant rhetoric and policy positions, and a notorious primary reelection campaign spot titled "They Keep Coming," Pete Wilson did not endorse Proposition 187 until September. But he had done much to help it qualify for the ballot the previous July.[51] With both President Bill Clinton and Kathleen Brown—the top of the national and state Democratic tickets—as well as organized labor strongly opposing the proposition, all Democratic candidates felt pressure to fall in line. After singling out immigration as contributing to the state's fiscal crisis, and running a campaign commercial accusing her opponent in the Senate race of being soft on immigration, Dianne Feinstein, with visible reluctance, came out against 187 in October. The big Latino march against the proposition thus went forward in a context of at least official Democratic support. The result was historic—perhaps the biggest protest march in LA history up to then, according to the *Los Angeles Times*, which placed the participants at seventy to eighty thousand.[52] Gutiérrez, de León, and Núñez, with the support of Cedillo, especially, but also Contreras and Durazo, had, indeed, well outdone the great Chicano Moratorium.

Record-setting protest march against Proposition 187, from East LA to downtown Civic Center, on October 16, 1994. This photo appeared in color and above the fold on the LA Times *front page. The sight of so many Mexican flags set off heated debate. Photo by Andy Scott/*Los Angeles Times.

Forging Future Leaders and Dividing the City

Among those drawn into the march against 187 were emerging activists and future LA Latino leaders Eric Garcetti and Alex Padilla, who were twenty-three and twenty-one years old, respectively. They had both grown up in the San Fernando Valley, albeit from distant corners of it, and had never crossed paths. Both had also gone to elite universities across the country, Eric to Columbia and Alex to MIT. But Eric's father was pioneering LA County District Attorney Gil Garcetti, while Alex's father was an immigrant Mexican cook and gardener. Their paths to political careers would differ greatly, but within seven years they would be brought together as colleagues on the LA City Council, with Alex getting there first, and one succeeding the other as the first two Latinos to serve as LA city council president.

In 1994, they both found themselves in the thick of that fall's political action—Eric working in the Kathleen Brown campaign for governor, Alex in Art Torres's campaign for insurance commissioner. Of the two, Alex was the more deeply affected by the new wave of hostility to Latino immigrants that he had come home to after graduating from MIT not five months earlier. He felt that the Wilson campaign and then 187 were attacking his own family, his immigrant parents in particular. The young Padilla had a golden degree in mechanical engineering, but between the ongoing and permanent contraction of the aerospace industry in Southern California and the suddenly threatening political climate, he had started looking around for another career he might want to pursue. He won a prestigious fellowship that placed him in a series of one-month positions that amounted to an extraordinary tour of LA Latino-empowerment institutions and operations. These included the Torres statewide election campaign, the County Federation of Labor, and the newsroom of Univision TV's flagship station, KMEX. So, both Garcetti and Padilla were fated to see from the inside, while still at impressionable ages, their candidates get swept away by that year's anti-immigrant wave.

At the end of October, nine days before Election Day, the *Times* divided both its editorial board and its newsroom by opposing 187 in its endorsement editorials but also supporting Wilson's reelection.[53] Whatever the considerations concerning the incumbent and his challenger, Kathleen Brown, the Wilson endorsement seemed gratuitous at best, as the paper had not taken an editorial position in a gubernatorial race in decades. The paper's senior Latino editor and columnist, Frank del Olmo, led an internal rebellion, and his dissenting column was published the following day. He rejected his editorial board's attempt to distinguish between Wilson's reelection campaign and the proposition: "Please note how I link the two campaigns—Wilson the candidate and 187 the ballot measure. That is pivotal to my reasoning and to the fundamental difference I now feel with some of my superiors. For I am speaking as a Mexican American, and in the eyes of the vast majority of Mexican Americans—California's largest single ethnic group at 6.1 million people—Wilson's campaign and Proposition 187 cannot be separated. Lord knows, the Wilson campaign has made no effort to separate the two in the minds of anxious voters."[54]

In the end, the great California political drama of 1994 was one front in a larger war over the country's future. Representative Newt Gingrich of Georgia nationalized the congressional elections by enlisting all Republican candidates behind his "Contract with America," which included provisions denying federal services and benefits to both documented and undocumented immigrants. He even cast the struggle for control of Congress in warlike terms, and he won. Gingrich and his party brought forty years of Democratic control of the House to an end, and he took over as Speaker. Representatives Xavier Becerra and Lucille Roybal, just elected in 1992, enjoyed a single term serving in the House majority before being consigned to the minority for the next six.

The LA-based resistance movement conjured up by Kevin de León, Fabián Núñez, their One Stop Immigration colleagues, and Gilbert Cedillo obviously failed when both the proposition and Wilson won by landslides. Willie Brown was effectively proved right when he lost his majority in the state Assembly. State Senator Art Torres's electoral career ended with his loss in the insurance commissioner race. Nevertheless, over time a consensus would emerge among political analysts that the combination of Wilson's rhetoric, his reelection campaign, and Proposition 187 proved to be a Pyrrhic victory for the Republican Party in California. A federal court first enjoined the proposition and then found it unconstitutional, so it was never allowed to take effect. Wilson's successor as governor, Gray Davis, canceled any appeal of the court's ruling by California. And the great majority of the state's Latino voters were now on record as united in defense of the undocumented, consequently turning that position into a litmus test for Latino Democratic candidates.

Twenty-five years later, a retrospective series on the battle of 187, produced by the local PBS affiliate and sponsored by the California Community Foundation, by then run by Antonia Hernández, celebrated the state's political transformation since 1994. That had resulted in Democratic supermajorities in the state legislature; an astonishing series of six Latino Speakers of the Assembly, Fabián Núñez among them; the first Latino state Senate president pro tempore since the 1880s, Kevin de León; and five statewide elected officials. The vastly expanded Latino Legislative Caucus produced a twenty-fifth anniversary video on the proposition that it cheekily titled "Thank You, Pete Wilson," in which over two dozen caucus members told how Proposition 187 had threatened their families and motivated them to enter politics, just as it had Núñez and de León.[55] Others similarly inspired included former Assembly Speaker Anthony Rendon, now–US Senator Alex Padilla, former Secretary of Health and Human Services Xavier Becerra, and former LA Mayor and US Ambassador to India Eric Garcetti, whose further experiences and contributions are traced in the coming chapter. Those advances would not ensue until the next two decades. In the 1990s, a couple more reactionary ballot initiatives would again challenge the community and its leaders. But what came next, just two years later, was the recovery of the Assembly majority, largely due to the mobilization of new Latino voters, and the election of the first of those six Latino Assembly Speakers.

A vastly expanded *California Latino Legislative Caucus thanks Pete Wilson in a video they produced on the twenty-fifth anniversary of Prop. 187. In the center are Senator María Elena Durazo and Caucus Chair Lorena Gonzalez.*

Chapter 8

Expansion, Diversification . . . and Comeback

California voters' dual landslide endorsements of Pete Wilson and Proposition 187 seem hardly imaginable in the 2020s from our "sanctuary state" vantage point. But in retrospect, we can see a number of key advances from around that time that paved the way for Latinos to overcome, just two years later, the unprecedented setbacks of 1994. That comeback, in turn, helped propel further advances and genuine breakthroughs as the California Latina/o-empowerment project drew in a burgeoning cast of characters over a widening expanse of political geography. In this chapter we will consider many new faces, some of whom were fated to go astonishingly far, well into the next century. Among them is a young man we should get to know well, who became California's first Latino US senator before turning fifty, and a young woman from Texas who, in LA, not only became a global TV superstar but also a premier national Latina activist.

As we have already seen, the 1992 elections multiplied Latino—and especially Latina—representation in the state Assembly. Within those aggregate leaps forward, Latina/o representation was both diversified and expanded in multiple aspects. For the first time, what had started two decades earlier as the Chicano Legislative Caucus became truly Latina/o with the election of Hilda Solis and Liz Figueroa. Solis—who eventually rose to become the highest-ranking Latina ever in US government as secretary of labor under Barack Obama—was truly Latina, being of both Nicaraguan- and Mexican-immigrant parentage.

The '92 elections, in fact, marked the start of an unprecedented dozen years of sustained growth and geographic expansion of Latino Democratic representation in the state legislature.[1] The Latino caucus grew with every election from 1992 to 2004. After a single term in the Assembly, Hilda Solis went on to succeed Art Torres in the state Senate in '94. Torres had left his seat open that year to run for insurance commissioner, in an ill-fated attempt to become the first California Latino elected statewide in the twentieth century. Instead, Hilda became the first Latina elected to the California Senate. Liz Figueroa was the first Salvadoran American elected to the state legislature. Both Solis and Figueroa also represented geographic expansion, as Hilda was firmly rooted east of East LA in the San Gabriel Valley, and Figueroa in the San Francisco Bay Area—more specifically the East Bay. Months after their election in 1992, Cruz Bustamante won another political breakthrough in a Central Valley special election to catch up with the '92 Assembly entering class. In spite of all the organizing by the farmworkers movement since 1962, the state's vast Central Valley had not elected a Latino to the Assembly in decades.[2] Now, in the '90s, half a decade later, the valley would boot out a Republican incumbent and elect a second Latino Democrat to the Assembly, as well as its first Latina, to succeed Bustamante. In yet another breakthrough, Bustamante would be elected lieutenant governor.

The reactionary wave election of 1994 itself was not without Latino advances in addition to that of Solis in the state Senate. Gilbert Cedillo and his union Local 660 invested heavily not only in the march against Proposition 187, but also in his old comrade Antonio Villaraigosa's election to the Assembly. Villaraigosa would go on to become Speaker and then, in the next decade, the first Mexican American mayor of Los Angeles since the 1800s. Villaraigosa succeeded Richard Polanco in his district, while Polanco himself also won an upgrade to the state Senate in a larger district that had not previously elected a Latino. Although he never supported Villaraigosa, Polanco's continuing leadership of the Latino Legislative Caucus made possible most of the Latina/o gains in the legislature throughout the 1990s.[3] In still another advance that foreshadowed a political earthquake soon to come, that same year Santa Ana, in Orange County, elected Mexico City–born Democrat Miguel Pulido as mayor. The "OC" had long been a stronghold of resentment and resistance against anything associated with LA or Democratic politics, but demographic change and years of organizing, bolstered by LA's Hermandad Mexicana, among Santa Ana's burgeoning Mexican-immigrant population were eating away at the bases of white Republican power in the heart of the county.[4]

Sixth Duo—Alex and Tony

Political duos have been a hallmark of the California Latino-empowerment experience—most famously in the case of Cesar Chavez and Dolores Huerta, but also, as we highlight in *Power Shift*, in the cases of Richard Alatorre and Art Torres in the 1970s–'80s, Cedillo and Villaraigosa in the '70s–'90s, and María Elena Durazo and Miguel Contreras in the '80s–'00s, as well as with the emergence in the '90s of Fabián Núñez and Kevin de León. A sixth promising empowerment duo, Alex Padilla and Tony Cárdenas, got its start in the '94 general election.[5] Padilla had his month-long stint in the Art Torres campaign as part of the public-service fellowship he was awarded that began that fall. Campaign manager Dario Frommer—another LA Latino who would go on to his own notable career as a legislator—charged Padilla with setting up a phone bank in the San Fernando Valley as part of the Torres campaign's field effort. A complete rookie in such matters, Alex asked Frommer what a phone bank was and what it entailed. Duly informed, Padilla grabbed a Torres campaign mailer and scrutinized its list of endorsers. He spotted the name of Richard Alarcon, himself just elected to the LA City Council the year before, in the first Latino breakthrough in the East San Fernando Valley, which would be followed by many more. Alex called the Alarcon office, which recommended Padilla reach out to one of Alarcon's supporters—a young realtor named Tony Cárdenas, who, like Alex, was from the same area of the East Valley, known as Pacoima, and a graduate of San Fernando High.

Tony Cárdenas's real-estate office, with its many desks and phones that went unused after hours and on weekends, was perfect for a campaign phone bank. That the office had been recommended to Padilla by the area's new LA city council member—whose election Cárdenas had supported the year before—and that it would be used for political heavyweight Art Torres's historic statewide campaign, made it easy for Cárdenas to agree. Tony was a socially committed and politically engaged community businessman. He located his realty office a short walk from his old high school, so students could easily intern and visit there and see successful, young Chicano professionals in suits working in an office. Besides, Tony hit it off personally with Alex. Both had been trained as engineers but chose not to pursue a career in that field, which had fallen on hard times in post–Cold War Southern California. Both their fathers were immigrants from the Mexican state of Jalisco. And Tony was happy to help a fellow San Fernando High "Mighty Tiger" who, ten years his junior, was fresh out of college. They found they had even grown up within blocks of each other and had gone to the same elementary school.

The Torres campaign field effort was a joint learning experience for them. They spent hours chatting in a conference room while the phone bank Alex had set up did its work—all of which set the stage for a joint turning point: The following summer Cárdenas decided to run for what was due to become an open Assembly seat in 1996, and asked Padilla to manage his campaign. Despite having experienced the Torres defeat together, they had both caught the political bug. Tony's business was successful enough to give him the means and flexibility to run, while Alex was motivated by the need to resist the nativist movement headed by the newly reelected governor.

Nevertheless, Padilla objected that with just a month's experience with a major field effort, he did not know how to manage a campaign. Cárdenas replied that surely his young friend would seek elected office himself someday, for which there was no better preparation than running a campaign. At that time, however, Alex's life might well have taken another course. He had interviewed with a firm that produced the LA Lakers pregame show, a sports media gig that would involve traveling with the team to away games. To a young man who had gone back to living with his parents in Pacoima, it sounded ideal. But time passed without a follow-up from the firm, so Alex cast his lot with Tony. The call finally came the following Monday. The firm had gone with someone else for the Lakers job but had since landed a new contract with the LA

Raiders—a team not only in the dominant sport and league in the country, but historically special to Mexican Americans.[6] The production firm now needed Alex, but he was committed to his friend and to the cause of Latina/o political empowerment, so he turned down not just a plum job offer, but a whole other life.

What was certain was that both Alex and Tony had already embarked on lives dramatically different from those of their parents. Although their families moved to Pacoima at different times in the post–World War II era, both arrived when the community was steadily becoming a predominantly African American fringe of the San Fernando Valley. The area had long been part of the city of Los Angeles, but like Chavez Ravine, it had some of the characteristics of unincorporated East LA and the colonia phenomenon elsewhere—a mix of homes that at one time included converted Quonset huts, tents, and shacks. As tract homes were built for Black World War II veterans, the district became known as "LA's first Black suburb." Pacoima would come to house 90 percent of the Valley's African American population by the time Alex graduated from high school.[7] Pioneering Mexican American rock-and-roller Ritchie Valens briefly put Pacoima on the pop-culture map during his short career in the late 1950s, but substantial Mexican migration to the area started only in the 1970s. Alex's family moved there from North Hollywood in 1978, after he'd had a year of preschool. The neighborhood elementary school in Pacoima found him to be both too far ahead and uncomfortably tall for its kindergarten, so it placed him in first grade. For the next dozen years of public education, Alex would be the youngest and still the tallest boy in every class.

Five-year-old Alex was assigned, along with the other "Mexican" first graders, to the "ESL"—English as a second language—class, with textbooks in Spanish. Proceeding at his own pace, he "zipped" through all the assignments in Spanish and finished second grade, so he was given English textbooks and assigned the next year to a third-grade class taught in English. When he got to fourth grade, his new teacher found him still far enough ahead of the class that she scrambled to get him transferred to a better school altogether, a magnet school in the neighboring community of Arleta, on the other side of the roaring Interstate 5. It took the combined efforts of a wife-and-husband team of teachers in adjacent classrooms to secure Alex's father's permission, get him tested right at the deadline, and have him transferred. "It changed the trajectory of my life," Alex told us. "From then on, I wasn't the smartest kid in the school." He completed both elementary and junior high in Arleta's magnet schools, but then he chose to rejoin his friends at San Fernando High—another fateful move.[8]

Crack and Baseball

What came to be known as the crack epidemic developed in areas of Los Angeles throughout the 1980s and into the '90s. Padilla learned years later that for a time in his youth, the LAPD considered an intersection a half block from his family home to be the Valley's worst for drug dealing, prostitution, and other gang activity. The sound of hovering LAPD helicopters was common at night. The 2015 "gangster rap" film set in mid-1980s South Central LA, *Straight Outta Compton*, captured well the scene in Alex's immediate neighborhood, he would later say. To keep him away from gangs and trouble, Padilla's mother told him he had a choice: sign up to be an altar boy, or play baseball in the church-based Valley Catholic League, which paralleled Little League. He developed into a dominating pitcher, towering over the other boys from his perch on the mound, and played every season all the way to his freshman year in college. Baseball introduced Alex to the rest of the San Fernando Valley and beyond; he once played as far away as Banning, two counties over to the east. But on returning from games, his dad would sometimes have to dodge crack peddlers who would rush to the car and even jump on the hood, trying to make a sale. His neighbors' and family's response to the situation was to form a neighborhood watch group. Alex would accompany his mother on the walk over to meetings in a neighbor's converted garage, and he liked to listen. As his parents were not yet citizens, elections never brought a knock at the door by a campaign volunteer, or mailers in the mailbox. Neighborhood watch meetings were Alex's introduction to politics and government, especially when they featured a representative of the LAPD or city attorney's office. He came to understand that Pacoima and the Valley were part of LA.

Latinos' heavy use of public parks on weekends gave his aunt and uncle the chance to earn extra income and Alex to learn an extra skill. On Friday nights they would make piles of burritos to sell from a couple of little Radio Flyer wagons they pulled around all the Valley parks. While years of pitching habituated Alex to performing in front of an attentive and sometimes vocal crowd of both supporters and detractors, hawking burritos got him used to approaching strangers with a sales pitch. He learned that the faster they could sell, the sooner he could get back home. These childhood experiences would eventually serve him well in developing a political career.

Baseball also taught Alex lessons. Well into one game, he appeared frustrated as he came off the mound, and his coach asked what was wrong, since they were winning. "I can't strike anybody out!" he replied. "You're a smart guy, Alex," his coach said. "Answer me two questions. If all you throw are strikes, what's the minimum you need to get out of an inning?" The answer was nine, of course. "But if each batter grounds out, how many pitches would you have to throw?" The answer was three. "Alex," his coach concluded, "which is smarter? You have seven teammates behind you. Use them!" The lesson in teamwork, delegation, and practical tactics over heroics was valuable; nevertheless, Padilla would forever remember his one complete game as his best performance, not so much for the win but for having hurled eighty-four pitches. Poise, stamina, and sustained concentration under pressure would also serve well a young man who one day would be thrust into the role of acting mayor of Los Angeles in a national crisis.

If gangster rap was, for a time, the soundtrack and movie version of life in his obscure immediate neighborhood, another film—*La Bamba*—gave Pacoima a very different sound and public image, just as Alex was entering high school. The Ritchie Valens musical biopic told the true story of this Mexican American high schooler who had just started a sensational career as a rock-and-roll singer, guitarist, and songwriter when he was killed in a plane crash while on tour. Brought to the screen by writer-director and Chicano cultural legend Luis Valdez, the movie included scenes filmed on location in Pacoima the summer before Alex started at San Fernando High. He knew fellow students who were cast as extras. Millions of Mexican Americans across the LA area, not to mention far beyond, knew the traditional Mexican song adopted as the title track, but before seeing the new hit movie, they had no concept of the Valley or Pacoima. The most famous of the East LA bands, Los Lobos, covered the Valens version of the song for the movie, and in their extensive touring became evangelists for the film, soundtrack, and Valens legend. From then on, Alex was from somewhere, from the same neighborhood and schools as the great and tragic Ritchie, part of the backstory to the even bigger hit song "American Pie" and its poignant notion of "the day the music died."

As a student, Alex happened to like math, suggesting he indeed had a talent for focus and concentration. Teachers suggested he should consider engineering. He was fortunate to be growing up in an era when LA schools, for the most part, no longer assumed Spanish-dominant students to be less intelligent, not "college material," and fated for lives of nonprofessional work. He and his best friend in high school talked regularly about college, where to go and what to study. He knew a recent graduate who was the first from his high school to go across the country to MIT. That success story urged Alex to apply there as well. When this slightly older friend returned to the high school on a recruiting trip for the university, and specifically focused on Alex, he made the sale. Both Padilla and his best friend applied and were admitted. The day after his graduation in the summer of 1990, Alex boarded a plane for just his second time, a cross-country red-eye to a new life.

Ivy-Adjacent, Ivy *Pachanga*

MIT—the Massachusetts Institute of Technology—is often said to be "next to" Harvard in Cambridge, which can be read in two ways, as MIT has been rated in some surveys as the top university, or the second- or third-best, in the country and even in the world. Alex Padilla won admission there to study engineering, a field in which the university is regularly ranked first in the nation. He enjoyed the side benefit of its proximity to Harvard, and especially his participation in the sprawling student network known as the East Coast Chicano Student Forum (ECCSF), which he came to lead. More than anything else, Padilla's four-year, elite-level immersion "back East" prepared this kid from Pacoima not only for a public life but also to begin to play a leadership role on the national stage when he was still only in his twenties.

Alex Padilla studied engineering at MIT. Here, on the right, he wears a cap that says Pacoima and poses with a photograph of Emiliano Zapata. Courtesy of the Padilla family.

Before the 1970s, the country's oldest and historically most exclusive private colleges and universities in the Northeast lacked enough Mexican American students to form their own organizations. As their presence began to grow, most of these students' experiences were shaped by several common factors. First, all or nearly all who were enrolled at the Ivies, MIT, the "Seven Sisters," and other schools in the Northeast came from immensely long distances in the Southwest. Furthermore, the first generation of these students in the 1970s–'80s quickly learned that they were beneficiaries of the social movements of the 1960s, the Black and Chicano civil rights movements in particular. That, in turn, accounted for the fact that Black students had arrived earlier and were considerably more numerous, organized, and familiar with the history and dynamics of majority-minority group relations and politics. Consequently, when Mexican American students in this strange and challenging environment congregated and began to organize themselves, they tended to embrace a politicized Chicano identity, even if few had arrived with such a consciousness.

The presence of Puerto Rican students had a dual effect of both introducing the Chicanos to the idea of belonging to a broader Latino community and making vividly clear each subgroup's many differences with the other. In addition to much else, one difference between them and both the Puerto Ricans and most of the African Americans was immensely practical: Few, if any, Chicanos could afford to fly home for both Thanksgiving and Christmas. This reality gave rise to a new and distinctively Northeastern Chicano institution and tradition—the boisterous Thanksgiving *Pachanga,* hosted by the Chicano student community of a different Ivy every year. In the 1980s, Chicano students from Harvard and MIT down to Georgetown, in Washington, DC, formed the ECCSF coalition. Initially, this was to pair their established Thanksgiving huddle with a conference, which then grew into an annual series of two and even three convenings focused on a range of social, political, and academic issues.

In his first year, Alex became involved with MIT's Chicano student organization, La Unión Chicana por Aztlán (LUChA), attended his first Pachanga, and played first base on the freshman baseball team.[9] After that, he set baseball aside to concentrate on his demanding schoolwork, continued to participate in LUChA, and eventually had to decide whether to seek to lead that organization or to chair the intercollegiate ECCSF coalition instead. He came down on the latter, which made him a regional Chicano student leader in elite Northeastern higher education by the age of twenty. Shortly before his last Thanksgiving Pachanga/forum, an issue flared up that had the Chicanos at Cornell calling out for help. They asked all the sister organizations to petition their own university presidents to pressure Cornell's to respond to a campus controversy. As ECCSF chair, Alex organized his maiden press conference and sent out his first release—like Kevin de León across the country, using a random press release as a template. The hurriedly improvised effort was successful enough to be covered by *The Boston Globe.*

Back in LA, Politics Calling

Due to his family's role in the neighborhood watch program, Padilla got his first taste of electoral politics while back home on his last spring break prior to his graduation. It was 1994, but the harshest and most visible anti-immigrant aspects of the campaigns for Wilson's reelection and Proposition 187 were still to come. A renowned Valley activist, Irene Tovar, called Alex's mom, looking for help with the field effort for the campaign defending the leader of the state Senate, who was the target of a punishing recall effort financed by the National Rifle Association. Padilla's mother volunteered him for a few days of working door to door in a different Valley neighborhood. He did not know then that by the fall, he would be called upon to organize another aspect of a field campaign close to home, nor that over the next three years he would manage three campaigns for the state legislature, direct a statewide coordinated field operation for the Democrats, and then run for office himself before the decade was done.

Had he still been in the state legislature in 2019, Alex would certainly have appeared in the powerful "Thank You, Pete Wilson" video, produced by the Latino Legislative Caucus for the twenty-fifth anniversary of Proposition 187. The video makes vivid how the 1994 elections set the terms for the life's work of over a generation of Southern California Latino leaders and activists.[10] For Martha Escutia it meant—in addition to advancing her own legislative agenda and career—bolstering and then leading the Latino caucus in expanding the map of representation. For Kevin de León it meant first working in labor to advance Latino empowerment and immigrant rights and then getting Fabián Núñez elected to the state Assembly. Most immediately in the mid-1990s, for Alex Padilla it meant growing the ranks of Latino elected officials by managing a series of victories that even got the attention of *The New York Times*.[11] "That's what it was about after [Proposition] 187," Alex would later recall, "getting more Latinos elected." But Proposition 187 was also part of a trio of statewide ballot measures designed especially to mobilize white male discomfort with a changing California. The second such initiative would coincide with the Tony Cárdenas campaign, which Alex agreed to manage.

The success of Proposition 187, and Wilson's use of it to turn around his previously disastrous standing in the polls, energized a pair of conservative Bay Area academics who had been trying for years to fight affirmative-action policies through state legislation. They succeeded in winning over to their efforts a Wilson-appointed member of the UC Board of Regents, Ward Connerly, but their legislative proposal failed in the summer of 1994. A right-wing legislator heavily involved with Proposition 187 had already advised them to go the route of a ballot initiative, and when that measure won, they scrambled to mount a similar effort for what they dubbed the "California Civil Rights Initiative." They were aiming for November 1996 and benefited from picking up a pair of major endorsements along the way. Connerly got the Regents to vote to end affirmative action, and Wilson to support their ballot measure. This time, Wilson was trying to set up a campaign for president, although many leading Republicans were wary of supporting his hard-right stand, as they had been before regarding immigration.

Seen from 1995, when Padilla took on the Cárdenas campaign, the outlook for the Latino community was mixed going into the 1996 election cycle. That it was a presidential election year was a plus; that would itself mobilize more voters, as it had in '92—a banner year for Democrats, women, and Latinos. But this was a reliable "D" district, so Tony's contest would be in the primary. The organizers of the ballot measure against affirmative action were aiming for the fall. Of greater concern was how the voters would see Tony, who had no political or government experience and seemed very young. Through the Art Torres campaign, Tony and Alex had gotten to know state Senator Richard Polanco, head of the Latino caucus, who in turn arranged for them to meet Gilbert Cedillo at his union HQ. This duo struck Cedillo as so green that he thought they might be there to talk about a student-government election. Cedillo had yet to figure out what the visit was about when Polanco called to see how it went: "Did they make the ask?" Cedillo: "What ask?" Polanco had sent them to ask for the backing of Gilbert's union for Tony's campaign, but they seemed to fail to work up the nerve. As Alex would later say in an interview, as they made the rounds to drum up support, he and Tony were laughed out of some offices.

The Cárdenas–Padilla duo nonetheless went on to round up the needed support and won the March primary election convincingly—so much so that Padilla did not need to stay on for the general election in November. They were beneficiaries of what had emerged by the 1990s as an LA Latino power network of organized labor, business, and several professions with a presence at high levels in elected office, complemented by political expertise. Polanco and his caucus were key, as were Padilla's ties to labor. His father had been a member of HERE Local 11, headed by María Elena Durazo. Alex's fellowship also assigned him to work at the County Federation of Labor, directly with Miguel Contreras—the Fed's new political director as well as Durazo's husband.[12] The duo hired Councilman Alarcon's political consultant, James Acevedo, who had also been a Coro Fellow and was a master at field operations. Tony's landslide election in November was part of the Democrats winning back the majority in the state Assembly. But the truly historic consequences of this partisan comeback would not be secured until Assembly Democrats, which included twenty-four freshly minted members-elect, caucused two days later. An immediate breakthrough, however, resounded from coast to coast, but would remain a source of controversy all the way into 1998.

In another instance of Latino LA's expanding empowerment project, Hermandad Mexicana had sent its top organizer to Santa Ana in Orange County in 1982 to assist primarily undocumented Mexican immigrants with their housing issues. By 1984, organized renters were protesting their apartments' substandard conditions and the evictions precipitated by the city's enforcement of code violations. By the following January, this new tenants' rights movement launched a rent strike that spread and continued into 1987 with the support of Catholic parishes, a broad coalition, and Hermandad's litigation. The coalition's goal was to reorganize Santa Ana's municipal government. In 1986, it launched a voter-registration drive in advance of a special election that featured a referendum that would have reformed city government. The referendum failed in a close vote, but Mexican-immigrant businessman Miguel Pulido was elected to the Santa Ana City Council that November. Although Pulido was not part of the tenants' rights movement, he benefited from that mobilization and the new voters it brought into electoral participation. All along, Hermandad Mexicana was involved in the battle over federal immigration reform in Washington and was instrumental in assisting the undocumented with the legalization process that began in 1987, and it followed that up by assisting with citizenship promotion and voter registration. These years of work climaxed in 1996 with an all-out drive to defeat the Republican incumbents in the state Assembly and Congress who represented the districts that included Santa Ana, and to replace them with Lou Correa and Loretta Sanchez.

While LA had elected its first Latino to Congress in 1962, Orange County still had not, over a third of a century later. That suddenly changed in 1996, when Loretta Sanchez, a member of the Anaheim City Council, upset veteran right-wing Republican Robert K. Dornan, known as "B-1 Bob" for his bombastic demands for increased defense spending and expensive new weapons systems. There was no doubt that both Miguel Pulido's breakthrough election as mayor of Santa Ana in 1994, Sanchez's take-down of Dornan in '96, and Lou Correa's election to the state Assembly in '98 were based on both the growth of the Latino population and, especially, Hermandad's intensive community organizing.[13] Dornan claimed Sanchez had been fraudulently elected by illegal votes, which precipitated investigations locally by the district attorney and by Congress itself. Both investigations failed to find sufficient evidence to substantiate the allegations.[14] President Clinton's reelection, the first for a Democrat since 1944, combined with the collapse of Governor Wilson's attempt to run for president on an anti-immigration platform, Democrats' recovery of the state Assembly, and the Dornan congressional upset, amounted to what appeared on election night, from a California Latina/o point of view, as a stunning, clean sweep. Two days later, just hours after the state Assembly's Democratic Caucus voted Cruz Bustamante Speaker-elect, MALDEF President and General Counsel Antonia Hernández opened her organization's annual fundraising gala in LA, declaring that she felt like heavyweight boxer Evander Holyfield, who had lost his championship title in 1994 but then won it back in 1996.[15] Bustamante would assume the speakership when the Assembly reconvened the following month.

LA's the Place

The political comeback of 1996 was not limited to the fortunes of California Latino Democrats. The setbacks of 1994 severely damaged the Clinton presidency, but his strong reelection in '96 was certainly a personal comeback, even if Congress remained under Republican control and would severely restrict his ability to effect policy advances in a second term. For this and other reasons, the country's preeminent Latino political leader, Clinton's HUD Secretary and former San Antonio Mayor Henry Cisneros, did not relish the prospect of serving another four years in Washington.[16] But the political landscape in his home state of Texas looked even less promising for him. George W. Bush had ousted incumbent Democratic Governor Ann Richards in the 1994 wave, marking the start of a complete Republican takeover of Texas state government.[17] California, on the other hand, and LA in particular—in spite of its recent riots, wildfires, and earthquakes—still appeared to offer opportunities of various sorts, in addition to its long-held fame as a land of self-reinvention. The afternoon following Clinton's second inauguration, Cisneros and his wife, Mary Alice, boarded a flight from Washington to LA with that very intention in mind. And as he would learn in the coming years, Henry was not the only Texas-born-and-bred Latino talent to make that move around that time.

HUD Secretary Henry Cisneros and President Bill Clinton. Photo by Wally McNamee/Getty.

As a former career politician and public servant, Cisneros could hardly seem more different from former TV megastar Eva Longoria, but there are certain parallels. Both were born and raised in Mexican American South Texas and attended Texas A&M University, albeit at different campuses and decades apart. Both experienced a major change in career goals while still in college. Although on radically different tracks, their careers drew both of them into political activism and national Latina/o leadership roles. And at nearly the same time, but at different stages of their lives, they moved to LA, where they eventually met. Longoria's life began changing direction during Henry's last year as HUD secretary, when she entered and won the Miss Texas A&M University–Kingsville (TAMUK) pageant, and went on from there to be crowned Miss Corpus Christi USA. She graduated with a bachelor of science degree in kinesiology but put that profession on pause when she won a talent contest that took her to LA, where Eva chose to stay.[18]

It is likely that nobody ever made a more informed and well-considered choice to move to LA than Henry Cisneros did. To begin with, in college in the 1960s, he had gone from dreaming of becoming an astronaut/engineer to becoming a passionate urbanist, a student and scholar of city planning and administration—at a time when the country was in the throes of a national urban crisis. He went on to earn master's and doctoral degrees in the field and served four terms as mayor of San Antonio before becoming secretary of Housing and Urban Development. In his four years as HUD secretary, Cisneros made working visits to two hundred cities and every state in the country. His bond with his native San Antonio was unbreakable, but having spent a month in LA in the aftermath of the 1994 Northridge earthquake, he found the city "beautiful" and its people "stimulating." "I loved living in LA," he told us. "I chose to go to Univision."

In one of its several major changes in ownership, Spanish-language media conglomerate Univision was acquired by an investor group headed by LA-based media mogul Jerrold Perenchio. Although Perenchio was a Republican, he was advised that Cisneros would be a Univision president "out of central casting." The Cisneros brand was that of the business-friendly mayor of San Antonio with a national profile who had a talent for making private-sector development tangibly benefit the less-advantaged sectors of the city, which in San Antonio meant its Latino majority most of all. Although Univision's corporate headquarters was in Washington and its TV network production was in Miami, Perenchio himself ran his various businesses from LA's glitzy Century City on the Westside, and he wanted his Univision president and COO working down the hall. However much hiring Cisneros was seen as ostentatiously confirming the Univision network's political activism on behalf of its heavily immigrant Latino audience, Perenchio made it clear he did not want Cisneros to have a public political role. Thus, during his four years in LA, Henry's activism went on behind the scenes. Network news nightly coanchor Jorge Ramos continued to be the company's de facto political face, and with Cisneros's key internal support, he became even more so. Ramos's ability to advance a Latino political viewpoint on the air was necessarily limited on the nightly, half-hour general news program he shared with María Elena Salinas, but Cisneros successfully lobbied to establish an hour-long Sunday political chat show, like all the English-language network news departments had. With Ramos solely in charge, *Al Punto* became the first such network program in Spanish.[19]

The Politicization of Eva and Lorena

Growing up and being educated in South Texas, in a family rooted there for seven generations, Eva Longoria was not exposed to or taught about such things as the Chicano movement or its take on the Mexican American experience. As she was finding her way to break into and advance an acting career in Los Angeles, however, she came to know other Latinos pursuing a range of roles in "the business," among them David Damian Figueroa, a youngish man who was well-connected with social and political activists in the LA Latino community. Having himself come to LA from the Mexican American borderlands to the east, Figueroa was ideally positioned to help raise Longoria's sociopolitical consciousness and reputation. He was from an Arizona farmworker family and had himself worked in the fields as a child. He had also lived in South Texas and had family there, and he had participated in talent contests as a singer. From the first time he saw the city suddenly come into view, while driving in from the east on Interstate 10, he found LA liberating and thrilling. There, David Damian, as he is universally known, became both a publicist for actors and singers and a communications strategist for advocacy organizations. He eventually came out as gay, and he and his partner would host salon-like parties for a mix of Latino artists, entertainers, and activists. It was at one of these that David Damian introduced Eva Longoria to Dolores Huerta.

In that milieu, Eva began learning about not only the farmworkers' movement, but the full range of the Mexican American experience and the many social causes Huerta was involved in. Eva was enthralled by what she heard, and both Figueroa and Huerta urged her to read the Chicano studies classic *Occupied America: A History of Chicanos*, by pioneering Cal State Northridge professor Rodolfo Acuña, and encouraged her to take a class with him. The book set Longoria's mind on fire and led her to write a fan letter to the professor. They chatted by phone, during which Acuña urged Eva to enroll in his university's Chicano studies master's degree program, designed for working adults to complete in three years. She also began attending Latino activist events and learning about the principal organizations and their work. Her earliest philanthropic role—as the celebrity spokesperson for Padres Contra El Cancer—was ethnic but safely apolitical. In time, she would assume key positions with national Latino advocacy organizations, plunge into presidential-politics fundraising and vote promotion, cofound an unprecedented Latino political action committee, and become the Democratic Party's most prominent Hollywood activist. Along the way—while starring in what was for a time the most popular TV program in the world—she would fulfill in person all the course requirements for her advanced degree in Chicano studies and spend hours with Henry Cisneros working out her plan for her master's thesis.[20]

Lorena Gonzalez, originally from Oceanside and Vista, north of San Diego, was in the late 1990s another newcomer to LA who would also have a future as a prominent Latina leader.[21] Daughter of a marriage between a socially conscious, activist nurse and an immigrant farmworker, Lorena first ventured north for college at Stanford. There, she fell in love with a talented baseball player who was drafted by the Baltimore Orioles.

They married and moved back east. Whip smart and needing something to do, Lorena applied and was admitted to a doctoral program at George Washington University in DC. Somewhat like Martha Escutia before her, however, Lorena came to realize that an academic life was not for her. The news of Proposition 187 back home in California, combined with advice from a professor, made her think that, given her interests, law school would be a better fit. Pregnant, but with her marriage failing, Lorena applied to and was admitted to UCLA Law, moved to Los Angeles, and spent the next three years as a single-mom law student. When the time came to plot her next move, she was surprised to learn that a Latino had been elected lieutenant governor, and she set out to find a way to get a job working for him. That sent her back north, this time to Sacramento, but it would not be long before she would find herself once again in LA.

Padilla's "Three-Peat" and a Third Proposition

The 1996 Tony Cárdenas–Alex Padilla primary campaign was such a success that some key tables were turned—the very next year, when Gil Cedillo decided to run in a special election for another suddenly vacated Assembly seat, he went to see Cárdenas to ask to borrow Alex, who was then on Tony's staff.[22] The Cedillo election, with a first round in late 1997 and a runoff in January 1998, marked another sort of breakthrough. This contest took Alex far outside his home turf, up against the campaign of longtime Eastside activist and LA Unified School District Board Member Vickie Castro. But now Padilla and Cedillo had alongside them an unprecedented, independent expenditure (IE), organized-labor field effort powered by María Elena Durazo's Local 11 and other heavily immigrant unions coordinated by the County Federation of Labor, headed by her husband, Miguel Contreras. This election, as with the Cárdenas Assembly race before it, was all about the primary, so Alex was free before the end of 1997, but would be pressed into service again at the start of 1998—another pivotal political year for California Latinas and Latinos.

That January, in a very '90s LA sign of the times, Cedillo succeeded Louis Caldera, who had supported taking driver's licenses away from California's undocumented-immigrant residents. Gilbert would spend the next fifteen years in both houses of the state legislature, fighting to undo what Caldera had wrought. With this second successful campaign to his name, the tables kept turning and politics kept calling for Alex. He now turned to another campaign he had agreed to manage—Councilman Alarcon's bid for what would be an open seat in the state Senate. This would be the toughest race of the three for Padilla, as Alarcon faced former Assembly Majority Leader Richard Katz in the June 2 Democratic primary. That bitterly hard-fought win would be, in LA Lakers sports lingo, Alex's "three-peat," making his record as a campaign manager three for three, and incidentally opening up Alarcon's city council seat in a special election the following year.[23] But much else was happening that winter and spring that made the next year seem a world away. The whole Assembly class that had entered in 1992 was termed out, including Speaker Bustamante, who was running for lieutenant governor. At the end of February, Antonio Villaraigosa succeeded in pushing Bustamante out of the speakership, putting the Assembly under new management.[24] Martha Escutia was running for the state Senate, and a very promising aide to Polanco was running to succeed her in the Assembly.

On the same primary ballot was a proposition that would effectively ban bilingual education in public schools—the third in less than four years that threatened another policy setback for Latinos and other language minorities. Dubbed "English for the Children," Proposition 227 was also endorsed by Governor Wilson—to the chagrin of its author. Ron Unz, a young, "geeky ideologue," millionaire tech entrepreneur, lamented that Wilson's support made his proposition look like a "'third strike' against Hispanics, after Propositions 187 and 209."[25] Like the two previous ballot measures, 227 passed in a landslide, but at least the end of Wilson's governorship was now on the horizon.[26]

Alex and Hilda Make Their Move

With the primary campaign over, Alex was immediately looked to as a potential candidate to succeed Richard Alarcon on the LA City Council, and he chose to run. Now all of twenty-six years old, Padilla would face a Latina lawyer twice his age in the April 1999 special election, who surprisingly had on her side the outgoing incumbent Alarcon—whom

Padilla had just managed to help get elected to the state Senate. Alex won decisively but did not clear the 50 percent threshold needed to avoid a runoff. Padilla took the second round in June with a two-to-one blowout and was sworn in as an LA city council member in July 1999—exactly fifty years after Ed Roybal made the breakthrough that had gotten LA and California Latina/o political empowerment started. Roybal had run on the slogan "Give a Young Man a Chance."[27]

Decades, centuries, and millennia have no natural meaning, but a vague sense of acceleration and anticipation seemed inescapable in the late 1990s. President Clinton had endlessly characterized the second term he sought in 1996 as a "bridge to the twenty-first century."[28] Beyond that rhetoric, as 1999 wore on, the US public at large was troubled by the imaginary threat of an electronic apocalypse called "Y2K," when the year would roll over to 2000 at midnight on New Year's Eve. If we look in the realm of Latino empowerment for a real marker that accompanied this numerical transition, we can see multiple dimensions of the Latino power shift converging: the community's embrace of the defense of immigrant rights; the rise of Latino leadership in organized labor; the ascent of specifically Latina leadership across the board; the mobilization of immigrant workers and the transformation of labor's policy and practice toward them; and the LA-Latino-led shift by labor to dramatically enhanced electoral activism. The AFL-CIO held its last convention of the century in LA in the fall of '99. Its host was the County Federation of Labor, headed since 1996 by Miguel Contreras. As we recounted in our first book, Contreras wound up in this position thanks to the role he had played in overseeing the rocky leadership transition of HERE Local 11, which was rooted in the conflict between its old-guard white leaders and the insurgent mobilization of its Latina immigrant members, led by María Elena Durazo.[29] That experience converted Contreras—a veteran of the United Farm Workers—to the cause of reforming the labor movement to organize immigrants and defend the rights of the undocumented among them.

Contreras and Durazo led the effort to push the AFL-CIO convention to abandon the Federation's traditional hostility toward immigration and undocumented workers. Specific proposals were adopted for debate in labor forums across the country, and then made official the following February at the AFL-CIO Executive Committee's annual winter meeting, held in New Orleans. In a span of four months—bridging, so to speak, two decades, centuries, and millennia—the US labor movement moved into a new era of renewed and expanded inclusion and organizing, effectively adopting the LA Latino model of labor and community solidarity, the model that Bert Corona and his Hermandad Mexicana had pioneered and advocated for decades. That model had momentum, and the Durazo–Contreras duo always had new goals. The "Super Tuesday" primary elections of 2000 loomed just weeks after the historic success of their efforts within the AFL-CIO, but this year the presidential contest was not their main concern—it was the San Gabriel Valley congressional seat occupied by conservative Democrat Matthew "Marty" Martínez. His district largely overlapped with that of state Senator Hilda Solis, who, nearly three decades younger, was far more closely allied with labor. Both of Hilda's parents had been longtime union members and activists, and she had a much more robust record of legislative accomplishment in her eight years in Sacramento than Martínez had in his eighteen in Washington. Nevertheless, it was unusual for a long-established incumbent to be challenged by a member of their own party. But for politically activist LA labor, this was a demonstration election. Contreras was open about the lesson he and the unions were out to convey, and the opportunity was well chosen. Martínez was not only weak from a labor and immigrant-rights point of view, he was pro-gun and anti-abortion. After losing the March primary, he only amplified labor's political lesson by increasingly voting with the Republican majority and even switching parties.[30] Marty's bitter and spiteful last ten months served to position Hilda well for big things to come—but not until after two Republican presidential terms largely defined by George W. Bush's "war on terror."

City Council President Turned Acting Mayor

When Alex Padilla was sworn in, the council was under the authority of its seventy-five-year-old president, John Ferraro—the longest-serving member in LA history, having joined the body well before Alex was born. Fate then seemed to intervene, not once but twice, to dramatically catapult Alex onto the national stage, giving his already rapid rise another boost. First, Ferraro succumbed to cancer less than two years later, in April 2001, necessitating the election of the first new council president in fourteen years. As it was a mayoral election year, with seventy-year-old, two-term incumbent Richard Riordan unable to run again, Ferraro's passing compounded the sense that the city was in the midst of generational political change.

Just a week before, former State Assembly Speaker Antonio Villaraigosa, forty-seven, had placed first in the mayoral primary, and would face City Attorney James Hahn, fifty, in the June runoff. Padilla had supported the victorious Hahn, and the June runoff determined that the council, in its new term to start in July, would have a record four Latino members out of fifteen. Despite his youth, but in tune with the times, Padilla took the initiative, discreetly convening, perhaps for the first time ever, the other three Latino members to consider acting together. They divided up the task of consulting with the rest of the council and met again. They found that if they voted together, along with two to three other supporters they had identified, only Alex himself would be within striking distance of winning the council presidency. They decided to get to work to reach the necessary eight votes to win. Now Alex was up against the fourteen-year veteran councilwoman who, since Ferraro's death, had been serving as interim council president by seniority. On July 4, 2001, his colleagues elected Padilla the youngest city council president in LA history. He moved decisively to reorganize committee assignments, creating a considerable stir in at least one case. Allied with the new mayor, James Hahn, who had just taken office himself three days before, the two most powerful city officials made clear that a new generation was indeed in charge at City Hall.

Two months and a week later, the terrorist attacks of 9/11 made that reality bracingly clear. Mayor Hahn was on his first lobbying visit to Washington for the city, and while he was away, the council president automatically became acting mayor, a legal provision that normally passed unnoticed. An emergency call early that Tuesday morning—combined with the sight on live TV of the airliner crash into the second World Trade Center tower—thrust Padilla into high gear, but he found traffic jammed surrounding City Hall. After spotting a staffer coming out to meet him, Alex jumped out of his car, tossed the staffer his keys, and ran the rest of the way to his office and the city's Emergency Operations Center. With all but tactical military aircraft grounded, the mayor would be stranded in DC for the next two days. It fell to Padilla to lead and address the city. As the *Los Angeles Times* reported, "in the absence of Mayor James K. Hahn, Padilla has been omnipresent on Los Angeles radio and television. He has assuaged and assured over and over, in English and Spanish, displaying far more polish than his 28 years and his rocky start as council president might have suggested."[31]

Los Angeles City Council President Alex Padilla addresses the city from Police Department headquarters as acting mayor on September 11, 2001. Courtesy of ABC7 Los Angeles.

Joining the Cast

The start of the new century saw rising young LA Latina/o leaders take their places on trajectories that would ultimately make them outstanding players in their community's empowerment experience for decades. Already they represented the ongoing dimensions of this political project's expansion and diversification, but they could not have imagined the battles they would have to fight, the setbacks they would experience, and the unprecedented advances they would achieve. Alex Padilla was not only key to building up the expansion of Latino empowerment to the East San Fernando Valley, as LA city council president he was already starting his twenty-first century with a historic breakthrough. Padilla stunningly reached this position with the support of an especially promising new entrant into the empowerment movement, Eric Garcetti, son of the first Mexican American district attorney, who had just left office the previous December. Garcetti represented both diversification and expansion, as he was raised in a different part of the San Fernando Valley, while his mother was Jewish of European origin and raised on the Eastside in Boyle Heights. As such, Garcetti seemed symbolic of the new, diverse, and increasingly interrelated Los Angeles. His initiation to city council politics was as part of the impromptu Latino huddle that secured Padilla's election as council president on Garcetti's first day in office.

*Adopting a resolution sponsored by first-term Los Angeles City Council Member Eric Garcetti, pictured here, in February 2003, Los Angeles became the largest American city to oppose the US war in Iraq, a month before the invasion ordered by President George W. Bush. Photo by Myung J. Chun/*Los Angeles Times *via Getty Images.*

Hidden among the new faces, busily assembling the incoming mayoral administration of Jim Hahn, was an especially striking representative of diversification and expansion—Westside LA Latina immigrant Nathalie Rayes, born in Venezuela to a Lebanese Druze immigrant family. After completing a public policy master's degree program at UCLA and a State Department fellowship that placed her in Cairo for a year, Nathalie had been scooped up by then–San Fernando Valley City Council Member Mike Feuer. Feuer, who lost his first bid for city attorney in the same election Hahn won for mayor, handed Nathalie off to the Hahn transition team, among which she did not take long to stand out. She literally sat with Garcetti at his place at the horseshoe in City Council Chambers to show him how to work the system, and she quickly became Mayor Hahn's foreign policy advisor. He soon promoted Rayes to deputy chief of staff.

Garcetti would eventually succeed Padilla as city council president, and between them, Padilla, Garcetti, and Rayes would win statewide and citywide elections, become close allies of and advisors to governors and US presidents, lead national organizations, and garner positions as mayor and US senator, as well as appointments to two ambassadorships. But to achieve all that, they would first be severely tested by the most threatening political backlash to Latinos ever, and they would give the resistance struggle their all.

Chapter 9

New-Century Action: Sactown Hearings to National Megamarches

As the century and millennium got vigorously underway in 2001, with new administrations first in Washington and then in Los Angeles, a number of LA-based Latina and Latino leaders looked well positioned to make future advances in their careers, but the next major empowerment step for the community was hard to make out. Of the historic first two Latino Speakers of the state Assembly in the twentieth century—tellingly, the *last* two Speakers of the century—the second, Antonio Villaraigosa, had stepped down in 2000. Tony Cárdenas's bid to succeed him failed, and the next two Speakers would not include a Latina or Latino. After four years in LA heading the Spanish-language media conglomerate Univision, Henry Cisneros had just returned to San Antonio, where he would launch a new business and not seek public office again.

Over at *La Opinión*, the '90s had started out full of promise, with the Times Mirror Company's acquisition of a 50 percent stake in the Spanish-language daily and Monica Lozano's elevation to editor. The *Times* had experimented with publishing a bilingual weekly since 1989 but found, as others had before them, they could not break even in a market dominated by *La Opinión*'s loyal readers.[1] Then, as partners, the *Times* and *La Opinión* attempted to coordinate their distribution systems to boost both papers' circulation, but that did not work out, either, and Times Mirror vetoed *La Opinión*'s plans to diversify into radio.[2] The city had changed and would continue to become more Latino, limiting the *Times*'s penetration in its home market. In the mid-1990s, Lozano moved over to her family paper's business side as associate publisher, but then the unexpected acquisition of Times Mirror by Chicago's Tribune Company in 2000 meant *La Opinión* suddenly had a new and unfamiliar senior partner.[3] Unnoticed at the time, Tribune was developing its own ideas for publishing in the Spanish-language market; in 1998 it launched a daily in New York City called *Hoy*, to compete with the country's oldest newspaper in Spanish, *El Diario La Prensa*—a paper comparable in many ways to *La Opinión*.[4] The outlook was mixed at best.

Latina/o leadership had fundamentally reformed the unions' policy toward immigrants and succeeded in electing labor warrior Hilda Solis to Congress, but she and other promising Latino members remained boxed in during a dozen-year stretch of Republican majority control of the House.[5] Villaraigosa's 2001 bid to become mayor of LA seemed headed for historic success after the first-round election, but then failed in the second. The state's top Latino elected official since the 1800s was Lieutenant Governor Cruz Bustamante of Fresno, who took office in 1999, but the brightest rising star of California Latino political leadership in 2001 was Alex Padilla. He shone in the glare of 9/11, yet Padilla was still the youngest of all and just beginning his run as LA city council president. Bustamante planned to first run for reelection in 2002 and then try to succeed Gray Davis as governor in 2006, when they would both be termed out of the positions they held. But as we know with the benefit of hindsight, those plans were fated to be dramatically terminated by Arnold Schwarzenegger in 2003.

Although his aspirations would not be realized, nor would his career endure for long, Bustamante had, nonetheless, already contributed to the Latino-empowerment project in several ways, not the least of which was recruiting Dean Florez from the Central Valley to run for state Assembly. Furthermore, as Speaker from December 1996 to February 1998, he significantly improved the position of several Latina/o assembly members in the legislative committee system.[6] Since 1999, he and his office had also been developing another future standout Latina leader, Lorena Gonzalez, who joined his staff as a Capitol Executive Fellow fresh out of UCLA Law School.[7] After an intense year working closely with the lieutenant governor in Sacramento, Bustamante sent Gonzalez back to LA to run his Southern California regional office. The year was 2000, when the lieutenant governor was simultaneously running for reelection, preparing to run for governor after that, and helping host the Democratic National Convention in LA, the city that in the '90s had emerged as the country's premier stronghold of Latina/o political empowerment. As Bustamante's top aide in LA, Lorena could not have gotten better experience and opportunities to develop her own emerging career.

Thus, despite some outward signs of Latina/o political stasis in California at the start of the century, LA retained not only the institutional power but also Latinas and Latinos in major positions who could cultivate new leadership and engineer future empowerment breakthroughs. Although the fifth of our six LA-based dynamic duos of political empowerment, Kevin de León and Fabián Núñez, had not been widely visible since the pivotal march against Proposition 187 in 1994, they had landed in greatly improved positions immediately afterward. With a key boost from Gilbert Cedillo, de León was hired by the California Teachers Association (CTA)—the state's largest union—and Núñez by the County Federation of Labor, to work with its political director, Miguel Contreras. In retrospect, Núñez certainly appears to have also gotten on an ideal track to prepare him for a path to the next major advance in California Latina/o political representation. From there, he would be able to boost de León onto his own trajectory of ascent.

Contreras had become the Federation's first Latino executive secretary-treasurer in 1996, due to the untimely death of the Fed's visionary and relatively young head, Jim Wood. Contreras, in turn, appointed Núñez as his successor as the Federation's political director, placing him in the middle of the "Latino-labor alliance" he was forging in tandem with his wife and fellow activist labor leader, María Elena Durazo.[8] Contreras and Durazo, the fourth of our six LA-based Latino-empowerment duos, were using that alliance to build an "unprecedented political mobilization machine" in the metropolis.[9] Over the next four years, Núñez became a crack operative of that machine, helping many Latino candidates win office. In particular, the Fed's political operation was central to the historically innovative campaigns that elected Cedillo to the

Assembly in 1997–98 and Hilda Solis to Congress in 2000. Núñez then took a job managing government affairs for the mammoth LA Unified School District. Two years in that position further prepared him for his own historic role in public office. A tailor-made opportunity arose when Cedillo chose to run for state Senate in 2002, leaving his Assembly seat open. Fabián called on his old *compa* Kevin to manage his campaign. De León had not run a campaign before, but after years with the CTA, had acquired more experience than Alex Padilla had when he managed Tony Cárdenas's Assembly campaign in 1996. Besides, between the two of them, Núñez could count on ample support from labor, and he won in a landslide. This transplanted San Diego duo was now half into its LA politician phase.

But at least since the 1970s, Latina/o political empowerment in Greater LA and California had meant more than building an electorate, developing the means of mobilizing it, and finally achieving representation in elected office for the community—it also meant *using* that representation ever more boldly to make and change policy, reforming both government and nongovernmental power structures and practices. That Latinas and Latinos were acquiring real power showed most of all when they were willing and able to use it and "push the envelope" to, and past, its limits.

The Question Man, the Megabillionaire, and the Oracle Debacle

> *It's the questions you ask,*
> *in the right form, that have the most power.*
> —Dean Florez[10]

The most gripping California political drama of 2002 was in large part orchestrated by second-term Central Valley Assembly Member Dean Florez. Eligible for a third term, like Cedillo in LA he opted instead to run for an opening in the state Senate before somebody else beat him to it. Longtime incumbent Senator Jim Costa was terming out of his seat, which represented both Dean's and the neighboring assembly district to the north. Costa was a friend and ally who supported Florez as his successor. Since his senate district included Fresno, the Valley's biggest city, the combined area was much more urban and securely Democratic than Dean's assembly district by itself. This allowed Florez to win the March 5 primary in a landslide and render the November general election a formality, which meant he was free to use his last year in the Assembly as he pleased. As chair of the Joint Legislative Audit Committee, Florez had a big gun handy to take on virtually any issue or special interest he deemed worthy. Just a month after the primary, a fat target came right into his sights.

In early 2000, at the height of the "dot-com bubble" in the computer-tech industry, Larry Ellison was on top of not only California but indeed the world, as he was briefly ranked the richest billionaire alive, and his company, Oracle, was challenging Microsoft as the dominant business-software corporation.[11] Also pulling the highest executive salary in the country, in the scores of millions of dollars, Ellison reached his peak wealth ranking due to annual bonus "megagrant" awards of millions of shares of stock options, grants that came into vogue during the bubble.[12] But the dot-com bust that followed was compounded for Oracle by "tremendous pressure . . . to lower prices." As tech stocks tumbled in value, Ellison's fortune began shrinking fast, even if it remained immense. Besides that, his company's near–$100 million contract with California government was under investigation by the state auditor.[13] In her April 2002 report, the auditor found that California was paying significantly more for its "enterprise lease agreement" (ELA) with Oracle than for the individual software licenses it replaced, separately purchased by over a hundred state agencies. Furthermore, the ELA was alleged to have been hurriedly negotiated under pressure from the company, which was known to employ aggressive tactics favored by its hard-charging, yacht-racing CEO. Ellison was reportedly "horrified" by the auditor's analysis, but worse was to come.[14]

Governor Gray Davis, up for reelection that fall, had to act to contain the damage the report could do to his administration's image. Then Davis learned his technology advisor—against the governor's written policy—had accepted a campaign contribution from an Oracle lobbyist days after the contract had been agreed to. The governor went ballistic, ordering the Highway Patrol to raid the offices of his own Department of Information Technology, suspending its director, forcing out his technology advisor, and calling on the attorney general to investigate. The May 2 raid was being covered on live TV when "Oracle's Washington-based senior political operative" called Ellison and his chief of staff to alert them. In the words of Ellison's authorized biographer, Oracle was "now embroiled in a major political scandal," one that would metastasize into "the worst crisis the company had faced in more than a decade."[15] Enter Dean Florez and his Joint Audit Committee.

That Florez would jump on this opportunity cohered with over three decades of his learning and experience of politics and government. When he was growing up in La Colonia Mexicana, a mile and a half outside the city limits of Shafter, Dean's parents were too focused on work to show any interest in politics, but he spent countless after-school, weekend, and summer hours with his paternal grandmother. Even after his parents' years of hard work allowed his family to move into Shafter, he continued taking the school bus back to his grandmother's in the colonia. His Nana was obsessed with two great worlds of competition and combat: sports and politics, which she followed daily and discussed over dinner. She was a big fan of the LA Dodgers, never missing a game on radio or TV, as well as of the Kennedy brothers, each of whom had served in the US Senate and either had or would run for president. The most Dean knew of Los Angeles was from long bus trips he took with his grandmother to sit in top-deck cheap seats in Dodger Stadium. Both there and at home, his Nana fastidiously marked every pitch and play in her scorecard book. Equally devoted to politics, she sent her monthly donation to a "Kennedy Club," clipped political stories from newspapers, and walked the colonia before every election to inform neighbors how to vote. Dean walked with her. A particular standout memory was of the Watergate hearings in the summers of 1973 and '74, especially the former.

Those Senate Watergate Committee hearings are well remembered for two questions that echo practically undiminished four decades on: Senator Howard Baker's repeated "What did he know and when did he know it?" regarding Nixon and the Watergate break-in, and Minority

Counsel Fred Thompson's "Mr. Butterfield, are you aware of the installation of any listening devices in the Oval Office of the president?" The latter moment changed the course of history. Although throughout his youth, Dean, like his parents, had little interest in politics, he watched the hearings with his Nana and absorbed a lesson that would get revived for him in college and stay with him all the way through his career as a California legislator: The greatest tool, skill, or weapon in our adversarial system of government, law, and policymaking is to *ask the right question.*[16]

Not surprisingly, sports became Dean's real passion and the arena in which he excelled. An exceptional runner, in high school Florez set records in both track and as a wide receiver in football. Recruited by Arizona State, his ticket out of Shafter seemed secure until the first game of his senior year, before classes had even started. A big teammate struggling to grind out an extra yard fell on Dean's right leg and broke it in two places. The break was so severe that his parents said they heard the snap from where they sat in the bleachers. Dean left the field on a stretcher before the game was over, and spent the next six months in a quarter-body cast and traction. Florez would not see his school again until March, and then in a wheelchair. He was walking by summer, but instead of heading to Arizona State for football camp, Dean started working at the same Mobil Chemical plant in Bakersfield as his father. That fall, Florez enrolled at Bakersfield Community College, where he had both an intellectual and political awakening, an epiphany of sorts, in a class on political theory. In a reflective mood since the tragic turn in his life, he found himself captivated by a professor's Socratic approach to big ideas like justice. Dean learned the critical importance of asking probing questions. He would later say it was in that class that he earned his "first legitimate A."

Despite a whole year without sports and having gained an enormous amount of weight, Florez was able to revive the internal discipline of an accomplished athlete, and for the first time began running long distance. He recovered enough to make the college cross-country team, and by the next spring he was back to running his old track events well enough to be admitted to UCLA on a track-team scholarship. His experience at the big university in the megacity would further change his life. Previously apolitical Dean was pulled into Chicano student politics, of the sort invented on LA's Eastside. His timing was fortuitous, as UCLA MEChA had united with other minority organizations to form the Third World Coalition. The *MEChistas* saw in Dean a *pocho* who could speak mainstream political lingo and be a crossover candidate for student government. They not only politicized him but even radicalized him. Florez also had the support of star male athletes he knew from the campus weight room. The result was that Dean, after first being elected to the student council, next became the first Latino elected president of the Associated Students UCLA.

Florez planned to follow his days as the radical-activist big man on campus with three years at Yale Law to study not so much law but *jurisprudence*, the philosophy of law. He had an aspirational role model in Supreme Court Chief Justice Earl Warren, raised in his mother's hometown of Bakersfield. Dean's mom was a graduate of Bakersfield High, as was Warren. The chief and former governor passed away in the summer of 1974, as the Nixon impeachment hearings reached their climax. Dean watched them with his Nana (it was too hot to play outside). The historic resonance that took over both national and local news that summer was inescapable: Warren, the late, great Californian; Nixon, the bad one, whose resignation was celebrated over dinner at Nana's house. A decade later, in college, Florez would read every biography of a Supreme Court justice he came across. *Justice*—one of the ideas that in class at Bakersfield College awakened the serious student in Dean. *Simple justice*—from a phrase of John F. Kennedy's that became identified with Warren's greatest achievement: his court's unanimous decision in *Brown v. Board of Education* and the opinion he wrote for it, the foundational court ruling of the civil rights movement. Dean allowed himself to imagine that it could be a straight shot for him from Yale Law to the Supreme Court to a place in history, but he got drawn down a different path.

While speaking at a rally in downtown LA to protest US policy in Central America, Dean caught the notice of state Senator Art Torres. The senator, who had a significant record of recruiting young talent who would go on to historic careers of their own—including Gloria Molina and Hilda Solis—was impressed with Florez. Torres's chief of staff invested the effort to get Florez to defer his first year at Yale Law School to be a Capital Fellow in Sacramento, assigned to the senator's office. The two had a certain affinity, as Torres had been student president at several schools he attended, a fellow admirer of Earl Warren since his own college days, and a socially committed Chicano lawyer who had worked for California Rural Legal Assistance and the UFW.[17]

Before even deciding whether to accept the fellowship, Florez had learned through the interviews that Torres chaired the Senate Special Committee on UC Admissions. Dean took the fellowship and arrived in Sacramento with a capital idea: How about a Torres committee field hearing on racism in the UC system, staged on campus at UCLA? The previous May, elections to determine Dean's successor as student body president had exploded in violent upheaval. Another Latino backed by the Third World Coalition won the scheduled elections, but then the outgoing student council retroactively determined him to be academically ineligible and scheduled a new round of voting. A protest rally on the day of the new vote devolved into a riot, with fights and destruction of most voting centers. Still another election had to be held under heavy security.[18]

The senator whom Dean went to the Capitol to work for had visited UCLA in June to investigate racial tensions on campus, the student-elections conflict, and allegations of institutional racism. Dean, having just graduated after two intense years of activism, proposed to Torres that he follow up his quick campus visit with a full hearing. The chair and other legislators on his committee would pose the right questions to a parade of witnesses, ranging from undergrad and grad students to professors, administrators, and even Chancellor Charles Young. Torres had no trouble understanding the value of a potentially dramatic field hearing.[19] The five-hour exercise at UCLA that October resounded around the UC system and sold Dean on what he could do in Sacramento. He began proposing one field hearing after another to the senator, and he put off law school for good. But after several years of honing his skills in this arena, the time came when the senator himself suggested to Florez that he should prepare for the next step in his career. Feeling too old to start law school, Dean now set his sights on Harvard Business. Knowing his major weakness as a business school applicant was having studied virtually no mathematical subjects—no statistics or quantitative analysis—Dean pitched himself to the school as uniquely expert on the regulatory environment in which business is conducted; in other words, the role of government, policy, and politics in regulating the private sector. He could share his expertise for the benefit of his classmates and even of his professors.

Hearing examines racism

Grievances aired, solutions offered

By Shana Chandler and Tina Anima
Staff Writers

Racism took center stage on campus Tuesday as State legislators probed allegations of racism and ethnic insensitivity throughout the University of California system.

Senator Art Torres chaired a five-hour state Senate committee hearing in a crowded hearing room on campus. The hearings are part of a series designed to look at higher education in the UC system.

Torres and other members of the Senate Special Committee on UC Admissions heard testimony from undergraduates, graduates and official representatives from throughout the system.

"The grievances we heard (today) are real," said Marjorie Green, Western States education director and a

LYNETTE TSAI/Daily Bruin

State Senator Art Torres gives the opening statement at "Racial/Ethnic Tensions on University of California Campuses", a public hearing held Tuesday at the Faculty Center. Former UCLA student body president Dean Florez is on the left.

racial and ethnic insensitivity

fessor of English.

The cover of the October 5, 1988, UCLA Daily Bruin *featured staffer Dean Florez and state Senator Art Torres at the hearing on racism in the UC system. Photo by Lynette Tsai. Reproduced with permission from* Daily Bruin.

After a few years working municipal finance for an investment banking firm, first back East and then in LA, Florez increasingly felt pulled back toward politics and his hometown. First, while Dean was in his last term at Harvard in 1993, a fellow Latino Central Valley Democrat, Cruz Bustamante, was elected to the Assembly in the next district up, centered in Fresno. Next, MBA in hand, Florez was hired by a New York firm that needed a West Coast regional manager to break into municipal finance there. Come 1994, Florez was ensconced in the executive suite of a downtown LA skyscraper as his former boss, Senator Torres, was running for statewide office. But what put him on the ground back in Shafter was his mother's decision to run for the city council there in 1996. Though his Nana had been the political one throughout Dean's childhood, his mother, Fran, eventually became a community leader in her role as manager of the Bank of America branch in Shafter, which organically drew her into public affairs.

While Dean was reintegrating himself into California goings-on, the state legislature was in upheaval, both at the top and in the historically Democratic Thirtieth Assembly District, which includes Shafter. The Republican incumbent was vulnerable on several counts, including being a Southern California transplant and still largely financed by Orange County money, in a district with a slightly Democratic majority among registered voters. Bustamante, who knew Florez from when they were both legislative staffers, recruited him to serve on the California High-Speed Rail Authority, setting Dean up for a potential Assembly run in his home district. Dean could run as an authentic Thirtieth District homeboy, but he would also be able to tap into external money, which Speaker Bustamante pledged to provide. Bustamante, however, was out as Speaker in February of 1998, and Antonio Villaraigosa was in. Florez and Villaraigosa knew each other only as opponents in the 1991 election that had pitted their respective mentors, Art Torres and Gloria Molina, against each other for LA county supervisor. Antonio bluntly informed Dean that he would not make good on the support Bustamante had promised.

Not long after, first-term Assembly Member Tony Cárdenas, along with Alex Padilla, who was again on his staff, drove to Dean's campaign office in Shafter to size up his prospects. Florez had thoroughly broken down and assessed the district's electoral geography and patterns. After determining that winners of either party tended to carry the district by about seven thousand votes, he had set as his fundamental strategic goal to register at least fifteen thousand new voters and get at least half of them to the polls. Alex scrutinized the maps, breakdowns, and data taped up all around on the office walls, noting that if Dean could get 10 percent more here and 7 percent more there, he could win. "This guy was speaking my language," Dean later recalled. This all reflected the data-driven techniques Florez had learned in LA while working for Art Torres and the multiple campaigns he had been lent out to, techniques that were not used in the Valley. Tony finally asked, "How are you on money?" Dean shared that the support he had expected to get from Bustamante was not coming from Villaraigosa, and he was far behind the incumbent on fund-raising. "We can help with that," Tony responded. Alex stayed in Shafter for a couple more days to dig further into Dean's district and campaign, while Tony worked on arranging for the needed funds.

The money did not start flowing into the Florez campaign accounts until the last third of October, when he was still hundreds of thousands of dollars behind the incumbent—but it was precisely then that the progress the campaign had made registering voters since the year before became clear in private polling, and the first big check led to over half a dozen more. In the final two weeks of the campaign, Florez outraised the incumbent better than five to one, reporting over $750,000 in new contributions—including from the fund that Speaker Villaraigosa controlled. Dean's campaign hired every temp worker available in Bakersfield to knock twice on the doors of every identified supporter in the district, won by a near-landslide, and was still able to return the Speaker's check, uncashed.

In Sacramento, Florez had come to see astutely framed, prepared, and conducted hearings as more valuable than legislation, for not only addressing but even resolving a range of public issues, especially those concerning oversight of existing policy or government practice. In running his Joint Legislative Audit Committee, Dean found that scheduling state officials to testify in a hearing and giving them sufficient time to prepare was often enough, by the time they appeared before him, to effect a needed change in their agencies' practice, without having to resort to legislation. The big Oracle software enterprise lease agreement case presented Florez with the opportunity to review and reform the state's practices in contracting with private corporations. He brought three investigative journalists onto the committee staff to dig deep into both sides of the case, the corporate and the governmental, in preparation for an epic set of hearings. The committee obtained and examined thousands of pages of documents. The public phase of Dean's investigation, the hearings, stretched over two months and entailed questioning thirty witnesses.[20] The main result was the rescission of the state's contract with Oracle and full reimbursement by the corporation. But there was collateral damage. According to Florez, Assembly Speaker Herb Wesson had implored him to end his hearings, as the governor was unhappy with his staffers being hauled before the committee and the attendant negative publicity as the fall campaign season drew near. Dean refused, and only ended the hearings on his own time, which he followed with a stinging opinion column in *The Sacramento Bee,* strongly implying that corrupt practices were spreading in state government, unchecked due to a lack of leadership and commitment from the governor's office.[21] Two days after the column ran, Speaker Wesson yanked Florez off the Joint Audit Committee he chaired. Dean later learned he had been banished from the Assembly Democratic Caucus as well.

The committee's investigation of the "Oracle debacle," as it was called, besides being Dean Florez's 2002 state Assembly swan song, prior to his election to the state Senate, displayed both the reach and limits of legislative committee hearings as a policy tool, resource, and weapon. But it also showed something of the range of contributions Latina/o leaders were making, not only to their community's empowerment but to the political development of, in this case, the state as a whole and its government. This is not to say, however, that this sort of contribution outweighed the legislative agenda Florez also brought to the Capitol for the benefit of his particular constituencies, such as farmworkers, the agricultural economy, and Central Valley communities. From his first year in office, Florez fought for and achieved legislation establishing safety standards for the transport of farmworkers by labor contractors, farmworker exposure to pesticide drift, the regulation of labor practices in conditions of extreme heat, and the application of the federal Clean Air Act to farms. He also fought to establish overtime pay for farmworkers, as was required for all other wage labor, although this bill was vetoed by a new governor, who was elected in another instance of the familiar phenomenon of right-wing political backlash.

The Schwarzenegger Backlash

Both Governor Davis and Lieutenant Governor Bustamante won reelection in November 2002, but unlike in their first election in 1998, this time neither of them reached 50 percent of the vote. The "dot-com crash" that followed the internet boom of the late 1990s was hurting the state economy and especially tax revenues, precipitating a series of budget deficits and cutbacks.[22] When Davis partially addressed his budget crunch with an increased vehicle registration fee, a rich right-wing member of Congress from San Diego County launched a recall drive against the governor. When such a petition qualifies to mandate a recall election, candidates who aspire to replace the elected official appear on the same ballot. Just before the deadline to file, Arnold Schwarzenegger announced on *The Tonight Show* his candidacy to replace Davis. This presented Bustamante, who had already spent years preparing to run for governor in 2006, with a dilemma. Polls indicated majority support for recalling Davis, and Schwarzenegger's celebrity made him the instant favorite to win the contest to take the office. Bustamante could not escape the spotlight, as by law it was up to him to set the date of the special election. He could simply unite with all other Democratic Party officeholders against the recall and risk that, if it succeeded, Schwarzenegger would become governor and run as the incumbent for reelection in 2006. Alternatively, Bustamante, who had a strained relationship with Davis from the start, could run himself to replace the governor. He decided to do both, running on the slogan "No on Recall, Yes on Bustamante."

Bustamante set the recall election to take place in October, giving candidates, himself included, ten weeks to campaign to potentially replace Governor Davis. The recall was a challenge radically unlike what the lieutenant governor had planned and been working toward, and what Lorena had imagined and become part of in joining his staff. Politically, Bustamante was a Central Valley centrist whose strategy since high school for getting through life, as well for getting ahead in politics, was to not take sides.[23] That made him unlike his own parents, who had been activists in the farmworkers' movement. But Bustamante's centrism made his chances of getting through a California Democratic primary for governor a tough proposition. Lorena immediately became the progressive on the lieutenant governor's staff. His renowned campaign consultant, Richie Ross, saw Lorena as a resource for preparing Bustamante to get through a Democratic primary and arranged to have the two of them spar in mock debates. They needed to find a way for Bustamante to express policy positions that would be acceptable to him and not anathema to Democratic primary voters. But all that training would do him no good in a free-for-all recall election pitting the lieutenant governor against a celebrity Republican outsider, who ignored Bustamante in favor of running against the sitting governor—a stance Cruz could not take.

Governor Davis would not condescend to campaign for the office he had been reelected to less than a year before, choosing instead a posture of being busy doing his job governing the state. But he could not ignore that he was down in the polls and losing support from Latino voters in particular. Latino legislators, led by Gilbert Cedillo, leaned on Davis to sign Cedillo's bill restoring driver's licenses to immigrant California residents without regard for their federal immigration status—a bill he had vetoed twice before. Now, when Davis signed this bill in September, in the middle of the recall campaign, Schwarzenegger—a heavily accented Austrian immigrant—pounced and turned his effort to oust Davis into an anti-immigrant backlash, promising to overturn the new law before it could take effect in January. Schwarzenegger's success promptly ended Davis's political career and effectively canceled Bustamante's political future.

Nevertheless, the years of experience Gonzalez acquired while serving on Bustamante's staff in Sacramento and running his Southern California office in LA provided her with exceptional training and a vast array of immensely valuable professional relationships. She was at the center of his 2002 election campaigns, as well as the recall, advised him on a wide array of issues, and staffed him at state and national conventions and official trips both in and beyond the state, including to Mexico. Toward the end, she established and ran his new office in San Diego and there made her own first bid for office, running for city council and losing narrowly.[24] She left the lieutenant governor's staff for good in 2006, when he reached the end of his two terms and chose to run for insurance commissioner. At that point, Lorena was recruited to serve as political director of the San Diego and Imperial Counties Labor Council, the state's second-largest labor federation. She would go on from that position to become secretary-treasurer of the labor council and subsequently again run for office, which would send her back to Sacramento to begin another phase in her leadership journey.

Assembly Member Lorena Gonzalez speaks at press conference on April 18, 2018, in support of bill restricting mandatory arbitration clauses in employment contracts that block public disclosure of workplace misconduct in sexual harassment cases. Photo by Liz Hafalia/The San Francisco Chronicle*/Hearst Newspapers via Getty Images.*

La Opinión Goes to War

In 2000, Tribune Company executives cheerily told *La Opinión*'s leaders they planned to be more supportive of the Spanish-language paper than bad, old Times Mirror had been, but it did not take long for their designs for domination to become apparent. *La Opinión* management started getting to know the Tribune Company's Spanish-language platforms *Éxito* in Chicago and *Hoy* in New York, sounding out possibilities for content sharing and other joint projects. As Tribune had four directors on *La Opinión*'s board, the media conglomerate had full access to the paper's internal workings, books, and strategic planning. But by 2003, Tribune's thinking became apparent when it converted *Éxito* into *Hoy Chicago*. Its model was to develop a national newspaper, in some ways like a tabloid version *USA Today* in Spanish, that essentially differed only in having a city name attached to the common *Hoy* brand—*Hoy New York*, *Hoy Chicago*, and so on—in each of the Latino-heavy markets in which Tribune had an English-language paper. It got around to presenting its plan to the Lozanos, who had a five-to-four majority on the *La Opinión* board. Tribune proposed to buy out the 50 percent share the family retained, liquidate the paper, and launch *Hoy Los Angeles* in its place. It offered to have Monica transfer over to the *LA Times* to direct its new Spanish-language division. The *Hoy* chain would be controlled by the publisher of the original New York property, Louis Sito.

Led by Monica, the Lozanos answered with a hard "no." Tribune's *Hoy* model was unacceptable to a family that had been proudly publishing newspapers for ninety years. They would have to find outside investors to help buy back the 50 percent share Tribune had acquired when it bought out Times Mirror, and that called for an alternative model and a plan to compete beyond LA with what Tribune was putting together. *Hoy New York*, selling at half the price, reported having rocketed past *El Diario* in circulation. Tribune was evidently out to raid *La Opinión*'s national advertisers with its multimarket product. Between its *LA Times* infrastructure and cookie-cutter tabloid, an LA *Hoy* could be cranked out as soon as its distribution was ready. A promising path forward materialized for *La Opinión* in July, when a group of investment firms announced its acquisition of *El Diario La Prensa*. Monica knew *El Diario*'s editor-turned-publisher, Rossana Rosado—they had parallel careers in the same business. Rosado welcomed her paper's new owners, whom she described as "going to war" with Tribune's *Hoy*. A national partnership with a model contrary to *Hoy*'s was the move for the two historic papers to make.

The investors agreed that a national network of distinct papers organic to metropolitan Spanish-language markets was the natural alternative to a fast-food chain of *Hoys*. Stressing heritage, identity, and deep community ties, a federation of existing newspapers could leverage demonstrated Latino brand loyalty and community relationships against the shiny new object with a cut-rate price. In a press conference on January

15, 2004—their father Nacho Lozano's seventy-seventh birthday—Jose and Monica announced the birth of ImpreMedia, the first national Spanish-language newspaper company, which they would come to stress was, in fact, a multiplatform media corporation embarked on acquiring a native presence in the top-ten Latino cities. The occasion also marked the transfer of the position of publisher and CEO from Jose to Monica, with their dad looking on. The paper his own father had founded eight decades earlier would go on in the new century.

Monica Lozano announces launch of ImpreMedia, accompanied by Los Angeles Mayor James Hahn, City Council Member Antonio Villaraigosa, and City Council President Alex Padilla. Courtesy of Aurelia Ventura, photographer.

The Lozanos' unveiling of ImpreMedia beat Tribune's expected launch of its LA *Hoy* by over six weeks. On the very day of the latter, Monica led another news conference at which, as the *Times* reported, she "declared war" on Tribune's upstart tabloid, "telling the publisher of... *Hoy* to 'bring it on.'"[25] She set up a campaign-style "war room" at the paper to monitor and gather intelligence on every move Tribune made in relation to *Hoy*, and she set out to renew contracts and agreements with advertisers and cross-promotional and community partners, wherever possible locking in exclusivity within the home market. The campaign included a new series of articles, radio and TV commercials, billboards, and ads on bus benches stressing *La Opinión*'s rootedness in and commitment to the community.

At the same time, increasingly loud rumors were circulating that both Tribune's main New York property, *Newsday*, based in Long Island, and the original *Hoy* it printed and distributed, had been inflating their paid-circulation figures for years. *Newsday* reporters investigated, and that summer the paper ran an exposé on its own illicit business practices. Publishers of both the main paper and *Hoy* were sacked.[26] The mastermind of Tribune's *Hoy* model and others at the two papers eventually pled guilty to federal fraud charges originally brought by the Securities and Exchange Commission.[27] *Hoy Los Angeles* was not required to report paid-circulation figures for the first six months of sales, but before the year was out, it tellingly announced that the cover price would be removed from the paper, which, starting in 2005, would be distributed free of charge.[28] War over.

Parallel Careers

Starting with her appointment to the University of Southern California Board of Trustees in 1992, and extending to the 2020s, Monica Lozano pursued a virtual parallel career sharing her insights and judgment on the management and direction of education in Los Angeles and the state. Almost as soon as Gray Davis succeeded Pete Wilson as governor in 1999, he appointed Lozano to the State Board of Education, of which she eventually became president. At the time of her appointment, the biggest challenges the gargantuan Los Angeles Unified School District (LAUSD) was struggling with were overcrowding in its high schools, an especially high Latino student dropout rate, and the particular problem of getting a major new high school built and opened that had been under construction for over a decade. Lozano and others founded the Alliance for a Better Community, a high-level Latino leadership organization in LA, to address the severely troubled school project that ultimately cost over $400 million to complete—the country's most expensive.

When the high school finally opened in 2008, the project's history of extreme dysfunction called for a rebranding.[29] The school's name was changed in honor of the late pioneer of Latina/o political empowerment in LA and the state, Edward R. Roybal. It took this huge new school's completion, along with a number of others, to end decades of staggered, year-round schedules to accommodate the growth in the number of students in the LAUSD over the thirty-five years it had gone without a new high school. Meanwhile, Governor Davis effectively promoted Lozano to the University of California Board of Regents. Over a decade later, then-Governor Jerry Brown reappointed Monica to the UC Board for a second twelve-year term, which then elected her chair.

Along the way, Lozano compiled an extraordinary record of board directorships at other for- and nonprofit entities, including the National Council of La Raza (which she also chaired), The Walt Disney Company, Bank of America, the Rockefeller Foundation, Target, and Apple. After stepping away from her position as CEO of Impremedia, Monica capped her educational and executive careers by taking over the presidency of the San Francisco-based College Futures Foundation, which she led through the COVID-19 pandemic until her retirement, but she continued to serve on several corporate boards. Her successful leadership of what had been her family's daily paper, and then saving it by fashioning the first US Spanish-language newspaper company, served as the basis for Monica Lozano's appointment as the first Latina director on, and often chair of, one high-level board after another, well into the twenty-first century.

The State Latino Leadership Academy?

With the sudden growth of its Latino Legislative Caucus in the 1990s, capped with the election of its first two Latino Speakers from 1996 to 2000, and the election of one of them as lieutenant governor in 1998, the state Assembly seemed confirmed as California's de facto academy for the development of Latina/o political leadership. But the collapse of Antonio Villaraigosa's bid to become mayor of LA in 2001, followed by the abrupt derailing in 2003 of Cruz Bustamante's plan to become the state's first Latino governor, called into question whether perhaps their consecutive speakerships might have been a fluke, and whether California voters would elect Latino legislators to major executive positions.

The first question was answered early in 2004, when his colleagues made first-term member Fabián Núñez Speaker of the Assembly. This third Latino Speaker in a span of six years established a trend that was underscored by his serving over four years in the position—the longest tenure since Willie Brown, who still holds the all-time record. And there were other lessons in Fabián's success. One was the critical importance at this time of his base in organized labor—LA-centered, immigrant-heavy, Latino-led labor. The other was the continuously increasing political weight of LA itself, beyond Latino empowerment. Fabián was not only the third Latino Assembly Speaker, but also the fourth consecutive Speaker from Los Angeles—and would be followed by four more from LA County. This unprecedented quarter-century domination of the state Assembly by LA Democrats was closely intertwined with rising Latina/o, immigrant, women's, and LGBTQ+ empowerment in the post–African American civil rights era.[30]

Also in 2004, but in another LA-dominated arena, Eva Longoria graduated from starring in a daytime soap opera to a primetime, worldwide hit, with her role in *Desperate Housewives* on ABC. Longoria was already more than a star actor; she was emerging as a producer and director of both TV and film, and as a strategic bridge between the Latina/o-empowerment project and the top tier of the entertainment world. She was involved with national Latino advocacy organizations such as MALDEF and NCLR, and in 2006 played a critical role in reviving NCLR's groundbreaking, nationally broadcast *ALMA Awards*, which she produced and hosted through 2014. In time, she would come to lead Latina/o support for Barack Obama's 2012 reelection and the election of Latinas and Latinos to public office across the country. She also mobilized her fellow Latina actor colleagues to promote Latina/o voting in national elections.

The second question—whether voters would elect a Latino legislator to a major executive position—was answered the following year (2005), when in his second run, Antonio Villaraigosa was elected mayor of LA, besting the incumbent he had lost to in 2001. A range of factors contributed to this uncommon turnaround, as an incumbent executive is usually hard to dislodge. From a Latino-empowerment perspective, a factor of particular note is that Villaraigosa made a greater effort and invested more resources mobilizing his Latino base, instead of taking it for granted. In 2001, rather than running as a Latino aspiring to make history, he positioned himself as a mainstream candidate who happened to be Latino, and he worked tirelessly to assemble the most diverse coalition possible. This strategy, however, did not spare Antonio from being subjected to a late campaign attack smearing him with drug and gang associations, nor from being portrayed by a top African American leader as a mysterious stranger to the Black community.

In 2005, besides Villaraigosa's greater outreach to Latino voters through Spanish-language media, through both paid advertising and "earned media," some significant conditions had changed. Among them was Univision flagship TV station KMEX's enhanced commitment to community empowerment. Since 2002, its news department had had a new director, Jorge Mettey. As the day of the runoff election approached, Mettey branded the station's coverage of the mayoral rematch with notes of history and urgency, using the phrase *Ahora Es Cuando* ("The Time Is Now"). Regular programming carried promotional spots for the station's enhanced electoral coverage. Without mentioning Villaraigosa by name, it featured familiar anchors and reporters urging the audience to vote, with each in turn giving a different reason, such as *Para Que Te Respeten* ("To Be Respected"), and ending with the *Ahora Es Cuando* mantra.[31]

The KMEX vote-promotion campaign culminated on election night with the 6:00 p.m. local newscast, which began when the polls would still be open for two more hours. The audience was greeted with the unheard-of message that they should leave their homes and go vote, or take someone else to the polls who had not yet voted. The entire broadcast was devoted to this message, including commercial breaks filled with promotional spots giving reasons for voting. Throughout the telethon-like thirty-minute program, the anchors theatrically glanced at a clock, stated the countdown of the diminishing time left to get to the polls, and intoned "The time is now." The emotional payoff for this effort came later that night, when during its special electoral coverage, the station announced the news of Villaraigosa's historic victory.

What remained to be seen, then, was if and when Latinas/os might again be elected to statewide office, or if the 1998 election of Bustamante as lieutenant governor—the only Latino elected statewide in the twentieth century—was the fluke. A decade would pass after Villaraigosa's win before that question could be similarly answered, when Alex Padilla took office as secretary of state—only the second Latino elected to statewide office since the 1800s. But again, in retrospect, we can see how the pieces were falling into place for future advances. In 2006, Padilla graduated from the LA city council presidency to state Senate, and Kevin de León was elected to the Assembly. In far-off Redlands, in a first step in what would develop into a career of leadership on the national stage, young Pete Aguilar was selected among eleven candidates to fill an empty seat on the town's city council.[32] But as strategically significant and necessary as these political developments were for what was to come, and however intense the efforts of those involved in effecting them, insofar as scale and visibility are concerned, they paled in comparison to the huge numbers of immigrants who mobilized largely on their own in the spring of 2006, which revealed the vast growth and development of a distinct and parallel world of leaders, activists, organizations, and masses of participants.

Parallel Universes of Activism and Empowerment

In a span of eight weeks from March to May 2006, over 3.5 million mainly undocumented Mexican immigrants and their supporters marched in hundreds of protests across the country. They were demonstrating against a House bill passed the previous December that was intended to crack down on undocumented immigrants and immigration.[33] The largest of the protests was in Los Angeles on May 1, with an estimated 650,000–700,000 protesters marching to and surrounding City Hall. Taken together, these marches constituted, to that point, the largest protest movement concentrated in a short period in US history. This phenomenal, if relatively short-lived, episode brought out several realities, in particular in the cases of the immense LA protests in March and May, and their contrast with the Chicago marches.

Besides its unprecedented dimensions, the most important overall aspect of this resistance movement was its immigrant-led character, fundamentally unlike the 1994 LA march against Proposition 187, and radically unlike the 1970 Chicano Moratorium movement against the Vietnam War. The principal organizers of the 1994 protest were US-born Latino leaders, several of whom went on to prominent careers as elected officials in the state legislature and LA City Council. Latino officials and labor leaders, however, were notably absent from the first of the two LA protests on March 25, 2006. Immigrant leaders, activists, and organizations, powerfully boosted by Spanish-language media, surprised predominantly US-born LA Latina/o political leadership with the biggest demonstration in the city's history. Over the preceding twenty years, Mexican immigrants had been organizing themselves into numerous "hometown associations," which they called *clubes*, increasingly with the encouragement of the Mexican consulate general and their own hometown and home-state governments in Mexico.[34] Indeed, for a substantial period, their hometown pastors also urged emigres from their villages to raise money to support their parishes and fund improvements to their churches and facilities. Over time, these clubs came together in home-state federations that undertook a range of projects both in their hometowns and in their communities in the US.

This rising self-organization of Mexican and other Latin American immigrants was complemented by the growth of Spanish-language media of every sort. When the December 2005 immigration bill passed in the House of Representatives, the alarm went out through the media and immigrant organizations that, should it become law, mass detentions and deportations could follow. The first protest was held in Washington, DC, on March 6, with a reported 30,000 participants. The next, in Chicago, was said to have mobilized as many as 300,000. A competitive dynamic set in, with LA activists determined to surpass Chicago on March 25, which they did, with as many as 500,000. In several cities across the country, protests of 20,000–50,000 were the largest they had ever seen. In LA especially, a key to the mass mobilizations was the emphatic encouragement of Spanish-language radio, whose audiences had come to surpass that of English-language radio stations.[35] In this effort, Jorge Mettey's KMEX news department went back to work, as it had during the mayoral election the year before, encouraging participation in the marches in the guise of promoting news coverage of them. Both radio DJs and TV news personalities banded together in broadcast shows of unity and common purpose. On the day of the first LA march, *La Opinión* ran the biggest banner headline in its history: *¡A Las Calles!* ("To the Streets!").

A telling difference between the first protest in Chicago on March 10 and the one in LA two weeks later was that Chicago Mayor Richard M. Daley marched in the first rank in his city, while LA Mayor Antonio Villaraigosa did not agree to address the rally outside his City Hall until practically the last minute. Indeed, the Chicago rally was also prominently attended by Illinois's governor and senior senator, as well as dozens of aldermen and state legislators. The LA rally could not have been more different in this regard, and there were other notable differences besides. The Chicago march was far more diverse, including representatives of the city's big Polish and Irish ethnic communities, which signaled a causal difference with LA. Chicago has long identified itself as a proudly immigrant city, while Los Angeles was for generations the least immigrant or immigrant friendly of major US cities. This environmental factor contributed to a tendency by Mexican Americans in LA and much of the Southwest to distinguish themselves from Mexican immigrants, while in Chicago a culture of identification as "Mexican" regardless of country of birth is far more prevalent. As a result, Mexican immigrants and Latinos/Mexican Americans in LA have, to a great extent, different leaders, activists, organizations, and even issue agendas, although virtually all US-born Latino political leaders embrace the defense of immigrant rights.

Major Spanish-language news media, especially the leading TV stations and networks and largest metropolitan newspapers, have served as the most notable bridge between the Mexican-immigrant world in LA and in other cities, and the Latino/Mexican American political world. These media have readers and audiences composed primarily of immigrants, but they give US and Latino politics extensive coverage, and as we saw in the case of the 2005 LA mayoral election, have strongly encouraged voter participation. Another bridging institution has been LA-based NALEO—the National Association of Latino Elected and

Appointed Officials—which for decades has conducted campaigns promoting both citizenship and voter participation. NALEO, in particular, tried to channel the energy of the spring 2006 protest marches into civic engagement, promoting the slogan *Hoy Marchamos, Mañana Votamos* ("Today We March, Tomorrow We Vote"). But as much as or more than anyone else, NALEO leadership knew the degree to which Latino political influence was limited by the lack of citizenship among millions of legal resident immigrants. This awareness would bring NALEO and KMEX together in 2007 to devise an innovative national campaign of citizenship promotion of unprecedented reach, as we shall see in the next chapter.

Politically, 2006 ended on a high note for most Latina/o members of Congress and the Democrats, as Nancy Pelosi led a national wave election that recovered a majority of the House after a dozen years under Republican control. Among the Latina/o representatives, Xavier Becerra of Los Angeles especially had invested years of effort trying to ascend into the leadership circle of the Democratic Caucus, and finally, under fellow Californian Pelosi, made his first entry as assistant to the leader. The next two terms would be particularly eventful, even dramatically so, with Pelosi in charge of the House, first battling with lame-duck President George W. Bush, and then in a doubly historic partnership with President Barack Obama.

Part IV
Always Another "Final Battle"

IF WE WIDEN THE SCOPE, the gains of the early 2000s look impressive. Alex Padilla became LA city council president in '01; Fabián Núñez, California Assembly Speaker in '04; Antonio Villaraigosa, LA mayor in '05; and Eric Garcetti, second Latino LA city council president in '06. Record mass protests killed the H.R. 4437 immigration bill that spring; and that fall, Democrats—which included all seven California Latino representatives—reclaimed control of the US House.[1] But many leaders agreed there was still a pressing need to involve more of their community in civic life, win greater representation, and advance key and persistent policy priorities—in access to healthcare, education, environmental justice, retirement security, immigration reform, and more. Looking ahead to the open presidential contest in 2008, they focused on a chronic weakness in Latina/o political-empowerment efforts. Even after the 1980s reforms of the Census, voting rights, and legalization of undocumented residents and migrant farmworkers, millions of eligible Latino immigrants took far too long to become citizens and voters—or never did at all.

The parties and a few election campaigns occasionally engage in voter registration, but since the mid-1990s, neither they nor government had done anything to promote citizenship.[2] In LA in 2007, a broad coalition launched a national effort to spur Latino-immigrant naturalization, followed by linked campaigns promoting registration and, ultimately, voting in 2008. Known as *¡Ya Es Hora!*, the results of this three-stage initiative contributed to a pivotal national breakthrough—the election and reelection of Barack Obama in 2008 and 2012—which itself produced big advances for Latinas/os in elections, appointments, and policy. But Obama's historic wins unsurprisingly sparked an unprecedented backlash, which, if it managed to take over the Republican Party, might well persist indefinitely. Early battles ensued over immigration in neighboring Nevada and Arizona in 2010, and that year Democrats again lost control of the House.

The continuing backlash carried Donald Trump and his movement to power in 2016. Determined resistance by Latino leaders and California helped contain policy damage and won back the House in 2018. This resistance then brought a new administration into office in 2020 that included record-breaking Latino representation at the highest level. But this was not enough to vanquish the backlash, which retook the House in 2022. Then a much more prepared Trump, now with the Republican Party fully under his control, returned to power in 2024 with a far more radically loyal team. This reinvented regime rushed to begin mass deportations and acted by fiat to cancel programs, policies, and laws, including constitutional birthright citizenship. The Trump movement's second presidency meant the resistance would have to fight on, to yet another "final battle."

Chapter 10

From ¡*Ya Es Hora!* to "Yes We Can"

Among the greatest Latino-empowerment strategies forged in LA was the *Ya Es Hora: ¡Ciudadanía!* campaign of 2007–08.[1] NALEO, founded in Washington by Representative Ed Roybal and colleagues in 1976, had moved its headquarters to his home district in Los Angeles in 1987, just as the immigration reform that had passed the year before began legalizing millions of undocumented immigrants and farmworkers, with LA as the epicenter. The organization was thus optimally positioned to focus on this boom in new legal immigrants. Legalization is the most important single advance in the quality and security of life of an undocumented immigrant and their family, but it is not political empowerment. NALEO's priority has long been to promote the follow-on empowering steps of naturalization, voter registration, and voting. The organization works with government agencies, mass media, and other groups in these efforts, as well as in urging participation in the decennial census and advocating for the appointment of Latinos to government positions. The immigrant-rights marches of spring 2006 underscored the need and hunger of millions of Latino immigrants for a political voice. But they had to take to the streets precisely because so many of them—whether undocumented or lawful permanent residents (LPRs)—lacked the status to channel their concerns and demands into the formal political system.

On one level, that extraordinary protest movement succeeded, while on others it failed.[2] It played a critical role in stopping the Sensenbrenner bill (H.R. 4437), which, after passing in the House and being sent to the Senate, was referred to the Judiciary Committee and never heard from again.[3] The stunning March 25 protest in LA, in particular, appears to have closed the door in the Senate Judiciary Committee to the possibility of a similarly draconian "enforcement-only" Senate bill, which could have passed and then been reconciled with the House bill, as the Republican majority leader at that time, Bill Frist, threatened. Organizers in LA, aware of Frist's imminent action, set the date of the protest march for the Saturday before the committee was to finally take up the issue. According to people who were present at the Judiciary Committee meeting, the news of the record-busting, five-hundred-thousand-strong LA march charged the atmosphere in the hearing room.[4] The committee had not acted on the comprehensive immigration bill that Senators John McCain and Edward Kennedy had presented the year before, which included "amnesty" and a "pathway to citizenship," nor on H.R. 4437, which had been referred to it earlier that year. Most Democrats kept a low profile on the issue, and Committee Member Dianne Feinstein indicated she would vote against McCain–Kennedy. But Republican Senator Arlen Specter, who served only this single 2005–06 Congress as judiciary committee chair, suddenly showed interest in getting the matter resolved before Majority Leader Frist intervened with his own bill. Specter adopted McCain–Kennedy for himself to introduce to the full Senate, Feinstein flipped her vote, and the bill passed the committee by the end of the day.[5]

In the weeks that followed, hundreds more marches swept the country. In spite of deepening public polarization on immigration, the Specter version of McCain–Kennedy passed the full Senate in May, but it was irreconcilable with the House's Sensenbrenner bill and never went to conference. Thus, the immigrant-rights mobilization in the streets helped kill a harsh, enforcement-only House bill, but did not advance the immigration reform that the undocumented needed. The protesters' demands for immediate amnesty for all undocumented immigrants not only marked one extreme of the country's polarization on the issue, it also reflected a major gulf between the local activists' world and the DC-based immigration-policy advocates' world. The former sought to maximize pressure by mobilizing the most grassroots protesters possible, while the latter prized making the best deal achievable, with the most allies, in a context of pursuing multiple policy goals, not just this one. A similar breach had characterized the long struggle to achieve the immigration reform of 1986, then between the litigators, like MALDEF, which took a more activist approach, and the lobbyists, like LULAC and NCLR, who accepted the inevitability of compromise. The divergence could also be seen in another aspect of the street marches: the chants and signs of *Hoy Marchamos, Mañana Votamos* ("Today We March, Tomorrow We Vote"), attempting to connect the protests to that fall's midterm congressional elections.

A major, pro-immigration-reform, interethnic coalition with national reach was launched in mid-May, with "an ambitious campaign to register 1 million new voters."[6] By early fall, however, it was apparent that there would be no significant increase in the number of Latinos on the voter rolls by November.[7] Undocumented immigrants could be mobilized to protest, but could not register to vote. Besides that, lawful permanent immigrants, eligible to become citizens and voters, were slow to do so. NALEO grappled with how to harness the energy and anger of the marches, first to accelerate Latino naturalization, and then to follow with registration and voting.[8] Unlike in other historic movements that produced reforms for women, labor, and African Americans, protest was far from enough to effect another reform for undocumented immigrants.[9]

A corresponding gap between two worlds, or parallel universes, of Latino LA was particularly visible that year from the perspective of the politically integrated sector of the community, which was involved in primary election campaigns at the same time that the politically marginalized, immigrant sector marched in the streets. Among the former, Alex Padilla was moving strategically from the LA City Council to the state Senate, Kevin de León was on his way to the state Assembly, and Xavier Becerra was reelected to Congress, where he would become a special assistant to Speaker Pelosi when the Democrats retook control of the House. But such campaigns mobilized a tiny fraction of the masses of Latinos who marched in the streets. This is not to mention a key future national Latino leader's ascension to a small city council an hour's drive east of LA without mobilizing any voters at all. Pete Aguilar took his first political career step that year, when the Redlands City Council chose him to take a vacated seat as an interim member, the youngest ever to serve on that body.

In the midst of that fall's campaign season, a pair of NALEO staffers met over lunch with Jorge Mettey, the news director of LA's Univision flagship station, KMEX, to grouse once again about the continuing underparticipation and underrepresentation of Latinos in civic life, elections, and government. Under Mettey, the KMEX news department had intensively addressed both the politically integrated and marginalized worlds by heavily promoting voting in the previous year's LA mayoral election, and in 2006 emphatically urging responsible, mass participation in the city's two giant immigrant-rights marches.[10] For its part, NALEO had enjoyed a small boom in naturalization rates in California in the aftermath of the 1994 battle with Governor Pete Wilson over Proposition 187. But now, a dozen years later, the age-old tendency of Mexicans in particular to take much longer than other immigrants to apply for citizenship was back.[11] NALEO had studied the problem the year before and conducted focus groups with immigrants. Their main takeaway was that of the several factors that had long contributed to the reluctance of Mexican immigrants to naturalize, chief among them was that they felt no *urgency* to acquire US citizenship. It could wait.[12]

Journalists everywhere know the elements of narrative drama: how to attract attention and stir emotion. Nowhere is this more the case than in Mexico, the land that gave the genre of sensationalized crime reporting a name more vivid than "yellow journalism," the country of the *nota roja*, and in particular the grisly tabloid weekly *¡Alarma!*[13] The methods of drama are universal, date to antiquity, and can be put to every imaginable use—including to advance an end as wholesome as civic engagement. Mettey knew well the power of his medium and had demonstrated it. He branded his TV station's coverage of the election that made Antonio Villaraigosa LA mayor with the slogan *Ahora Es Cuando!* He followed that by urging participation in the immigrant-rights marches with a promotional spot that featured a dozen of the principal TV news anchors and reporters in the LA market. Each of the familiar and trusted faces, close up, one after the other, stated a simple reason for joining the protest march. Seeing these famous competitors together, each speaking either earnestly or enthusiastically directly to the viewer, was itself riveting, as the spot built to a climax. It ended with the broadcast personalities locking arms and chanting in unison *Únete! Únete! Únete!* ("Unite! Unite! Unite!").[14]

Mettey not only believed in thinking big and dramatically, he lived for it. He proposed to his young NALEO friends a bold campaign to naturalize a million new citizens in the LA market in time to vote in 2008, and imagined a telethon-like ticker that would appear in a corner of the TV screen, constantly updating, showing progress toward the campaign's goal.[15] He had his newsroom come up with a brand name for the effort, and they gave him a list of suggestions, which he shared with NALEO. No decision had been reached by the time they were ready to pitch the campaign for the first time to a roomful of representatives of Latino community organizations. As they were about to step into the meeting, the NALEO-istas hastily picked the last option on the list: ¡*Ya Es Hora!*[16]

Embracing Permanence and Citizenship

Time and conditions were right in LA for a broad, united push to come together to promote and facilitate Latino-immigrant naturalization, especially for a coalition and campaign with legs to go national. Eighty years on from the founding of *La Opinión*, the attitudes of many Mexicans, as well as those of their homeland government, toward becoming US citizens were in transition. As we have recounted, whereas the LA daily's founder had staunchly believed in and urged Mexican immigrants to see their presence in the US as only temporary, and they should preserve their national identity unaltered, control of the paper had passed to a second and then a third generation of the Lozano family, which was thoroughly integrated into US society and politics.[17] Over the decades, the paper had steadily shifted its focus from news in Mexico to that of the US. By the 1980s, it was endorsing candidates in US elections. By the 1990s, the paper included California voter-registration forms. And by the first decade of the twenty-first century, it was sponsoring impactful, pre-electoral polls of voters' candidate preferences. In the aftermath of the legalization of millions of undocumented Mexicans in the late 1980s, their government, too, came to accept their permanence north of the border. As a result, in the 1990s, Mexico overhauled policy toward its diaspora, encouraging its emigres to organize for mutual assistance and to defend themselves against discrimination and nativist hostility. To encourage their naturalization in the US, in 1996 Mexico amended its Constitution to allow its emigres to adopt the citizenship of the country they lived in without losing their Mexican nationality.[18]

Mexico's Support

The Mexican government, at different times, pushed rebellious citizens out of the country en masse; at others, it sought their return and resisted even their temporary migration to the US; and at yet others, it favored their circulatory migration as guest workers, a.k.a. braceros.[19] *The US government also repeatedly altered its policies toward Mexican migration. Several factors have contributed to a lasting change in Mexican policy since 1990, beginning with expansion and reinvention of its consular network in the US. Mexico's LA consulate general was the test lab for reforms focused on better serving the country's diaspora. The Mexican Foreign Ministry's new Program for Mexican Communities Abroad assigned its first "community consul" to LA in 1990, a man from Mexico City who had completed a master's degree in international relations at the University of Southern California. Using the consulate's database, compiled from identification cards issued to nationals within its jurisdiction, the community consul coordinated visits from mayors and governors of the expatriates' hometowns and states of origin and convened dialogues between them. This was used to accelerate the formation of hometown clubs, which were then organized into home-state federations.*[20]

The Vicente Fox administration (2000–06) upgraded the Foreign Ministry's program into the Institute of Mexicans Abroad, paired with the office of a special advisor within the presidency, held by a Mexican American.[21] *Following the September 11, 2001, crisis, the consular ID card was upgraded into a secure form of identification that could be recognized by local law enforcement, acceptable for entering government buildings and opening bank accounts. Consulates lobbied local government and business to accept the upgraded cards as secure, government-issued photo identification. In*

2002, this new Matrícula Consular *was a turning point for the Mexican diaspora, and other countries emulated it. Undocumented immigrants in California had been denied state-issued driver's licenses since 1993, making their lives far more difficult, a condition exacerbated by security measures adopted after 9/11. But once they could open bank accounts and acquire credit cards, they began building credit histories, which allowed them to make major purchases, soon to include buying homes, and obtain micro-business loans. These changes in Mexican policy contributed materially to the permanence of the country's emigres in the US.*

A decade later, at the end of 2006, when NALEO and KMEX convened LA-based organizations to join in an effort to urge Latino immigrants to become citizens and help them through the process, the *¡Ya Es Hora!* (YEH) slogan fit the mood and moment so well that it was adopted enthusiastically. Jorge Mettey's aspirational and motivating goal was to mobilize the naturalization of a million new citizens, out of the over eight million eligible legal immigrants at that time.[22] Participating institutions had both the will and the capacity not only to rise to the challenge, but to also project it beyond LA and California altogether.[23] Since taking charge of the news department in 2002, Mettey had brought a new feature to KMEX called *A Su Lado* ("On Your Side"). It introduced a practical topic of concern to viewers during the 6:00 p.m. local newscast, and then had a phone bank ready to take questions for several hours into the night. The feature was launched with large-scale assistance from the Service Employees International Union (SEIU) regional office, then under the leadership of Executive Vice President Eliseo Medina and his special assistant, Ben Monterroso. The first topic was immigration issues, a subject that the union, and especially these leaders, were committed to. Headquartered in LA, this regional division of SEIU was indeed already prepared for what was to come years later as well. It had played a key role in engineering the AFL-CIO's policy turnaround on undocumented immigrants at its national meeting in LA. Furthermore, in that pivotal year of 2000, Medina and Monterroso founded the Latino-focused initiative to mobilize voters called *Mi Familia Vota*.[24] They lent the union's phone-bank facility for the *A Su Lado* TV feature and helped mobilize ninety volunteers to staff phones to answer questions about immigration policies, practices, and available resources.[25]

Once KMEX had upgraded its own phone system to handle dozens of calls at once, Mettey installed a phone bank in the studio to stage a monthly *A Su Lado* feature on changing topics such as health, accessing public services, education, workplace rights, and so on. After each topic was introduced during the local newscast, the station ran reminders for several hours to urge viewers to call in to learn more. Univision stations in other cities adopted the feature as well. By the time *Ya Es Hora* launched in January 2007, following the hundreds of immigrant-rights marches across the country the year before, and with an open presidential election ahead, the daunting process of applying for US citizenship was a topic that fit the format perfectly.

NALEO already had decades of experience helping immigrants become citizens and boosting their civic engagement. Since as far back as 1985, when it was still headquartered in Washington, the organization operated a toll-free national hotline for questions about naturalization.[26] By 2000, operating from LA, NALEO had installed a phone bank at its headquarters near downtown, to conduct its own "get out the vote" (GOTV) campaign in the final weeks of that year's presidential election, as well as to serve as an Election Day hotline to field reports of irregularities at the polls.[27] The organization repeated and expanded its GOTV efforts to five other metro areas in 2002 and 2004.[28] Thus, KMEX and NALEO were both known, experienced, and trusted messengers to the community, which they had socialized to take their cues on matters of both personal and public concern. Several local organizations also offered help with naturalization on a walk-in basis; they would distribute NALEO-produced citizenship packets and provide experienced volunteers for KMEX's now-weekly phone-bank feature, visible live during the station's early-morning program and nightly local news, and in announcements into prime time. The morning program additionally featured a community member seated at a table with an immigration advisor as they worked together on camera to fill out a naturalization application. NALEO's phone bank continued to respond to naturalization questions twelve hours a day during the week.

Since the early 1990s, NALEO had also perfected the method of large-scale citizenship workshops, conducted like health fairs in a variety of community locations. *La Opinión* joined the YEH effort as a matter of course, having been central to the legalization-promotion campaign of 1987–88. SEIU also joined as a national cosponsor. Together, these institutions organized, promoted, and staffed the workshops to provide in-person assistance, with volunteer lawyers on hand to consult on legal issues. KMEX aired live updates on location from the workshops, urging prospective applicants to come by, much as it had urged citizen viewers the year before to vote in the mayoral election.

The National Council of La Raza (NCLR) joined the YEH coalition, injecting another layer of professionalism. Participating community organizations had to get training in advising on the naturalization process and sign a memorandum of understanding with the campaign before they could be listed as "Citizenship Centers" on the websites of the national coordinating institutions.[29] Each of the campaign's national cosponsors reproduced the YEH model in other cities where they had a presence: Univision and Entravision where they had TV stations, NALEO where it had regional offices, ImpreMedia where it published newspapers, NCLR where it had affiliated community organizations, and SEIU where it had Latino, immigrant-heavy union locals. The YEH internet home page managed by NALEO presented a comprehensive directory with listings and links to all the qualified participating local organizations providing services, links to upcoming workshops in nine states and the District of Columbia, and a wealth of instructional materials. Seven of the TV stations had pages on their own websites, all or in part prominently dedicated to the citizenship drive within their markets.[30]

At the end of January 2007, after the public launch of YEH, US Citizenship and Immigration Services (CIS) proposed a sharp increase in naturalization application fees.[31] Although the Bush administration made the announcement discreetly, the YEH campaign and Spanish-language media in general seized upon it as likely to suppress naturalization as the 2008 elections approached—perhaps on purpose. Whatever the intent behind the agency's timing, both the prospect of the fee hike and the six months it would take to approve and implement it helped intensify

At top, 2006 sign made by the Mexican American Political Association (MAPA) and Hermandad Mexicana Latinoamericana. Below, screenshot of 2007 NALEO YEH citizenship campaign internet home page. Courtesy of Hermandad Mexicana and NALEO, respectively.

the sense of urgency YEH sought to create. The administrative approval process had to allow two months of public comment, which effectively set two deadlines the campaign could repeatedly call attention to—the start of the public comment period to prepare for, and its end, which could theoretically mean when the fee hike might be implemented. Thus, a period of suspense ensued, until the size of the increase and the actual date it would take effect were announced at the end of May. At that point, prospective citizens were given two more months to begin the naturalization process before fees went up. This half-year experience of alarm bells ringing allowed for activists, elected officials, the YEH coalition, and Spanish-language media to repeatedly whip up anger, concern, and motivation to acquire citizenship in time to vote in 2008.

Results and Impacts

While citizenship applications had already been rising over the course of 2006—especially as of March, when the immigrant-rights protests began—this trend sharply accelerated starting precisely in January 2007, the month *Ya Es Hora: ¡Ciudadanía!* was launched with its weekly phone banks on KMEX. That month, applications soared 79 percent nationally over the previous January, and more than doubled in the LA area for the whole first quarter.[32] By June, nationwide citizenship applications were at over 150,000, also more than double what they had been the year before. In July, the last month before the fee increase, nationwide applications broke all records and expectations, surpassing 460,000—well over six times those made the year before.[33] This surge consisted of more than Mexican or Latino immigrants, of course, and could not all be attributed to the YEH campaign, especially since another, well-funded coalition, the We Are America Alliance (WAAA), had been launched the previous May, on the heels of the marches. Among its multiple goals, WAAA promoted naturalization among immigrants of all origins.[34] In February, after YEH had just gotten underway, NALEO made a presentation on its campaign to the WAAA leadership. WAAA leaders were skeptical and held off committing any support to YEH until the starter effort in LA had moved into high gear and was showing results. On that basis, WAAA joined as another national sponsor of YEH, and YEH became part of the WAAA coalition.[35]

In the end, the YEH coalition could, in fact, point to over a million citizenship applications in seven months, from its launch in January 2007 through July; in August, fees for adults increased from $330 to $595, resulting in a crash in new applications. The 1.15 million applications submitted in those seven months were two and a half times those for the same period in 2006. In the final three and a half months of May–July, applications received were three and a half times those of 2006, which caused processing time to as much as double, to a year and a half. By the end of 2007, the number of completed applications pending a decision—the naturalization backlog—had more than doubled from the year before, reaching 1.1 million.[36] These processing delays happened in spite of the fee increase, which was premised on providing the resources needed to reduce the backlog.

The timing of that fee hike, however, proved doubly functional for the YEH campaign. It provided a focal point for the naturalization efforts, requiring close cooperation among a large number of actors, and a rationale for the sense of urgency they needed to convey to the masses of the undocumented. Additionally, it provided a perfect pivot point for the transition from promoting naturalization to mobilizing voter registration. The August 2007 hiatus allowed for the preparation of the next iteration of YEH, swapping *¡Ciudadanía!* with *¡Regístrate!* for the next twelve months, at which point the third and final YEH phase, *¡Ve y Vota!*, would kick in. In a happy coincidence for Democrats in the fall 2008 general-election campaign, the Latino vibe of YEH harmonized with the Obama campaign's "Yes We Can" slogan—itself borrowed from the United Farm Workers' *Sí Se Puede!*

The delay in processing the surge in citizenship applications, however, made it impossible to determine how many new citizens were able to vote in 2008 as a result of the YEH campaign, even if the increase in the Latino vote was impressive. That year, over two million more Latinas and Latinos voted in the presidential election, approaching the long-sought goal of ten million votes nationwide.[37] However arbitrary and inherently meaningless the notion of breaking into "double digits" may be, the reality is that surpassing the ten million benchmark would notably alter how Latina/o electoral clout would be noticed, discussed, and covered by news media. For the next four years, the national Latino vote was considered sure to well surpass ten million in the next presidential election, an expectation that would influence political plans and decisions made from the local level to the White House.

Chapter 11
Empowered Latinos

California Latino empowerment could be seen advancing on two distinct levels in the spring of 2006. On one level, the national immigrant-rights movement planned and carried out the biggest series of street protests in US history.[1] On another, veterans of the historic resistance to Proposition 187 a dozen years earlier in Los Angeles were immersed and ascending in institutional and electoral politics and policymaking. On New Year's Day that year, the first Latino president of the LA City Council, Alex Padilla, handed his gavel over to the second Latino to serve in that position, Eric Garcetti—both had marched against Proposition 187 in 1994. When the record-breaking protests in LA took place later that spring, Padilla was busy running for the state Senate as he completed his last year on the council. Those marches traced a route from East LA to LA's Civic Center, culminating at and famously surrounding City Hall—where Antonio Villaraigosa, himself a former immigrant-rights activist, now sat behind its biggest desk in its biggest office, in his first year as mayor. But in 2006, he emerged from the iconic tower he had contemplated from a distance forty years earlier, as a boy delivering newspapers in City Terrace, to address the multitude that had, in effect, followed him there.

At the same time, Martha Escutia, who had also marched in 1994, was now beginning the last year of her two terms in the state Senate, after serving her limit of three terms in the Assembly. In Sacramento, Escutia had pioneered legislation concerning children in the areas of environmental justice and food in public schools. Also that year, the Fabián

Núñez–Kevin de León organizer duo of the 1994 march, with the former now serving as Speaker of the state Assembly, were working to elect the latter to that body. Neither of them had ever served as an intern or staff member there; both entered as outsiders who made their names as protest leaders turned labor organizers. Once on the inside, both were able to become *policy* leaders and make historic contributions unique to California. De León's policy achievements would show how vast, impactful, and interrelated California's political and public policy world is—encompassing not only LA and Sacramento but Washington and the country as well—and how the role Latinas/os play in it is evolving. In de León's case, his causes would directly engage, both positively and negatively, both presidents in power—Obama and Trump—when he served in the state legislature.

Mayor Villaraigosa boldly kicked off a new phase of Latino policy assertiveness in LA, clamoring for an unprecedented role in addressing problems plaguing the public schools. Though he would ultimately become better known as "the subway mayor" for his astonishing leadership in advancing the development of the city's Metro system during the Great Recession, his efforts in education were more directly and unambiguously about and for the Latino community and its progress.[2] In his successful second run for the office in 2005, he called for LA's mayor, like his counterparts in New York and Chicago, to have authority over the massive, troubled metropolitan-area school district. Just as the immigrant-rights protests were getting underway in March 2006, Mayor Villaraigosa declared in a press conference that improving schools—and especially the high school dropout rate—was "the new civil rights issue of our time."[3] The LAUSD (the country's second largest) disputed the mayor's claim that a majority of its high schoolers failed to graduate, and the district board resisted submitting to his bid to gain authority over it, which had no legal basis.[4]

Antonio, however, retained clout in Sacramento. His ally Speaker Núñez got the legislature to pass a bill giving Villaraigosa oversight of the district through his control of a new "Council of Mayors" of the dozens of cities LAUSD served. The board countered with litigation, which struck down the law. It nevertheless agreed in negotiations to give the mayor oversight of sixteen low-performing high schools and their feeder schools. Villaraigosa furthermore delved into school-board elections in battle with his former employer, the teachers union.[5] He garnered sufficient influence over the board to get his own education advisor, Ramón Cortines, appointed district superintendent. Their efforts produced results, and Villaraigosa continued to fight—even after leaving office—to win the authority for California mayors that he felt they needed to overcome teachers unions' opposition to basic reforms.[6] He made his first run for governor in 2018, touting among his signal achievements as mayor the school district's improved graduation rates and test scores—a theme he would reiterate in 2024 when he announced a second run.[7]

Lion in the Policy Thicket

Kevin de León, born in downtown Los Angeles but raised in San Diego, is not shy to admit that, like his political partner, Fabián Núñez, he can be seen as a carpetbagger, rather than a homie of the LA district he ran to represent in 2006. They first got to know their adjoining districts not by living in them but by organizing the historic mass resistance to Proposition 187 in LA in 1994, when they were working for One Stop Immigration in Boyle Heights. After their years at One Stop, they took jobs in organized labor. Núñez was the first to run for office in 2002, with de León managing his campaign for the Assembly. Then, while he was still a freshman, Fabián rocketed to the position of Speaker.[8] As he approached his first election as the leader responsible for protecting and growing his Assembly majority, Núñez was all-in for getting his childhood friend to join him in Sacramento. De León, however, would have to best an opponent with a magical name: Christine Chavez, another carpetbagger and Cesar Chavez's granddaughter.

De León is a thoroughly urban man. Not only was Cesar Chavez never his role model, before Kevin got to college, he did not even know who the legendary UFW leader was—the great Mexican boxer Julio César Chávez, yes, for sure, but not the California labor icon. "Ignorance is bliss," he is given to repeating in interviews, in which he also insists that if not for affirmative action he would never have had the opportunity of college, much less a political career. It was perhaps an ironic sign of the times that immigrant-rights activist de León snuffed out Christine Chavez's political aspirations with an urban-labor-backed landslide. In his first term in the Assembly, de León demonstrated the value of incorporating diversity that affirmative action can bring, not only to higher education but to a variety of fields, perhaps especially in formal policymaking and the management of a broad range of institutions.

Raised by a single mother, Kevin considered her older sister to be his "second mom." He felt so attached to this *tía* that once he had sufficient income, he started sending her a monthly check to help with expenses. One time while visiting, after he was elected to the Assembly, he asked his aunt, by then in her seventies, why she still worked long hours every day cleaning houses, like his mother had. Didn't she have some kind of retirement plan? His tía responded with a withering glare that wordlessly said to him, *¡Qué pendejo!* How can a college graduate and elected official ask such a stupid question? She broke her silent pause to say she had no other income but a scant Social Security check and what Kevin lovingly sent her. She *had* to keep working to cover expenses, most of all her medications. His aunt's piercing gaze took de León aback. She unforgettably made him feel small, even "tiny."

Back in Sacramento, he told his chief of staff, Dan Reeves, that they had to come up with an answer for workers who do not have employer-provided retirement plans. Thus began a decade-long policymaking journey of astonishing complexity. This was a field de León was utterly unfamiliar with, but he took a deep dive. Dan and Kevin spent months on the challenge, settling on the notion of a state-backed retirement savings instrument for workers whose employers do not offer any similar benefit, but they discovered that federal regulations did not allow states to sponsor such programs. They decided to take their case to DC and arranged to meet with Obama's secretary of labor, Hilda Solis. Their meeting with the secretary, and their follow-up communications with her staff, went nowhere. But de León and Reeves kept working the idea, consulting widely, and became known within specialized policy circles as advocates for an innovative approach to the retirement problems some workers faced.

When Tom Perez succeeded Solis at the Labor Department, they tried again. Perez, an energetic career civil rights and labor attorney, instantly grasped the need and the challenge. Days later, Secretary Perez called de León directly to inform him that he had briefed President Obama on the proposal to change federal regulations to allow states to sponsor their own retirement savings accounts. It was a Friday, and Perez said the president would announce on Monday, in an appearance in the Rose Garden, that he was directing his secretary of labor, along with the heads of other relevant departments such as the Treasury, to undertake the reforms needed to establish such financial instruments. The regulatory changes cleared the way for de León to fashion his bill, which financial institutions and their allies in the legislature strongly contested, to establish what would become the CalSavers program.[9] De León says that, of all he has accomplished throughout his career, this is the achievement that he is proudest of, but that remains the least known.

Novice lawmaker de León introduced his retirement savings bill in 2008, only to see it die in the Appropriations Committee "Suspense File" hearing.[10] He continued into his second two-year term to refine and promote his proposal, building an increasingly broad and diverse coalition of support, even as he tried but failed to follow in his partner Fabián's footsteps as Speaker. Unexpectedly losing the speakership contest was a blow that made de León shift gears. The chance arose for him to run for the state Senate in 2010, instead of seeking another Assembly term. When Kevin won, he promptly became deputy majority leader. De León went on to substantially modify his approach to his retirement plan; a new, expert board, headed by the state treasurer, would be created to study the proposal and, if found feasible, design the program. This phase would be funded by foundation grants and other nongovernmental sources, avoiding the Appropriations Committee hurdle. The board would then run the program if an authorizing statute became law. The later bill would also create a state trust to serve as the program's financial account.

Enter Speaker Pérez

KDL was set to become the next Speaker of the Assembly in 2010 when a first-term Latino member from LA—representing an adjoining district and boasting even stronger union backing—pulled off a stunning upset.[11] *John Pérez, a native of Northeast LA and first cousin of former Speaker and second-term Mayor Antonio Villaraigosa, had enormous presence, quick mind, booming voice, and aggressive union-leader style. Besides having been political director of the California Federation of Labor, Pérez had served over a decade on the board of the influential California League of Conservation Voters and was a well-connected Democratic Party activist to boot.*[12] *Thus, John had joined the Assembly with substantial political capital to leverage in 2008. Pérez became the first openly gay Speaker, a fact that, combined with his size, made for a stunning first meeting with the governor. Although Schwarzenegger had learned the hard way that he could not intimidate Fabián Núñez, he still used his physique and acting skills to that end with others. John entered the governor's office well-prepared, having consulted with outgoing Speaker Karen Bass and Senate Pro Tem Daryl Steinberg. Schwarzenegger strode right up to John, belly to belly, but the Speaker stood his ground. As he recounts it:*

> Arnold, our first official meeting, welcomes me to the office; we never sit down. He starts putting his finger on my chest... standing right in my face, telling me all the things he's going to make me do. I leaned into him, and I'm taller than him, even when he wears his cha-cha heels.... I said, "Governor, you must have misread the press. It said I was a fag, not a wimp. You push me too hard, and I'll knock you on your ass." ... I grew up watching *Pumping Iron*, where he mind-f*s Lou Ferrigno.... I heard from Karen [Bass] how he would treat her and Daryl in budget negotiations.... He liked to get in people's face. He liked to get in their head. He liked to get them off center. I had to get him off center. The calculation in my mind is, he's either going to back down, or he's going to hit me. If he hits me, I'm going to hit him back. If he beats me up, I got beat up by the Terminator. That's not a big deal. If I kick his ass, he got beaten up by a fag.... From a risk calculation, I had nothing to lose.... Seriously, you hear there was a fight between the Speaker and Arnold Schwarzenegger, you don't care who the Speaker is.... I literally get into his face. He gets in mine a little more.... We're

there, literally, staring each other down. He finally takes a breath and goes, "That's good. I like that."[13]

Governor Schwarzenegger congratulates Assembly Speaker Pérez after signing his bill creating the California Health Benefit Exchange, the country's first state-sponsored health insurance marketplace under the terms of the Affordable Care Act, in Los Angeles on October 1, 2010. Photo by Ringo Chiu/Zuma Press, Inc./Alamy Stock Photo.[14]

The need for a program like de León was proposing had been documented by university and think tank studies and gained support from labor and business, advocacy organizations, and philanthropic foundations. Kevin got his revised bill passed before the end of his first four-year Senate term, and Governor Jerry Brown signed it in 2012. The full California Secure Choice Retirement Savings Investment Board was formed over the course of 2013 and first met officially that September.[15] Both the process that ensued and its product were pioneering examples of public-private partnerships in developing policy and providing a vital service, in this case retirement security, to millions. This policy achievement—like many California innovations—went on to be studied and emulated by other states.

The agency came into being in 2017—nine years after de León introduced his original bill—now financed by a startup loan from the state General Fund and able to hire staff under the authority of its board. More precise design and development followed, which included establishing governing rules and regulations for all aspects of the program, as well as additional means of public input. The public-private partnership dimension continued with United Way as a key collaborator, bolstered by more foundation support to design and fund regionally specific outreach plans. The staff set up ongoing stakeholder advisory work groups, public comment periods, and workshops.

Going into 2018, both Senator de León and Treasurer Chiang embarked on campaigns for higher office. Now in his last year in the state Senate, Kevin chose to challenge California's senior US senator, Dianne Feinstein, who was running for her last reelection. Chiang sought to succeed Jerry Brown as governor. Even while campaigning, however, both continued to champion the new program in advance of its coming enlistment periods. The agency launched a pilot version of this new state service in late 2018. De León, teaming up with Chiang, devoted his final days as a state senator to outreach events from Sacramento to San Diego.[16] The employer-enlistment phases, by size of firm, began in 2019. When general enrollment for California workers opened that summer, de León, by then "pro tem emeritus," joined new state Treasurer Betty Yee in Sacramento for yet another public launch event. After over a decade of work, on July 1, CalSavers became available to millions of Californians.[17]

The Obama Breakthrough

As the open presidential election of 2008 neared, key California and Los Angeles–based Latina and Latino leaders began to diverge over whether to support second-term Senator and former First Lady Hillary Clinton for the Democratic nomination—as most Latino leaders and voters did nationally—or instead back relatively unknown first-term Senator Barack Obama. LA Mayor Antonio Villaraigosa was a major supporter of Clinton and served as a national co-chair of her campaign, while City Council President Eric Garcetti came out early for Obama. Dolores Huerta strongly supported Clinton and worked to line up other Latina/o endorsements for her. María Elena Durazo, however, the powerful head of the LA County Federation of Labor, became Obama's most prominent Latina supporter and co-chaired his campaign.[18] Although Durazo and the County Fed had engineered the election of Hilda Solis to the House in 2000, Solis nonetheless split with Durazo, sticking with Clinton in the 2008 primary. Her rising House colleague Xavier Becerra, however, threw his lot in with Obama. State Senator Gilbert Cedillo was the only major California Latino legislator to back Obama over Clinton in the primary. *La Opinión,* led by publisher Monica Lozano, topped off Obama's high-level California Latina/o support with an attention-grabbing endorsement editorial that angered the fiery Huerta.

Obama's campaign pledge to make immigration reform a top priority in his first year in office, perhaps even in his first one hundred days, was a major consideration for Durazo, Cedillo, and *La Opinión.*[19] He also strongly supported restoring access to driver's licenses for all residents, irrespective of their immigration status—at that time Cedillo's decade-long elusive goal.[20] Seen in retrospect, some of these electoral alignments proved to be a consequential investment for LA Latina/o political empowerment in both the short and long term. Durazo's influence in the Obama transition was essential to the historic naming of Hilda Solis to be secretary of labor, and the new Obama administration's continued support of her nomination against Republican resistance in the Senate.[21] Obama's running mate, Joe Biden, as senator for Delaware, had previously had neither the need nor the opportunity to develop relationships with Latinos. But as Latino support for Obama in the primary expanded to the Obama–Biden ticket and then the administration, a foundation was laid for a continuing relationship between these leaders and the subsequent Biden presidential campaign, transition, and administration in 2020–21. Representative Becerra, as assistant to House Speaker Nancy Pelosi, would be a key part of the strenuous effort to pass Obama's Affordable Care Act (ACA), which in turn set up his surprise nomination a decade later to be the first Latino secretary of health and human services in the Biden administration.[22] LA Mayor Eric Garcetti would be instrumental in the naming of other LA Latino cabinet members in Biden's 2020–21 transition.

Obama's surprise nomination of Hillary Clinton to what is traditionally considered the top cabinet position further cemented and widened his and Biden's Latino support in their first term.[23] Having Clinton as secretary of state allowed for the nomination of her supporters to diplomatic posts, such as onetime MALDEF President Vilma Martínez, also of LA, to be ambassador to Argentina.[24] Eva Longoria had backed Clinton in the 2008 primary, but she later became one of the top fundraisers for Obama's reelection in 2012 and Biden's election in 2020. Thus, between them, Obama and Clinton consolidated substantial Latino support for and ties to their administration early on, sending Obama's job-approval rating among Latinos soaring to over 80 percent in early 2009.[25] The president, however, set aside his promised immigration reform that year while single-mindedly pursuing his top priority, healthcare reform. The lack of progress on immigration was exacerbated by the administration's stepped-up enforcement, which meant more, and more visible, raids on workplaces in search of undocumented employees, and increased deportations. Obama authorized hardened enforcement as a political strategy to enhance his ability to support a comprehensive immigration-reform bill that he expected to emerge in Congress. As a result, Obama's job approval among Latinos began to significantly decline, spurred by a novel factor in the long-standing immigration-policy debate. Obama's senior Senate colleague, Richard Durbin of Illinois, had introduced his "DREAM Act" in each Congress since 2001, but could never get it passed.[26] Durbin's bill stimulated the emergence and visibility of the Dreamer movement, which for the first time helped push the issue of immigration reform to the top of Latino voters' policy priorities.[27]

Obama's Affordable Care Act, a.k.a. "Obamacare," dominated congressional politics throughout 2009, as the president clung to hope that it might draw a modicum of Republican support. The bill passed in the House in November, while it took until Christmas Eve to pass in the Senate. The political struggle then continued throughout the winter, as the two chambers had to reconcile their differences. Through a series of party-line votes, the act finally reached the president's desk in March—while all along, the immigration issue continued to fester, in particular in California's neighboring states of Arizona and Nevada.[28]

Local backlashes and fierce resistance struggles in those states beckoned and motivated California Latino solidarity and assistance. In Arizona, the sheriff of Maricopa County, whose seat is Phoenix, began an extended, high-profile crackdown on undocumented immigrants in 2005, which courts would later rule included illegal racial profiling of Latinos.[29] Sheriff Joe Arpaio devoted years to ostentatiously apprehending and displaying in humiliating fashion the undocumented immigrants his department apprehended. Arpaio's cruel theatrics helped advance a bill in the Arizona legislature that was more draconian than California's Proposition 187 had been. That 2010 law made the immigrant crackdown a mandated duty of all public officials, enforceable by private lawsuits.[30] California Latino legislators responded by engineering the passage of their own law barring official state travel to or contracting with business based in Arizona.

The same year in Nevada, a candidate challenging the incumbent US Senate Democratic majority leader, Harry Reid, unleashed an aggressive campaign targeting undocumented immigrants that was even more extreme than California Governor Pete Wilson's 1994 reelection effort. Reid responded by staking his reelection on Latino voter turnout, relying on the capacity developed in previous years, in particular by the hotel workers union, which had adopted the LA model of immigrant electoral mobilization.[31] Reid won, but his Senate majority was reduced to fifty-one. In the House, Speaker Nancy Pelosi lost seventy seats and with them her majority.

Supporters of the DREAM Act and the Dreamer movement went into overdrive to get their bill passed in the lame-duck session following the election, while Democrats still controlled both houses of Congress. Although the act had bipartisan majority support, in both Congress and public opinion as well as from the White House, it was not enough to overcome a Republican filibuster in the Senate. Latino frustration with the lack of progress on immigration policy mounted, and Obama's Latino job approval slid to under 50 percent in the summer of 2011. His polls improved in early 2012 to around 60 percent, but this would not be enough going into his reelection that fall. Republican Senator Marco Rubio of Florida both forced the issue and gave Obama an opening when in June the senator announced he was preparing his own bill to provide protection to Dreamers. The president was scheduled to address the annual meeting of the National Association of Latino Elected and Appointed Officials (NALEO) that summer, a gathering of thousands of government officials from across the country, and the stakes had just gone up. In the days between Rubio's announcement and the convention, Obama announced his Deferred Action for Childhood Arrivals (DACA) program, which could protect nearly a million undocumented immigrants brought into the country as children.[32]

The immense challenge of creating a system to rapidly process hundreds of thousands of DACA applications came under the purview of Alejandro Mayorkas, then-director of the Homeland Security Department's US Citizenship and Immigration Services (USCIS). Mayorkas, born to a Jewish Cuban family in Havana that fled the Revolution when he was a toddler, grew up in, was shaped by, and made his career in Los Angeles.[33] His agency started taking applications later that summer and throughout the fall election campaign. Whether by coincidence or design, this process unfolded at a time of maximum political impact. A highly visible outreach campaign mobilized hundreds of thousands of immigrants to apply for this novel and critical benefit. The president's job-approval rating among Latinos then began a steady ascent and reached 75 percent around the time of his November reelection.[34] But this was not the only novel element that mobilized Latino support for Obama in 2012.

Up to this election cycle, with the exception of the more affluent Cuban American community, campaigns and candidates saw Latinos as a substantial potential source of votes, but not of campaign funds. Obama's first term happened to coincide with the first step toward fulfilling the goal of a national museum in Washington dedicated to Latino history and culture. That step was the long-delayed creation of an official commission—launched in 2009, the first year of the Obama presidency—to study the feasibility of such an institution, which brought together twenty-three appointed members from across the country. Among the various factors these commissioners would have to consider would be the significant role of private fundraising to create and maintain cultural institutions of this sort, as was readily apparent in existing examples and in those underway, like the United States Holocaust Memorial Museum, the National Museum of the American Indian and the National Museum of African American History and Culture on the National Mall. This new Latino museum commission fatefully brought together Eva Longoria, at the height of her television career, and star architect and Democratic activist Henry Muñoz of San Antonio. Their work together over the succeeding years resulted not only in a report that vetted the proposed national museum; they decided to top that achievement by joining forces to elevate the Latino role in the next presidential election. They committed to raising $5 million for the 2012 Obama reelection campaign.[35] But that turned out to be a woeful underestimate of the resources they could mobilize among the Latino community. In the end, they managed to raise over $30 million for Obama.[36]

Eva Longoria announces the creation of the National Museum of the American Latino Commission, on which she served, on October 13, 2009, in Washington, DC. Congress members Hilda Solis and Xavier Becerra appear on her right. Photo by Paul Morigi/WireImage/Getty Images.

After the great success of Eva's partnership with Henry Muñoz in fundraising for Obama—which gave her a speaking role at the Democratic National Convention—she and Muñoz founded the Latino Victory Fund (LVF) political action committee. Latino Victory became the first ongoing vehicle to bolster the election of Latinas and Latinos to public office across the country. LVF has recorded numerous successes, including the election of the first two Latinas to represent Texas in Congress, and threw its growing clout behind high-level appointments to public office as well. Longoria had an even bigger role in the 2016 Democratic convention, and by 2020 she was the most visible celebrity activist in the party. Early in 2020, Nathalie Rayes, who was already serving on the Latino Victory board of directors, left her corporate job to lead the organization herself—a move she made specifically to devote herself full-time to the effort to oust Trump from the presidency.

Then-President and CEO of Latino Victory Nathalie Rayes speaks at Vote Like a Madre event on August 13, 2022, in Coral Gables, Florida. Photo by Alexander Tamargo/Latino Victory Project via Getty Images.

Although Obama's DACA action bolstered Latino support for his reelection, it did not end the pressure for comprehensive immigration reform. In a nationally televised town hall sponsored by Univision in September of that campaign season, anchor Jorge Ramos bluntly challenged the president, stating he had failed to deliver on his promise of immigration reform in his first year in office—and by then, his first term was in its final months. In fact, DACA did not even quiet the Dreamer movement. Instead, the outreach and mobilization to apply for DACA grew and energized it. Far more young immigrants applied than had ever, or would have ever, become activists—and in so doing, they became aware of their stake in the politics of immigration policy. The Dreamers and their many supporters knew well what Obama made clear from the start: DACA did not legalize them, it only temporarily stayed their "removal" (a.k.a. deportation) from the country, and it did nothing at all for their parents. The movement continued to press for a real, legislated solution for themselves (i.e., the DREAM Act) and began loudly agitating for a policy reform for their parents and undocumented immigrants in general.

The president's impressive margin of victory over Mitt Romney, who had led in the polls earlier in the year, pushed the Republican National Committee (RNC) in a promising direction. The RNC issued an "autopsy" report on its loss that argued the party had to compromise on immigration reform to address its disadvantage, relative to the Democrats, with the growing Latino electorate.[37] Bipartisan talks on comprehensive immigration reform emerged in the Senate, but Obama's job-approval rating resumed the slide seen in 2009–12 before DACA. In 2013, the bipartisan "Gang of Eight" senators succeeded in crafting a reform bill that passed their chamber with a two-thirds supermajority. Nevertheless, extremists in the House, who had dubbed themselves the Tea Party Caucus, refused to yield.[38]

As the 2014 midterm elections approached, prominent Latina/o leaders notably ramped up the pressure on the president. Janet Murguía, head of UnidosUS, took to the airwaves to loudly complain that in spite of DACA, which offered only temporary protection to a small fraction of the long-term resident undocumented population, the administration's immigration enforcement continued apace, indeed setting a new record for immigrant "removals," or deportations. Murguía made headlines by dubbing Obama the "deporter in chief." The president began publicly pressing House Speaker John Boehner to allow hearings and a vote on the Senate bill. After having put the issue off since the year before, Boehner finally announced in June that the House would take no action on immigration legislation in that session, provoking Obama to respond furiously. The president ordered that new executive measures be developed for his consideration by summer's end. While Obama appeared to be repeating his 2012 play that had helped with his reelection, this time vulnerable Democratic senators pleaded that they could be hurt by it; *they* were on the ballot in November, not him. Obama agreed to hold off on taking action until after the midterms—but that September saw his own job approval among Latinos sink to the lowest point of his presidency, just 47 percent.[39]

President Obama seemed resolved to not end the year with his job approval underwater with Latinos as well as with whites, where it had been since mid-2009. Two weeks after the 2014 midterms, he not only announced an extension and expansion of DACA but also added a new program, Deferred Action for Parents of Americans and Lawful Permanent Residents (DAPA), and a broad reordering of immigration-enforcement priorities. Altogether, Obama's overhaul of immigration policies and practices by executive action would completely reverse the enhanced-enforcement strategy of his first term, potentially shielding nearly 90 percent of the resident undocumented population. Furthermore, while Obama was addressing policies of particular concern not only to Latinos but to several countries in Latin America, he went on to take another bold step with broad regional appeal. Less than a month following his moves on immigration, the president announced on live television the restoration of diplomatic relations with Cuba—severed over a half century before—and before his term ended, he would be the first US president to visit the island since the 1920s.[40]

Obama thus chose to launch what he called the "fourth quarter" of his presidency with historic policy innovations of particular interest—if not in the same way—to both US Latinos and Latin America. Could it be coincidental that an unprecedented movement to take the country back in the opposite direction in these and other areas would be announced six months later, with a crackdown on migration from Mexico and border control as its lead issues? Most of the country would observe the rise of this movement over the next two years, dismissing the possibility that it could come to power—until in 2016, it did.

Chapter 12

Collision, Defeat, Resistance, Comeback

JANUARY 2015 MARKED THE COMPLETION of six years of the Obama presidency and start of its "fourth quarter." Although the 2014 midterm elections had given the opposition complete control of Congress, and in spite of the huge challenge of trying to win a third straight presidential election, Democrats nonetheless appeared to have a good chance of retaining the White House in the coming open contest of 2016, with former Secretary of State Hillary Clinton as their likely nominee. In the words of a leading political analyst, Obama's "coalition of transformation"—with the Latino vote looming larger every cycle—still looked ascendant over its opposing "coalition of restoration."[1] At least regarding the presidency, Republicans at that time seemed adrift, with no compelling leader.

A broad sense of national progress appeared to be building at multiple levels, especially in the economy. When Obama had taken office in 2009, in the depths of the Great Recession, the country was suffering stunning job losses every month.[2] By January 2015, however, the economy had registered over four years of continuous job growth. Looking to 2016, Republicans—visibly casting about for both a "standard bearer" and an issue to run on—increasingly sounded unlikely to be able to campaign on the state of the economy.[3] On other fronts, and for Latinos in Southern California in particular, a sense that government could be reformed to act in ways that made life better was also already evident in healthcare and expected on immigration policy as well.

In 2010, over 40 percent of Latinos aged eighteen to sixty-four lacked health insurance, by far the highest proportion of any race or ethnic group measured by the Centers for Disease Control, and well over twice the rate of non-Hispanic whites.[4] As discussed in the previous chapter, however, Obama's signature healthcare reform was passed that same year, while he still enjoyed congressional majorities. Although the ACA stumbled in 2014 when its national healthcare exchange website crashed on debut, due to the leadership of then-Assembly Speaker John Pérez, California had brought its own pre-existing, state-run health insurance marketplace into compliance with the new federal law years before. Within the state, the remarkable Latino-led, nonprofit healthcare provider AltaMed Health Services surpassed all other entities in ACA enrollments.[5] Nationally, enrollment in ACA programs reached nearly 12.6 million by the end of 2014 and was headed for nearly 23 million by the end of 2015, and the president came to embrace the "Obamacare" nickname. On the immigration front, in January 2015, the Department of Homeland Security was preparing to process millions of undocumented residents for protection from deportation, under the terms of the expanded DACA program and the new DAPA executive action announced the previous fall.[6]

Toward the end of the month, a bevy of Republican presidential aspirants gathered in Des Moines for the right-wing "Iowa Freedom Summit," a preview and warm-up for the state's first-in-the-nation contest still a full year away. The following evening, the *Los Angeles Times* posted its online coverage with a curious headline: "Analysis: Rosier Views on Economy Pose a Challenge for Republicans."[7] The article appeared on the next morning's front page with a more pointed head spanning three columns—"2016 Strategy for GOP: Play Down the Economy"—followed by an explanatory subhead: "Voters Are Feeling Better, Creating a Dilemma for Party's Presidential Hopefuls." Such was the state of political play at the time that, although Donald Trump was among those who spoke forcefully at the Iowa "summit," he did not rate a mention in the *Times*. On its front page, the *Des Moines Register* reported that Scott Walker and Ted Cruz were "the best received" at the gathering, and that "even Chris Christie . . . got an enthusiastic standing ovation." It was not until the jump to page 14 that the local paper's report turned to Trump, almost as an afterthought, referring to him as "a Manhattan-based real-estate developer and reality TV star"—in other words, notably unqualified. Further on, it added, "With a mix of bravado and apprehension, the speakers rhetorically jostled over who was the most conservative and could 'take down Hillary'"—Obama's presumptive successor.[8]

Collision Course

> *Republicans better wake up, and for the first time in my life appeal to white Americans!*
> —Ann Coulter
> May 26, 2015[9]

A couple of years earlier, at another right-wing confab, notorious columnist-provocateur and book author Ann Coulter declared she had become a single-issue voter—against immigration.[10] The blonde bomb thrower was in open, albeit somewhat lonely, rebellion at that time against her party's leaders. As recounted in the last chapter, Obama had succeeded in reversing his alarming slide in approval among Latino voters in 2012 with his first DACA executive action—a move that helped reelect him. That result seems to have traumatized Coulter.[11] The Republican National Committee then made matters worse for Coulter with its autopsy report calling for the party to adapt to demographic change and embrace immigration reform, and then the bipartisan "Gang of Eight" senators sponsored a comprehensive reform bill that passed with a large majority.[12] Coulter's opposition on immigration began metastasizing into a broader rejection of her party as a whole—or at least of its "establishment" leadership—for drawing a lesson that was to her the opposite of what it should have learned from its 2012 defeat. By Coulter's lights, what Republicans needed to do most was *openly appeal to white voters.*[13]

She had her issue, but now, in 2015, at the start of the next electoral cycle, Coulter saw no candidate worth supporting. In the three months since Obama had unveiled his expanded protections for undocumented residents, she had been curiously silent on immigration in her syndicated weekly column. In February 2015, however, on the heels of the Iowa "summit," she abruptly shifted back into anti-immigrant high gear. Observing what to her was a field of feckless pretenders to the Republican nomination, Coulter had a political epiphany. She suddenly reverted again to pounding the immigration issue week after week. In her first column that month, she tore into what seemed like the whole range of candidates. Coulter denounced their conciliatory positions on access to driver's licenses and in-state public college tuition. She especially unleashed her wrath on Governors Jeb Bush, Chris Christie, Mike Huckabee, and Rick Perry but did not entirely exempt Senators Rick Santorum and Marco Rubio. Odd as it may seem coming from hard-right Coulter, she proclaimed that in recent years Mitt Romney had been "the only Republican who has ever opposed the media and big campaign donors on immigration" and lamented that since his surprisingly lopsided loss to Obama in 2012, Republicans had "kicked [Romney] to the curb." Notably, Trump was the one presidential aspirant she did not mention in this column.[14]

Two weeks later, Coulter went hard after congressional Republicans, declaring that if they could not stop Obama's new immigration executive actions, "there is no reason to vote Republican ever again."[15] In May, Coulter announced she had a new book, *¡Adios, America! The Left's Plan to Turn Our Country into a Third World Hellhole,* coming out on June 1.[16] She complained the major TV networks refused to give her a promotional interview. But then she got a break from an unlikely source. Univision nightly news coanchor Jorge Ramos invited Coulter to appear on his afternoon English-language chat program, *America with Jorge Ramos,* to discuss her book and immigration.[17]

True to her practiced schtick, Coulter was energetically offensive to her host's live Latino audience. In addition to calling on Republicans to appeal to white voters "for the first time in my life," she also called Mexican culture "deficient," marked by incestuous rape, and said immigrants were more dangerous to Americans than Islamic State (ISIS) terrorists. Trump took to Twitter to praise the book, and then exactly three weeks later launched his unorthodox campaign for president. Coulter had hooked her man, and Trump had his issue.[18] Numerous journalists credited Coulter's book for Trump's rhetoric and strategy of running on immigration, although given his widely reported aversion to reading and his notoriously compulsive daytime TV watching—together with his tweet that same day—it is a fair bet that he saw Coulter's performance on the Ramos program.

In the aftermath of Obama's reelection, and the RNC's and Republican senators' response to it on immigration, Coulter had dramatized a populist way to attack both immigrants and Republican leaders from the right. This one issue could serve as a vehicle to draw the attention and notoriety she thrived on, but her rhetoric needed major amplification and a disruption of the emerging Republican presidential debate. Could her approach to immigration serve as the big gun for an outsider candidate to attack (and run with against) *all* the politicians seeking the 2016 Republican nomination—the whole field? Indeed, it did. Over most of the subsequent decade, the match between Coulter's and Trump's interests and styles, their disruptive synergy and symbiosis, would prove to have the power to upend US national politics in ways not seen since the 1960s and the trauma of Vietnam, or the early 1950s and McCarthyism, and perhaps not even since the debate over slavery that led to the Civil War. That summer, Coulter began appearing as a warm-up act at Trump campaign rallies.[19]

Ramos tried valiantly on his program to exorcise the anti-immigrant demon possessing Coulter, challenging the wild premises of her outrage and prescriptions—allegedly thirty million undocumented immigrants, rampant criminality, American culture overwhelmed, the need for a triple-layer fence around the country—but to no avail. After Trump launched his campaign with the same claims of Mexican criminality and the charge that Mexico was intentionally exporting rapists, other criminals, and drugs to the US, Ramos tried again, handwriting Trump a personal request to appear on his program. Trump responded by posting and mocking the invite on Twitter. The image displayed Jorge's personal cell phone number—a hostile act known as "doxing." Univision publicly canceled its agreement to broadcast Trump's Miss World beauty pageant—to which Trump responded by filing a half billion dollar lawsuit and barring Univision employees from his Doral golf resort, just a mile up the street from Univision's news headquarters in Miami-Dade.[20] Everything Coulter and Trump set out to do worked: Her book became a bestseller, widely covered in the media, and Trump had the attention he needed. The rest of the Republican presidential field was suddenly deprived of oxygen.

Ramos plotted his next move. Seeing Trump campaigning, climbing in the polls, stumping and holding press conferences in Iowa, Jorge conferred with his producer and decided to confront him there. Trump had promised to deport the officially estimated 11–12 million undocumented residents of the country, strip their US-born children of citizenship, and build a wall along the nearly two-thousand-mile border with Mexico. Ramos flew to a campaign presser to challenge Trump on those pledges, which he saw as blatantly false promises he could neither legally nor practically carry out. In short, Ramos would tell Trump to his face that he was running on lies and insistently ask why.

Less than a half minute after Ramos rose from his front-row seat to ask his questions, Trump executed his first symbolic deportation on live TV. After yelling repeatedly to "sit down" and "go back to Univision," with a wordless gesture to a giant security guard, the candidate had the newsman physically pushed out of the room. At the time, many saw the press-conference clash as potentially marking a turn in Trump's campaign coverage to something more critical, but at least to some, it seemed odd that it had been precipitated by a star TV journalist of a Latino news operation based in conservative Cuban American Miami, where Trump was well established.[21] But the conflict at hand was not between Trump and Latino Miami so much as it was between Trump and *Latino LA*.

Ramos, certainly, and even the Univision news department up until then, had been shaped by the Latino empowerment-movement experience of twentieth-century Los Angeles. The network's flagship station KMEX's news and community relations had played a historic role in that experience, as we have shown. By confronting Trump, the hyper-alert and methodical Ramos served as an early-warning system, a sort of twenty-first-century Latino Paul Revere, calling attention to the instigator of a new backlash against immigrants and Latinos. In so doing, in the summer of 2015, Jorge and his network kicked off the most visible

Latino resistance to Trump, which got more broadly and vigorously underway—in California, especially—upon his upset election in November 2016.

State of Resistance/#StateofResistance

It is up to us to pass policies to firewall Californians . . . from the cynical, short-sighted, and reactionary agenda . . . rising in the wake of the election. We must be defiant whenever justice, fairness and righteousness require. Californians do not need healing. We need to fight.
—Assembly Speaker Anthony Rendon
December 4, 2016[22]

While Trump was building his campaign over the summer of 2015, second-term state legislator Anthony Rendon, PhD, of the small Latino cities immediately southeast of downtown Los Angeles, was lining up votes to become the next Speaker of the California Assembly. That would make him the fifth Latino Speaker ever—all five had reached that office in a span of twenty years since 1996—and for the first time, place both chambers of the legislature under Latino and Southern California leadership. Although he shared some traits with his political forebears going back two generations, Rendon's career had begun only three years earlier in a political world transformed by Latinos and other people of color. First elected in 2012, when Obama was reelected president, Rendon flipped his district, helping his party achieve a historic, Latino-led two-thirds Assembly supermajority.[23]

As we have already seen, Martha Escutia had come over from East LA two decades before that to initiate the Southeast Cities' Latino-era empowerment in state politics.[24] By mid-2012, former Assembly Speaker Antonio Villaraigosa had begun his eighth year as LA mayor, and his cousin John Pérez was in the middle of his own speakership in Sacramento. Gloria Molina was in her sixth and last term on the county board of supervisors. Lucille Roybal-Allard—daughter of political pioneer Ed Roybal—had been elected ten times to represent that area in Congress, and she was running for reelection again. Rendon knew all about the struggles that had brought Latinos to that level of empowerment and the challenges they'd had to overcome. The thrust of political history all around him resonated with the same ancient concept and value that gripped Dean Florez a few years earlier: *Justice*, as explored in Plato's *Republic*. The idea made Florez want to study law, while it led Rendon to pursue a doctorate in political theory. This outlook, and the reality he knew, contributed mightily to the widely held conviction that Donald Trump was simply not electable to the presidency of twenty-first-century United States.

Rendon began his speakership in March 2016, when both the Republican and Democratic presidential nominations were still being fought out. Although Trump had led his competitors in the polls since the year before and was ahead in the delegate count, Texas Senator Ted Cruz was not far behind and remained in the race until May. On the Democratic side, Vermont Senator Bernie Sanders was committed to quixotically pursuing that nomination all the way to the convention.[25] By then, the state's top Latino leaders—LA Mayor Eric Garcetti, Secretary of State Alex Padilla, Senate President Pro Tem Kevin de León, and new Speaker Rendon—each in their first term in these lofty positions, were focused on and involved in the Hillary Clinton campaign, giving little thought to the strange drama on the Republican side surrounding Trump's march to power. All were genuinely shocked the night of November 8 when the election result was called. In a victory of greater significance to their futures than they could have then imagined, California Attorney General Kamala Harris was easily elected to the US Senate over their friend and member of Congress Loretta Sanchez of Orange County. But instead of joyfully celebrating her early win with the laughter and dancing she would later become famous for, as the stunning presidential returns came in, Harris nervously ate her way through a large bag of Doritos.[26]

The next morning, Rendon and de León expressed their dismay in a strongly worded joint statement.[27] The first concrete expression of the state's commitment to resisting the incoming administration came three weeks later, however, from another office in the state capitol, when Governor Jerry Brown announced his nomination of veteran LA

Congressman Xavier Becerra—originally of Sacramento—to succeed Harris as attorney general.[28]

As chair of its Democratic Caucus and with a quarter century of seniority, Becerra had risen to become the top Latino in the House. Representing Northeast LA, Xavier was on track to sooner or later become *the first Latino Speaker of the House in US history*—until Jerry Brown persuaded him to return to his hometown to lead his state's legal resistance to Trump.[29] Three days later, Rendon opened the new Assembly session, pledging "to pass policies to firewall Californians" and their values from the Trump regime. Rendon, de León, and colleagues unveiled their first action that day in a press conference—legislation to provide tens of millions of dollars to fortify legal defense of the state's undocumented-immigrant residents.[30]

Assembly Speaker Anthony Rendon, center, discusses a pair of proposed measures to protect immigrants, during a news conference in Sacramento on the first day of the new legislative session, December 5, 2016. Lawmakers urged President-elect Donald Trump to refrain from pursuing mass deportations and introduced urgent legislation to fund immigration lawyers and help public defenders protect the state's immigrants. Photo by Rich Pedroncelli/Associated Press. Copyright 2016, The Associated Press. All rights reserved.

The next month, Rendon and de León announced they would bolster incoming AG Becerra's legal efforts by hiring former US Attorney General Eric Holder, then in private practice specializing in civil rights, to advise the legislature on how to protect California policies from Trump administration challenges. In a Senate confirmation hearing, de León pressed Becerra to make a long-term commitment to his new role, because "the state is about to enter into a battle with the incoming administration of President-elect Donald Trump, who has threatened to roll back many California policies on issues including the environment and immigration."[31] The Senate pro tem also got to work on legislation that would become known as making California a "sanctuary state," whose agencies, to the extent legally possible, would refuse to support federal immigration enforcement.[32]

California Secretary of State Alex Padilla was among those who had thought Trump's election was inconceivable. The day after, he found his staff in what seemed like a state of shock. Padilla gathered them together to provide a sense of direction. From his formative experience in sports, he had learned how to lose, recover, and resume preparations for the next engagement and all the rest to come. In formulating what to say, Padilla drew on this experience and both his and others' continuing interest as sports fans. His agency would take as its motto the ethos of the "Bad Boys" Detroit Pistons of a quarter century earlier: "No Easy Buckets." They would fight anything the incoming administration either said or tried to do affecting Californians' voting and elections. Whatever the prospects of success in any particular dispute, the situation called for a full-court press. First up was the claim Trump was given to making: that noncitizens voting in California had cost him the majority of the popular vote nationwide. Indeed, the margin of his landslide loss in the state exceeded that of his loss nationally. If California's votes could be subtracted from the national total, Trump would have won both the popular and Electoral College results, instead of only the latter. Padilla and his office pushed back on each and every allegation that noncitizens had voted in California.

Since taking office in 2015, Padilla had become active in the National Association of Secretaries of State—the country's oldest society of public officials—and had cultivated relationships with his Democratic peers in other states.[33] With the advantage of a four-year term in by far the largest economy of any state, he was able to support the election and reelection of a number of other Democratic secretaries of state. Padilla found himself immediately at odds with his opposite number in Kansas, Republican Secretary of State and Trump ally Kris Kobach. In spite of having won and taken power, the Trump administration and congressional Republicans—who controlled both houses—continued making allegations of voter fraud and calling for investigations. This was a campaign to delegitimize voting systems in blue states, which culminated in Trump's executive order in May 2017 creating his "Voter Fraud Commission," chaired by Vice President Mike Pence, with Kobach as vice chair and executive director.[34] The commission tried to obtain the states' voter rolls, but the great majority of them followed California's lead in refusing to cooperate. The National Association of Secretaries of State adopted a resolution defending their agencies' sovereign role in protecting voter information. Trump "abruptly" disbanded his commission the following January.[35] Six months later, Padilla was elected western region vice president of the secretaries of state association.

Fourth Horseman of the Resistance

Of the various means California used to resist the Trump administration, the state's own Justice Department—with a staff of over a thousand lawyers, second in size only to the federal DOJ—was clearly the main force. Jerry Brown was governor when Trump was first elected in 2016, and both he and the state were fortunate they could turn to longtime Congressman Becerra to step in to succeed Attorney General Kamala Harris, who had just been elected to the US Senate to succeed the retiring Barbara Boxer. Northern Californian Becerra had begun his governmental/political career right out of Stanford Law as a Capital Fellow, assigned to then–state Senator Art Torres, who represented East LA. Torres was himself a lawyer, originally from Boyle Heights, before his family moved to suburban Monterey Park, just to the east.

Senator Torres—one of the *Los Diez* pioneers of California Latina/o political empowerment—firmly connected Becerra to both the Chicano movement and the professional political dimensions of LA's Greater Eastside history. Art was a 1960s student body president at East Los Angeles College (ELAC). In law school at UC Davis, he connected with Dolores Huerta while serving as lobbyist for California Rural Legal Assistance, and then he worked a stint for the UFW. Becerra graduated from Capital Fellow to become administrative assistant–field deputy in East LA to Senator Torres, before taking a position in downtown Los Angeles as a deputy attorney general for the state. Like Torres, who moved back to the Eastside to run for office, Xavier saw his political future in LA, where he first ran for an open Assembly seat in 1990, and then for Congress in 1992.

The Atlantic *magazine profiled Xavier Becerra shortly after his confirmation as attorney general of California, dubbing him the "warrior" for a state on a collision course with the Trump administration. The story was illustrated by this drawing of Becerra riding a bear and brandishing the California state flag like a spear. Courtesy of John Cuneo, artist.*[36]

The governor did not personally know Becerra when he had to nominate a replacement AG, but tapping Xavier proved a master stroke in multiple ways. It signaled to California Latinos that their top representative in the House would take charge of defending them and the state against a decidedly nativist incoming Trump administration—while leaving the governor free to do whatever was necessary to secure federal assistance as needed. Those needs came up immediately, in the form of damaging winter rainstorms and, even more devastatingly for Brown's successor, Gavin Newsom, increasingly severe wildfires. It is unlikely the governor realized just how much he was contributing to coupling together Latino and California resistance to Trump. With Padilla as secretary of state, de León as Senate president, and Rendon as Assembly Speaker, by adding Becerra as AG—the role with the most formidable weapons to deploy—Brown was completing the four horsemen of the California Latino resistance.

Attorney General Becerra led California to file or join 123 lawsuits against the Trump administration, and his department won over two-thirds of them. The suits primarily concerned policy on the environment, immigration, and healthcare, as inventoried by the nonprofit news organization *CalMatters*.[37] The crowning achievement of this bulging portfolio of litigation was the Supreme Court's ruling in 2020 that saved DACA protections for nearly seven hundred thousand immigrants brought into the country as children, approximately two hundred thousand in California.[38] This case was particularly meaningful for the state, as the original lawsuit against the Trump administration was filed in the name of the Regents of the University of California, and ultimately the primary litigants were the university system and the state. A principal advocate for the lawsuit on the UC Board of Regents was former Assembly Speaker John Pérez, board chair at that time. Pérez was in attendance, along with UC President Janet Napolitano and a number of DACA recipients who were UC students and alumni, when the Court heard oral arguments in the case the previous November.

The Battle for Arizona

The Supreme Court's ruling on DACA happened to be decided the year that saw the outbreak of the global COVID-19 pandemic, as well as the police murder of George Floyd in Minneapolis and the consequent eruption of the Black Lives Matter movement that swept the country. The pandemic proved consequential for the electoral showdown that pitted the Trump administration seeking reelection against the opposition-party resistance. The Democrats, observing and supporting public health directives, held their national presidential nominating convention on TV and online, and suspended in-person field efforts across the country. Eva Longoria, who had twice before addressed the DNC, served as the opening night host.

DACA recipients and supporters on Supreme Court steps cheer immigration rights activists who rallied in front of the Court in Washington, DC, November 12, 2019, following oral arguments over Trump's executive order to abolish the Obama-era program. Photo by Scott Henrichsen.

As California, a deep-blue state, is not in play in presidential elections, activist Californians were called upon to devote their efforts to other states, principally neighboring Nevada and Arizona, which resulted in an upsurge in digital outreach and the use of innovative techniques such as peer-to-peer (P2P) texting, which allowed for personal text conversations similar to those that traditionally took place in door-to-door canvassing. Pandemic restrictions vastly increased the availability of both volunteers and registered voters with time on, and phones in, their hands for such electoral efforts.

Nonetheless, critically important initiatives independent of the party or presidential campaign intensified their voter mobilization work, supported both remotely and in person by organized labor and other activists in or from California. The numerically principal force in this effort was UNITE HERE, the umbrella union for the local that had pioneered immigrant mobilization in elections in Los Angeles and Las Vegas. Also of great importance and inspiration was the organization Living United for Change in Arizona (LUCHA), which had been devoted to mobilizing the Latino community since the passage of SB 1070 in 2010. That law required law enforcement to demand immigration documents of anyone they suspected of being undocumented, and, if they failed to do so, allowed any citizen to file a private lawsuit against the officers. LUCHA activists described their organization as modeled after the Latino community's response to Proposition 187 in California.[39]

The battle of Arizona in the 2020 presidential election came to a nationally electrifying climax on the night of November 3, when the major cable network most supportive of Trump surprisingly was the first to call the state in favor of Joe Biden. Although Fox News would not call the overall electoral result until the next morning, if proved true, the win in Arizona was considered pivotal and widely seen as resulting from a decade-long effort by LUCHA and others to flip the state. The national map now appeared to have a complete blue fishhook, or reverse J, made up of the West Coast states, Arizona, New Mexico, and Colorado, anchored by the California corner. One side in this contest reveled in the result, while the other refused to accept it.

Chapter 13

We Had Next—Briefly

HAD THE RESULTS OF THE 2020 election not been reversed four years later, the colossal mobilization that buried the incumbent president under a record avalanche of over 81 million votes—in the midst of a horrendous pandemic—might have been long celebrated as a great national triumph and repudiation of Trumpism.[1] The ancient notion that history is written by the victor, however, is confounded to the extent that the 2024 result was premised on the "Big Lie" that the previous result was a "steal." The resistance had won big, but the die-hard backlash, clinging to its version of history, was not vanquished.

The great reversal of 2024 qualified the meaning of the 2020 result and what it had achieved. What remains undiminished is that many Latina/o leaders considered beating Trump's first reelection attempt as perhaps the greatest national priority Latinos had ever faced, and that effort was successful in confirming that effective resistance can bring major gains for Latinos. Nevertheless, while we can continue to stress breakthroughs like the record four Latinas/os—three from Greater LA—named to the Biden–Harris presidential cabinet, we cannot ignore that this historic advance could neither be extended nor built upon in a second term.

We can likewise still highlight the role played by the Democratic Latino vote, and by support from California, in winning Nevada for the fourth time, and most critically flipping Arizona in 2020; but the 2024 backflip in those states complicates the picture. Alex Padilla's appointment as the first Latino senator from California—he went on to be elected outright in 2022—is a lasting breakthrough, as is his appointment to the Senate Judiciary Committee, and his becoming the state's senior senator in 2023, at the age of fifty. But those advances were soon hobbled by his party losing control of both the Senate and the White House in 2024. Furthermore, in another major advance, three LA Latina/o leaders who played key roles in the 2020 election and in assembling the new administration were rewarded with important ambassadorships, but their service was painfully cut short.

Ironically, these achievements resulting from the 2020 election also contributed to the setback of four years later. The main figures involved were in whole or part recused from the 2024 contest. Whereas throughout 2020, California Attorney General Xavier Becerra was filing more lawsuits and piling up wins over the Trump administration, as HHS secretary he was severely constrained from visibly campaigning or raising funds for his president or vice president in 2024. LA Mayor Eric Garcetti was a national co-chair of the Biden–Harris campaign in 2020, but 2024 found him serving as US ambassador to India. Nathalie Rayes took charge of Latino Victory and led it to endorse and financially support Biden–Harris in 2020, but four years later she, too, was far away, serving as US ambassador to Croatia. Prodigious campaign fundraiser and advisor Cynthia Telles, like her father before her, was US ambassador in Costa Rica. All these appointees took quality staffers with them to their new gigs, thereby also extracting them from the 2024 cycle, which was marked by a rightward drift of Latino votes.

It is impossible to know what any of these appointees might have done, had they not been part of the administration, to address the Democratic Party crisis in 2024 over whether Joe Biden should run for reelection, or if it would have made any difference. Given the early warning signals in pre-electoral polls that Biden was losing support from Latino voters, it is possible that, as fellow Californians, they might have been able to accelerate the transition to what became the Kamala Harris campaign, as well as help increase Latino turnout and diminish the record proportion of Latino voters who stayed home or went to Trump.[2]

Among the principal Latino appointees of the Biden presidency, the experience of Department of Homeland Security (DHS) Secretary

Alejandro Mayorkas may be the most unfortunate. In 2020 he was a supremely talented and well-connected LA "Super Lawyer" in private practice, supporting and advising the Biden–Harris campaign.[3] With extensive and intensive DHS experience in the Obama administration—having set up and administered the DACA program—as Biden's nominee he had to overcome vitriolic Republican opposition to be confirmed, and then took over a huge department in disarray. The Trump years saw a parade of *six* DHS secretaries, the last four of whom were "acting," without Senate confirmation.[4] Due to a combination of factors, Mayorkas was almost immediately confronted with waves of asylum seekers at the southern border, made into a crisis by an asylum process in ruins in his department.[5] As he undertook to painstakingly rebuild the asylum infrastructure and observe both US statutory law and treaty obligations, Mayorkas suffered a nonstop onslaught from congressional Republicans, was repeatedly hauled before hostile congressional committees, and was ultimately impeached by the Republican majority in the House of Representatives.[6] Although by mid-2024 Mayorkas was able to dramatically reduce border crossings between ports of entry, the allegations that he and Biden had thrown the border open, were failing to enforce immigration laws, and had been lying to Congress were endlessly repeated and played a major role in the election.

Nevertheless, we should recognize that thanks to the single Biden–Harris term and Mayorkas's tenure at DHS, millions of desperate asylum seekers were able to apply for protection from deportation for themselves and their children, and to schedule interviews with an asylum officer. They also became eligible for work permits for the duration of their asylum process. Thanks to the enormity of the Biden–Harris electoral mobilization in 2020, the Senate Democratic Caucus grew to fifty members through the simultaneous and historic wins of African American candidate Raphael Warnock and Jewish candidate Jon Ossoff in Georgia's January 2021 runoff election. Together with Kamala Harris, who assumed the vice presidency, giving her the tiebreaking vote in the Senate, Alex Padilla and his new colleagues were sworn in on the Senate floor at the same time. The sight of a new Latino, a new Black, and a new Jewish member—all firsts for their states—entering the US Senate simultaneously, sworn in by the country's first Black, Asian, and woman vice president, captured and immortalized the significance of the 2020 presidential election—and that was not all.

Back in 2017, having been attorney general of the largest state, Kamala Harris was granted an exceedingly rare opportunity as a first-year rookie to become California's *second* member of the Senate Judiciary Committee, along with Dianne Feinstein.[7] The high-profile committee afforded Harris a national platform during confirmation hearings of Trump's Supreme Court nominees. She tried to capitalize on the recognition she had won through those hearings to launch her presidential campaign in 2019, but that effort did not make it to the 2020 primaries. The two experiences together, however, earned her Biden's historic invitation to be his running mate. Thus, on January 20, 2021, the path of political ascent that Harris had blazed appeared to be an especially promising one for Alex Padilla to follow. Vice President Harris swore in Alex as her successor in the Senate shortly after the Biden–Harris inauguration on the west front of the Capitol. Although Padilla was trained as an engineer, not as a lawyer, he was allowed to succeed Harris on Judiciary, also as a freshman. Notable as well was Padilla's later election by his fellow Democrats to the position of ranking member of the Rules Committee. That position put Padilla, in a sense, on par with Mitch McConnell, the committee's chair, and a notch above his fellow Democrat Charles Schumer—both former Senate majority leaders.

The ongoing nature and national import of California Latina/o political empowerment appeared to be accelerating at the start of the Biden–Harris administration, as if the success of the resistance had given the empowerment project continuing momentum. This was again made vivid a month after the inauguration, when Senator Padilla had the privilege of introducing his friend and colleague Xavier Becerra at the latter's confirmation hearing for secretary of health and human services. They are the first Latinos to ever serve in these positions and have much in common. That they had both been legislators who represented LA districts in Sacramento and Washington, and then simultaneously served as statewide California elected officials, overshadowed another commonality, too minor and local to be noticed: Neither of them were products of LA's Eastside, where sustained California Latino empowerment was born. This detail became more apparent with other empowerment advances in 2022 and 2023. At the start of 2023, Representative Pete Aguilar of Redlands, east of Los Angeles in Southern California's citrus belt, was sworn in as chair of the Democratic Caucus of the House of Representatives—a position previously held by Xavier Becerra—making Aguilar the highest-ranking Latino in his chamber of Congress. The following summer, state Assembly Member Robert Rivas of Salinas succeeded Speaker Anthony Rendon of metropolitan LA.

Time was when an aspiring Latino Speaker of the state Assembly had to come from, or have the blessing of, Eastside LA leaders. The same pattern applied to appointed positions at either the state or federal levels. Back in the 1970s, President Jimmy Carter nominated as US ambassadors graduates of the Eastside's principal, rival high schools—Esteban Torres of East LA's Garfield High to represent the US in Paris before UNESCO, and Julian Nava of Roosevelt High in Boyle Heights as ambassador to Mexico.[8] Those unprecedented appointments reflected the clout of Eastside Latino leaders and the influence they had in presidential elections.[9] As mentioned before, LA Latina/o leaders did not lack for influence in the Biden–Harris campaign, but none of the trio of Garcetti, Rayes, and Telles, also named ambassadors, were products of the Eastside, nor were cabinet appointees Mayorkas, Becerra, or Isabella Guzman.

The great breakthrough appointment of this era for California Latinas/os was Judge Patricia Guerrero, nominated by Governor Newsom in 2022 to be chief justice of the state Supreme Court. She was the first Latina ever on that court, and just earlier the same year, the first Latina named to the state appeals court. Guerrero is a product of the Imperial Valley, over two hundred miles southeast of LA, and received all her higher education in the San Francisco Bay Area. On the state Supreme Court she succeeded another product of the Imperial Valley, Jerry Brown appointee Mariano-Florentino Cuéllar, who pursued his higher education in Ivy League schools and at Stanford. In Guerrero's case, at least, Newsom was explicit about naming a justice from the Imperial Valley, consonant with his broader emphasis on state government's engagement with all of California's thirteen regions.[10]

Chief Justice Patricia Guerrero delivering the 2025 State of the Judiciary address to the California legislature. Copyright California Courts.

These trends in California Latinas/os holding elected and appointed offices, at both the state and federal levels, are more meaningful taken together with the much-discussed trend of increased Latino voting for Trump in the elections of 2016, 2020, and 2024. As this and our previous book have shown, generations of activists, leaders, and voters were faithful to the progressive political culture forged in Boyle Heights in the post-Depression, post–World War II, Latino "Greatest Generation" era, which was exported around the state by Community Service Organization (CSO) as it built a Latino electorate through the 1960s. Both CSO founder Ed Roybal and Cesar Chavez, who later became its staff director, grew somewhat disenchanted with scrupulously nonpartisan CSO. They started new organizations—the Mexican American Political Association (MAPA) and the United Farm Workers (UFW)—that revived a more idealistic and fighting spirit in the empowerment project; they were joined in the late 1960s by the more militant Chicano student movement. Other influences like urban organized labor and immigrant-rights activism also helped maintain and reenergize Latino progressivism into the new century. But with the benefit of hindsight, it seems inevitable that the spread of Latino empowerment into areas unlike and far from LA's highly urban and politicized Eastside would eventually develop independent leaders and viewpoints.

That the expansion of the Latina/o-empowerment project beyond Eastside LA has affected the project's political culture and ideological inclinations can be seen in some concrete historical steps. Among the most successful Latino elected officials not from the core of the Eastside are Senator Padilla and former Assembly Speaker Anthony Rendon. As related in chapter 8, Padilla played a major role in the 1998 midterm electoral cycle, before running for office himself. He and his political partner, Tony Cárdenas helped Dean Florez first get elected that year in the San Joaquin Valley district he was originally from. Padilla and Cárdenas, of the San Fernando Valley, were intentionally building an alternative LA Latino power base to that of then-Speaker Antonio Villaraigosa of the Eastside, who was reluctant to support Florez. While Florez learned everything he knew about politics from his time in LA and working for Eastside heavyweight Art Torres in Sacramento, to attain and retain office he clearly positioned himself as a politically moderate Central Valley homeboy.

Similarly, Anthony Rendon of the Southeast Cities was from metropolitan LA, but not the core of Eastside. He moved to the "Inland Empire" for his doctoral program at UC Riverside. In the 1998 election, Padilla headed the statewide coordinated Democratic field campaign, with gubernatorial candidate Gray Davis at the top of the ticket. When Pete Aguilar, still in college at the University of Redlands, joined that field effort in the San Bernardino area, he was paired with Rendon. The three, Padilla, Rendon, and Aguilar, became and have remained close friends and political allies ever since. Aguilar eventually sought nonpartisan local office in Redlands as an authentic local centrist, albeit labor friendly. Local leaders, such as Florez in the Central Valley and Aguilar in the Inland Empire, are Latino Democrats, but not Eastside LA–barrio Democrats. Their positioning, discourse, campaigns, and advocacy gave Latino voters in their districts somewhat different signals and messages from what their counterparts experienced in Eastside LA.

Under the circumstances, given years of wrenching developments at the national level in this century since 9/11, it is not particularly surprising that some proportion of new voters and infrequent voters—including Latinos, and especially those away from big-city barrios—could be drawn to even a radically different type of populist leader such as Trump, who went out of his way to appeal to traditionally Democratic voters.[11] That difficult twenty-first century experiences fostered many Latinos' attraction to populist outsider candidates was also manifested in the 2020 Democratic primaries—in which Bernie Sanders beat Biden among Latino voters in every state, including in conservative rural counties that Trump later won in November. But, however diminished, there would still be Latinos and others determined to resist a second Trump presidency, especially as the new administration attempted to roll back progressive advances on a wide range of fronts.

Resistance State, Round 2, and the Firestorm in LA

Upon Trump's reelection in November 2024, Governor Gavin Newsom and his hand-picked attorney general, Rob Bonta, flew into action, indicating a heightened level of preparation and commitment to resist, born of the experience and standard set by the state and its Latino leaders during the first Trump presidency. Newsom had nominated Bonta, an immigrant Filipino American member of the state Assembly, to succeed Xavier Becerra as AG when the latter returned to Washington to join the Biden cabinet in 2021. Now Newsom called on the state legislature to convene in special session in December, when it would gather for its members' inauguration, to authorize emergency appropriations for AG Bonta's defense of the state's interests against the incoming federal administration, and to bolster legal assistance to the state's undocumented residents. By contrast, in 2016 then-Governor Jerry Brown had struck a moderate tone—other than his nomination of Becerra as AG—in response to Trump's first election.[12]

Bonta and his department had been preparing for a potential Trump comeback for months, and for years regarding the potential threat of a federal law limiting abortion rights.[13] Bonta's frequent references to his parents' activism in the farmworkers' movement spoke to how the Latino-empowerment experience continued to inform the state's political culture well into the new century.[14] He bluntly warned local law enforcement not to violate state law by assisting federal immigration authorities to detain and deport the state's undocumented residents, and pledged to defend officers against administration pressures and threats of legal action. The legislature, however, proceeded cautiously, particularly the Assembly, led by Speaker Robert Rivas. True to the commitments he made to win the votes he needed to become Speaker, Rivas stressed what he saw as the need to consult patiently with all his chamber's members, in contrast to the more authoritative leadership styles of past LA Latino Speakers.[15] As a result, the legislators failed to approve the funds Newsom sought for the state's legal defense before adjourning for the holidays. When they reconvened in January 2025, however, the world would suddenly change on them in unimagined ways.

On the second day of the new legislative session, January 7, 2025, the first and most destructive of an unprecedented cluster of wildfires broke out in the Pacific Palisades district of Los Angeles. Driven by intense winds, multiple fires quickly spread and led to mandatory evacuations that continued for weeks, involving hundreds of thousands of residents in various parts of the city and county. It soon became clear that the legislature would have to address the most destructive fire in US history, as well as defend California values against the new administration that was due to take power within a couple of weeks. Newsom had to return to the approach he used under similar circumstances during the first Trump administration—to make every effort to placate the president for the sake of obtaining the support the state needed following a major natural disaster. Trump, still only president-elect, took to beating up on the state, insulting the governor, propagating disinformation, and conditioning federal assistance on policy changes in California that bore no relation to the fires or public safety.

Fortunately for the state and LA, Newsom had experience navigating an emergency political and policy division of labor with his AG. Bonta would focus on defending California whenever possible against the designs of the new administration, while the governor managed his relationship with the threatening incoming president. Newsom ignored Trump's lies and insults while standing up an informational website on the fires, using his own campaign funds instead of state monies. He asked Trump to visit LA to see the vast destruction the fires had wrought, and although uninvited, Newsom met Trump at the airport as he came off

Air Force One. By late February, Newsom asked Congress for almost $40 billion to reconstruct destroyed areas of LA city and county.[16]

For his part, Bonta and some of his fellow Democratic AGs (D-AGs) from twenty-two other states and Washington, DC, had been preparing for a year, should Trump win the election, to take action as soon as he did anything they agreed to challenge in court. In November 2016, most D-AGs had been as shocked as the rest of the world by Trump's electoral upset. Xavier Becerra had not even been nominated to the position by then-Governor Brown until December and, all told, did not take office for over two and a half months after the election, pending his confirmation by the legislature. But neither was Trump ready to take over, nor did he have a team to prepare quick action for him to launch at the outset. In 2017, small ad hoc groups of state AGs prepared lawsuits in uncoordinated fashion, which left most work to be done by California's big department of over a thousand attorneys, supported by thousands more in staff. By September 2018, *The Washington Post* could report that the D-AGs had become "the muscle of the resistance," but there was still more they could do, should the need again arise.[17]

Back in 2002, California's then-AG, along with a couple of small states, founded the Democratic Attorneys General Association (DAGA). Over the decades, DAGA became a fully staffed professional advocacy operation, headquartered in Washington, that also worked to elect and reelect D-AGs across the country. The association was not used as a vehicle to coordinate lawsuits against the first Trump administration. In early 2024, however, concern began to mount that Trump just might pull off a comeback. By then, only one DAGA member remained who had been in office during Trump's first term, and at the association's annual meeting, he implored the other AGs to start preparing for a possible second, including securing extra funding to hire more lawyers. Bonta had already begun work along these lines since 2022, when the Supreme Court overturned the constitutional right to abortion, opening the door to a legislated national abortion ban. Several of his counterparts stepped forward to join in more comprehensive preparatory work, using the Heritage Foundation's Project 2025 as a blueprint of what was to come if Trump were reelected.[18]

By the summer, the AGs were meeting weekly online, readying briefs and litigation strategies for each potential issue, with all DAGA members participating. After the November election, the weekly meeting ramped up to daily, every afternoon. Through this work, they were poised to act, although they did not anticipate the torrent of executive orders Trump issued on Inauguration Day. On his first afternoon as president once again, among Trump's dictates was his order revoking birthright citizenship. Having to respond to the specifics cited in each order, the AGs worked all night to be able to collectively file their first lawsuit against the administration the following morning, to prevent the order from taking effect.[19] Many more lawsuits were in the works. The terms of the conflict between California and the Trump administration were set in the first twenty-four hours of the four challenging years to come, but this time both the state's arguments and its allies were fired up and ready to go.

Epilogue
After the Transition

When Pete Aguilar nominated Hakeem Jeffries to be Speaker of the US House of Representatives *fifteen times* over four days and nights during the first week of January 2023, the new Republican majority there was in disarray. They won control of the chamber in the previous fall's midterm elections, but their predicted "red wave" failed to materialize, leaving them both divided and with just a precarious nine-vote margin.[1] Courtesy of Donald Trump, US national politics had been on a seven-year roller-coaster ride with no end in sight, the twists and turns to come scarcely imaginable. Disorder in the House of Representatives had much to do with the disgraced ex-president's announced bid to stage a comeback. No one could have guessed that a couple of years hence, the country would again find itself in much the same situation as at the start of Trump's first term—being led by a historically unpopular president with an extremist agenda, but who by then would openly claim, "I run the country and the world."[2]

Twice impeached, but not yet criminally indicted that January, Trump had still not fully recovered from the scandal of his efforts in 2020–21 to illegally stay in power, which precipitated his second impeachment. The ex-president favored Kevin McCarthy, leader of the House Republicans since 2019, for Speaker, but neither man had control of all their party's representatives. McCarthy had to make unprecedented concessions to extremists in his conference, including the politically fatal one of a rule that would allow a single member to trigger a vote to depose him—a trigger pulled nine months later.[3]

The renewed Republican chaos in October put House Democrats—especially Aguilar—in a fighting mood, judging from their response to his then sixteenth and seventeenth speeches again nominating Jeffries. Far-right Representative Jim Jordan was at that time the top radical trying to replace McCarthy. Aguilar's latest speeches—described by news media as "fiery" and "amazing"—addressed Jordan's nomination directly. He pointed out that in the Republican's sixteen years in the House, Jordan had failed to introduce a single bill that had a chance of becoming law.[4] Aguilar subtly linked Jordan to the far right's political project dating to Newt Gingrich's 1994 "Contract with America," and more openly to Trump's by-then-ninety-one criminal indictments: "If the goal is to continue a thirty-year march to hollow out our democratic institutions, weaken our democracy, and embolden extremists, there's a candidate for you. If the goal is to continue taking marching orders from a twice-impeached former president with more than ninety pending felony charges, then there is a candidate for you."[5]

Aguilar's Democratic colleagues responded with raucous standing ovations, none more spirited than by Speaker Emeritus Nancy Pelosi, leader of Aguilar's home-state delegation. Pete was just the third Latino to reach the position of Democratic Caucus chair—all three under Pelosi's leadership.[6] As minority leader when Trump was first elected, Pelosi found a worthy successor to Xavier Becerra in the young Pete Aguilar—a Southern California Latino with the potential to go all the way in House leadership. Becerra, then Democratic Caucus chair and former assistant to the leader, left the House in 2017 to take Kamala Harris's place as California attorney general, when Harris joined the Senate. Six years later, *Politico* reported that Pelosi was "thrilled" by Aguilar's rise to caucus chair and "eager to discuss his ascent."[7] She had supported him since his first, unsuccessful run for Congress in 2012, helped him get on the all-important Appropriations Committee in 2019, and named him to the Select Committee on the January 6 Attack, which she formed and funded in 2022. Her confidence in Jeffries and Aguilar was underscored by her decision later that year to step down in January as the House Democrats' most accomplished leader, making room for Jeffries to become minority leader, and Aguilar caucus chair, of the 118th Congress.

To be sure, the rise of Pete Aguilar of Redlands exemplified the expansion of the California Latina/o political-empowerment project beyond LA, but in our current national circumstances it has come to mean much more. Aguilar's ascent also positioned him to play a national role in what had seemed to be the post-Trump era, in part defending Latino progress against what remained of the Trump-led backlash. But now it means more than that as well. That much also applies within California to Speaker Robert Rivas of Salinas, who was elected to the state Assembly four years after Aguilar was elected to Congress. Although Trump had announced his candidacy and was building his third campaign when Aguilar gave the first of his many speeches nominating Jeffries, he was not then widely expected to win reelection—especially not as his many indictments would be revealed and he faced the prospect of spending much of 2024 in court. But win he did, and in so doing redefined the current phase of US political history. Trump's return thrust Aguilar further into a prominent national role, not only in defense of Latino progress, but indeed in defense of American democracy against a threat never before seen or imagined. The strength and resilience of the Latino-empowerment project in battling this backlash—with new leaders like Pete Aguilar at the fore—has become one of the factors that could determine no less than the survival and quality of democracy in America.

How We Got Here

The Pelosi–Aguilar alliance was partly based on the recognition by Northern California's top Democratic leaders' that the state's resistance to Trump and his movement required a prominent role for Southern California Latino leaders. This was evident in Jerry Brown's nomination of Xavier Becerra to become the state's first Latino attorney general, and Gavin Newsom's appointment of Alex Padilla as California's first Latino US senator. Political continuity from Becerra to Padilla to Aguilar both revealed and concealed important features of the state's Latino politics. On one hand, the disposition of this trio to vigorously resist the Trump-led backlash was deeply rooted, reaching all the way back to the start of the state's Latina/o political empowerment on the Eastside of Los

Angeles. Aguilar, the youngster of the three, was a successor to Becerra as a Latino Democratic caucus chair. Becerra, in turn, was a direct successor to Ed Roybal, of LA's Boyle Heights, the first of California's Latino members of Congress. Becerra, as well, had been given a boost by Nancy Pelosi, who appointed him assistant to the Speaker, before he ascended to caucus vice chair and then chair. In the 1990s, Xavier had also headed the Congressional Hispanic Caucus (CHC) founded by Roybal in the 1970s. For his part, when Aguilar entered Congress in 2015, he immediately saw the CHC as *familia,* his family on Capitol Hill, and chose to serve as its vice chair in his freshman term.[8]

San Francisco Chronicle

SFCHRONICLE.COM | Wednesday, December 23, 2020 | CONTAINS RECYCLED PAPER | $2.00 ★★★★★•

Historic pick for Senate

New senator: Secretary of state has blazed trails in politics for 20 years

By Alexei Koseff

SACRAMENTO — When he heads to Congress as California's newest senator, it will be a full-circle moment for Secretary of State Alex Padilla. After launching his career as an aide to Sen. Dianne Feinstein, the Los Angeles Democrat will now serve alongside the woman who gave him his first job in politics.

Padilla has risen steadily through local and state elected office in the two decades since then, frequently breaking new political ground. He made history Tuesday when Gov. Gavin Newsom appointed him to fill the seat being vacated by Vice President-elect Kamala Harris. Padilla

Padilla continues on A10

Russell Yip / The Chronicle 2015

California Secretary of State Alex Padilla was chosen to fill the U.S. Senate seat of Vice President-elect Kamala Harris.

Congress: Padilla will be first Latino to represent state in upper chamber

By Alexei Koseff

SACRAMENTO — Alex Padilla, the son of Mexican immigrants who rose over two decades in politics to become California secretary of state, will be the first Latino to represent the state in the U.S. Senate.

Gov. Gavin Newsom appointed Padilla, 47, a Democrat from Los Angeles and a longtime political ally, on Tuesday to fill the Senate seat being vacated by Vice President-elect Kamala Harris. It is a historic choice in a state where Latinos now make up the larg-

Senate continues on A10

» **Replacement:** Governor taps Black assemblywoman for secretary of state. **A11**

San Francisco Chronicle *front page with photograph of Alex Padilla under banner headline, "Historic Pick for Senate," December 23, 2020. Photo by Russell Yip/*San Francisco Chronicle*, 2015.*

Alex Padilla, who bonded with Aguilar in the 1998 California Coordinated Campaign election field effort, had served as president of the other, lasting, and much bigger political organization Roybal founded in the '70s, the National Association of Latino Elected and Appointed Officials (NALEO), headquartered in LA. The statewide '98 field campaign, directed by Padilla, paired Pete with then–graduate student Anthony Rendon, who was pursuing his doctorate in political theory at nearby UC Riverside. This duty was Pete's first direct step, while still in college, toward a career in politics and government, which won him an appointed state job in 2001.[9] In 2009, when Aguilar was the youngest of Redlands' nonpartisan, five-member city council and aspired to be voted mayor by his colleagues, then–State Senator Padilla called with an important ask: that Pete endorse San Francisco Mayor Gavin Newsom for Governor.[10] Pete reacted gingerly, saying, "Look, I just got on a pretty conservative city council, and Gavin's a pretty liberal mayor, right?" Newsom was then the partisan Democratic head of the country's most progressive city, and at that time best known for having directed his city clerk to defy state law and issue marriage licenses to same-sex couples. The mayor himself famously officiated over the first of those marriages in City Hall. He also marched in picket lines with workers on strike against San Francisco's most famous hotels. After some consideration, Aguilar concluded that "you roll with your friends in this world," granted his endorsement, and hosted a "meet and greet" for the Northern Californian he himself had yet to meet. Over a decade after they worked together in 1998, Pete, Alex, and Anthony kept in frequent contact with an ongoing text-message chain.

Aguilar's passing hesitation over endorsing Newsom was indicative of the different political reality he faced as an elected official in the Inland Empire, well to the east of the LA megalopolis, where Alex and Anthony were from, and a world away from what was then even more lefty San Francisco. Years later, this aspect of his identity was submerged in Washington as a result of being lumped together with all the other California Latinas and Latinos in Congress, most of whom represented metro Los Angeles. That Aguilar, a non-Angeleno, rose to chair the whole House Democratic Caucus, and was taking big steps to succeed Pelosi as leader of the California delegation, was a major development. He created the California House Majority Fund, his own vehicle to help finance candidates to flip districts in his state from red to blue—just what Pelosi had helped him pull off a dozen years earlier in his own Republican district.[11] Aguilar became caucus chair when he was over a decade younger than Becerra had been, and in half the time, greatly enhancing his prospects of eventually reaching the speakership. In 2023–24, however, when Pete Aguilar debuted on national TV in the January 6 committee hearings, was voted caucus chair, and nominated Jeffries for Speaker, he and his colleagues assumed this was all happening in a post-Trump political era.

But because of the 2024 election, it turned out to be smack in the middle of an unexpectedly extended and intensified Trump backlash, as well as the resistance to it. History had rushed Pete into an unimagined new role.

New Era, New Resistance, New Competition

Within weeks of the formal start of the second Trump presidency, the course of Latino political development was already in a new era, although it would be hard to pin down exactly when it began. The new administration kicked off with a storm of draconian executive actions that had been in preparation for years and left no time to sort out just when or how it was that the major elements of this new death match kicked in; but at least several could be identified. From the start, the second Trump term was far more radical and staffed with more unquestioning loyalists than the first; the new regime also came to power with greater support than before and succeeded in enhancing political divisions among Latinos and other groups; the steady geographical expansion and diversification of California Latino empowerment had installed new, top-tier political leadership no longer beholden to LA's Eastside; and an entirely different and opposed Latino political project was an emerging part of the new regime.

Much of the power of the new administration, compared to 2017, was the dramatically altered balance of energy between it and its opposition. The new Trump regime's frenetic pace served as "shock and awe" to both suppress resistance and intimidate the main constraint on its power, which in the absence of any congressional check would have to be the courts. The administration deliberately stoked fear that it could at any time precipitate a constitutional crisis by defying a court order—which it bet that judges, and most of all the Supreme Court, would try hard to avoid. But as we saw in the last chapter, California's official legal dimension of the resistance was thoroughly reorganized and ready for a second Trump term. Rob Bonta, Xavier Becerra's successor as California attorney general, was fortified not only by Becerra's example and legacy in fighting the first Trump administration, and the big and supremely experienced staff at his disposal the day he took over, but by November

2024 he also had the collective strength of twenty-two other state AGs from across the country, with whom he started meeting online every afternoon to coordinate Democratic states' legal response to moves the administration made that could be challenged in court. This well-resourced company of legal talent was in no way intimidated by either Trump's threats or his lawyers.[12]

By 2025, another layer of committed resistance on the ground in California was asserting itself more robustly than anything seen in 2017. Back then, two Bay Area legal-services collaboratives, in response to the first Trump administration, merged to grow their reach in Northern and Central California. By 2025, however, the California Collaborative for Immigrant Justice had further widened the scope of its work to more comprehensively and directly combat detention and the Immigration and Customs Enforcement (ICE) agency itself, through advocacy, litigation, and empowerment of vulnerable immigrant communities. Furthermore, it had greatly developed its Rapid Response Network hotline, with over twenty local hubs providing emergency legal services, from Sonoma and Napa Counties in the north to San Diego in the south.[13] In San Diego and LA, some eighty organizations formed another coalition to provide similar support, with the added features of community patrols—especially around schools—on the lookout for ICE raids, and a series of street protests in downtown LA. Calling itself the Community Self Defense Coalition, this and other forms of resistance to the threat of mass deportations appeared to have deterred or delayed planned ICE operations in Chicago and LA, drawing criticism and threats of legal action from the Trump administration's "border czar" Tom Homan.[14]

The Rubio Factor

The most prominent aspect of an alternative, right-wing Latino political project allied with the regime was Trump's quick nomination of his Cuban American former opponent, Senator Marco Rubio, to be secretary of state—the top position in the cabinet—making him the highest-ranking Latino ever in US government. This appointment, unanimously confirmed by the Senate within hours of Trump's inauguration, made Rubio fourth in the line of succession to the presidency.[15] That he was taken seriously when he ran for the Republican nomination in 2016, was also seriously considered as Trump's potential running mate in 2024, and is from the key state of Florida, make Rubio a highly likely repeat candidate for president in 2028. Such a campaign would surely make a historic effort to draw Latino votes nationwide. Trump's indication that he does not consider Vice President J. D. Vance to be his successor boosted the expectation that Rubio will make another run, starting as soon as the 2026 midterm elections are over.[16] Throughout their early months in office, the two men appeared to be vigorously competing to win Trump's favor with relentless public flattery.

The prospect of a second Rubio candidacy was further fueled by exit polls indicating that Trump might have won as much as 46 percent of the Latino vote—considered by many analysts and commentators to have been key to his reelection in 2024—combined with continuing rapid growth of the Latino electorate. But several factors undermining the prospects of a potential second bid for the Republican nomination were also clear at the start of Rubio's turn as secretary of state. First, he was too consumed with trying to establish his authority in the diplomatic field, both within the Trump regime and internationally, to devote time to begin cultivating either a Latino or non-Latino domestic base of support outside of Florida. His early internal difficulties were reflected in his reported open clash with Elon Musk, who undercut Rubio's ability to accomplish anything in the world by crippling US foreign aid and closing US embassies and consulates.[17] These challenges were exacerbated early in Rubio's tenure by the multiplication of his responsibilities due to disorder within the administration, combined with his unbridled eagerness to please Trump. This conjuncture led to his being named interim director of the US Agency for International Development, National Security Advisor, and even interim director of the National Archives.[18]

Furthermore, Rubio was burdened with Trump's many provocative foreign policy pronouncements and actions, which produced conflicts with formal US allies, crowned by utter chaos in US trade policies toward virtually the whole world. Concerning any intention of Rubio's to specifically appeal to Latino voters in a future presidential campaign, Trump roiled those prospects with offensively aggressive statements about Latin American countries—such as in relation to the Panama Canal, Mexico, and Colombia—which Rubio had no sway over, or even advance knowledge of in some cases. The mounting evidence that Rubio was not remotely leading in foreign policymaking and had to awkwardly reverse himself on a range of critical positions, most notoriously in relation to Russia and its war of conquest in Ukraine, was most problematic of all.[19] Musk was a problem for him on this front, as well, given his direct involvement with Ukraine since at least 2022.[20] With both Trump and Musk given to making international deals—and threats—on the fly, world leaders and diplomats had little reason to think the nominal US secretary of state reliably spoke for his government.[21] It must have come as no little relief to Marco when Musk was pushed out of the administration by June.

Another certain source of problems for Rubio, should he attempt to run again, concerns the administration's many sweeping, legally challenged, and even brutal moves on immigration enforcement. Under pressure from Trump to create the impression of great progress on his promise to carryout mass deportations, Rubio turned to revoking international student visas *en masse*, in many cases using absurd pretexts and alarming police-state methods, and threatened to do the same to work-visa holders.[22] As a candidate, Rubio would have many administration actions and statements to answer for, in addition to his humiliating policy reversals and the many ways he appeared to not have control of his own putative domain.

Resistance of the Ready and Willing

Overall, Latino resistance to Trump appeared slowed and diminished in the months following the 2024 election, but that condition was not entirely due to the result. The outcome was unexpected but followed a long period of waning enthusiasm for fighting Trump. Since 2017, President Biden, for all his historic legislative success, proved incapable of communicating effectively to the nation on any issue, and consequently spent most of his presidency "underwater" in the polls. As we noted in the preface to this book, there is significant evidence that Latino voters' trust in government, once impressively high, had collapsed well before the election, even months before the pivotal Biden–Trump debate in June 2024.[23]

Biden's late withdrawal from the race and the substitution of Kamala Harris sparked an astonishing surge of enthusiasm but proved insufficient to repeat the record-setting, election-winning turnout of 2020. Effective resistance to a Trump comeback called for new tools, strategies, and reorganization. We have seen how at least one part of this was already in place—the new generation of leadership in the House, as well as in the California Assembly—with more on the way in the 2026 elections. Jeffries and Aguilar, having taken charge of the Democratic opposition in the House in 2023, did not have enough time to win back their chamber's majority in 2024, but were hankering to have another go in 2026—especially in their respective states of New York and California. Their work started immediately.

Other relevant developments were either in place or falling into it. Aguilar's effort to flip five Republican seats in California was complemented by the state Federation of Labor, headed by Lorena Gonzalez, which focused on the same five seats. Together, they managed to help flip three. An incremental but major change on the Senate side was the election of Ruben Gallego in Arizona, in spite of Trump's backflipping the state at the presidential level. This completed another sort of "California corner"—of Latina/o senators, including Padilla, Catherine Cortez-Masto of Nevada, and Ben Ray Luján of New Mexico. Cortez-Masto, Padilla, and Luján were each practiced in helping elect candidates in states other than their own.[24]

Another reorganization in the Latino political power network was the return of Cristóbal Alex to Latino Victory (LV). Alex had been LV's first president and CEO until he left to join the Biden campaign in 2020, when Nathalie Rayes succeeded him. Following the November 2024 setback, Alex returned to chair LV's board, simultaneously with the appointment of a new CEO. Work on the 2026 midterms was underway before the holidays. On the metropolitan level, Monica Lozano led the creation of the L.A. Local News Initiative, a consortium announced in September 2024 and launched in 2025.[25] From the viewpoint of the resistance to Trump, the need for this initiative was dramatized by the accelerating decline of the *Los Angeles Times* since it had been acquired in 2018 by billionaire doctor and Trump friend Pat Soon-Shiong. The year before Soon-Shiong's purchase of the *Times*, it had published a six-part series of front-page editorials titled "Our Dishonest President," which dissected, in addition to Trump's dishonesty, his authoritarianism, war on journalism, and penchant for conspiracy theories.[26] During the fall 2024 campaign, however, Soon-Shiong ordered a massive round of editorial staff layoffs, vetoed the paper's endorsement of Kamala Harris, and brought CNN's top Trump apologist, commentator Scott Jennings, onto its editorial board. The editor of the paper's editorial pages resigned over the editorial board's spiked Harris endorsement, and thousands of readers canceled subscriptions.[27]

The "California Corner" of Latina/o US senators.

In addition to the above acts of positioning and repositioning for the four years of Trump's second term, as well as for the midterm elections of 2026, what remained to be seen was what effect Trump's radical form of rule, and growing resistance to it, would have on the Latino community, its leadership, the open 2026 California gubernatorial race, and the unfinished business of Latino empowerment. According to one poll at the 100-day mark, Trump may have completely lost the gains he had made among Latinos since his first election in 2016.[28] Just as the White House opened a week of celebrations of those first 100 days, it was hit by a raft of polls also showing Trump had fully squandered the majority support he enjoyed in January for the first time since having entered politics. Indeed, more than one poll showed Trump had the lowest approval rating ever recorded for a president at that point in a term, going back eighty years.[29] The next day, Trump's own Commerce Department had to report that after thirty-three previous quarters of steady growth, the US economy shrank in Trump's first quarter.[30]

A major poll of Latinos released two weeks later did not confirm the across-the-board collapse of Latino approval of Trump, but the poll's "internals" revealed a strategically critical loss of support among young Latino men. Latino men aged eighteen to thirty-four had been Trump's best and most targeted demographic in 2024, which voted for him by a near-landslide eleven-point margin (54–43). By late April, overall support for Trump among these voters had reversed to an eleven-point deficit (44–55), and an even worse seventeen-point deficit on his handling of the economy.[31]

Trump's first 100 days and beyond were an unprecedented experiment in aggressively expanding presidential power and rule by decree; a test of public support for or tolerance of efforts to dismantle and contract whole sections of government; and a drive to ideologically purge and remake education at all levels. Of most relevance to us here is the test of the value voters place on democratic government in principle. The most fundamental premise of the project of Latina/o political empowerment is that civic inclusion, participation, representation, and a voice in and influence on the making of public policy are indispensable. In this view, the opposite conditions of exclusion, invisibility, and voicelessness are debilitating and unacceptable.

The 2026 elections in California promise to offer several specific tests of the political impact of the second Trump term and the role of Latinos in the fight over the country's direction. In the first instance, there is the usual midterm referendum on the administration in power, in the form of the contest for control of Congress. Would Pete Aguilar as chair of the House Democratic Caucus, and Lorena Gonzalez in command of the California Labor Federation, succeed in helping flip more Republican-held seats, in addition to the three flipped in 2024? Would doing so overturn Republican control of the House, as happened in 2018? Would Speaker Robert Rivas retain his supermajority in the state Assembly?

The governor's race is shaping up to be especially complicated, historic, and commanding of national attention. By the spring of 2025, at the time of this writing, the contest had already attracted over a dozen announced candidates—including three Latinos—while several other statewide races still had none.[32] Two aspects are of particular import from a Latino perspective—a rematch between Antonio Villaraigosa and Xavier Becerra a quarter century after they competed in an open contest for mayor of Los Angeles, and the prospect that Kamala Harris might also enter the race. As in the 2001 LA mayoral cycle, Becerra did not announce his candidacy until well after Villaraigosa had launched his campaign. Once again, these two men are politically and ideologically much alike. That they and Harris were all part of a Democratic California consensus across most policy issues—a.k.a., "California values"—combined with the congressional midterms referendum on the Trump administration, make it highly likely that the contest will be dominated by the question of who could better lead the state's renewed resistance during the final years of the second Trump term and whatever might follow.

The second Trump presidency, with its shockingly aggressive approach to US allies and neighbors in the world, also has the potential of provoking a new front of Latino, and specifically Mexican American, resistance paired with pressure for inclusion. Foreign policy is historically and inherently an elite political domain, one that Mexican Americans as a community have never specifically organized themselves to influence on a sustained basis.[33] But there are indications that, independently of Trump's undiplomatic provocations, the will, capacity, and opportunity of Mexican Americans to participate in foreign affairs have developed substantially over the past decade. As noted in chapter 13, Biden named a trio of LA Latinas and Latinos to US ambassadorships in Asia, Latin America, and Europe.[34] Among these, Ambassador Nathalie Rayes, following her service in Croatia, undertook in 2025 to fashion a comprehensive and ongoing Mexican American initiative in support of defending and strengthening the bilateral US relationship with Mexico.

Complementing the diplomatic experience and expertise Ambassador Rayes brings to this initiative is, as noted earlier, the election of Latina/o senators in the four Southwestern corner states, three of which share a border with Mexico. The enhanced role the Senate plays in US foreign policy makes the current conjuncture an unprecedented opportunity for Latino/Mexican American engagement in US-Mexico relations. Among those already working with Rayes to develop this initiative were former Assembly Speaker Fabián Núñez and President and CEO of AltaMed Health Services Cástulo de la Rocha, both of whom are well known and highly regarded in Mexico.[35] Given Rayes's experience in diplomacy and in advancing Latino representation in elected and appointed office, combined with the unprecedented challenges to the bilateral relationship Trump and his team issued and threatened in their early months, this new initiative had the potential to develop into a major advance in Latina/o empowerment.[36]

Thus, as suggested at the start of this book, the aspirational world of Latina/o political empowerment today finds itself colliding with a contrary movement and national administration that is guided and supported by a hardened, cynical view of government, one that seeks to delegitimize and significantly dismantle it. Latino political development is irreconcilable with cynicism toward government and other prominent sectors, such as higher education, the professions, corporations, communications media, and cultural institutions, that Latinas and Latinos have struggled for generations to be included and visible in. The prospects of and for continued Latina/o political empowerment and development depend fundamentally on whether Latinas and Latinos accept or reject political cynicism and the current, ongoing assault on democratic government.

Postscript

Los Angeles, June 2025

AS WE PUT THIS BOOK into production, California and LA were struggling to recover control of not only their own public safety, but their narrative and identity as well. The Trump administration's promised mass deportations provoked spontaneous community pushback in San Diego on Friday, May 30, when dozens of Immigration and Customs Enforcement (ICE) agents raided a pair of Italian restaurants in the heart of that city, right before the dinner rush. Masked and armed agents in tactical gear closed the streets, surrounded each establishment, and handcuffed all employees before demanding their IDs.[1]

Neighbors and passers-by, noting the road blocked by large, unmarked vehicles in the street, began to gather and question the agents outside the restaurants. By the time ICE started pulling out several handcuffed workers and loading them into a van, the crowd had swelled and become increasingly angry, recording the operation on their cellphones and chanting "shame!" The agents called in backup armed with assault rifles, as if for a military-style "extraction" from hostile territory. They fired flashbang grenades into the thin crowd around them in the street and then fled the scene at high speed with their human prey. San Diego civic leaders, from the mayor on down, were outraged by the gratuitous display of force.[2] But perhaps more significantly, Los Angeles was bathed for days in press coverage and social-media umbrage that primed large sectors of its residents with fear and anger. A week later, the scene shifted to LA.

ICE began a weekend of Los Angeles-area raids at a garment factory and other locations the next Friday, June 6—the anniversary of World War II's D-Day. The operations tripped the alarms of both the organized immigrant-defense networks and general social-media subcommunities, dramatically heightening local wariness and readiness, and producing a large gathering of protestors at the downtown LA Federal Building and its adjacent Metropolitan Detention Center.[3] ICE launched another major raid the next day—a Saturday, when most residents were off work—at a Home Depot in the overwhelmingly Latino Southeast city of Paramount. Reports of the ICE presence drew nearby residents and activists to the scene, including provocateurs out to take advantage of the organized rapid-response protest. As the ICE agents loaded both store clerks and customers into vans, the confrontation with neighbors and activists became increasingly aggressive, before a long file of ICE vehicles fled at high speed, the last of which were pelted with rocks.[4]

That night the White House, with Trump reportedly monitoring cable TV coverage, ordered thousands of National Guard troops and active-duty Marines to LA to back up more mass-deportation raids and inhibit protests against them.[5] US Representative and Chair of the Congressional Hispanic Caucus Nanette Barragán, whose Forty-fourth Congressional District includes Paramount, became a ubiquitous presence on news programs explaining the community's view on the raids, the deportation campaign, and local protests.[6] The Home Depot operation intensified the weekend of extended and proliferating confrontations between authorities and protesters, both there and in downtown LA, that continued through the following Monday night. By all appearances, a proverbial long, hot summer was underway.

Just a half-month earlier, the acknowledged architect of Trump's mass deportations, Deputy Chief of Staff Stephen Miller—himself from Santa Monica, on metro LA's Westside—had berated fifty senior ICE field commanders from across the country for reportedly pursuing known criminals. "What do you mean you're going after criminals? *Why aren't you at Home Depot?*" he demanded. Miller ordered another doubling of ICE's arrest rate to 3,000 people per day, so to reach the regime's goal of a million deportations in its first year.[7] During the 2024 campaign, Miller had repeatedly said his plan would employ federalized National Guard troops, and that the consent of governors, as historically required by law and practice, would not be needed.[8]

Come Monday, Governor Gavin Newsom and Attorney General Rob Bonta promptly announced the state's lawsuit against Trump and his Secretary of Defense Peter Hegseth for commandeering the California National Guard without a request from or coordination with the governor, compounded by their sending hundreds of active-duty Marines to LA. Even before the immigration-enforcement crisis erupted, however, CNN reported that the Trump administration was preparing to cancel federal funding for programs in California across the board, potentially starting the very day—D-Day—that the ICE workplace raids precipitated the first protest in Central LA.[9] It appears, then, that the Trump team had prepared not one but at least two strategies to initiate major conflict with California on that day. There was no report, however, that the budget cancellations were implemented, and Governor Newsom said later that he'd had a fully cooperative phone call with Trump late that night, Friday, informing him of the day's events, but the president showed no interest in discussing anything happening in LA and said nothing about the National Guard.[10]

Nevertheless, the next night, Saturday, the White House issued its presidential memorandum federalizing the Guard—without mention of any state or city—placing it at Hegseth's discretion for the purpose of "the protection of Department of Homeland Security Functions."[11] The memorandum further authorized deployment of both the Guard and active-duty armed forces anywhere that protests against those functions "are occurring or likely to occur based on current threat assessments and planned operations." On Sunday June 8, Trump said in response to a reporter's question, "We're going to have troops everywhere."[12]

That same afternoon, Jorge Ramos announced on social media that after a six-month absence from journalism since his retirement as nightly coanchor of Univision News, he was flying back to LA to report independently on the deepening crisis.[13] When Congress reconvened the following Tuesday, Representative Pete Aguilar used his time in an Appropriations Subcommittee hearing to question Hegseth on the deployment of troops to LA, precipitating a widely reported and heated exchange on national TV.[14] As the crisis unfolded, protests against ICE operations spread across the country, drawing worldwide attention.[15] At this early stage, at least, the widespread response to events in LA appeared to signal the birth of a new national movement reminiscent of the last year of Trump's first term, when Black Lives Matter surged in the wake of the police murder of George Floyd in Minneapolis.[16] And yet, the intensity of these events did not mean that Latino political development in California had entirely reverted, even for the time being, to again being mainly protest-driven and solely about resistance. Latinas and Latinos—in California, certainly—had advanced too far in their political development for that to be the case, and evidence of this was also at hand.

Over the same weekend, state Senator Monique Limón of Santa Barbara secured the votes among her Democratic colleagues to be elected on Monday, June 9, 2025, as the first Latina Senate president pro tempore in state history, a position held only once before by a Latino.[17] Her election was internal to the supermajority Senate Democratic Caucus, which made Limón pro tem-elect, with the actual succession to take place in 2026, as is the usual practice in the California legislature. Limón's ascent was notable on multiple levels. It meant that for the first time since 2018, both chambers of the legislature would again be led by a pair of Latinos at the same time. It furthermore confirmed what we have argued in this book—that California Latina/o political empowerment has transcended its twentieth-century origins in Los Angeles.

And yet, despite this landmark instance of California Latino political progress, ICE accelerated immigration raids that same day in the LA area, contributing to a night of intensified vandalism downtown, which moved Mayor Karen Bass to impose a curfew in a limited part of downtown for the following night. The drama not only continued but intensified further when three days later, DHS Secretary Kristi Noem staged a provocative press conference in the Wilshire Federal Building on LA's Westside. Noem declared, "We are staying here to liberate the city from the socialist and the burdensome leadership that this governor and this mayor have placed on this country." "Definitely fighting words," wrote the reputed "dean" of the state's Capitol press corps and senior LA *Times* political columnist, George Skelton.[18]

It so happened that Senator Alex Padilla was in a conference room down the hall, waiting for a scheduled briefing by military officials who were in the Noem presser. Padilla went to listen and had just entered the room when he heard Noem's rhetoric about increasing ICE's operations in Los Angeles to "liberate" it from its democratically elected leadership, rhetoric the *Times* called "right-wing lunacy" in the headline they gave to Skelton's column. Alex was standing at the back of the small room with a National Guardsman and FBI agent, who had escorted him from where he had been waiting. The senator took a step forward to ask a question, interrupting Noem's remarks, when he was immediately pushed back by someone appearing to be an ICE agent, and then also pulled from behind by another security guard. Padilla kept talking, still trying to ask his question and identifying himself, while being roughly jostled to the door and into the hallway. After being pushed a few steps down the hall, the men ordered him to kneel and then forced him face down on the floor to apply handcuffs. Multiple cellphone videos captured different angles of the incident, which were played repeatedly on news programs and widely shared on social media. The incident remained alive into the next week, as Senator Padilla's colleagues spoke out about it, and then Alex himself did so on news programs and in the Senate chamber.[19]

Alex Padilla's expulsion from the Noem press conference in LA came just days short of the tenth anniversary of Trump's announcement in New York City in 2015 that he was running for president—a declaration that stressed his intention of campaigning, and eventually governing, on the demonization of Mexican immigration in particular and in ridding the country of millions of undocumented immigrants. As such, the persistence of this theme, both rhetorically and practically, ensured that it would remain central to the definition of the Trump era in US politics and to our understanding of the role of backlash in Latino political development.

That this past decade has been so disturbingly bookended by the physical suppression of questioning by prominent Latino leaders—Jorge Ramos in 2015, Alex Padilla in 2025—evidenced the role of crude political theater in the politics of backlash and in its efforts to construct an authoritarian state. And yet, the elevation of a Latina to the top position in the California Senate precisely at the height of this turmoil can be read as indicative of broad support in the state's dominant party for combatting backlash with *both* resistance and inclusion. The elevation of Xavier Becerra to attorney general in 2016–17, Alex Padilla to US senator in 2021, Pete Aguilar to House Democratic Caucus chair in 2022–23, and now Monique Limón to California Senate pro tem in 2025–26, constitutes in no small measure a strategy of resistance by inclusion. The ensuing course of the unfinished journey of Latina/o political empowerment—on its own terms, with the approach of midterm and statewide elections in California and beyond, as well as in the context of the ongoing national struggle over the direction of the country—points to the need to always maintain and apply a balanced understanding and mastery of both the politics of inclusion and the politics of resistance.

Notes

Preface: Latino Politics in Transition

i. In using the identifier "Latino" in the title of this book, and often "Latina/o" in the text, we signal the dilemma between economy of expression and our strong desire for gender inclusivity. We had a compounded dilemma in titling our first book, which used both the terms "Latinos" and "America." While "Latinx" and "Latine" are increasingly used as gender-inclusive alternatives, they have yet to be widely accepted by the vast community that identifies as Latina or Latino. We respectfully ask readers to keep in mind both our dissatisfaction with inappropriately gendered and chauvinistic language, and the fact that these problems remain unresolved and troublesome in our society.

ii. From a national perspective and in historical order, the most significant independent communities of origin in the continental US (i.e., not counting Puerto Rico) include Albuquerque, San Antonio, Los Angeles, New York City, Miami, and Chicago. Highly significant empowerment experiences also developed in state capitals and Washington, DC, relatively independently of Latino communities in these cities and metropolitan areas.

iii. Villaraigosa, who in 2024 announced his second bid for governor, is the last remaining leader featured in *Power Shift* to have come out of LA's Eastside barrios.

iv. *Los Diez* ("The Ten"): Edward Roybal, 1916–2005; Esteban Torres, 1930–2022; Richard Alatorre, 1943–2024; Art Torres, 1946–; Gloria Molina, 1948–2023; Richard Polanco, 1951–; Miguel Contreras, 1952–2005; María Elena Durazo, 1953–; Antonio Villaraigosa, 1953–; and Gilbert Cedillo, 1954–.

v. The late Kenneth Burt titled his exhaustive history, to which we are indebted, *The Search for a Civic Voice: California Latino Politics.*

vi. The 1994 backlash and 1996 comeback, the Democratic recovery of control of the state Assembly, and election of the first of two consecutive Latino Speakers, are covered in chapters 7–8. The 1996 election arguably marked the beginning of the end of a significant role for the Republican Party in California politics.

vii. State leaders have invoked "California values" with increasing frequency in the Trump era. The state institutionalized this concept in law in 2017, in relation to immigration enforcement, with the California Values Act (SB 54), more widely known as the "sanctuary state" law. See "The California Values Act—SB 54 (de León)," California Immigrant Policy Center, December 1, 2021, https://caimmigrant.org/timeline/the-california-values-act-sb-54-de-leon/.

viii. Second and third generation in a political sense, not in terms of immigration and nativity. The "founding father," so to speak, of sustained California Latina/o political empowerment, Edward Roybal, counted the generations of his family in New Mexico back to the seventeenth century. See Ayón and Pla, *Power Shift*, 25–27.

ix. Brownstein, "Is Donald Trump Outflanking Hillary Clinton?" Ronald Brownstein memorably tagged the trio of Pennsylvania, Wisconsin, and Michigan as a "blue wall" that sustained Democratic presidential fortunes.

x. An alternative framing, which we believe cannot be justified at this time, would be to see a lifetime's worth of progressive Latino politics as now passing from the scene, conforming to the "life cycle" model commonly applied to social movements.

xi. "Landslide" is used here to refer to a win *significantly* over 50 percent—i.e., 55 percent of votes or better.

xii. Nichols, "If Less Than 115,000 Votes"; and Wasserman, "Key Takeaways." Trump won the core swing states of Pennsylvania, Wisconsin, and Michigan by a combined total margin of less than 230,000 votes, which means that a switch of as few as 115,000 votes could have reversed the result in the Electoral College.

xiii. Estimates of the Latino vote for Trump vary significantly, and major sources differ widely in methodology. See the widely available National Election Pool exit poll conducted by Edison Research, CNN, "Election 2024: Exit Polls" (46 percent for Trump); Lodhi et al., "AP VoteCast: How America Voted in 2024" (43 percent for Trump); and African American Research Collaborative and BSP Research, "2024 American Electorate Voter Poll" (37 percent for Trump).

xiv. Roper Center for Public Opinion Research, "US National Election Day Exit Polls"; and Bowman and Goldstein, *The Exit Polls*.

xv. As this book argues, major developments in California Latino political and policy priorities include the embrace of farmworker unionization in the 1960s–'70s, adoption of defense of undocumented immigrants in the 1970s–'80s, and the close alliance with urban organized labor in the 1980s–2000s.

xvi. Ayón and Pla, *Power Shift*, 280–81. We called this a "tradition," contrasting with Hofstadter's definition in *The American Political Tradition*. We use the term "progressive" to mean elements of what was associated in the twentieth century with the Progressive movement and later referred to as "liberal," not the recent appropriation of the term by those on the left who consider progressivism to mean blanket anti-corporate and anticapitalist "democratic socialism." "Latino progressivism" here refers to the politics of inclusive, sustained and sustainable, reformist sociopolitical progress advanced through activism, organizing, mobilization, and activist government by the leaders, initiatives, and legislation examined in this book.

xvii. Our use of "barrioization" departs from Camarillo's "barrioization thesis" in his *Chicanos in a Changing Society*.

xviii. The Latina/o pioneer leaders of *Los Diez* featured in *Power Shift* either moved away from LA's Eastside and later returned, or came to LA as adults. Edward Roybal and Esteban Torres moved as children to Boyle Heights with their families, subsequently moved out, and later moved back to the Eastside to run for office. Richard Alatorre and Art Torres, born in Boyle Heights, moved away and later also came back to the Greater Eastside for their political careers. Gloria Molina moved away from East LA with her family but later defied them and came back on her own to become an activist. Richard Polanco was born and raised in East LA and went away to college but came back to pursue his community-focused career. María Elena Durazo and Miguel Contreras, born and raised in the state's agricultural Central Valley, moved to LA as adults and became top labor leaders. Gilbert Cedillo and Antonio Villaraigosa were born and raised on the Eastside, attended UCLA on the Westside, returned, and eventually ran for office after careers in labor. Some leaders featured in this book have similar stories of Eastside LA community attachment.

xix. The aggregate national "shift" primarily reflected the absence in 2024 of millions who had voted in 2020, followed by new voters, and in third place, voters who switched parties. Equis Research refers to the last of these as "Biden defectors," i.e., those who voted Biden–Harris in 2020 but then flipped for Trump in 2024. Equis Research, "May 2025 Poll on Latinos, Trump and Immigration."

xx. Román and Vargas Poppe, *Latinos and the Great Recession*.

xxi. Notably, caravans of Central Americans, with increasing numbers of Cubans, Haitians, and eventually Venezuelans in large numbers, and others seemingly from all over the world.

xxii. Stimulus checks were also sent under Biden, but without his signature. After the election, he said that was a mistake. McCann Ramirez, "Biden Says He Regrets."

xxiii. Drawing on several sources, the Pew Research Center found a marked decline in Latinos' trust in government from a high during the Clinton presidency in the 1990s, nearing 60 percent, to 30 percent and lower under Biden; see "Public Trust in Government: 1958–2024." The Partnership for Public Service found a more concentrated and stunning collapse of Latino trust in government—the most among all measured racial and ethnic groups—during the Biden administration, from 45 percent to 23 percent; see "The State of Public

Trust in Government 2024." This finding, albeit using relatively small samples of minority groups, should have set off alarms among the whole Democratic political class in the spring of 2024, but passed unnoticed.

xxiv. Bernal, "Koch-Affiliated Libre Initiative;" and Danailova, "Latino Republicans, Empowered by Election."

xxv. President Biden appointed Dr. Cynthia Telles ambassador to Costa Rica, Nathalie Rayes ambassador to Croatia, and LA Mayor Eric Garcetti ambassador to India, as discussed in chapter 13.

Introduction: Worlds in Collision

1. Edward Roybal, featured in our first book, was the first Latino elected to significant office in twentieth-century California, to the LA City Council in 1949. He served there until elected to Congress in 1962, in which he served until 1993.
2. Speaker Emeritus Nancy Pelosi, herself a proud appropriator, considers Aguilar something of a policy soulmate for his appreciation of the significance of that role in Congress; see Martin, "This California Democrat Might Be the Future of the Party." Much of Roybal's reputation as a House member was due to his service and accomplishments as an appropriator, for which he was honored by having the campus of the Centers for Disease Control in Atlanta named after him.
3. Jeffries is the first person of color to head either party in the House, whether as Speaker or minority leader. Aguilar served on the Redlands City Council from 2006 to 2014. California Assembly Member Richard Alatorre, representing Los Angeles, was critical to electing Willie Brown, of San Francisco, the first Black Speaker in 1980. The Aguilar–Jeffries alliance recalls the Alatorre–Brown alliance, but it has not yet achieved control of the House. Brown ruled the California Assembly for a record dozen years. Nancy Pelosi is the only woman to have served as Speaker of the House of Representatives.
4. House Republicans were led at that time by Representative Kevin McCarthy of Bakersfield.
5. "AOC" upset Representative Joe Crowley in the 2018 New York primary elections, knocking him out not only of the House leadership but electoral politics altogether. The presence and roles of Latina/o members in the House leadership under Pelosi is striking. Crowley's predecessor as caucus chair was Xavier Becerra, who left Congress in 2017 to become California attorney general. Crowley's deputy or vice chair was Linda Sánchez, who represents a suburban district split between LA and Orange Counties. Jeffries moved up to caucus chair after Crowley, and Aguilar followed as vice chair.
6. President Biden preempted that threat by granting the entire committee an advance pardon.
7. A case could be made that Alejandro Mayorkas, secretary of Homeland Security under Biden, had the highest-ranking position of a Latino Democrat thus far. Republican Latinos have held higher positions: Alberto Gonzales as

attorney general under George W. Bush, and Marco Rubio as secretary of state under Trump.

8. We see the dominant trend of institutional Latino-empowerment efforts as a decentralized political movement or project, whose coherence can be captured with emphases on place, leadership, goals, and strategy. In this book, as in our first collaboration, we take a Los Angeles- and California-centric perspective, although the experiences recounted in both books extend significantly beyond, to Washington, DC, and other Southwestern states. A completely distinct Latina/o political empowerment movement is rooted in Miami and the state of Florida, protagonized by Cuban Americans and channeled through the Republican Party. For a brief, recent introduction, see Orta, *From Havana to DC*.
9. The partisan character of this movement is due to several factors, starting with the historically far greater openness of the Democratic Party to ethnic political organization and mobilization, the legacy of New Deal policies and politics, the role of organized labor, and even Democratic administrations' relations with Latin America. The tradition of Latinos registering as Democrats and voting primarily for Democratic candidates is comparable to the partisan nature of the dominant strains of both Jewish American and African American politics, but in all three cases, that partisan affiliation has become increasingly contested. On Latino Republicans nationally, see Cadava, *The Hispanic Republican*.
10. This aspect of the backlash is emphasized by the special role the issues of immigration and border control have played in the Trump movement, campaign, and presidencies, especially in the relentless and increasingly aggressive demand for mass deportations. Overall, however, this backlash is obviously also a reaction to the Barack Obama presidency, advances made by women and the LGBTQ+ community, and a variety of other changes wrought in the development of American-style modernity. Regarding women, see Rubin, *Resistance*.
11. Roper Center, "US National Election Day Exit Polls"; and Bowman and Goldstein, *The Exit Polls*.
12. This was often repeated in the broadcast coverage and podcast analyses of the 2024 election, as well as anticipated in articles such as Amezcua, "Chasing the 'Latino Vote.'"
13. Barreto and Segura, *Latino America*, 33.
14. Reagan appointed Cisneros, then-mayor of San Antonio, to the special "Kissinger Commission" on Central America.
15. Contrasting most of all with Mexico City, which has been the premier stronghold of Mexico's political left since at least the 1990s. Mexican migration to the US from Mexico City and other large urban areas was scant during the twentieth century, but it began increasing significantly with rising crime and drug-cartel violence in the twenty-first century.
16. Those of Mexican origin are by far the majority of the US Latino population, but the bulk of the rest has similar origins in Central America and the Caribbean.
17. Although many people of Mexican origin did settle in or near LA, it is in this that Mexican immigrants have historically differed significantly from those of

other Latin American countries, who predominantly settled within large cities such as New York, LA, Miami, and others. Here, by "immigrants" we refer to the first generation from Mexico and other countries of Latin America; "migrants" refers to those who migrated to California from other US states. Many of those of Mexican origin who settled in Los Angeles *County* did so outside of LA *city* limits, and indeed outside of any city, in farmworker labor *colonias,* when the county was agriculturally the most productive in the country. See Behrens, "Until the 1950s, Los Angeles County Was the Top Agricultural County."

18. California's *colonias* should not be confused with the more recent phenomenon, mainly in Texas, of *border colonias.* Although both started out as self-built shantytowns, typically outside city limits and lacking basic services, California's agricultural labor colonias began proliferating in the World War I era, from the Sacramento Valley in the north down to Orange County in Southern California. Texas border colonias began sprouting up in significant numbers in the late 1980s–'90s as a result of enhanced border enforcement, which impeded what had been daily informal border crossing by Mexican workers commuting to jobs on the US side.
19. Historian Stephen Pitti and demographer David Hayes-Bautista trace the birth of Latino politics in California to the mid-nineteenth century in different locations, but without continuity to the empowerment efforts that in the mid-twentieth century achieved ongoing representation in public office. See Pitti, *The Devil in Silicon Valley*; and Hayes-Bautista, *La Nueva California.* Kenneth Burt considered the historic First National Congress of the Mexican and Spanish American Peoples of the United States (a.k.a. *El Congreso*), convened in Los Angeles in 1939, to be "The Birth of California Latino Politics," and its California and national president, Eduardo Quevedo, to be the Latino-empowerment project's original pioneer. After an initial flurry of significant activity, however, that organization died in 1942, fifteen years before the founding of the Community Service Organization (CSO) in Boyle Heights. Quevedo ran repeatedly for office in the 1940s but was never elected. See Burt, *The Search for a Civic Voice*; and chap. 6 in García, *Mexican Americans.*
20. The exceptions include Sánchez, *Boyle Heights,* and Bernstein, *Bridges of Reform.* This movement evolved significantly over time, but its major modifications were also largely fashioned in LA, namely, the adoption of California farmworkers as a central cause, the shift to the defense of undocumented immigrants as an even higher priority, and the largely simultaneous development of a strategic alliance with organized labor. A California-centric treatment that examines each of these transitions in detail is Shaw, *Beyond the Fields.*
21. See chapter 5 of *Power Shift* on the long struggle to get the US census to include a complete count of the Hispanic/Latino population. This reform, in addition to a range of other policy, political, and business uses, was key to fashioning legislative districts that allow Latino voters to elect representatives of their own choosing. The first complete count in the 1980 census was used in the redistricting processes of 1981–82, and has been repeated every ten years since.

Furthermore, achieving this reform required an intense coalitional effort that brought together Latino leaders and organizations of diverse national origins to negotiate a shared ethnic identifier—“Hispanic”—and then promote participation in the census in their corresponding communities. We called the historic result of this exercise in the politics of inclusion “strategic rebranding,” as it fundamentally advanced Latino empowerment.

22. As discussed in chapter 2, “Bracero Program” is the informal but commonly used label for the Mexican Farm Labor Program of 1942–47 and its successors through 1964. In spite of its official name, during World War II the program admitted more temporary railroad workers from Mexico than farmworkers. Extensions of this guest-worker arrangement had other official names, and it eventually came to be known simply as Public Law 78.
23. Jordan, “Univision Gives Citizenship Drive Unusual Lift.”
24. Longoria has addressed each DNC since 2012, but her role in 2020 was particularly notable. That year Longoria opened and hosted the convention on its first night. Along with Henry Muñoz, Longoria cofounded the Latino Victory Fund (LVF) as a political action committee. The organization, now called Latino Victory (LV), currently encompasses three entities: Latino Victory Fund, the political arm; Latino Victory Project, focusing on leadership development and voter engagement; and Latino Victory Foundation, a 501(c)(3) that “engages in research, non-partisan civic engagement, strategic communications, and leadership development.” “About Us,” Latino Victory, accessed June 20, 2025, https://latinovictory.org/.
25. Schwarzenegger actually used the stage name Arnold Strong in his first film and a series of bodybuilding pamphlets. His campaign took on a backlash character when he pledged to overturn a Latino-backed bill, which Davis had signed into law but had not yet taken effect, that would have restored access to driver’s licenses to residents, regardless of their federal immigration status. The core elements and dynamics of the “strongman” as an authoritarian political leader are rigorously analyzed in Ben-Ghiat, *Strongmen*.
26. Ayón and Pla, *Power Shift*, 247–251.
27. The Republican bill (H.R. 4437, passed December 16, 2005), widely associated with its main sponsor, Representative James Sensenbrenner, was a product of furious right-wing opposition to President Bush’s efforts in both 2001 and 2005 in favor of comprehensive immigration reform.
28. Zepeda-Millán, *Latino Mass Mobilization*, 1–2.
29. In California’s Constitution, the lieutenant governor is the titular president of the state Senate, who, like the vice president in relation to the US Senate, has only rare ceremonial functions. The actual chief executive of the California Senate is elected by the senators from among their ranks, in the same manner as the Speaker of the Assembly. *Pro tempore* means “for a time,” and is written as “pro tempore” but commonly shortened to “pro tem.”

Chapter 1: Where to Begin

1. This is without counting the Broadway (1957) and movie (1961) productions of *West Side Story*. *In the Heights* premiered off Broadway in 2007, won the Tony Award for Best Musical in 2008, and toured the country the following year; the film version opened nationally in 2021. An exceptional guide to the two versions is Miranda, Alegría Hudes, and McCarter, *In the Heights*. That same year saw publication of the long-awaited history by Sánchez, *Boyle Heights*.
2. The colonia phenomenon is not limited to ethnic Mexican farmworkers, nor, depending on definition, to self-built settlements in the state. As the "citrus belt" surrounding Los Angeles emerged in the 1880s, Chinese immigrant workers pioneered such communities, which soon aroused violent nativist hostility. Their leading role in California agricultural labor steadily declined due to the combined effects of nativist attacks, discriminatory local legislation, and a series of racist federal immigration policies known as the Exclusion Acts. See Garcia, *A World of Its Own*, 54–56. In his landmark Orange County study, Gilbert González categorized citrus-belt labor settlements into company towns, settlements on company tracts within larger communities, and communities built on noncompany land. It is not clear if he considered them all to be colonias, and he preferred the general term of "worker villages." See González, *Labor and Community*, 9. Since the 1990s the distinct phenomenon of "border colonias" has dominated policy concerns, academic attention, and media coverage. Those are overwhelmingly to be found in Texas, along the border with Mexico, and are mainly a consequence of US border control policy developments in the 1990s. See Ayón, "Impact of Mexican Migration."
3. The foundational work on this subject is by Carey McWilliams, with his books *Factories in the Field*; *Southern California Country*; and *North from Mexico*, 217–21. Ernesto Galarza made useful contributions to understanding the phenomenon in *Farm Workers and Agri-Business in California, 1947–1960*. Gilbert González went beyond what had come before with his *Labor and Community*. Garcia, *A World of Its Own*, is still the most recent addition to this literature.
4. Vanessa Madrigal-Lauchland has written insightfully about community struggles against "generations of social and institutional erasure," and the "archival silences" that attend marginalized and physically destroyed communities. Madrigal-Lauchland, "Shifting Meanings of Stockton's Barrio del Chivo."
5. Two years after this reality was exposed by the mass shooting, San Francisco's ABC TV station produced a documentary and a number of related items on the continuing situation of farmworkers living in extremely substandard conditions on the mushroom ranches. See Peña and Guerrero, "Hidden Crisis."
6. Huerta, Gallegos, and Torres were born in Dawson, New Mexico; Aguilar, Colorado; and Miami, Arizona, respectively. On *Salt of the Earth*, see Lorence, *The Suppression of Salt of the Earth*.
7. The Treaty of Cahuenga, a.k.a. "Articles of Capitulation," was signed on January 13, 1847. See Harlow, *California Conquered*, 231–32.

8. The paper now bills itself simply as *The Mercury News,* with a small-type tagline right above, "The Newspaper of Silicon Valley," as if the actual geographical name was not Santa Clara Valley. "Silicon Valley" was coined by a journalist as a humorous take on the valley's real name, but the connection soon became lost even to residents of the Bay Area.
9. Johnston, *Mercury and the Making,* 15.
10. Pitti, *Devil in Silicon Valley,* 25.
11. Campbell, *An Empire for Slavery.*
12. Henderson, *A Glorious Defeat*; and Greenberg, *A Wicked War.*
13. McWilliams, *North from Mexico,* 132–33. Andrés Castillero was a Mexican Army officer actually born and raised in Spain.
14. See section by Castañeda in "A History of Mexican Americans in California."
15. Johnston reduces to a caption of an engraved illustration the basic field process of using mercury to draw gold from quantities of soil bearing it, in his *Mercury and the Making,* 26.
16. Smith, *History of the Comstock Lode.*
17. As Johnston put it, "Like haciendas built throughout Spanish colonies in the Americas, New Almaden was built on the backs, especially early on, of a workforce that perhaps was held in peonage, limited in opportunity by racial and ethnic bias in early California" (*Mercury and the Making,* 27).
18. The first session of California's new state legislature passed a "Foreign Miners Tax," which, as Johnston put it, "was enforced largely along racial and ethnic lines, with Chinese, Mexicans, and Central and South Americans bearing the brunt." As he further notes, this "institutionalization of racism" benefited New Almaden, "which provided them a stable and skilled workforce that had few options for improved conditions elsewhere in the state" (*Mercury and the Making,* 14). On the violence this law immediately unleashed on Mexican prospectors, see Pitt, *Decline of the Californios,* 60–64.
19. Pitti cites a source putting the extent of the tunnels as "hundreds of miles," in *Devil in Silicon Valley,* 55.
20. Johnston, *Mercury and the Making,* 15, 26, 49–50, 98.
21. "Californio" was the term and local identity adopted by the Mexican residents of the territory of Alta California, analogous to the Tejanos of Texas. See Pitt, *Decline of the Californios.*
22. Pitti, *Devil in Silicon Valley,* 48–49.
23. This case astoundingly went as high as to involve President Lincoln and the Supreme Court. See Ascher, "Lincoln's Administration and the New Almaden Scandal"; and Shutes, "Abraham Lincoln and the New Almaden Mine."
24. The fee was purportedly a toll for using the road into the property. The use of the company store was forced upon the workers by a ban on products purchased off company property.
25. Pitti, *Devil in Silicon Valley,* 62; and Campbell, *From Cinnabar to Quicksilver,* 62–63.

26. Campbell, *From Cinnabar to Quicksilver*, 60–61; and Johnston, *Mercury and the Making*, 32. The process of drawing mercury from the ore known as *cinnabar* called for stoking constantly roaring furnaces around the clock, seven days a week. The ore was roasted until the mercury trapped within not only returned to a free liquid state but evaporated and was caught in overhead vents and then condensed back into liquid, at which point it was bottled.
27. Pitti, *Devil in Silicon Valley*, 62.
28. Kay, "Tracking a Toxic Trail."
29. Pitti, *Devil in Silicon Valley*, 57–59.
30. Hayes-Bautista, *El Cinco de Mayo*.
31. Hayes-Bautista et al., "Empowerment, Expansion, and Engagement," 12, 68n32.
32. Hayes-Bautista et al., "Empowerment, Expansion, and Engagement," 10, 17.
33. Pitti, *Devil in Silicon Valley*, 63–71.
34. Pitti, *Devil in Silicon Valley*, 70–71; and Johnston, *Mercury and the Making*, 149.
35. Borrowing from Johnston, who concludes his introduction by observing that "California is the Golden State, and always will be. However, California is also the Quicksilver State" (*Mercury and the Making*, 149).
36. Henderson, *Beyond Borders*.
37. On the "colonia complex," see Carey McWilliams, *North from Mexico*, 197–202; and chap. 2 in Garcia, *A World of Its Own*.
38. Esteban Torres, featured in our first book, was also born in 1930, in an Arizona mining town. After his Mexican-immigrant father was deported during the Depression, Esteban's remaining family moved to California. The loss of his father haunted him, but the move from deeply segregated Miami, Arizona, to Boyle Heights was for Torres a dreamlike change in quality of life. See Ayón and Pla, *Power Shift*.
39. This account of Dolores Huerta's background and experience draws on recorded interviews with her (conducted by the authors on December 16, 2020; March 19, 2021; April 16, 2021; April 23, 2021; and February 4, 2022), as well as other sources as noted.
40. For the most complete history, see Pappas, *Crosses of Iron*.
41. Varney, *New Mexico's Best Ghost Towns*, 46, 49.
42. The Welfare Committee was originally appointed by the company's Welfare Department, which also published the town paper, *The Dawson News*, before it adopted elections. See *The Dawson News*, "Phelps Dodge Corporation."
43. "Hispano" is the preferred identifier of those New Mexicans whose ancestry in the territory predates annexation by the US—in other words, those who are not descended from immigrants to the US, but rather from settlers during the centuries of Spanish colonialism.
44. See Smith, *Coal Town*, 53–56; and Pietro Scarafiotti, "About," "Dawson New Mexico" Facebook group, accessed March 2, 2020, https://www.facebook.com/groups/556793837833040/permalink/1431734110339004/.

45. Associated Press, "Democrats Gain Control of Legislature"; West, "Labor Forgets Fight During Legislature"; and Associated Press, "Rio Grande Pact Approval Forecast."
46. Phelps Dodge announced the imminent closure of its last working mine at the site in the midst of the winter 1950 national coal strike. See Smith, *Coal Town*; and Pappas, *Crosses of Iron*.
47. Green, *Company Town*.
48. Ayón and Pla, *Power Shift*, 155.
49. Chinese immigrants were famously first used in building the transcontinental and local railroads from the 1860s to the 1880s, after which they drifted into farmwork. Nativist pressures and laws led to successive waves of immigrant workers from other Asian countries before farm labor came to be dominated by Mexicans. See McWilliams, *Factories in the Field*.
50. Quoted by McWilliams, *Factories in the Field*, 99.
51. McWilliams, *Factories in the Field*, 124–25. The colonial relationship gave both Filipinos and Puerto Ricans the right to migrate to the US.
52. Galarza, *Farm Workers and Agri-Business in California* and *Merchants of Labor*.
53. Galarza, "Burning Light," 31.
54. McWilliams, *North from Mexico*, 228. Shafter's Mennonite farmers encouraged their farmworkers to form a colonia outside city limits, but at some point they allowed children of farmworkers to attend school in Shafter, to the benefit of Dean Florez's family and others.
55. The Oxnard colonia was established at its present longtime location by residents of its razed predecessor. Similarly, the three colonias of LA's famed Chavez Ravine grew as a consequence of Mexicans being pushed out of what was known as Sonoratown of the old Plaza area, with the development there of Union Station and its environs. In the early 1950s, those colonias were destroyed as part of an urban redevelopment plan to build public housing—but in a shift to the right, the LA City Council canceled the housing project. For decades afterward, former residents of the Ravine gathered in annual reunions in Elysian Park. See Nusbaum, *Stealing Home*.
56. Thompson, *America's Social Arsonist*, 73; and Pitti, *Devil in Silicon Valley*.
57. Thompson, *America's Social Arsonist*, 80.
58. Thompson, *America's Social Arsonist*, 113.
59. Until that time, every election since 1928 had an incumbent president on the ballot—first Franklin Roosevelt and most recently Harry Truman.
60. Gellman, *President and the Apprentice*.
61. Pawel, *Crusades of Cesar Chavez*, 36. See US Citizenship and Immigration Services, Citizenship Resource Center, "Apply for Citizenship: Exceptions and Accommodations: English Language Exemptions," https://www.uscis.gov/citizenship/exceptions-and-accommodations. This exemption is commonly referred to as the 50/20 exception, which was later augmented with a 55/15 exception.
62. The 3,000 who had gone through the CSO citizenship program joined another 5,000 naturalization applicants for the Hollywood Bowl ceremony. See

Los Angeles Daily News, "Teacher Proud" and "8,000 to Take Oath"; and Burt, *Search for a Civic Voice*, 151.

63. Ross, *Conquering Goliath*, 4.
64. Thompson, chap. 10 in *America's Social Arsonist*.
65. The preceding references to the town of Shafter and its Colonia Mexicana, as well as all subsequent discussion of Dean Florez in this and other chapters, draw on recorded interviews with him (conducted by the authors on November 10, 2020; November 16, 2020; December 9, 2020; December 15, 2020; and February 9, 2022).
66. Rosalio Muñoz, famous for his leading role as a draft resister and organizer of the historic 1970 Chicano Moratorium Against the Vietnam War, became the first Chicano UCLA student body president by inheriting the office when the elected president stepped down. Florez was the first Latino *elected* to the office.
67. See Fry and Harter, "California Overtakes Japan."

Chapter 2: Building an Electorate and the Dream of Empowerment

1. Rainey, "Eternal Soldadera." Much of this chapter and many details contained in it are based on the authors' interviews with Dolores Huerta (conducted on December 16, 2020; March 19, 2021; April 16, 2021; April 23, 2021; and February 4, 2022), as well as sources listed in these notes.
2. CSO was founded in 1947 in the Eastside LA neighborhood of Boyle Heights, as an outgrowth of Edward Roybal's failed campaign for city council that year. See Ayón and Pla, *Power Shift*, 50–52.
3. Huerta walked Kennedy to the ballroom where campaign workers and supporters were gathered. The ABC News live feed from the Ambassador Hotel shows them together, but Dolores gets separated from the senator, and he initially appears at the podium flanked by his wife, Ethel. Overcoming the throng with some difficulty, the diminutive Huerta can be seen making her way to Kennedy's side. See "19680605 ABC-LA NETWORK FEED—RFK 1968 California Primary Victory Speech Ambassador Hotel," June 4, 1968, posted May 22, 2018, by Woodrow, YouTube, 29 min., 12 sec., https://youtu.be/AhDQhlvwGgw.
4. There is no agreed-upon name for the wider Mexican American/Latino-empowerment cause that is comparable to what is understood as the (African American) civil rights movement. There is a significant literature on the Chicano movement, also referred to in the community as *El Movimiento*, and to a lesser extent as *La Causa*, but "La Causa" is mainly used in reference to the UFW. Some do refer to a Chicano, or Mexican American, civil rights movement.
5. The initial organization established in 1962 was the National Farm Workers Association (NFWA), which did not define itself as a labor union. In 1966, the NFWA merged with the predominantly Filipino American Agricultural Workers Organizing Committee (AWOC) to become the United Farm Workers of America.

6. More layers would be added to this foundation in the late 1960s and '70s, and new routes of empowerment and leadership development would branch off the original road. Those would include The East Los Angeles Community Union (TELACU), founded in 1968; the Chicana feminist network *Comisión Femenil Mexicana,* organized in 1970; the California Chicano (later Latino) Legislative Caucus, founded in 1972; and Hispanas Organized for Political Equality (HOPE), founded in 1989. Empowerment efforts founded elsewhere would also move to or come to be run out of Los Angeles, including MALDEF, NALEO, and the Southwest Voter Registration and Education Project.
7. Available accounts and records give somewhat differing versions of these events. See Peña Harden, "Lifetime of Labor Activism"; Snodgrass, *Beating the Odds,* 224; Bardacke, *Trampling Out the Vintage,* 119; and Beagle, "Siete Lenguas."
8. Lucas, "The Battle of Los Angeles."
9. McWilliams devotes several chapters of *North from Mexico* (206–31) to drawing out the connections between the wartime atmosphere, the internment of the Japanese community, and the turn to racist attacks on Mexican American young men. See also chaps. 3–4 in Starr, *Embattled Dreams.*
10. This is how Dolores recalls the events of 1942, when she was twelve years old, and as they are depicted by most published sources. See, among many others, Snodgrass, *Beating the Odds,* 224. Another version has that Richards acquired the hotel and renamed it for himself, before he and Alicia were married. See Bardacke, *Trampling Out the Vintage,* 119.
11. Bardacke, *Trampling Out the Vintage.* The mustering of skid-row transients for farmwork, a.k.a. a "shape-up," is discussed extensively in London and Anderson, *So Shall Ye Reap,* passim; in Stockton specifically, 49; photograph, 64.
12. Many sources, including government documents and the Library of Congress, refer to the "Bracero Program" in upper case, but diverge on whether its legal name was the Emergency Farm Labor Program or the Mexican Farm Labor Program, and whether it was first formally established by a US presidential executive order, a negotiated and signed bilateral agreement, or an exchange of diplomatic notes. Of numerous sources consulted, none cite a named and dated original document. For a useful, fact-filled overview, see McElroy and Gavett, *Termination of the Bracero Program.*
13. The Mexican Farm Labor Program of 1942–47 allowed nonseasonal, nonagricultural workers, with contracts up to eighteen months before a required return to Mexico. By the last year of war, when just under 50,000 braceros were admitted, over 58,000 worked in agriculture, primarily in the West, and nearly 62,000 on railroad crews, primarily in the Midwest and East. See Gamboa, *Bracero Railroaders;* Martin, "Mexican Braceros and US Farm Workers"; and Galarza, "Guide to the Ernesto Galarza Papers."
14. Geiger, *German Prisoners of War.*
15. Peña Harden, "Lifetime of Labor Activism," 20.
16. Records show James and Alice Richards as registered Democrats in the 1940s, so it remains unclear how or why Dolores would have initially registered as

Republican. She explained in an interview with the authors that there was a tradition among Hispanos in New Mexico, going back to Lincoln and the Civil War, to affiliate with the Republican Party, which is, in fact, the case both there and in California. See Ayón and Pla, *Power Shift*, 34, 40n29; and Hayes-Bautista et al., "Empowerment, Expansion," 15, 18.

17. The physical community of Stockton's "Goat Valley" was lost to freeway construction and redevelopment by around 1960, according to former residents who keep its memory alive with an organizing committee, reunions, social media groups, and exhibits, such as at Stockton's Chicano Studies Center. See Carpizo, "Recordando"; and Madrigal-Lauchland, "Shifting Meanings."
18. Thompson, *America's Social Arsonist*, 126.
19. Thompson, *America's Social Arsonist*, 110; and Pitti, *Devil in Silicon Valley*, 150–52.
20. Marcoida, "CSO San Jose Juan Marcoida."
21. Levy, *Cesar Chavez*, 104–5; Pawel, *Crusades of Cesar Chavez*, 35, 490; Thompson, *America's Social Arsonist*, 114; and Pitti, *Devil in Silicon Valley*, 167.
22. Thompson, *America's Social Arsonist*, 72–73, 126.
23. Burt, chap. 6 in *Search for a Civic Voice*.
24. There are accounts of Latina leaders of the short-lived Congress of the Mexican and Spanish American Peoples of the United States (a.k.a. *El Congreso*) engaging in sporadic lobbying in Sacramento, but nothing like the dedicated lobbying Huerta began doing in the 1950s. On the former, see García, chap. 6 in *Mexican Americans*; Daniel, *Chicano Workers*, 8; and Burt, chap. 1 in *Search for a Civic Voice*.
25. Beagle, "Siete Lenguas."
26. Garcia, *From the Jaws of Victory*, 28; Rose, "Dolores Huerta," 9; and Bardacke, *Trampling Out the Vintage*, 119.
27. Velasquez et al., "Interview with Dolores Huerta," 2.
28. Piore, "Dual Labor Market." Economists and demographers have long studied how the interaction of factors such as race, undocumented immigration, and state policies structurally created and maintain dual labor and job markets, by segmenting undesirable work into categories of dead-end, relatively high-turnover jobs. See also Hall et al., "Job Mobility among Unauthorized Immigrant Workers."
29. The NLRA is also known as the "Wagner Act."
30. Daniel, *Bitter Harvest*, 261.
31. On the concept and history of "total war," see Chickering et al., *A World at Total War*. Imported contract labor had been outlawed since the 1880s, when the first immigration laws were passed and immigration from China was cut off completely.
32. Martin, "Comparison of California's ALRA."
33. Galarza, *Farm Workers and Agri-Business*, 35.
34. Mize, "Workplace Identities." In Mireya Loza's book, *Defiant Braceros*, braceros are portrayed very differently, with a primary focus on individual-level

defiance, particularly regarding their sexuality. But besides being individualistic, the braceros' defiance, in Loza's insightful reconstruction, was of Mexican institutions (cultural, political, and governmental) more than of the US-managed program, employers, or labor contractors. In her examination of the failed effort to organize braceros, Loza also makes the case for how well the program served the growers' interests. Her reference to Mize's work on braceros' memories and silences furthers the argument that the bracero program was a "total" or totalizing institution. See Loza, *Defiant Braceros,* 141.

35. Garcia, *Operation Wetback.*
36. Nobel Prize–winning Swedish economist Gunnar Myrdal published *An American Dilemma: The Negro Problem and American Democracy* in 1944. See the 1996 reprint by Transaction Publishers.
37. Kiser, "Bracero Program"; and Cohen, *Braceros,* 216–18. Twenty-eight undocumented farmworkers were killed in a plane crash while being deported from California in 1948. Woody Guthrie famously lamented the tragedy and racist handling of the victims—whose names were not reported and bodies went unclaimed—in a song that became a folk standard, covered dozens of times by star artists and groups. See Hernandez, *All They Will Call You*; and Khokha, "Immortalized by Woody Guthrie." Thirty-two braceros were killed in 1963 when the truck transporting them was broadsided by a train. A member of Congress commissioned Ernesto Galarza to conduct an investigation. See Flores, *Grounds for Dreaming.* On both these and other accidents that killed numerous farmworkers, see Arellano, "Ghosts of Migrant Dead."
38. Kiser, "Bracero Program"; Hawley, "Politics of the Mexican Labor Issue"; and Elmore, *Claiming the Cross.*
39. Bronder, *Social Justice and Church Authority*; and Rendon, "Archbishop Robert E. Lucey." That priest, Robert E. Lucey, founded and led both the Bishops' Committee for the Spanish-Speaking and the Conference on Spanish Speaking People of the Southwest. For the bigger picture of the Catholic Church's turn to advocacy for Mexican Americans, see Elmore, *Claiming the Cross.*
40. Archbishop Lucey introduced Saul Alinsky and Edward Roybal to each other at one of his conferences in San Antonio. See Ayón and Pla, *Power Shift,* 37–38.
41. Levy, *Cesar Chavez,* 89.
42. On McCullough, see London and Anderson, chap. 4 in *So Shall Ye Reap.*
43. Thompson, *America's Social Arsonist*; and Garza, *Organizing the Chicano Movement.*
44. Pawel, *Crusades of Cesar Chavez,* 50–51.
45. On Alinsky and Ralph Helstein, who headed the UPWA, see Horwitt, *Let Them Call Me Rebel*; and Ross, *Conquering Goliath.*
46. Levy, *Cesar Chavez,* 36–39, 54–56.
47. Ross, *Conquering Goliath,* 18–21.
48. In that one year, "literally hundreds of training centers, air and naval bases, supply depots and administrative headquarters were established" up and down the state. See Starr, *Embattled Dreams,* 67–68.

49. Levy, *Cesar Chavez*, 36–39, 55–56; and Pawel, *Crusades of Cesar Chavez*, 13, 16.
50. Levy, *Cesar Chavez*, 129–30; and Pawel, *Crusades of Cesar Chavez*, 56. This is despite the fact that at its July 1957 meeting in LA, the CSO board had formally decided to "engage the farm worker issue" and named Ernesto Galarza chair of a committee to study the Bracero Program. See Burt, *Search for a Civic Voice*, 156–57. Galarza sent all CSO chapter presidents a copy of his first book on the program and was several years into his long campaign to abolish it. Chavez might not have gotten the memo, so to speak, precisely because he was on Alinsky's payroll, not CSO's.
51. Levy, *Cesar Chavez*, 89.
52. Ross, *Conquering Goliath*, 7. Ross recorded his discussions with Cesar, which were later edited by Chavez speechwriter Marc Grossman into this short book. It captures Cesar's experimental farmworker organizing in Oxnard, and it is a critical and primary source of insight into Chavez's development as organizer and leader, essential for understanding how his Oxnard experience redirected his life.
53. Burt, *Search for a Civic Voice*, 165–71; and Folkart, "Enrique (Hank) Lopez." Attorney General Pat Brown was the gubernatorial candidate, and LA activist-lawyer Hank Lopez ran in and won the Democratic primary for secretary of state. Lopez was an associate and a friend of Edward Roybal and served as legal counsel for CSO.
54. "Del Buono Heads Service Group," *Oxnard Press-Courier*; and "New Citizens in Colonia," *Oxnard Press-Courier*.
55. Burt, chap. 8 in *Search for a Civic Voice*.
56. Ross, chaps. 5, 10–12 in *Conquering Goliath*.
57. Ross, *Conquering Goliath*. The book never makes clear if the jobs "key" meant combating the growers, who controlled hiring; the government, which imported the braceros; the braceros themselves; or all three. That ambiguity would afflict both the perception and reality of Cesar's and the UFW's responses to undocumented migrant farmworkers all the way into the 1980s, long after the Bracero Program ended.
58. Burt, *Search for a Civic Voice*, 156–57.
59. Levy, *Cesar Chavez*, 142.
60. Levy, *Cesar Chavez*, 142; Pawel, *Crusades of Cesar Chavez*, 60; and Ganz, *Why David Sometimes Wins*, 83. As Chavez said to Levy, "Our biggest break came when we got the growers to agree to hire people at our office. That was the most beautiful victory. We forced the growers' association to come and pick our people up right in front of our office. We became a hiring hall. We had them!"
61. "Leadership and Popular Movements," Center for the Study of Democratic Institutions.
62. "Dolores Huerta Talks About Republicans," in García, *A Dolores Huerta Reader*.
63. "Letters from Dolores Huerta to César Chávez," in García, *A Dolores Huerta Reader*.
64. The Amalgamated Meat Cutters and Butcher Workmen of North America.

65. Sanger, "Interview with Dolores Huerta"; and Huerta, interview with the authors, February 4, 2022.
66. London and Anderson, *So Shall Ye Reap*, 91.
67. London and Anderson, *So Shall Ye Reap*, 91; and Ganz, *Why David Sometimes Wins*, 65.
68. Ganz, *Why David Sometimes Wins*, 6; and Ganz, interview with the authors, November 8, 2018.
69. London and Anderson, *So Shall Ye Reap*, 95.
70. London and Anderson, *So Shall Ye Reap*, 47–56, 95–96.
71. Ganz, *Why David Sometimes Wins*, 65–67; Sanger, "Interview with Dolores Huerta"; London and Anderson, *So Shall Ye Reap*, 49; and Huerta, "Interview No. 1577," 8–9.
72. Jacobs, *A Rage for Justice*, 75–77. According to Jacobs, "in Burton's hands, the once-soporific legislative hearings became an effective weapon."
73. Jacobs, *A Rage for Justice*, 77. Huerta told Jacobs that Burton's actions that day on behalf of farmworkers had "the fire of holiness."
74. Jacobs, *A Rage for Justice*, 78–79.
75. Jacobs opened his magisterial biography with a quote from the late Wisconsin Senator and Governor Gaylord Nelson: "I spent thirty-two years in elective office, and I only met one absolute political genius. That was Phil Burton." See Jacobs, *A Rage for Justice*, vii.
76. Jacobs, *A Rage for Justice*, 76.
77. Burt, *Search for a Civic Voice*, 199–202.
78. Jacobs, *A Rage for Justice*, 78–79; Burt, *Search for a Civic Voice*, 200; Fox, "Save Our Senior Noncitizens."
79. Leal, "Paving the Road to the White House," 29.
80. Thompson, *America's Social Arsonist*, 141.
81. Thompson, *America's Social Arsonist*, 140–41.
82. "Robert F. Kennedy," *Time*, October 10, 1960.
83. "Letters," *Time*, November 7, 1960.
84. Pawel, *Crusades of Cesar Chavez*, 64.
85. Pawel, *Crusades of Cesar Chavez*, 70–73; Levy, *Cesar Chavez*, 146–48; and Thompson, *America's Social Arsonist*, 142–43.
86. Ayón and Pla, chap. 5 in *Power Shift*.
87. Rose, "Dolores Huerta," 12–13. This volume also contains a collection of letters from Huerta to Chavez, from 1962 to 1964, their primary means of communication until she moved to Delano.
88. Burt, *Search for a Civic Voice*, 206–8.
89. Galindo, "How Dolores Huerta and Cesar Chavez Started."

Chapter 3: Plotting *La Causa*

1. Ganz, *Why David Sometimes Wins*, 4–5.
2. This strategic point, discussed in the previous chapter, is drawn out at length by London and Anderson in *So Shall Ye Reap*, by sharply contrasting the

community approaches employed by both Chavez in Oxnard and AWA in Stockton with the AWOC approach. Ganz, however, more clearly connects it to the organizing undertaken by Chavez, Huerta, and other CSO veterans in the San Joaquin Valley from 1962 through the launching of the strike in Delano in 1965. See 64–70, 99–103, and 113–16.

3. From Chavez letter to Fred Ross, quoted in Pawel, *Crusades of Cesar Chavez*, 70.
4. Garcia, *From the Jaws of Victory*, 28.
5. As Garcia has charted in detail, there were already ties of various sorts—including baseball leagues—between colonias in certain areas such as the citrus belt ringing Los Angeles. Garcia writes that "each colonia, regardless of size, maintained a baseball team that competed in a regional 'Mexican league' fully funded and staged by Mexican residents" (*From the Jaws of Victory*, 73). The CSO chapters' planned urban farm-labor committees anticipated, in a sense, the grape-boycott urban infrastructure that the UFW would build up years later across the country. See the discussion of the UFW's "boycott houses" in Garcia, *From the Jaws of Victory*, chap. 2.
6. Levy, *Cesar Chavez*, 144.
7. Pawel, *Crusades of Cesar Chavez*, 64.
8. Garcia, *Jaws of Victory*, 29–30; and Levy, *Cesar Chavez*, 147.
9. Levy, *Cesar Chavez*, 147.
10. Moore, *Slaves We Rent*, 132.
11. Thompson, *America's Social Arsonist*, 128–29. On Fred Ross's interim dream of a statewide CSO, see 109.
12. London and Anderson, *So Shall Ye Reap*, 46.
13. "Chavez and the UFW," *Rural Migration News*. This newsletter is understood to be authored by Dr. Philip L. Martin; much of this article is derived from his book *Promise Unfulfilled*, 4–6.
14. Ganz, *Why David Sometimes Wins*, 85. According to Pawel, after Chavez announced his resignation at the CSO convention, "Oxnard was out" as a choice for him because the patron who had offered $50,000 for him to organize farmworkers shifted her money to a new initiative in Oxnard led by activists that Chavez had brought into his CSO effort there. See Pawel, *Crusades of Cesar Chavez*, 79; and especially Barajas, *Mexican Americans with Moxie*, 18–19. According to Barajas, a delegation of Oxnard CSO activists called on Chavez in Delano, in a failed effort to persuade him to return to Oxnard.
15. Pawel, *Crusades of Cesar Chavez*, 82.
16. Another of the cofounders of the NFWA, Gilbert Padilla, recalled to Marshall Ganz that this is what Chavez said when he called to urgently summon him to the organization's headquarters. See Ganz, *Why David Sometimes Wins*, 124.
17. Bender, *One Night in America*, 12–22.
18. Ganz, *Why David Sometimes Wins*, 4–5; Bardacke, *Trampling Out the Vintage*, 179–82; London and Anderson, *So Shall Ye Reap*, 153–57; Pawel, *Crusades of Cesar Chavez*, 123–29; Levy, chap. 11 in *Cesar Chavez*; Garcia, *From the Jaws of Victory*, 48–50; and Thompson, *America's Social Arsonist*, 173–76.

19. See Middlekauff, *Glorious Cause,* on the use of this phrase to refer to the US War of Independence.
20. Vargas Santiago, "Uncontainable Zapata Iconicity."
21. See the full text, with an introduction by Valdez, in "Commentary of Luis Valdez."
22. Valdez, "Huelga en General."
23. Pawel, *Crusades of Cesar Chavez,* 130.
24. Bender, *One Night in America,* 29–35; Pawel, *Crusades of Cesar Chavez,* 167–68; and Mariscal, "Cesar and Martin, March '68."
25. Thompson, *America's Social Arsonist,* 195.
26. Levy, *Cesar Chavez,* 289.
27. Clarke, *Last Campaign.*
28. See Palermo, *In His Own Right,* 244; and Palermo, "Here's What RFK Did in California in 1968."
29. Bender, *One Night in America,* 38.
30. Bender, *One Night in America,* 39.
31. Pawel, *Crusades of Cesar Chavez,* 170.
32. Bender, *One Night in America,* 48.
33. In the final days of the Chavez fast, over ten thousand Chicano students walked out of Los Angeles high schools, throwing the district into crisis. Kennedy announced his candidacy challenging President Johnson less than a week after returning from Delano. Two weeks after that, Johnson unexpectedly announced he would not run for reelection. In the interval between the Kennedy announcement and the Johnson withdrawal, Dr. Martin Luther King was assassinated, setting off a wave of riots. Kennedy's assassination in June was followed that summer by successive days of street battles outside the Democratic National Convention in Chicago.
34. Garcia, *From the Jaws,* 132–33. According to Matt Garcia, in his first year in office, Nixon had the Defense Department more than double its purchases of grapes, while South Vietnam's imports soared eightfold. On the 1970 contract negotiations, see 108–10.
35. Pack, *Jerry Brown,* 256.
36. Pawel, *Browns of California,* 241.
37. Pawel, *Crusades of Cesar Chavez,* 322. According to Miriam Pawel, "preliminary results gave the UFW 192 victories, while the Teamsters won 119." See also Garcia, *From the Jaws,* 160.
38. Pawel, *Crusades of Cesar Chavez,* 243–44.
39. Pawel, *Crusades of Cesar Chavez,* 244–45. Reagan also ran a "favorite son" campaign in California for a similar reason—dissatisfaction with President Gerald Ford. One consequence was that Ford emerged debilitated from the Republican convention and in a deep hole in the polls against Carter.
40. Garcia, *From the Jaws,* 162–77. In *Power Shift* we incorrectly described this proposition as proposing a state constitutional amendment. Our thanks to Marc Grossman for pointing out this error.

41. Chatfield, "A Turning Point."
42. Pawel, *Crusades of Cesar Chavez*, 333.
43. On Tunney's extraordinary relationship with the Kennedys, see Tunney, "John Tunney Oral History."

Part II: Going National

1. Gratton and Klancher Merchant, "*La Raza*." At that time and for decades to come, census forms were not shown to residents but filled by hired enumerators going door to door. Enumerators could designate individuals' "race or color" without asking the question. Results were tabulated in this order: White, Negro, Mexican, and Indian, followed by nine Asian or Pacific Islander categories. See University of New Mexico Geospatial and Population Studies, "1930 Population"; and Schor, *Counting Americans*.
2. This was the first Latino mobilization on a national policy, not counting territory-based issues such as the struggle for New Mexico statehood or federal policies specific to Puerto Rico. These two cases strikingly contrast the sustained and successful struggle for inclusion in New Mexico with an even longer case in Puerto Rico of a Latino community split between a politics of inclusion and a politics of *resistance to inclusion* (as a state). We will examine these contradictory dynamics in our next book.
3. Organized labor had long opposed the Bracero Program and was joined by a broad coalition of organizations, many of which were religious. As discussed in chapter 2, CSO officially joined this effort in 1957, when it named Dr. Ernesto Galarza, the most prominent Mexican American activist on the bracero policy, to spearhead its initiative. Galarza's life and conjoined career of activism and scholarship was already the stuff of legend in his own lifetime and lives on in his many books. Dubbed "man of fire" by labor writers London and Anderson (see chap. 6 in *So Shall Ye Reap*), he was most recently lauded by O'Connell and Peters in *In the Struggle* (see chap. 3). See also Galarza, "Burning Light."
4. Kamasaki, *Immigration Reform*, is the definitive account of the emergence of a Latino lobby in national policy.

Chapter 4: Representation in DC and Pivot to Immigrant Rights

1. Garcia, *From the Jaws of Victory*, 171–72.
2. Carter had a huge lead in the polls following the convention, but Ford made impressive progress throughout the fall campaign, putting the outcome into doubt and enhancing public attention at the end.
3. Lyndon Johnson did not have a transition beyond the confines of the White House complex when he took over the presidency after the assassination of President Kennedy in 1963. Even when he won election outright in 1964 by a historic landslide, Johnson predominantly retained the Kennedy cabinet—with the notable exception of Attorney General Robert Kennedy, who had left to run for the open New York Senate seat that year.

4. Edmund G. "Pat" Brown was first elected governor in 1958. He was reelected in 1962 over Nixon, who had returned to California following his defeat in the presidential election of 1960 to John Kennedy. The elder Brown attempted a second reelection in 1966, but he lost to Reagan. Nixon's criminality is detailed in the new edition of Woodward and Bernstein, *All the President's Men*, and especially Graff, *Watergate*.
5. See Perlstein, *Reaganland*.
6. See Burt, *Search for a Civic Voice*, 300–301.
7. "Biography Sketch of Carmela G. Lacayo," Dr. Hector P. Garcia Papers.
8. TELACU, founded in 1968, stands for The East Los Angeles Community Union, the community development corporation that marked both a new stage and an expansion of Eastside Latino empowerment, beyond that achieved by CSO. See Ayón and Pla, *Power Shift*, 72–76.
9. Estrada had just moved to UCLA from Texas during the Carter administration's first year. He was appointed to the Census Advisory Committee on the Spanish-Origin Population for the 1980 Census, and later to a staff position at the Census Bureau. See Levine, "Oral History."
10. See discussion of Raymond Telles and the Alliance for Progress in chapter 6.
11. On Nava generally, see Burt, *Search for a Civic Voice*; on the politics of his appointment as ambassador, see 302–3. See also Nava's memoir, *My Mexican-American Journey*.
12. Kamasaki, *Immigration Reform*, 68-69.
13. The key provisions of the VRA are its Sections 2 and 5. Section 5 required jurisdictions "pre-clear" with the Justice Department any change in registration or voting procedures if less than 50 percent of their eligible population of a "protected class" was registered to vote. This placed electoral procedures throughout the South under DOJ supervision. Section 2, as interpreted by the Supreme Court, allowed lawsuits challenging electoral procedures throughout the country that could be shown to have been adopted with the *intent* to discriminate against a protected class. The 1975 extension of the VRA added Latinos to its specified protected classes, but the need to prove *intent*, as opposed to effect or result, was a high bar to clear. See Boyd and Markman, "1982 Amendments."
14. See Ayón and Pla, *Power Shift*, 103–12.
15. Ironically, the issue was thrust on Nixon, as well, by his own rogue INS. When Nixon nominated LA Latina businesswoman Romana Bañuelos to be treasurer, INS agents raided her foodstuffs plant to round up alleged undocumented workers on her staff. See "U.S. Raid Nets 36 Illegal Aliens," *New York Times*. For more on Bañuelos, see Ayón and Pla, *Power Shift*, 45.
16. See the one-page "policy primer" sidebar on "employer sanctions," the central provision of many efforts to stanch undocumented immigration, in Kamasaki, *Immigration Reform*, 53.
17. For the whole inside account of the immigration-reform battles, including the blitzing of Carter in 1977, see Kamasaki, *Immigration Reform*. "Comprehensive immigration reform" refers to a package of provisions dealing with not only

the resident undocumented population but also future flows, agricultural labor needs, sanctions on employers who knowingly hire undocumented workers, border control, etc., as opposed to "piecemeal" reform in these areas.

18. At different times, the US Labor Department's Bracero Program and private farm associations actively recruited farm labor from deep within Mexico, which was widely understood as having stimulated undocumented migration in parallel with the official program. Major Mexican American organizations did not oppose the mass deportation effort in 1954, officially known as Operation Wetback, and at least one major organization (the veterans group American G.I. Forum) actively lobbied for it. See Ramos, *American GI Forum*.
19. And accompanied by undocumented migrants often housed on ranches and farms.
20. London and Anderson, *So Shall Ye Reap*, 10. According to Philip Martin, "at least 100,000" braceros were sponsored by their employers for "green card" immigrant visas. What's more, these farmworkers "were well positioned to recruit friends and relatives to fill US farm jobs." See Martin, "Mexican Braceros." See also Ganz, *Why David Sometimes Wins*, 96, 106–7; and Bardacke, *Trampling Out the Vintage*, 140, 753n9. According to Bardacke, "the INS allowed California growers to distribute many of the green cards."
21. Ganz, *Why David Sometimes Wins*, 5–7, 94–96. Ganz describes the impending demise of the Bracero Program.
22. On the decline of bracero work permits and both growing immigrant visas and apprehensions of undocumented Mexicans, see the first table in Martin, "Mexican Braceros." Bracero work permits peaked in 1956 at just over 445,000 but declined to less than 180,000 by 1964, the program's last year. Legal immigration (i.e., the issuance of permanent resident visas, or "green cards") from Mexico rose significantly in the 1950s. Well over 500,000 green cards were issued over the years the Bracero Program was in effect, 1942–64.
23. The 1965 changes to the INA are detailed in Murphy, "Current Concerns."
24. Nepal, "Primer." Such was the case for decades, in spite of the existence since 1952 of the H-2 temporary worker visa program, which the 1965 reform split into the H-2A (for agriculture) and H-2B programs. These visas remained at relatively low levels, but H-2A in particular has dramatically expanded in the most recent period, approaching Bracero Program levels of over four hundred thousand farm labor visas per year.
25. For a Mexican American take on the "green carders" as a contentious issue in the late 1960s, see Ortego, "Mexican-Dixon Line."
26. Growers also had Mexican-migrant foremen and supervisors who recruited and directly hired seasonal workers, but over time they shifted to independent labor contractors, who insulated them from accusations of deliberately and directly hiring undocumented migrants.
27. Conway, "Step-Wise Migration." "Step migration" is a concept dating to the 1880s.

28. There are an estimated four to five hundred thousand undocumented farmworkers, while the whole undocumented population is estimated at over ten million. It is likely that the nonfarmworker undocumented population became a majority relatively soon after the end of the Bracero Program, around 1970, but methods of estimating the undocumented were very primitive back then, with huge ranges given.
29. Numerous accounts from both within and without have documented this outlook and practice. For example, see the detailed examination of views expressed in the UFW's official newspaper by Chomsky, "'But He Can't Work in Stockton'"; and organizer-author Bardacke, "UFW and the Undocumented."
30. Patiño Jr., "Time for Resistance," 81–82. "Border crossing cards," also known as "white cards," allowed bearers to spend up to seventy-two hours within twenty-five miles of the border for purposes of shopping and visitation. These "white cards" disallowed employment but were subject to abuse for that purpose. See also Herzog, *Where North Meets South*. Note that the meaning and use of the terms "white card" and "border crossing card" have shifted over the decades.
31. The most comprehensive source on Corona's long activist career is his oral history told to García, *Memories of Chicano History*. The bulk of his account of the development of Hermandad Mexicana, and the subsequent rise and fall of CASA, begins on 290.
32. Ayón and Pla, chaps. 9–10 in *Power Shift*.
33. As its all-caps suggest, "CASA" was was an acronym for *Centro de Acción Social Autónoma* ("Autonomous Social Action Center"), to which was appended "-HGT" (*Hermandad General de Trabajadores* ["General Brotherhood of Workers"]). For a wide range of details on the internal workings and fortunes of CASA, see Pulido, *Black, Brown*. See also "Guide to the Centro de Acción Social Autónomo," Online Archive of California.
34. CASA also used Hermandad's slogan *Un Daño Contra Uno Es un Daño Contra Todos*—"A Harm to One Is a Harm to All"—but more as an internal norm than its public rally chant *Somos Un Pueblo, Sin Fronteras*. While the two express similar sentiments, the *Sin Fronteras* slogan was more confrontational and contrary to conventional politics than the older *Un Daño*—which conveys mutual aid without challenging a precept of national sovereignty. See Patiño Jr., "Time for Resistance," 82n117; and Pulido, *Black, Brown*, 119.
35. See Pulido, *Black, Brown*, on CASA membership requirements.
36. On the concept of "linked fate," see Cox, "Most U.S. Adults Feel."
37. Ramírez, *To the Line of Fire!*; and García, chap. 2 in *Mexican Americans*. LULAC, formed from the merger of three preexisting Texas organizations in 1928, was to a significant extent created by World War I veterans.
38. García, chap. 3 in *Chicano Generation*; Davis and Wiener, chaps. 31–32 in *Set the Night on Fire*; PBS SoCal, "The Muñoz Family"; and Hernandez, "Loss of Innocence."

39. Gutiérrez, "'Sin Fronteras?,'" 20–22; and Calavita, *California's "Employer Sanctions."*
40. Gutiérrez, "'Sin Fronteras?,'" 17; Pulido, *Black, Brown,* 119; and Garcia, *Memories of Chicano History,* 305.
41. Many sources overpersonalize the dispute as simply between Chavez and Corona, when, in fact, the harshest acrimony was between CASA on one side and Chavez and the UFW on the other. CASA's *Sin Fronteras* ideology was radically at odds with UFW positions and Chavez's statements regarding undocumented Mexican workers, immigration law enforcement, and border enforcement. Yet even to state the conflict this way can be misleading, as can be seen in a careful reading of the "green carder" issue. In the late 1960s, especially, Chavez and the union stressed their opposition to cross-border farmworkers with green cards as much as or more than they did regarding the undocumented. At bottom, the issue was migratory workers who were not part of the communities the UFW organized, not their immigration status. But the UFW could report the undocumented to authorities and denounce their employers more harshly than it could do with the green carders, whose legal right to cross the border to work was little understood.
42. *Gooch v. Clark*; Geile, "NOTE"; and Fragomen Jr., "Permanent Resident Status." The Supreme Court twice ruled on the right of green card holders—in official terms, lawful permanent residents—to reside across the border and commute either daily or seasonally to jobs in the US.
43. Significantly, undocumented students and the US-born children of undocumented immigrants could not be accused of displacing locals in the way that undocumented workers are blamed for taking an allegedly limited number of jobs. Public schools are required to accommodate all school-age children in their assigned areas, as affirmed by the Supreme Court in *Plyler v. Doe* in 1981. As we have seen in the twenty-first century, the accumulation of undocumented immigrants brought into the country as children ultimately recast in dramatic fashion the issue of immigration enforcement. See Nicholls, *The DREAMers.*
44. Calavita, *California's "Employer Sanctions."* The Supreme Court ultimately overruled the California courts, finding the law not unconstitutional, but the state took no action to enforce it. The law remains on the books to this day. Calavita explains in detail how the law was primarily passed for symbolic political reasons in the first place, but the changing political climate dissolved its symbolic value.
45. del Olmo, "Chavez Union Does Turnabout."
46. As late as fall 1981, the union's representative in Washington testified in support of employer sanctions in a Senate committee hearing, in open conflict with both MALDEF and LULAC, who also testified on this issue. See Bower, "Statement of Stephanie Bower."
47. For a recent and provocative reassessment of Chapman, see Malcolm Gladwell, host, *Revisionist History*, podcast, season 3, episode 5, "General Chapman's Last

Stand," Pushkin Industries, June 4, 2018, https://www.pushkin.fm/podcasts/revisionist-history/general-chapmans-last-stand.

48. Gutiérrez, "'Sin Fronteras?,'" 24–25.
49. Gutiérrez, "'Sin Fronteras?,'" 26–28; and Kamasaki, *Immigration Reform*, 36.
50. On conceptualizing and illustrating Mexican American, Chicano, and Latino generations as such, see García, chap. 2 in *Mexican Americans*; García, *Chicano Generation*; and García, *Latino Generation*.
51. García, *Memories of Chicano History*, 249–50.
52. *Raza* and *la raza* are flexible terms that can be applied as narrowly as to a tribe and as broadly to all Latinos or Hispanics, and generally mean "the people" or "my people." Raza can also be used to mean "race," its cognate in English; however, "race" is understood differently in the US and Latin America. See the classic treatment by Degler, *Neither Black nor White*. *Migra* refers to immigration authorities.
53. ICE (Immigration and Customs Enforcement) is the successor agency to the INS, since the creation of the Department of Homeland Security in 2002.
54. Bender makes this point in a different way, noting, "In 1968, the farmworker movement and organizer Cesar Chavez dominated discourse and the societal view of Latinos," but "now, unchecked Mexican immigration is far and away the defining social and political issue for Latinos" (*One Night in America*, 102).
55. Truax, *Dreamers*; and Nicholls, *The DREAMers*.
56. Kamasaki, *Immigration Reform*, 59–64.
57. Ayón and Pla, *Power Shift*, 174–75, 192–93nn5–17. The case is *Madrigal v. Quilligan* (1975); see Hernández, "Chicanas and the Issue."
58. Ayón and Pla, *Power Shift*, 171–76. Molina and Yolanda Nava led the founding in LA of the first and most important chapter of the Comisión Femenil Mexicana Nacional.
59. David Boies, senior staffer to the Judiciary Committee. See Kamasaki, *Immigration Reform*, 92; and Hernández, "Interview with Antonia Hernandez."
60. Kennedy spoke to a LULAC meeting that night; see Kennedy's remarks at John F. Kennedy Library, "November 21, 1963—President John F. Kennedy at League of United Latin American Citizens Dinner," posted August 14, 2022, by HelmerReenberg, YouTube, 10 min., 53 sec., https://youtu.be/ENeQr4TdZNg.
61. Molina, interview with the authors, October 16, 2014.
62. Hernández, "Oral History Interview."
63. Ayón and Pla, *Power Shift*, 222.
64. Village of Arlington Heights v. Metropolitan Housing Development Corp, 429 U.S. 252 (1977). See Flores, introduction in *Latinos*.
65. Congress.gov, "S. 506—Fair Housing Amendments Act of 1979."
66. Boyd and Markman, "1982 Amendments"; and Johnson, "1982 Voting Rights Act." The VRA case was City of Mobile v. Bolden, 446 U.S. 55 (1980).
67. O'Connor and Epstein, "A Legal Voice"; and Márquez, *Politics of Patronage*.
68. Kamasaki, *Immigration Reform*, 92.
69. Kamasaki, *Immigration Reform*.

70. City of Mobile v. Bolden, 446 U.S. 55 (1980), 60–61, analyzed in exhaustive detail in Boyd and Markman, "1982 Amendments."
71. For a short discussion of the history of broader denial of discrimination experienced by Mexican Americans, counterposed with substantial evidence of it and efforts to fight it, see Kamasaki, *Immigration Reform*, 13–22 and 37–40. For Antonia Hernández's own summary, see her 1990 testimony opposing the confirmation of David Souter's nomination to the Supreme Court (Hernández, "Statement on Behalf"). By far the most thorough collection of key materials on the Latino experience with discrimination—but unfortunately not including the subject of voting—is Delgado, *Latinos and the Law*.
72. Kamasaki, *Immigration Reform*, 68–69, 168, 428n116.
73. The Section 5 decision was in the case of Shelby County v. Holder, 570 U.S. 529 (2013). See Bullock, Gåddie, and Wert, *Rise and Fall*; and Rhodes, *Ballot Blocked*. The Section 2 case was Allen v. Milligan, 599 U.S. ____ (2023) [sic]. See Thompson, "Voting Maps Throughout the Deep South."
74. The case was *Moore v. Harper*, No. 21-1271 (2023). See Liptak, "Supreme Court Rejects Theory."
75. Roper, "Voting Rights Extension."
76. Boyd and Markman, "1982 Amendments," 1,351, 1,358n61; and Pertschuk, *Giant Killers*, 156. We are indebted to Charles Kamasaki for generously sharing with us an unpublished fragment on the 1982 Voting Rights Act renewal from his book *Immigration Reform*, which led us to Pertschuk's account of public-interest legislative battles of the 1980s.
77. Kamasaki, *Immigration Reform*, 96, 129, 226.
78. Referring to Reagan's assistant attorney general for civil rights, William Bradford Reynolds. See Roper, "Voting Rights Extension," 191. See also Pertschuk, *Giant Killers*, 157.
79. Pertschuk, *Giant Killers*, 151–52.
80. Boyd and Markman discuss the hearings in detail ("1982 Amendments," 1,357–69); see also Roper, "Voting Rights Extension," 191–93; and Pertschuk, *Giant Killers*, 157–58.
81. Johnson, "1982 Voting Rights Act."
82. Hernández's gentle speaking style is vividly displayed in extended interviews such as Hernández, "Oral History Interview"; Hernández, "Our Stories, Our Impact"; and Hernández, "Podcast FULL INTERVIEW." But that style can be deceptive. As Kamasaki learned from interviews for his book, "a close colleague once characterized getting into an argument with her akin to being punched by 'a steel fist in a velvet glove'" (*Immigration Reform*, 93).
83. In legal parlance, the "state" refers to the government as a whole, as in the doctrine of separation of church and state. On this case, see Olivas, *No Undocumented Child*.

Chapter 5: Forging the Latino Lobby

1. Reasons include distance, climate and weather, salaries, and politics. Elected office in Los Angeles and in the California state legislature is considered professional, full-time work and relatively well paid. In Texas, which abhors "professional politicians," representative public office is predominantly considered and paid as part-time volunteer work. Historically, staff professionals, too, have been better compensated in California than in Texas. Political differences have also weighed heavily. There has *never* been a Democratic president from California. Before Kamala Harris, there had never even been a Californian on the Democratic ticket for either president or vice president. Finally, as noted, neither John Kennedy nor Jimmy Carter won California in either the primary or general election, but both won Texas, in 1960 and 1976, respectively.
2. The great exception to this is Santa Barbara native Carlos McCormick, who took a unique route (through Arizona) to become valuable to Senator John Kennedy, spearheaded the Viva Kennedy campaign in 1960, and took a role in the Kennedy administration. See Leal, "Paving the Road"; and García, *Viva Kennedy*.
3. This and other discussions of Escutia in this book draw on interviews with the authors (conducted on December 29, 2020; April 29, 2021; May 3, 2021; May 25, 2021; September 2, 2021; January 27, 2022; and April 9, 2024).
4. Kamasaki, *Immigration Reform*, 160.
5. Martha and a cousin told the story of their Papú for the radio series *StoryCorps*; Escutia and Jimenez, "They Called Him Papu."
6. Sahagun, "Day of Rage in East LA." For film of that day, see García and Ruiz, "Requiem 29."
7. Ayón and Pla, *Power Shift*, 139–42.
8. Ayón and Pla, *Power Shift*, 178, 194fn24–25. While Alatorre's committee had the legal authority to produce all the reapportionment and redistricting plans in concert with its Senate counterpart, the actual mastermind of the congressional map was Representative Phil Burton, whom Democrats in the State Legislature happily deferred to.
9. Craig, "Operation Intercept."
10. Calavita, *U.S. Immigration Law*; Saxton, *Indispensable Enemy*; Fine and Tichenor, "A Movement Wrestling"; and Haus, "Openings in the Wall." Institutionalized racist and anti-immigrant attitudes in organized labor are well documented, especially in the case of the AFL, organically rooted in that it was originally a federation of specialized guilds, later called "craft unions," which themselves were highly discriminatory.
11. Kamasaki, *Immigration Reform*, 50, 52–54; Fragomen and Wenk, "Legislative and Judicial Development"; and Hohl and Wenk, "Illegal Alien."
12. For overviews and reviews of the thirty-volume report, see Fragomen Jr., "Final Report and Recommendations"; Martin, "Select Commission"; and Schey, "Select Commission on Immigration."
13. Kamasaki, *Immigration Reform*, 70–76.

14. Kamasaki, *Immigration Reform*, 146.
15. Kamasaki, *Immigration Reform*, 188–89. Scholar Christine Sierra dubbed the CHC strategy during this period "Hispanic veto politics"; see "In Search of National Power," 140–45.
16. Ayón and Pla, *Power Shift*, 138–39, 194n36; and Goldmacher, "Waxman–Berman Machine."
17. Kamasaki, *Immigration Reform*, 160–61.
18. Kamasaki, *Immigration Reform*, 227. In his August 4, 2019, book presentation at the UnidosUS (formerly known as NCLR) annual conference in San Diego, Kamasaki called Torres the "unsung hero" of the Latino policy struggle over IRCA (author's notes). Martínez repeatedly flipped from Democrat to Republican and back in his life as a registered voter and officeholder. The website GovTrack reports, "From Jul 1982 to Dec 2000, Martínez missed 1,097 of 9,718 roll call votes, which is 11.3%. This is much worse than the median of 3.0% among the lifetime records of representatives serving in Dec 2000" (https://www.govtrack.us/congress/members/matthew_martinez/400595).
19. Civil Rights Commissioners Confirmation Hearing, C-SPAN, July 13, 1983, 7 hr., 12 min. https://www.c-span.org/program/senate-committee/civil-rights-commissioners-confirmation-hearing/66829. Martha testifies at 5:31:25.
20. Ayón and Pla, *Power Shift*, 71–77. Torres was the founding director of TELACU, which itself was one of the original seven affiliates of NCLR in 1968.
21. Kamasaki, telephone interview with the authors, September 11, 2022.
22. Kamasaki, *Immigration Reform*, 227.
23. Kamasaki, *Immigration Reform*, 125–30.
24. Pertschuk, *Giant Killers*, 153–58. The original source for this point is Pertschuk, but we learned of it thanks to Charles Kamasaki.
25. Márquez, *LULAC*; Kaplowitz, *LULAC, Mexican Americans*; O'Connor and Epstein, "A Legal Voice"; and Márquez, *Politics of Patronage*.
26. Ayón and Pla, *Power Shift*, 115, 121n60.
27. In her pioneering work, scholar Christine Sierra nevertheless includes the UFW as a part of the Latino lobby's "organizational core." See Sierra, "Latino Organizational Strategies." Sierra treats separately the role of Congressional Hispanic Caucus in the immigration-reform battle in "In Search of National Power."
28. Bert Corona vividly describes his members' meetings with legislators, highlighting their encounter with Senator Kennedy, in García, *Memories of Chicano History*, 305–8. See also Sierra, "Latino Organizational Strategies," 133; and Kamasaki, *Immigration Reform*, 277–79.
29. Kamasaki, *Immigration Reform*, 166–67.
30. Kamasaki, *Immigration Reform*, 165–66, 180.
31. The next year, Pepper became chair of the Rules Committee.
32. Ayón and Pla, *Power Shift*, 138–39.
33. Kamasaki, *Immigration Reform*, 223–24.
34. Kamasaki, *Immigration Reform*, 215–17.

35. The Panetta guest-worker proposal was essentially mirrored by an amendment sponsored by Pete Wilson in the Senate, which after a modification also passed easily. See Martin, "Good Intentions," and Martin, "CAW at 30." In *Power Shift*, we mistakenly wrote that the Wilson guest-worker proposal made it into IRCA, which it did not.
36. Kamasaki, *Immigration Reform*, 244–45.
37. Schumer first threw himself into an effort to "rescue" the bill in 1984, before he did the same, with greater success, in 1985. See Kamasaki, *Immigration Reform*, 239–41, 274–77; and Perotti, "Resolving Policy Conflict."
38. See the discussion of "green carders" in chapter 4.
39. There are some discrepancies among quality sources on the precise numbers of the undocumented who were legalized under IRCA, which can be attributed partly to the date of the source. Among those that offer the greatest detail and come very close to coinciding are Rytina, "IRCA Legalization Effects"; Kerwin, "More Than IRCA"; and Martin, "CAW at 30."
40. The SAW legalization program actually had two tracks. Initially, applicants had to show proof of employment in agriculture for ninety days each in the years 1984, '85, and '86. The second track required evidence of ninety days of employment in agriculture during the twelve months prior to May 1987.

Chapter 6: Inclusion Unbound

1. Brown's designated lieutenants were a "mod squad" from LA—Assembly Members Alatorre, Maxine Waters, and Mike Roos—one white (Roos), one Black (Waters), and one Chicano (Alatorre). The stories of the coup that won the speakership and Alatorre's forceful direction of the redistricting process are recounted in Ayón and Pla, chap. 6 in *Power Shift*. Brown's political patron, Phil Burton, who sought to become Speaker of the House in DC, was key to tripling Latino representatives in Congress from the Eastside.
2. Kamasaki, *Immigration Reform*, 300–301.
3. O'Connor et al., "Central American Immigrants." The Central American immigrant population in the US more than tripled in the 1980s, growing by almost eight hundred thousand, with the greatest concentrations of Salvadorans and Guatemalans in Los Angeles County.
4. Chinchilla and Stoltz Hamilton, *Seeking Community*. Undocumented urban immigrants arriving after January 1, 1982, would not qualify for the main legalization program. However, their mounting presence added to the Latino community's growing influence, swelling the audience for Spanish-language media, facilitating the creation of a second Latino-heavy city council district (won by Molina in February 1987—less than three months before the legalization window opened), and growing the Latino presence in the Catholic Church, as well as in other denominations.
5. Formally named *La Iglesia de Nuestra Señora de los Ángeles* ("the Church of Our Lady of Angels"). For a full history, see Pfeifer, "La Placita and the Evolution of Catholic Religiosity in Los Angeles," chap. 4 in *Making of American Catholicism*.

6. Morrison, "Father Luis Olivares Brought the Sanctuary Movement"; García, *Father Luis Olivares*; and Ayón's personal observation of the mass. Olivares not only challenged his Mexican and Mexican American congregation, he was also challenging his newly installed archbishop, Roger Mahony, who in spite of being supportive of refugees and immigrants, did not favor violating the law by providing sanctuary.
7. García, *Father Luis Olivares*, 380–89, 499.
8. United States Conference of Catholic Bishops, "Encuentro." The first three editions of the Encuentro Nacional Hispano de Pastoral were held in Washington, DC; the first, in 1972, convened over 250 participants, including "8 bishops, 130 priests, 54 women religious"; the second, in 1977, drew some 1,200 participants, among them 50 bishops; the third, in 1985, drew "over 2,000 participants from 123 dioceses," including 56 bishops. That conference, "III Encuentro," was part of a "national process of consultation among Hispanics" to develop the Church's National Pastoral Plan for Hispanic Ministry, which in LA stretched until June the following year (and elsewhere longer).
9. Hernandez, "50,000 Worshipers Gather."
10. del Olmo, "Latino Community."
11. National Conference of Catholic Bishops, *National Pastoral Plan*.
12. Rappatoni, "Pope Holds Poignant Dodger Stadium Mass"; and Morrison, "When His Holiness Was in Hollywood."
13. Ayón and Pla, *Power Shift*, 206–7, 209–10.
14. The heading of this section respectfully acknowledges Rodriguez's fine account, *Making Latino News: Race, Language, Class*.
15. The story of the 1980 census, which attempted the first complete count of the Hispanic population, is told in chap. 5 of Ayón and Pla, *Power Shift*, as well as in Mora, *Making Hispanics*.
16. In fact, prior to the elections of 2000, supreme power had never been peacefully transferred to an opposition party or ruling group in Mexico.
17. Mai-Duc, "In Taking on Jorge Ramos"; and Taylor and Lopez, "National Latino Leader?"
18. This account and other discussions pertaining to Monica Lozano draw on interviews with her (conducted by the authors on March 9, 2013; April 4, 2013; October 4, 2022; October 28, 2022; and January 5, 2023); her father Ignacio "Nacho" E. Lozano Jr. (conducted by the authors on February 16, 2013; February 23, 2013; and May 4, 2013); and her father and mother, Marta Lozano (conducted by the authors on March 23, 2013). Other sources include Garcia, *Rise*; Rivas-Rodriguez, "Ignacio E. Lozano"; di Stefano, "'Venimos a luchar'"; and Garza, *They Came to Toil*. For nearly a century, the two Ignacio E. Lozanos have been distinguished by referring to the father as "Don Ignacio" and the son as "Nacho" or "Nachito."
19. Table in Rivas-Rodriguez, "Ignacio E. Lozano," 76.

20. Rivas-Rodriguez, "Ignacio E. Lozano." *La Prensa* lost 70 percent of its daily circulation between 1930 and 1935. On the repatriation pressures and deportations of that time, see Sánchez, *Becoming Mexican American*.
21. Historians have characterized this mentality among Mexican immigrants as "Mexico Lindo," or "Beautiful Mexico," after a classic song that voices the wish to return, even if only in death. See Sánchez, *Becoming Mexican American*, 109.
22. The difference between circulation and readership is not widely understood, but it is comparable in television and radio to the difference between the number of devices tuned in to a program and its number of viewers or listeners, i.e., the total audience. At its peak, *La Opinión* was distributed through 13,000 points of sale.
23. García, *Chicano Generation*.
24. García, *Making of*.
25. Leal, "Paving the Road"; and García, *Viva Kennedy*.
26. Based on multiple conversations with Raymond and Delfina Telles, as well as interviews with their daughter, Cynthia Telles (conducted by the authors on February 11, 2013, and February 22, 2013).
27. Gerassi, *Great Fear in Latin America*.
28. Levinson and de Onis, *Alliance That Lost*.
29. Blasier, *Hovering Giant*.
30. García, *Making of*, 127, 133.
31. Telles continued to serve in prominent but not diplomatic positions in Washington until his retirement.
32. Smith, "Nacho Lozano."
33. Argentine Ernesto "Che" Guevara's paternal grandparents met in Buenos Aires but were both born in California. Their fathers were among those who joined the Gold Rush and then returned to Argentina. See Castañeda, *Compañero*. The new California state government of 1850 acted to drive immigrants away from mining gold, resulting in many Chileans living among Californios and Mexicans in mercury mining colonias, such as at New Almaden, and elsewhere.
34. An earlier military coup in Brazil in 1964 had generated an outflow of regime opponents to nearby democratic Southern Cone countries, but then 1973 brought coups in Uruguay and in Chile. The entire Southern Cone came under military rule by 1976, with a coup in Argentina. The last two of these were particularly brutal. Political opponents of the four dictatorships fled the region, many to Mexico City and other Latin American countries and Spain, and a significant number to San Francisco. See Guendelman, "South American Refugees."
35. Ignacio Lozano Jr. remained chair of the *La Opinión* board into the 1990s.
36. The noisy newsroom is the domain of the top editor, kept separate from the business side of a newspaper, which is the domain of the publisher, with offices for circulation, advertising, delivery, marketing, etc. Monica had a summer's experience in high school as an apprentice photographer working out of the newsroom, but she had been mainly out on assignments. Leticia and Jose had worked every summer in the paper, and then full-time on the business side,

and were interim copublishers while their father served as ambassador to Costa Rica for about a year. Although Leticia later had the nominal title of "editor in chief," she actually remained on the business side of the paper.

37. The drive between downtown Los Angeles and largely undeveloped Newport Beach in Orange County was especially long before the opening of Interstate 5.
38. Kamasaki, *Immigration Reform*, 299.
39. The nativist right quickly seized upon "amnesty" and used it propagandistically to oppose any form of adjustment of status or legalization. Many activists and MALDEF rejected the term precisely because the nativists stigmatized it to mean that the law was being suspended for criminals. While the offense of "entering without inspection" was illegal, it was not defined as a crime in the strict sense, and legalization had to be earned by meeting specific criteria, which included continuous residence and no criminal record, as well as enrolling in and completing English and civics classes.
40. Kamasaki, *Immigration Reform*, 214–15.
41. del Olmo, "Latino 'Decade' Moves into '90s."
42. Cited in Kamasaki, *Immigration Reform*, 215, from a *Los Angeles Times* profile.
43. Kamasaki, *Immigration Reform*, 215.
44. This section draws on the authors' interview with Ramos on December 21, 2020, and several of his books: *Stranger*; *No Borders*; and *Sin Miedo*.
45. González Gutiérrez, "Fostering Identities."
46. Ayón, "Migrants and the State"; González Gutiérrez and Ayón, "Mexico and the Mexican Community."
47. Linder placed the number from Mexico alone at 2.3 million ("The Amnesty Effect," 15). This sudden, mass legalization was widely seen as contributing heavily to a change in Mexican politics and policy concerning the country's diaspora in the US. See Ayón, "Migrants and the State."
48. Immigrant workers remit scores of billions of dollars annually to their families in Mexico, contributing to positive development outcomes in local-level measures of infant mortality, child illiteracy, school attendance, and poverty. Remittances to Mexico more than tripled between 1980 and 1990, reaching nearly US$2.5 billion annually, according to World Bank estimates. The increased earnings of legalized workers undoubtedly played a role. By 2021, remittances to Mexico rose to over $50 billion per year. See López-Córdova et al., "Globalization, Migration and Development"; and Aguilar Rangel, "Remittances in Mexico."
49. State of the Cities Data Systems, "SOCDS Census Data."

Chapter 7: Democratizing LA and Facing the Backlash of the '90s

1. California's "English Only" movement grew out of soil tilled since the mid-1960s by Ronald Reagan and San Francisco educator and scholar S. I. Hayakawa, elected to the US Senate in 1976. Both were strident opponents of the social and civil rights movements of the 1960s–'70s. In the late '70s, Democrats who controlled the state legislature frustrated Republican calls for English-language amendments to the California and US Constitutions. But the issue then sprouted

locally in San Francisco in 1983, in reaction to electoral materials required by the language provisions of the Voting Rights Act, and to the growth of the city's Chinese community and proliferation of its business signs. A vigorous movement garnered wide grassroots support in liberal San Francisco, which passed a nonbinding local proposition against the VRA language mandates. This success revived efforts in the legislature, culminating with the statewide ballot measure along the same anti-VRA lines, which passed by a landslide in 1984. That movement, however, still could not get the legislature to establish English as California's official language. That frustration led to the next ballot measure in 1986 to amend the state Constitution, which passed with a bigger landslide vote, over the opposition of nearly all Democratic leaders and major news media. The amendment and the intense political battle over it have been forgotten, largely because the Democratic-controlled legislature blocked bills for the statutory laws needed to implement it, but also because propositions to come in the 1990s were even more divisive and consequential.

2. In California, state judges are appointed by the governor for an initial term of four years, but they have to be "retained" by voters for each subsequent term.
3. Ostrow, "U.S. Inquiry Targets 1982 L.A. Council Redistricting."
4. Ayón and Pla, *Power Shift*, 190–91, 199nn84–87.
5. Stewart, "Advocate."
6. Boyarsky, *Big Daddy*.
7. Skelton, "Wilson Expands Reasons."
8. Simon, "Judge Kenyon Enlivened Case."
9. Arturo Vargas, electronic communications with author, July 25, 2023.
10. Simon and Muir, "Schabarum Snubs Aide."
11. Boyarsky, "Rocky Race of Sarah Flores."
12. Ayón and Pla, *Power Shift*, 226–28.
13. "1990 Census: California," *New York Times*.
14. United States Census Bureau, "1990 Census Apportionment Results."
15. Los Angeles County Auditor-Controller, "Incorporated Areas—Cities." Mike Sonksen captures the great diversity of these communities in "A Brief History on the Gateway Cities."
16. Ayón and Pla, *Power Shift*, 139–42.
17. Griego, "Plan to Combine Several Districts." As of August 1991, the Southeast Coalition seeking its own assembly district was composed of the "pint-sized" seven cities of Huntington Park, Maywood, Bell, Cudahy, South Gate, Lynwood, and Bell Gardens, plus the unincorporated community of Walnut Park, and the district could also include neighboring Commerce and Vernon. At that time, these communities were "divided among three separate Assembly districts, three state Senate districts and three congressional districts," including Lucille Roybal-Allard's assembly district but not Xavier Becerra's. In taking from Roybal-Allard's district, however, the Coalition's proposed district, designed by Escutia, would have consequences for Becerra's.

18. Chacon seemed to position himself as Alatorre's successor several years previous in taking over as chair of the Chicano Legislative Caucus, of which he had been a founding member in 1972. Chacon, in turn, handed that position over to a more likely successor, Alatorre staffer Richard Polanco. See Becker et al., *History, Development, and Policy Influence.*
19. Institute of Governmental Studies, "Redistricting in California."
20. Bebitch Jeffe, "Why Republicans May Rue."
21. Sterngold, "Citizenship Incubator."
22. California Secretary of State, "November 3, 1992, General Election." Escutia won 75 percent of the vote in the November general election.
23. The independent candidacy of businessman Ross Perot can also be said to have played a role in California and other states. See Stone and Rapoport, *Three's a Crowd.*
24. Baker et al., *Latino Political Representation.* The fifth was Denise Moreno Ducheny of San Diego.
25. Cadelago, "How Kevin Leon Became Kevin de León." De León appears to have first shared these and other details in a long and painful interview with *The Sacramento Bee* in 2017. He confirmed many of these details to us three and a half years later, in the first of our series of interviews, which stretched into 2021.
26. Herrera, "Kevin de León." Fabián Núñez described de León's living quarters, more vividly and horrifically than did KDL himself, to journalist Jack Herrera.
27. Cadelago, "How Kevin Leon Became Kevin de León."
28. De León's distinctly modest primary school in Logan Heights, Brooklyn Elementary, did not have enough teachers to have separate fifth- and sixth-grade classrooms.
29. Herrera, "Kevin de León."
30. For a detailed description, see California State Postsecondary Education Commission, *Equal Educational Opportunity.*
31. Skelton, "Wilson Urges Welfare Cuts."
32. Reinhold, "In California, New Talk."
33. Bunting and Miller, "Feinstein Raises Immigration Profile."
34. Klein, "New Edge on Immigration Debate."
35. The proposition would have made proof of legal immigration status a requirement to access public services and even to enter public buildings. Among its consequences would have been expulsion of scores of children from public schools. For an overview of the development of Proposition 187, see Arellano, "Prop. 187 Timeline."
36. Ramos, "House Divided Over Immigration."
37. Colin Grant plumbs and vividly brings to life the world of Harlem street-corner soapbox in his *Negro with a Hat.*
38. Wilson, "State of the State Addresses."
39. Weintraub, "Wilson Scales Back Request."
40. "Hairy arms" is the feint of planting something gratuitous and objectionable in a design submitted for approval to a client or superior who is likely to want to

make a change in the work product. The term allegedly originated with either a graphic design for a character in an animated Disney film, in which the artist drew hair on the character's arms, or with a photo of a proposed layout of a marketing design in which the designer purposely had his arm caught in a corner of the image. The art director in the first case, and the client in the second, demanded a single change before approval—lose the hair from the character's arms, or the hairy arm from the photo.

41. Vogel, *Shock Waves Through Los Angeles*. The 1906 earthquake that destroyed most of San Francisco was in fact stronger—7.9 on the Richter scale—but the epicenter was two miles offshore, and it was the ensuing fire that caused the most damage to the city.
42. Herrera, "Kevin de León"; and Ayón personal observation.
43. Herrera, "Kevin de León."
44. On the 1970 Chicano Moratorium, see Ayón and Pla, *Power Shift*, 74, 79–80nn38–41. That march took place entirely on the Eastside, culminating at a park in East LA. The 1994 march started at LA's eastern border and, in proceeding across Boyle Heights toward downtown, drew people out of their homes to observe, cheer, and even spontaneously join in. The scores of thousands of protesters streamed dramatically over the LA River to the side of City Hall, across from the *Los Angeles Times*'s fortress-like headquarters building.
45. On the 1994 planning, see Herrera, "Kevin de León."
46. Ayón and Pla, *Power Shift*, 266.
47. Martin, "Proposition 187 in California."
48. On the judgment of the Brown campaign, see Reese and Schnur, *1994 Governor's Race*, 4.
49. Skelton, "Brown May Be Catching Wave."
50. Reese and Schnur, *1994 Governor's Race*, 56–57. Brown called on President Clinton to double the number of border guards assigned to California, but also to close two interior checkpoints.
51. See the Wilson spot, along with a comparison to another for the 2016 Trump campaign, in Garofoli, "Trump's Campaign Ad Is Brash."
52. Ayón and Pla, *Power Shift*, 273n30, 273n32.
53. Grad, "The Prop. 187 Rebellion."
54. del Olmo, "A Dissenting Vote."
55. California Latino Legislative Caucus, "25th Anniversary of Proposition 187."

Chapter 8: Expansion, Diversification . . . and Comeback

1. Becker et al., "California Latino Legislative Caucus."
2. Raymond Gonzales of Bakersfield was elected in the same cycle as Richard Alatorre in 1972, and he was thus one of the five founding members of the Chicano Legislative Caucus. Gonzales, however, lost his bid for reelection in 1974.
3. Becker et al., "California Latino Legislative Caucus."
4. Haas, "Grass-Roots Protest."

5. This section and other references to Senator Padilla throughout this chapter draw heavily on a series of recorded interviews with the senator, which began when he was still California secretary of state and extended shortly beyond when Governor Newsom appointed him to represent California in the US Senate (conducted by the authors on September 9, 2020, Los Angeles, CA; September 23, 2020; October 14, 2020; November 18, 2020; and January 8, 2021), as well as other cited sources.
6. After the Los Angeles Rams left LA to play in Anaheim, the Raiders moved down from Oakland into LA's Memorial Coliseum. The team was led by the NFL's first Mexican American head coach, Tom Flores, and the first Mexican American quarterback to win a Super Bowl, Jim Plunkett. The Raiders promptly won their third Super Bowl in 1983 to cap their debut season in LA. In 1995, however, the Raiders moved back to Oakland.
7. Williams, "Poverty, Pride and Power."
8. Padilla, interview with the authors, September 9, 2020.
9. Having tired of the position after a decade, Padilla made the team without revealing he was a pitcher. The MIT coach called Alex's high school coach, then loudly complained to him about this and talked Alex into pitching again.
10. California Latino Legislative Caucus, "25th Anniversary of Prop. 187."
11. Whitaker, "Quick Climb Up."
12. Padilla's month at the County Fed happened to start the same day Contreras took over the position of political director.
13. On the Latino role in the political transformation of Orange County, see Haas, "Grass-Roots Protest"; Reyes, "Santa Ana Rent Strike"; Arellano, "O.C. Can You Say"; Arellano, "Nativo Lopez"; and Arellano, "Orange County Once Was."
14. Koszczuk, "Proof of Illegal Voters."
15. Author's personal observation of Hernández remarks at MALDEF event, November 7, 1996.
16. This section draws on our series of recorded interviews with Secretary Cisneros (conducted September 28, 2020; October 15, 2020; November 5, 2020; January 20, 2021; and March 21, 2022), in addition to other cited sources.
17. Ayón, "Texas Versus California."
18. Discussion of Eva Longoria is based on interviews with her close friend and onetime publicist, David Damian Figueroa (conducted by the authors on February 13, 2020), and Professor Rudy Acuña (conducted by the authors on May 20, 2020), in addition to many secondary sources, including Livingston, "Eva Longoria Is Famous"; Rennie, "Political Passion of Eva Longoria"; and Kahn, "Eva Longoria Calls the Shots."
19. *Al Punto* was also discussed in the interview with Jorge Ramos conducted by the authors on December 21, 2020.
20. Also discussed in interviews with Cisneros.
21. This and other references to Lorena Gonzalez draw on recorded interviews with her (conducted by the authors on September 29, 2020; October 20, 2020; and November 17, 2020).

22. This discussion and other references to Cedillo draw on interviews with him (conducted by the authors on February 5, 2021; February 11, 2021; August 5, 2021; and August 12, 2021).
23. Arellano, "San Fernando Valley Latino Political Machine."
24. Tempest, "Rapid, Sometimes Bumpy, Rise."
25. Hornblower, "Man Behind Prop. 227."
26. La Ganga, "Bilingual Ed Initiative."
27. Berumen, *Edward R. Roybal*, 95.
28. McCall, "Building a Bridge."
29. Ayón and Pla, *Power Shift*, 205–11.
30. Ayón and Pla, *Power Shift*, 243–44.
31. Nichols, "A Warrior for Workers"; and Merle and Olivo, "Solis Trounces Martinez."

Chapter 9: New-Century Action

1. The *Times*' Spanish-language weekly was named *Nuestro Tiempo*. This discussion draws on recorded interviews with Monica Lozano (conducted by the authors on October 4, 2022, and January 5, 2023).
2. As a 50 percent owner of *La Opinión*, Times Mirror had veto power over the paper's capital expenditures and obligations.
3. The Tribune Company's acquisition meant the sprawling Chandler family, owners of Times Mirror, were exiting the business after well over a century. The Chandlers followed the long procession of families who left the newspaper business—unwelcome news for the Lozanos, despite their many differences with the Chandlers and their paper.
4. Both New York's *La Prensa* and Ignacio E. Lozano Sr.'s San Antonio paper of the same name were founded in 1913, but the latter was sold off and ceased publication in the 1950s.
5. Republicans led by Newt Gingrich won the House majority for the first time in forty years in 1994. Nancy Pelosi led the Democrats to win back the majority in 2006.
6. As Speaker, Bustamante assigned Democratic members to committees and designated chairs.
7. Discussion of Lorena Gonzalez is derived in part from interviews with her (conducted by the authors on September 29, 2020; October 20, 2020; and November 17, 2020).
8. The "Latino-labor alliance" construct was popularized by journalist Harold Meyerson in the 1990s when he was an editor and columnist at the *LA Weekly*.
9. Wong, "Dynamic Political Mobilization."
10. Discussions of Dean Florez draw on interviews with him (conducted by the authors on November 10, 2020; November 16, 2020; December 9, 2020; December 15, 2020; and February 9, 2022), as well as a wide range of news and magazine articles, including Molen, "Voice of the People"; and Pollard, "Valley-dictorian."

11. On the bubble and the crash, see Lowenstein, *Origins of the Crash*. According to Ellison's hybrid biography/autobiography with Matthew Symonds, his net worth surpassed $50 billion, overtaking that of Bill Gates. See Symonds, *Softwar*, 4.
12. Lowenstein, *Origins of the Crash*, 48.
13. Vogel, "State Repeals Oracle Contract."
14. Symonds, chap. 25 in *Softwar*, 589.
15. Symonds, chap. 25 in *Softwar*, 583.
16. Tapper, "Fred Thompson Watergate Myth."
17. Ayón and Pla, *Power Shift*, 70–71.
18. Ahn et al., "Student Protest Turns to Destruction."
19. Having worked for UFW, Torres was well aware of the famous congressional field hearing in Delano that featured Sen. Robert Kennedy excoriating the county sheriff, and had himself staged a raucous hearing on pesticides with Alatorre in LA. See Torres, "Oral History Interview," 30–31.
20. Symonds, chap. 5 in *Softwar*, 601.
21. Florez, "Is the Capitol for Sale."
22. Lowenstein, *Origins of the Crash*.
23. Zarembo, "Approach Has Served Bustamante Well."
24. Gonzalez lost the election by fewer than a thousand votes.
25. Vincent, "Spanish Papers Square Off."
26. Ware, "Newsday, Hoy Axe."
27. Securities and Exchange Commission, "SEC Brings Settled Charges Against Tribune Company"; Securities and Exchange Commission, "Order Instituting Cease-and-desist Proceedings."
28. *Los Angeles Business Journal*, "Tribune to Give Away Hoy."
29. Blume, "New Name, New Life for Belmont School."
30. This is not to imply that African Americans were left out of this era of Democratic Speakers. Herb Wesson was the third of the first four in this period, and Karen Bass was the first of the second four. Furthermore, Wesson went on to serve as president of the LA City Council, while Bass, after serving in Congress, went on to be elected LA mayor.
31. This section is based on Ayón, "Mobilizing Latino Immigrant Integration," and his personal observations as a participant.
32. Redlands is approximately sixty-five miles east of Los Angeles.
33. Bada et al., eds., *Invisible No More*.
34. Ayón, "Migrants and the State."
35. Zepeda-Millán, *Latino Mass Mobilization*.

Part IV: Always Another "Final Battle"

1. Representatives Joe Baca, Xavier Becerra, Grace Napolitano, Lucille Roybal-Allard, Linda Sánchez, Loretta Sanchez, and Hilda Solis.
2. The US has been euphemistically described as having a "laissez faire" approach to citizenship and immigrant integration, when, in fact, its system has

historically been disinterested and arguably suppresses naturalization and permanent residence. An exception in 1995–96 was the "Citizenship USA" program of the Clinton–Gore administration, which came under attack by Republicans. See DeSipio, *Counting on the Latino Vote*; and Verhovek, "Immigrants' Anxieties."

Chapter 10: From *¡Ya Es Hora!* to "Yes We Can"

1. *Ya Es Hora: ¡Ciudadanía!* was the first of three phases leading to the 2008 elections, but our focus here is on the first, foundational, and arguably most important. The *Ya Es Hora* (YEH) brand was even extended into a fourth phase in 2009–10 to promote Latino participation in the 2010 census.
2. Chris Zepeda-Millán argues in detail how the movement was perceived as a failure, and he goes further to make the case that it "likely contributed to the increased subjugation of the vulnerable population it professed to defend" (*Latino Mass Mobilization*, 162).
3. Border Protection, Antiterrorism, and Illegal Immigration Control Act, H.R. 4437, 109th Cong. (2005), https://www.congress.gov/bill/109th-congress/house-bill/4437.
4. Sources cited in Zepeda-Millán, *Latino Mass Mobilization*, which offers a meticulous reconstruction of these events.
5. Zepeda-Millán, *Latino Mass Mobilization*, 167–69.
6. Shaw, *Beyond the Fields*, 240. The coalition, called We Are America Alliance, persisted for several years with the benefit of substantial foundation support. See Voss and Bloemraad, *Rallying for Immigrant Rights*.
7. Zepeda-Millán, *Latino Mass Mobilization*, 161–62.
8. Lawful permanent residents (LPRs) hold "immigrant visas," also known as "green cards," in the strict sense of the term. In the vast majority of cases, a legal immigrant becomes eligible to apply for citizenship after holding such a visa for five years without violating some terms concerning criminal behavior.
9. Browning et al., *Protest Is Not Enough*; and Zepeda-Millán, *Latino Mass Mobilization*.
10. Ayón, "Mobilizing Latino Immigrant Integration."
11. Taylor, "Naturalization Trail."
12. Zepeda-Millán, *Latino Mass Mobilization*; and Ayón, "Mobilizing Latino Immigrant Integration," 8n20. Other factors include a stubbornly held belief by immigrants that they will return to Mexico sooner rather than later, and that to acquire US citizenship is to scorn their heritage and identity.
13. *¡Alarma!* for years had the highest circulation of any publication in Mexico, and it was widely available and circulated on the US side of the border. See Balderston et al., eds., *Encyclopedia*, 48.
14. Vividly described by Dawn Garcia in her Stanford University master's thesis, "Spanish-Language Media," 67–68. Garcia kindly shared with us the video recording of the promotional spot she obtained from the TV station's news department.

15. Unlike charity telethons that display tickers indicating the total donations pledged, Mettey's ticker started at one million and ticked backward, like a countdown.
16. Ayón, "Mobilizing Latino Immigrant Integration," 7–8.
17. The succeeding generations deliberately remained bilingual and bicultural, as many Latinos have chosen to, while integrating into US society. Nacho Lozano's sister, Mary Alice, however, moved to Mexico with her mother, married a Mexican businessman, and acquired Mexican citizenship, which at the time required renouncing her US citizenship.
18. Ayón, "Migrants and the State." Many other factors were involved in change in Mexican policy, including the goal of containing emigre resentment of and anger toward Mexican government authoritarianism and corruption; the rapid rise and importance of emigre remittances to their families in Mexico; the danger that growing political competition in Mexico could become internationalized; and the unprecedented election in 2000 of an opposition president, Vicente Fox, who had campaigned vigorously among Mexican emigres in the US.
19. In the late 1920s, Mexico suppressed an armed counterrevolutionary movement known as *La Cristiada* and deliberately sought to drive *Cristeros* and their supporters to the US. See Young, *Mexican Exodus*. In the early 1930s, Mexico supported mass repatriation back to Mexico of its emigres in the US, at a time when both US federal and local policies, such as in Los Angeles, conducted a campaign of enhanced repatriation pressures. See Alanís Enciso, *They Should Stay There*. In the 1940s, as the US mobilized to enter World War II, Mexico initially resisted US efforts to import Mexicans as guest workers, before acquiescing. By the early 1960s, when Congress sought to end the Bracero Program, the Mexican government lobbied to keep it going and later sought to have it restored. See García y Griego, "Importation of Mexican Contract Laborers."
20. Ayón, "Migrants and the State."
21. Ayón, "Migrants and the State."
22. Rytina, "Population Estimates"; and Ayón, "Mobilizing Latino Immigrant Integration," 14–15. Meeting this goal appeared at least mathematically possible within the KMEX market alone, which was the original plan. Of the estimated 8.25 million eligible nationwide, some 2.65 million were from Mexico, meaning probably over a million in the LA area, especially when other Latino immigrants were taken into account.
23. The NALEO leaders, however, were concerned about the breathtaking ambition of this goal.
24. Ramírez, *Mobilizing Opportunities*, 109, 131, 146; and Shaw, "Eliseo Medina."
25. Mettey, interview with the authors, March 9, 2024.
26. Vargas, "Testimony of Arturo Vargas."
27. Zepeda-Millán, *Latino Mass Mobilization*.
28. Ramírez, *Mobilizing Opportunities*, 105–9.
29. Community organizations fell into two categories: "information providers," which primarily gave out NALEO citizenship packets, and "citizenship centers,"

which helped with completing the application, organizing needed documents, test preparation, and interview training. Ultimately, over four hundred organizations in twenty-three cities participated. See Vargas, "Testimony of Arturo Vargas."

30. Ayón, "Mobilizing Latino Immigrant Integration." NCLR at that time had nearly three hundred affiliated local community organizations.
31. Gelatt and McHugh, "Immigration Fee Increases in Context."
32. Jordan, "Univision Gives Citizenship Drive Unusual Lift."
33. Migration Policy Institute, "Citizenship Applications Surge During Summer 2007 Even Higher Than Initial Government Estimates," press release, February 26, 2008.
34. From what can be gleaned from the few sources that remain accessible, the WAAA's initial promotion of naturalization consisted of "handing out citizenship applications," and its communications strategy involved "hearing about citizenship at Mass, at union gatherings and at civic organization meetings" (Shaw, *Beyond the Fields,* 240).
35. Ayón, "Mobilizing Latino Immigrant Integration," 14.
36. Vargas, "Testimony of Arturo Vargas."
37. 9.7 million; see Lopez and Taylor, *Dissecting the 2008 Electorate.*

Chapter 11: Empowered Latinos

1. This is not to suggest that this movement had national leadership—the planning and protests emerged organically in decentralized fashion in the local conditions of Chicago, LA, and other cities. Indeed, a competitive dynamic set in between activists in different cities. Spanish-language media made them hyperaware of each other's efforts.
2. Berkowitz, "Subway Mayor."
3. Landsberg, "Dropout Rate as 'Civil Rights Issue.'"
4. Guzman-Lopez, "LA Mayor Gets Mixed Reviews."
5. Mehta, "How Antonio Villaraigosa Went."
6. Remington, "Villaraigosa: Give California Mayors."
7. La, "Second California Governor Try."
8. Núñez had chits to call in, having helped several of his new colleagues win elections when he was political director of the LA County Federation of Labor, which also strongly backed his bid for the speakership. The Assembly Democratic Caucus, furthermore, wanted a speaker who could serve as long as possible and would not be cowed by Governor Arnold Schwarzenegger, who was known to be physically intimidating. Fabián not only had the clout of organized labor behind him, but despite his small size, had fought a hundred amateur boxing matches in his youth.
9. Mendel, "New State-Run IRA."
10. California Legislative Information, "AB-2940 Retirement." All approved bills with a projected price tag above a very low threshold go into the "Suspense

File," which the Appropriations Committee takes up in a marathon hearing the following summer to decide the fate of each bill for that session.

11. McGreevy, "Setback."
12. The California League of Conservation Voters, which has since rebranded itself as California Environmental Voters, is famous for its annual Environmental Scorecard, "which grades every state legislator and the Governor on their environmental actions from the past year" (California Environmental Voters, "Scorecard").
13. Pérez, interview with the authors, August 10, 2021.
14. Pérez's bill, AB 1602, together with a Senate bill (SB 900), vastly expanded and brought California's existing health insurance marketplace into compliance with the Affordable Care Act, passed earlier that year, and made the exchange available before the ACA's national marketplace. The program was later renamed Covered California. See Rasmussen and Kominski, "Sources of Success in California's Individual Marketplace"; and Covered California, "The First 10 Years."
15. See the renamed CalSavers Retirement Savings Board web page (California State Treasurer, "CalSavers").
16. California State Treasurer, "Treasurer Chiang & Senator De León."
17. California State Treasurer, "Official Launch of CalSavers."
18. Abcarian, "Obama Gets Major Labor Endorsement."
19. Clinton won substantial majorities of the Latino vote in the 2008 Democratic primaries, but the Obama campaign made significant efforts to compete for Latino voters in Clinton strongholds in big cities and states in which delegates were elected in caucuses. Democratic presidential primaries award delegates to candidates in proportion to votes cast, rather than the Republican practice of "winner take all," allowing Obama to steadily accumulate delegates in states he lost, as well as in those he won. See Hamburger and Wallsten, "Obama's Grass-Roots Latino Strategy."
20. Hamburger and Wallsten, "Obama's Grass-Roots Latino Strategy." Clinton and Obama split on the driver's license issue in their debate in Los Angeles on January 31, 2008. Cedillo had originally introduced his driver's license bill, AB 60, in 1997, his first year in the state Assembly. He did not succeed in getting the bill passed and signed until 2003, by then-Governor Gray Davis, who was at that time facing the recall effort led by Arnold Schwarzenegger. Schwarzenegger's big win in the recall vote resulted in the legislature rescinding the bill before it could take effect. It would take until 2013 for the bill to be signed again, this time by Governor Jerry Brown, and until 2014 for it to take effect. See Ayón and Pla, *Power Shift*, 246.
21. The Obama team stood by Solis but dropped its support for Thomas Saenz—former MALDEF head and chief counsel to Mayor Villaraigosa—to lead the Justice Department's Civil Rights Division, when he came under fire from Republicans on the Senate Judiciary Committee, which would have had to confirm him.

22. Ayón and Pla, *Power Shift*, 262–63. In 1993–94, Becerra was part of the failed effort to pass Bill Clinton's healthcare reform, albeit as a mere first-term member of the House. He had been an informal student of the health profession since his undergraduate years at Stanford, where he met his future wife, Carolina Reyes. After completing law school at Stanford, he moved with Carolina to Cambridge, where she studied medicine at Harvard. He later moved to Los Angeles when appointed as a deputy to the California attorney general. Reyes joined him in LA, they married, and he made his first run for office in 1990 for the California Assembly. When pioneering Congressman Ed Roybal decided not to seek reelection in 1992 and redistricting split his district in two, he encouraged both his daughter Lucille and Becerra to run to succeed him. Both were elected and moved to Washington. In Congress, Becerra landed a seat on the powerful Ways and Means Committee and was able to cultivate support from healthcare-industry political action committees.
23. The Presidential Succession Act specifies that the secretary of state, if qualified as a natural-born US citizen, is the first member of the cabinet in the order of succession.
24. Ayón and Pla, *Power Shift*, 244.
25. McCarthy, "Hispanics' Support for Obama Climbs."
26. Development, Relief, and Education for Alien Minors. See American Immigration Council, "Comparison of the DREAM Act"; and Herszenhorn, "Senate Blocks Bill."
27. Ayón, "Latino Diasporas." In polls, Latino registered voters have typically put economic issues, education, and healthcare above immigration as their policy priorities. Immigration reform surged as a top concern during the height of the Dreamer movement.
28. Hopper, *Presidential Framing in the 21st Century News Media.*
29. Greene Sterling and Joffe-Block, *Driving While Brown.*
30. Magaña and Lee, eds., *Latino Politics and Arizona's Immigration Law SB 1070.*
31. Jelen, "Nevada: The Tea Party Takes on Harry Reid."
32. Deferred Action for Childhood Arrivals (DACA) is a program within the Department of Homeland Security (DHS) that provides protection from deportation to undocumented immigrants who could show they were sixteen years old or younger when they were brought into the country. DACA was not established as an executive order, but rather as a memorandum of guidance on immigration enforcement by DHS Secretary Janet Napolitano during the Obama administration.
33. Mayorkas graduated from Beverly Hills High and Loyola Law School. He served as US attorney for Central California during the Clinton administration. Based in LA, he was the youngest of all lead US attorneys at that time. Mayorkas returned to private practice during the George W. Bush administration. During the first Obama administration, Mayorkas was appointed director of USCIS, which created and ran DACA, after which he was promoted to deputy secretary of DHS in Obama's second term. Mayorkas reentered private practice in

the Trump years and then returned to Washington when Biden nominated him to be DHS secretary. Republican senators tried to derail his confirmation but failed. House Republicans later succeeded in impeaching him on a party-line vote. The Democratic Senate quickly disposed of the House Republicans' specious articles of impeachment. See Grisales, et al., "Senate Kills Articles of Impeachment."

34. Ayón, "Latino Diasporas." Polls measured Obama's share of the Latino vote in November 2012 at 71–75 percent.
35. National Museum of the Latino American Commission, "Final Report."
36. Thomas, "Longoria, DNC Finance Chief Partner for Latinos."
37. Republican National Committee, *Growth and Opportunity Project.*
38. Weissert and Gomez Licon, "Immigration Reform Stalled."
39. Ayón, "Latino Diasporas."
40. Ayón, "Latino Diasporas."

Chapter 12: Collision, Defeat, Resistance, Comeback

1. Brownstein, "Coalition of Transformation."
2. While some estimates are even higher, the Bureau of Labor Statistics reported a revised 780,000 jobs lost—the largest job loss of the Great Recession—in the month Obama was inaugurated, January 2009. See Barker and Hadi, "Payroll Employment in 2009."
3. White, "GOP to Fix the Economy?" Indeed, the Republicans' incessant pounding on the slow pace of economic recovery from the Great Recession, which Obama inherited, failed to defeat his reelection in 2012, and in the next midterms of 2014, the Republicans hardly had a coherent economic message.
4. See Moonesinghe et al., "Health Insurance Coverage."
5. Vankar, "Affordable Care Act-Related (ACA) Enrollments"; Kominski, Nonzee, and Sorensen, "Affordable Care Act's Impacts." AltaMed had started out as La Clínica Familiar del Barrio in East LA in 1969. Under the leadership since the 1970s of former UC Santa Barbara student activist Cástulo de la Rocha, however, by the start of the Obama presidency AltaMed had established dozens of clinics in LA and Orange Counties. In 2013, in tandem with the launch of Covered California and before the ACA opened for business, AltaMed began setting up Health Insurance Resource Centers, in addition to its clinics, to assist enrollment in underserved communities. By the end of the Biden–Harris administration, AltaMed had expanded to nearly seventy health-services locations. See Karabin, "AltaMed Sees Number of Patients Grow."
6. Both the expansion of DACA and the addition of DAPA, announced at the end of 2014, were blocked from going into effect by federal courts.
7. Decker, "Rosier Views on Economy."
8. Jacobs, "Pitching for Conservative Votes."
9. Coulter, interview by Jorge Ramos, May 26, 2015.
10. Conservative Political Action Conference, 2013. More specifically, Coulter said she had become a single-issue voter against "amnesty," but also called for

a decade-long moratorium on all immigration. President Obama had approved the DACA executive action in the previous year.

11. Note her remarks at a 2015 Trump rally about the depression she had suffered since November 7, 2012.
12. Republican National Committee, *Growth and Opportunity Project*.
13. Coulter asserted this imperative as if it would be a change of course, when, in fact, Republican presidential candidates had won the white vote in every election since 1964.
14. As Coulter's column is syndicated, it appears under different titles written by the various papers it appears in. In the Jackson, Mississippi, *Clarion-Ledger* this column was titled "Latest Bush More Suited to the Presidency of Mexico" (February 5, 2015), while in the Casper, Wyoming, *Star-Tribune* it was titled "Three Generations of Imbeciles" (February 6, 2015).
15. Coulter, "GOP Double-Crosses Voters."
16. This was Coulter's eleventh book since 1998. Over nine years later, campaigning again for the presidency, Trump was still invoking "third world hellhole." See Sentner and Ward, "Third-World Hellhole"; and Coulter, *¡Adios, America!*
17. From 2013 to 2017, the news divisions of ABC and Univision collaborated on the cable and streaming service Fusion, which featured the Donahue- and Oprah-style live-audience series *America with Jorge Ramos*. Coulter appeared on the May 26, 2015, broadcast. Univision subsequently continued the series as *Real America with Jorge Ramos* on its own stations, and later also on Facebook Watch, and finally as just a podcast through the end of 2021.
18. Trump had raised the issues of immigration and the border in previous speeches going back at least to the year before, but apparently neither consistently nor emphatically, until his June 2015 campaign launch.
19. Civil rights, busing, and abortion were nationally disruptive issues at various times, but did not lead to a true outsider takeover of either major party or outsider presidency. The Vietnam War toppled an incumbent president, but that only led to the comeback of a former VP and presidential candidate of the other party. McCarthyism produced the first retired Army-general president, but by then he was president of an Ivy League university and recruited by both parties.
20. Perkins, "Donald Trump Sues Univision."
21. To that point, the only other major news media journalist to bluntly confront Trump with his record of offensive statements was Megyn Kelly, then of Fox TV, at a Republican candidates' forum. That a Miami-based Latino journalist would also do so at a press conference was out of step with that community's politically dominant Cuban American constituency, among whom Trump was popular. One of the best accounts of this episode was produced by the Canadian Broadcasting Corporation's *The National*, reported by anchor Peter Mansbridge ("Why Jorge Ramos Took on Trump," October 21, 2016).
22. Assembly Democratic Caucus, "Speaker Rendon Strikes Defiant Tone."

23. Like Edward Roybal in the 1940s, Rendon's path included community organizing; teaching college, like Richard Alatorre; and environmental advocacy, like John Pérez; but neither labor activism nor service on an elected official's staff.
24. The Southeast Cities actually had their own assembly district in the past, before most of their city councils came under Latino control. They were split up among several districts in the redistricting just a decade earlier.
25. Sanders ran for the Democratic Party nomination, but he was not and had never been a registered Democrat. Officially an independent, Sanders nevertheless was a member of the Senate Democratic Caucus and received committee memberships and even chairmanships on the same basis as all other caucus members.
26. Suter, "Harris Says in Fundraising Email."
27. Kevin de León and Anthony Rendon, joint statement, November 9, 2016, cited in Ayón and Pla, *Power Shift*, 2, 19n7. "Today, we woke up feeling like strangers in a foreign land, because yesterday Americans expressed their views on a pluralistic and democratic society that are clearly inconsistent with the values of the people of California."
28. Marinucci and Caygle, "Becerra Appointed California Attorney General."
29. Hakeem Jeffries, leader of the House Democratic minority at the time of this writing, was neither Becerra's deputy nor his successor in the caucus.
30. Cadelago and White, "Brown Bides Time."
31. McGreevy, "Becerra Tells Senators He'd Stick with Job."
32. Predictably, Trump's DOJ filed suit shortly after the legislation took effect. See Benner and Medina, "Trump Administration Sues California."
33. Brennan Center for Justice, "Trump's 'Voter Fraud' Commission."
34. Formally titled the Presidential Advisory Commission on Election Integrity.
35. Taylor, "Trump Dissolves Controversial Election Commission."
36. Cottle, "Golden State Warrior."
37. Ibarra and Christopher, "California's Lawsuits Against Donald Trump."
38. Ibarra and Christopher, "California's Lawsuits."
39. Barrón-López, "Machine to Turn Out Arizona Latinos"; Echavarri, "Closer Than Ever to Flipping Arizona"; and Candaele, *Building Power*.

Chapter 13: We Had Next—Briefly

1. That record vote total still stands. By contrast, the Trump–Vance ticket in 2024 won with 77.3 million votes.
2. Thomson-DeVeaux, "Are Black and Hispanic Americans Abandoning Biden?"; and Carrasquillo, "'Can I Just Vote for Her Instead of Biden?'"
3. The "Super Lawyer" designation is determined by annual voting by the profession. *Los Angeles Magazine* regularly publishes the LA list.
4. The appointment of one of these DHS secretaries was found to be unlawful.
5. See Bier, "Testimony of David J. Bier."
6. Alemany, "House Republicans Impeach Mayorkas."

7. A seat on that committee opened when Senator Al Franken resigned in December 2016. Harris was only the second African American woman to serve in the US Senate.
8. Torres had attended both East Los Angeles College (ELAC) and California State University, Los Angeles, but did not complete a degree. Nava started his higher education at ELAC but ultimately earned a PhD at Harvard and had an academic career. Both served in elected office, Torres in Congress and Nava as the first Latino on the board of Los Angeles Unified School District in the 1960s. Torres is among *Los Diez* featured in *Power Shift*.
9. As related in chapter 2, as far back as 1960, LA's and the state's Latino leaders and growing Latino electorate had developed impressive influence on the Democratic side in presidential elections, in part because California represented a huge cache of electoral votes that were often won by the Republican candidate.
10. Sumagaysay, "'Leave No Region Behind.'"
11. Davis, "Trump Stole the Democrats' Playbook."
12. Cadelago and White, "Brown Bides Time."
13. Jones and Gardiner, "Rob Bonta Finds His Calling"; and Michaelson, "California Sues Pres. Trump."
14. Esparza Loera, "Attorney General-Designee Rob Bonta."
15. Jones and Gardiner, "Robert Rivas' Waiting Game."
16. Udasin, "Newsom Asks Congress for Almost $40B."
17. Tumulty, "Down-Ballot Officials."
18. Bluth and Mason, "23 Dem AGs Think They've Cracked the Code."
19. Rector, "California, Other States Sue to Block Trump."

Epilogue: After the Transition

1. Of the country's 435 congressional districts, Republicans held 222 to the Democrats' 213, which meant that if either 10 Republicans abstained or 5 chose to vote with the Democrats, Jeffries could be elected Speaker.
2. Trump made this claim in an interview published in *The Atlantic*. Parker and Scherer, "'I Run the Country and the World.'"
3. The Democrats in Congress call their grouping a "caucus," while Republicans call theirs a "conference." Either can allow nonparty or nonvoting members of Congress to participate. Thus, so-called delegates representing territories such as Puerto Rico and the District of Columbia typically caucus with the House Democrats, and independent Senator Bernie Sanders caucuses with the Senate Democrats.
4. Jordan never had a bill even referred to a committee, much less given a hearing or a vote. See Fortinsky, "Aguilar Delivers Fiery Speech"; and Einenkel, "Rep. Pete Aguilar Gives Amazing Speech." The latter piece includes a full transcript of the first of Aguilar's two speeches.
5. In 1994, a split-level backlash swept US politics in California with Proposition 187, and nationally with Representative Newt Gingrich's "Contract with America" legislative program. It was a plan, literally signed by Republican candidates

in that year's midterm elections, that won them the House majority for the first time in forty years and made Gingrich Speaker. Many analysts and historians agree that Gingrich's approach inaugurated a new era of US politics conducted in a manner akin to warfare, with the relentless demonization of political opponents.

6. Robert Menendez of New Jersey was the first Latino to serve as chair of the Democratic Caucus, from 2003–2006, when he was appointed to fill a vacated Senate seat. Xavier Becerra, who like Menendez was first elected to Congress in 1992, chaired the Democratic Caucus from 2013–2017.
7. Martin, "This California Democrat."
8. This and other discussions of Chair Aguilar are based on interviews with Aguilar (conducted by the authors on September 6, 2023, and January 17, 2025), in addition to cited secondary sources.
9. The 1998 statewide coordinated field operation Padilla headed had gubernatorial candidate Gray Davis at the top of the ticket. Once he graduated from college, Aguilar was appointed deputy director of Governor Davis's Inland Empire regional office.
10. Newsom withdrew from the gubernatorial race when it became clear that former Governor Jerry Brown intended to stage a comeback. Newsom then redirected his efforts to his successful bid to be elected lieutenant governor.
11. Martin, "This California Democrat"; and Oreskes, "How the Mayor of a Small Inland Empire Town."
12. See Bonta, "California Sues Pres. Trump." The twenty-three Democratic attorneys general include Washington, DC's AG.
13. Uranga, "Immigrant Rights Activists Vow to Disrupt ICE Raids"; and the California Collaborative for Immigrant Justice website, https://www.ccijustice.org/.
14. Vives, "They Patrol L.A.'s Streets in Search of ICE"; and Macías, "Sesenta grupos se tomarán las calles contra La Migra en LA."
15. The order of succession to the presidency is vice president, Speaker of the House, president pro tem of the Senate, and then secretary of state.
16. Manchester, "7 Most Likely GOP Successors." Asked in an interview with Bret Baier that aired on Fox News on February 10, 2025, Trump said he did not consider Vance his political heir.
17. Swan and Haberman, "Trump Officials Clashed With Elon Musk"; and Bandouil, "Rubio, Musk Clash with Polish FM over Starlink."
18. See Wong, "Marco Rubio, Secretary of Everything."
19. See Mohyeldin, "Marco Rubio's Irrelevance in Trump World." Foreign policy specialists anticipated, months before he was sworn into office, that Rubio would be more figurehead than actual secretary of state; see Milne, "Trump Is His Own Secretary of State." Well into his second 100 days in office, mounting evidence confirmed that original expectation; see Stanley-Becker, "Trump's Real Secretary of State."
20. For an early take, see Toosi, "Marco Rubio Guide to Survival."
21. Saaliq, "Elon Musk Met with Modi."

22. Anderson, "Rubio Makes Immigration Threat."
23. Partnership for Public Service, "State of Public Trust"; and Pew Research Center, "Public Trust in Government."
24. To this end, Padilla had served as both western regional vice president of the National Association of Secretaries of State and president of the National Association of Latino Elected and Appointed Officials (NALEO). Luján led the Democratic Congressional Campaign Committee in the election cycle that recovered the House majority in 2018, while Cortez-Masto chaired the Democratic Senatorial Campaign Committee from 2019 to 2021.
25. Quick, "Ambitious Collaboration Boosts Journalism in Los Angeles."
26. Times Editorial Board, "Our Dishonest President."
27. Korach, "*LA Times*' Owner Courted CNN's Top Trump Defender."
28. The Pew Research Center poll put Trump's Hispanic net approval at 27 percent. See Pew Research Center, "Trump's Job Rating Drops," online appendix, "April 2025 Trump Approval Detailed Tables," https://docs.google.com/spreadsheets/d/1ad-90UPr75dNdHn5inG7epZHc_AOdTp4jPVVg1MBxUA/edit?gid=1374525747#gid=1374525747.
29. See Davis, "President Trump's Approval Rating: Latest Polls"; Alcantara et al., "Trump's First 100 Days, in 10 Charts"; Langer, "Trump Has Lowest 100-Day Approval Rating in 80 Years: POLL."
30. Sobczyk, "Trump's First Economic Scorecard."
31. Equis Research, "May 2025 Poll on Latinos, Trump and Immigration."
32. The third Latino in the race was Tony Thurmond, second-term superintendent of public instruction, who is of Panamanian descent.
33. Ayón, "United States Foreign Policy."
34. Cynthia Telles to Costa Rica, Nathalie Rayes to Croatia, and Eric Garcetti to India.
35. See the discussion of AltaMed in chapter 12. AltaMed has collaborated for many years with Mexican consulates in their offering of "Binational Health Week," aimed at addressing the health needs of Mexican immigrants.
36. This discussion is based on interviews with Rayes (conducted by the authors on April 10, 2025, and April 28, 2025), a prospectus by Rayes on this initiative, and conversations with others involved in preliminary planning.

Postscript: Los Angeles, June 2025

1. Stegall, "Federal Immigration Agents"; Weisberg and Mendoza, "ICE Agents Conduct Raid.
2. Vives, "ICE Agents with Assault Rifles"; Quezada and Bravo, "'Needlessly Reckless.'"
3. For an overview of the development of the immigration-enforcement crisis in metro LA, see Erden et al., "Maps and Timeline of the L.A. Immigration Protests." The imposing downtown LA Federal Building, in a twist of historical irony, is named for the great pioneer of California Latina/o political empowerment, the late US Representative and LA City Council Member, Edward R.

Roybal. There have been media accounts of immigrants being detained and held in the basement of the Federal Building upon reporting to ICE authorities for required check-ins. The building is also a federal courthouse. The large Metropolitan Detention Center (MDC), managed by the Federal Bureau of Prisons, is nearby in this US government complex. Many ICE arrestees are reportedly being held in the MDC, in addition to other federal prisoners pending court procedures or serving sentences.

4. Uranga and Vives, "What Really Happened?"
5. CNN's chief media analyst, Brian Stelter, called the operations a "Made-for-TV crackdown," noting that television personality Dr. Phil McGraw was embedded with ICE agents on their LA raids, and his camera crew was shooting footage in the style of war correspondents. This excursion was for a special report on McGraw's TV platform. Stelter, "Made-for-TV Crackdown."
6. Martínez, "As National Guard Deploys." Paramount is one of the heavily Latino-majority Southeast Cities of LA County, though not among those Martha Escutia mobilized for unification in a single assembly district for the 1992 elections. See the section "Redistricting Redux: Southeast Side Story" in chapter 7 for more on the general area.
7. Anderson, "Stephen Miller's Order"; Findell et al., "White House Marching Orders." Notably, it was the business press that led the media in reporting on the turn in the Trump administration's efforts to accelerate its mass-deportation objectives, of particular concern to business given the intensification of workplace raids.
8. Prokop, "The Architect."
9. Grayer, Cohen, and Klein, "Trump Preparing Large-scale Cancellation."
10. Duara and Kuang, "With Troops and Protests."
11. "Department of Defense Security," *Presidential Memoranda.*
12. Goitein, "'The Insurrection Act.'"
13. Jorge Ramos, "Lo que está ocurriendo en Los Angeles es muy grave," *Jorgeramosnews,* June 8, 2025, https://www.instagram.com/reel/DKptCb3N_rh/?igsh=NTc4MTIwNjQ2YQ==.
14. Forbes Breaking News, "Pete Hegseth Snaps at Aguilar."
15. Vertuno, "Protests Against Immigration Raids"; Smith et al., "As Immigration Raids Continue"; Beckett, "Los Angeles."
16. Doyle, "LA Demonstrations."
17. Wolffe, "California Senate elects Monique Limón."
18. Skelton, "Padilla Was Right"; Ehisen, "George Skelton."
19. Hubler, Medina, and Cowan, "Calif. Senator Forcibly Removed."

Acknowledgments

FORGING LATINO POWER, AS WITH our first collaboration, *Power Shift*, would not have been possible without the generous cooperation of many leaders who shared their perspectives and memories with us in multiple interviews: Rodolfo Acuña, Pete Aguilar, Howard Berman, Charles Kamasaki, Henry Cisneros, Kevin de León, Martha Escutia, David Damian Figueroa, Dean Florez, Marshall Ganz, Eric Garcetti, Gil Garcetti, Lorena Gonzalez, Dolores Huerta, Monica Lozano, Jorge Mettey, Alex Padilla, John Pérez, Jorge Ramos, Nathalie Rayes, Anthony Rendon, and Antonio Villaraigosa. Apologies to the many friends and colleagues who also helped along the way, unfortunately too many to list here—but we will try to on this book's forthcoming website.

These book projects owe their success to the brilliant and unwavering support of our team. Seda Yaghoubian guided this book with skill and dedication as project manager, while Anitra Grisales, our exceptional developmental editor for both books, brought vision, clarity, and care to every page. We're also grateful to Romie Vega for expertly coordinating interviews, to Debby Kim for managing key communications and logistics, and to Akiko Tamano, whose meticulous copy editing elevated the final manuscript. We've also been deeply enriched by the insight and generosity of many others through conversations and correspondence that helped shape our thinking.

David R. Ayón's Personal Acknowledgments

I owe much of what I've learned of California Latino politics to George Pla, of course, and am grateful for his commitment to our undertaking these books together. I've called our joint Power Shift project the greatest-ever continuing study of Latino politics—and we're far from done. Gilbert Cedillo and Marc Grossman have both been my tutors, tirelessly responsive to many calls and questions for over a decade. Charles Kamasaki was as generous as a friend and fellow author can be; in addition to writing the definitive history of the making of the 1980s IRCA immigration reform, he shared unpublished materials, answered many questions, brought me (by long-distance communications) into his Washington, DC Latino advocacy world, and connected me with Prof. Rosanna Perotti, attorney Bari Schwartz, and longtime activist Michael Treviño, who gave generously of their time.

Without Yolanda Nava, I would not have come to know and understand the empowerment experience she shared with our dearly departed Gloria Molina. My friend Cindy Montañez, who left us tragically young, was also a source for both books and of personal encouragement. Since *Power Shift* was published, we also lost Esteban Torres—who welcomed me into his home for my first interviews in 2010—and Richard Alatorre, both legends of LA Chicano/Latino history. My oldest friend and homie, attorney Fernando Tafoya, was both a source for this book and of endless good cheer and support.

Prof. Cristina Mora of UC Berkeley, herself a standout scholar of the Latina/o empowerment experience, believed in this project and gave it a home at the Institute of Governmental Studies, where I also had a year as a research associate while working on this book. The legendary Marshall Ganz gave me the opportunity to present *Power Shift* at Harvard, as well as an extended interview at his home for this second book. I again owe deep personal thanks to Monica Lozano, as well as to her departed parents Nacho and Marta, and Monica's sister Leticia.

George L. Pla's Personal Acknowledgments

This book emerged from a growing realization during the writing of *Power Shift*, as well as from our subsequent interactions with its readers: the remarkable history of California's Latino political brilliance was too expansive for a single volume, and readers wanted more. I'm deeply grateful to my coauthor, David R. Ayón—a brilliant scholar and steadfast partner—whose insight and commitment were essential to bringing both *Power Shift* and now *Forging Latino Power* to life, and to laying the groundwork for our books yet to come. I also want to personally acknowledge the "A" team: Seda Yaghoubian, whose professionalism and insight made our book possible; Anitra Grisales, the best editor ever; and Debby Kim, Romie Vega, and Lupe Sanchez for their commitment, expertise, and, most importantly, having the patience to work with me directly!

The result of over five years of work, *Forging Latino Power* arrives at a defining moment in American politics, society, and history, as debates over representation, justice, and power intensify. This volume introduces a rising generation of Latino leaders—from elected officials, organizers, and advocates to cabinet secretaries and diplomats—who carry forward the legacy and stand on the shoulders of the *Los Diez* pioneers of our first book, and who are transforming their communities from the ground up. Their stories offer young people more than inspiration; they prove that leadership can reflect their identities, speak their truths, and champion their futures.

It's an honor to have played a part in this history. I dedicate this work with love and gratitude to my family: my wife, Gail, whose steady support has uplifted every project; my children, Vincent and Lisa; my grandchildren, Vanessa, Daniel, Patrick, Damian, and Kane; and my great-grandchildren, Noah, Kaden, Jonah, and Sebastian. May this story serve as a legacy for them, and a window into the remarkable Latino leaders who transformed California and shaped the course of American politics.

Abbreviations

ACA	Affordable Care Act
ACLU	American Civil Liberties Union
AFSC	American Friends Service Committee
AG	attorney general
ALRA	Agricultural Labor Relations Act
ALRB	Agricultural Labor Relations Board
AWA	Agricultural Workers Association
AWOC	Agricultural Workers Organizing Committee
CASA	Centro de Acción Social Autónomo
CBO	community-based organization
CHC	Congressional Hispanic Caucus
CIR	comprehensive immigration reform
CRLA	California Rural Legal Assistance
CSO	Community Service Organization
CSU	California State University
CTA	California Teachers Association
DACA	Deferred Action for Childhood Arrivals
DAGA	Democratic Attorneys General Association
DAPA	Deferred Action for Parents of Americans and Lawful Permanent Residents
DHS	Department of Homeland Security
DOJ	Department of Justice
ECCSF	East Coast Chicano Student Forum
ELA	enterprise lease agreement
ELAC	East Los Angeles College
HOPE	Hispanas Organized for Political Equality
HUD	Housing and Urban Development (Department of)
ICE	Immigration and Customs Enforcement

INA	Immigration and Nationality Act
INS	Immigration and Naturalization Service
IRCA	Immigration Reform and Control Act
LAPD	Los Angeles Police Department
LAUSD	Los Angeles Unified School District
LCCR	Leadership Conference on Civil Rights
LDF	Legal Defense Fund (NAACP)
LPR	lawful permanent resident
LUChA	La Unión Chicana por Aztlán
LUCHA	Living United for Change in Arizona
LULAC	League of United Latin American Citizens
LV	Latino Victory
LVF	Latino Victory Fund
MALDEF	Mexican American Legal Defense and Education Fund
MAPA	Mexican American Political Association
MEChA	Movimiento Estudiantil Chicano de Aztlán
MIT	Massachusetts Institute of Technology
NAACP	National Association for the Advancement of Colored People
NALEO	National Association of Latino Elected and Appointed Officials
NCLR	National Council of La Raza
NFWA	National Farm Workers Association
NLRA	National Labor Relations Act
NGO	nongovernmental organization
SAW	Special Agricultural Workers (program)
SB	Senate Bill
SEIU	Service Employees International Union
UAW	United Auto Workers
UCLA	University of California, Los Angeles
UFW	United Farm Workers
UPWA	United Packinghouse Workers of America
USC	University of Southern California
USCIS	US Citizenship and Immigration Services (Homeland Security)
VRA	Voting Rights Act
WAAA	We Are America Alliance
YEH	*¡Ya Es Hora!*

References

Original Interviews

(All on Zoom and recorded unless otherwise noted.)

Acuña, Rodolfo. Telephone interview with authors, May 20, 2020 (notes only).

Aguilar, Pete. Interviews with authors, September 6, 2023; and January 17, 2025.

Berman, Howard. Interviews with authors, October 1, 2021; and October 7, 2021.

Cedillo, Gilbert. Interviews with authors, February 5, 2021; February 11, 2021; August 5, 2021; and August 12, 2021.

Cisneros, Henry. Interviews with authors, September 28, 2020; October 15, 2020; November 5, 2020; January 20, 2021; and March 21, 2022.

de León, Kevin. Interviews with authors, September 30, 2020; December 16, 2020; January 7, 2021; and September 17, 2021.

Escutia, Martha. Interviews with authors, December 29, 2020; April 29, 2021; May 3, 2021; May 25, 2021; September 2, 2021; January 27, 2022; and April 9, 2024.

Figueroa, David Damian. Interviews with authors, December 12, 2020; and February 13, 2020, by telephone (notes only).

Florez, Dean. Interviews with authors, November 10, 2020; November 16, 2020; December 9, 2020; December 15, 2020; and February 9, 2022.

Ganz, Marshall. Interview with authors, November 8, 2018 (audio only).

Garcetti, Eric. Interviews with authors, October 20, 2020 (audio only); and September 13, 2021.

Garcetti, Gil. Interview with authors, March 10, 2021.

Gonzalez, Lorena. Interviews with authors, September 29, 2020; October 20, 2020; and November 17, 2020.

Huerta, Dolores. Interviews with authors, December 16, 2020; March 19, 2021; April 16, 2021; April 23, 2021; and February 4, 2022.

Lozano Jr., Ignacio "Nacho" E. Interviews with authors, February 16, 2013; February 23, 2013; and May 4, 2013.

Lozano Jr., Ignacio "Nacho" E. and Marta Lozano. Interview with authors, March 23, 2013.

Lozano, Monica. Interviews with authors, March 9, 2013; April 4, 2013; October 4, 2022; October 28, 2022; and January 5, 2023.

Mettey, Jorge. Telephone interview with authors, March 9, 2024.

Molina, Gloria. Interviews with authors, October 16, 2014, Los Angeles; September 8, 2017, Los Angeles (notes only); September 10, 2017, by telephone (notes only); and September 11, 2017, by telephone.

Padilla, Alex. Interviews with authors, September 9, 2020, Los Angeles; September 23, 2020; October 14, 2020; November 18, 2020; and January 8, 2021.

Pérez, John. Interviews with authors, March 3, 2021; June 3, 2021; and August 10, 2021.

Pla, George. Interviews with David Ayón, July 14, 2020; September 22, 2020; and June 17, 2022.

Ramos, Jorge. Interview with authors, December 21, 2020.

Rayes, Nathalie. Interviews with authors, January 4, 2021; April 10, 2025; and April 28, 2025 (notes only).

Rendon, Anthony. Interviews with authors, December 14, 2020; January 13, 2021; and April 8, 2021.

Telles, Cynthia. Interviews with authors, February 11, 2013; and February 22, 2013 (audio only).

Secondary Sources

Abcarian, Robin. "Obama Gets Major Labor Endorsement." *Los Angeles Times*, January 16, 2008. https://www.latimes.com/nation/la-na-labor16jan16-story.html.

African American Research Collaborative and BSP Research. "2024 American Electorate Poll." https://2024electionpoll.us/.

Aguilar Rangel, Jazmin. "Remittances in Mexico Reach a Historic High." Wilson Center Mexico Institute, March 15, 2022. https://www.wilsoncenter.org/article/infographic-remittances-mexico-reach-historic-high.

Ahn, Eugene, Irena Auerbuch, and Peggy Lee. "Student Protest Turns to Destruction." *Daily Bruin*, May 27, 1988. https://dailybruin.com/2018/05/02/throwback-thursday-contested-usac-elections-of-yesteryear-triggered-racially-charged-protests.

Alanís Enciso, Fernando. *They Should Stay There: The Story of Mexican Migration and Repatriation During the Great Depression.* University of North Carolina Press, 2017.

Alcantara, Chris, Nick Mourtoupalas, Azi Paybarah, and Clara Ence Morse. "Trump's First 100 Days, in 10 Charts." *The Washington Post,* April 29, 2025. https://www.washingtonpost.com/politics/2025/04/29/trump-first-100-days-approval-rating/.

Alemany, Jacqueline. "House Republicans Impeach Mayorkas by a Single Vote." *The Washington Post,* February 13, 2024. https://www.washingtonpost.com/politics/2024/02/13/mayorkas-impeachment-seccond-house-vote/.

American Immigration Council. "A Comparison of the DREAM Act and Other Proposals for Undocumented Youth." June 5, 2012. https://www.americanimmigrationcouncil.org/research/comparison-dream-act-and-other-proposals-undocumented-youth.

Amezcua, Mike. "Chasing the 'Latino Vote': What Politicians Miss by Treating Voters as a Monolithic Bloc." *Perspectives on History,* American Historical Association, October 30, 2024. https://www.historians.org/perspectives-article/chasing-the-latino-vote/.

Anderson, Stuart. "Rubio Makes Immigration Threat to Revoke Student, H-1B And Other Visas." *Forbes,* May 05, 2025. https://www.forbes.com/sites/stuartanderson/2025/05/05/rubio-makes-immigration-threat-to-revoke-student-h-1b-and-other-visas/.

Anderson, Stuart. "Stephen Miller's Order Likely Sparked Immigration Arrests and Protests." *Forbes,* June 9, 2025. https://www.forbes.com/sites/stuartanderson/2025/06/09/stephen-millers-order-likely-sparked-immigration-arrests-and-protests/.

Arellano, Gustavo. "The Ghosts of Migrant Dead Haunt California. Let's Honor Them." *Los Angeles Times,* March 7, 2021. https://www.latimes.com/california/story/2021-03-07/migrant-crash-holtville-chualar-los-gatos-blythe.

Arellano, Gustavo. "Nativo Lopez, a Pioneering and Polarizing Latino Leader in O.C. and L.A., Dies at 68." *Los Angeles Times,* May 20, 2019. https://www.latimes.com/local/california/la-me-nativo-lopez-dead-hermandad-mexicana-20190520-story.html.

Arellano, Gustavo. "O.C. Can You Say . . . 'Anti-Mexican'?" *Los Angeles Times,* May 8, 2006. https://www.latimes.com/archives/la-xpm-2006-may-08-oe-arellano8-story.html.

Arellano, Gustavo. "Orange County Once Was an Anti-Immigrant Hotbed. What Changed?" *Los Angeles Times,* January 30, 2025. https://www.latimes.com/california/story/2025-01-30/orange-county-anti-immigrant-history.

Arellano, Gustavo. "Prop. 187 Timeline: The Rise and Fall of California's Anti-Immigrant Law." *Los Angeles Times*, October 29, 2019. https://www.latimes.com/california/story/2019-10-06/proposition-187-timeline.

Arellano, Gustavo. "The Rise and Stumbles of the San Fernando Valley Latino Political Machine." *Los Angeles Times*, February 27, 2024. https://www.latimes.com/california/story/2024-02-27/san-fernando-valley-latino-political-machine.

Ascher, Leonard. "Lincoln's Administration and the New Almaden Scandal." *Pacific Historical Review* 5, no. 1 (1936): 38–51. https://www.jstor.org/stable/3633317.

Assembly Democratic Caucus. "Speaker Rendon Strikes Defiant Tone for California as Assembly Reconvenes." Media release, December 4, 2016.

Associated Press. "Democrats Gain Control of Legislature." *Albuquerque Journal*, November 10, 1938.

Associated Press. "Rio Grande Pact Approval Forecast." *Albuquerque Journal*, January 15, 1939.

Ayón, David R. "Developing the U.S.-Mexico Border Region for a Prosperous and Secure Relationship: The Impact of Mexican Migration and Border Proximity on Local Communities." James A. Baker III Institute for Public Policy, Rice University, March 27, 2009. https://www.bakerinstitute.org/sites/default/files/2013-08/import/LAI-pub-BorderSecAyon-032709.pdf.

Ayón, David R. "Latino Diasporas, Obama's Executive Action Strategy and U.S.-Latin American Relations." In *Contemporary U.S.-Latin American Relations: Cooperation or Conflict in the 21st Century?*, edited by Jorge I. Domínguez and Rafael Fernández de Castro. Routledge, 2016.

Ayón, David R. "Migrants and the State, 1986–2006." In *Mexico's Democratic Challenges: Politics, Government and Society*, edited by Andrew Selee and Jacqueline Peschard. Stanford University Press, 2010.

Ayón, David R. "Mobilizing Latino Immigrant Integration: From IRCA to the Ya Es Hora Citizenship Campaign, 1987–2007." Wilson Center Mexico Institute, February 1, 2012. https://www.wilsoncenter.org/publication/mobilizing-latino-immigrant-integration-irca-to-the-ya-es-hora-citizenship-campaign-1987.

Ayón, David R. "Texas Versus California: Latino Politics and Relations with Mexico." In *The International Relations of California and Texas with Mexico and the World*, edited by Jorge A. Schiavon and Rafael Fernández de Castro. Routledge, 2023.

Ayón, David R. "United States Foreign Policy." In *The Oxford Encyclopedia of Latinos and Latinas in Contemporary Law, Politics and Social Movements*, edited by Suzanne Oboler and Deena J. González. Oxford University Press, 2015.

Ayón, David R., and George C. Pla. *Power Shift: How Latinos in California Transformed Politics in America*. Berkeley Public Policy Press, 2018.

Bada, Xóchitl, Jonathan Fox, and Andrew Selee, eds. *Invisible No More: Mexican Migrant Civic Participation in the United States*. Woodrow Wilson International Center for Scholars, 2006.

Baker, Lou, Lino E. Camacho, and Robert A. Salinas. *Latino Political Representation: The 1993–94 California Latino Legislative Caucus*. UC Berkeley: Chicano/Latino Policy Project, March 1995. https://escholarship.org/uc/item/9bj3332h.

Balderston, Daniel, Mike Gonzalez, and Ana M. Lopez, eds. *Encyclopedia of Contemporary Latin American and Caribbean Cultures*. Routledge, 2000.

Bandouil, Sonya. "Rubio, Musk Clash with Polish FM over Starlink in Ukraine, Accuse Him of 'Just Making Things Up.'" *The Kyiv Independent*, March 9, 2025. https://kyivindependent.com/rubio-musk-clash-with-polish-fm-over-starlink-in-ukraine-accuse-him-of-just-making-things-up/.

Barajas, Frank P. *Mexican Americans with Moxie: A Transgenerational History of El Movimiento in Ventura County, California, 1945–75*. University of Nebraska Press, 2021.

Bardacke, Frank. "UFW and the Undocumented." *International Labor and Working-Class History*, no. 83 (Spring 2018): 162–69. https://www.jstor.org/stable/43302716.

Bardacke, Frank. *Trampling Out the Vintage: Cesar Chavez and the Two Souls of the United Farmworkers*. Verso Books, 2011.

Barker, Megan M. and Adam A. Hadi. "Payroll Employment in 2009: Job Losses Continue." *Monthly Labor Review*, March 2010. https://www.bls.gov/opub/mlr/2010/03/art2full.pdf.

Barreto, Matt, and Gary M. Segura. *Latino America: How America's Most Dynamic Population Is Poised to Transform the Politics of the Nation*. PublicAffairs, 2014.

Barrón-López, Laura. "Inside the Machine to Turn Out Arizona Latinos—and Flip the State Blue." *Politico*, November 1, 2020. https://www.politico.com/news/2020/11/01/arizona-latinos-election-433796.

Beagle, Christine. "Siete Lenguas: The Rhetorical History of Dolores Huerta and the Rise of Chicana Rhetoric." PhD diss., University of New Mexico, 2015. https://digitalrepository.unm.edu/engl_etds/34.

Beam, Adam. "Farmworkers Fight Shaped California Attorney General Nominee." *U.S. News & World Report / Associated Press*, March 25, 2021. https://www.usnews.com/news/politics/articles/2021-03-25/farmworkers-fight-shaped-california-attorney-general-nominee.

Bebitch Jeffe, Sherry. "Why Republicans May Rue Their Heartfelt Support for Term Limits." *Los Angeles Times*, December 8, 1991. https://www.latimes.com/archives/la-xpm-1991-12-08-op-228-story.html.

Becker, Lawrence C., Tyler Hughes, and Jason L. Morin. *The History, Development, and Policy Influence of the California Latino Legislative Caucus*. Center for Southern California Studies, California State University, Northridge, 2016. https://www.csun.edu/center-for-southern-california-studies/latino-caucus.

Beckett, Lois. "Los Angeles, City of Immigrant Protests: Why It's No Surprise LA Rose Up Against Trump." *The Guardian*, June 11, 2025. https://www.theguardian.com/us-news/2025/jun/11/los-angeles-protest-history?CMP=Share_iOSApp_Other.

Behrens, Zach. "Until the 1950s, Los Angeles County Was the Top Agricultural County in the U.S." *PBS SoCal*, February 11, 2011. https://www.pbssocal.org/socal-focus/until-the-1950s-los-angeles-county-was-the-top-agricultural-county-in-the-u-s.

Bender, Stephen W. *One Night in America: Robert Kennedy, Cesar Chavez, and the Dream of Dignity*. Paradigm, 2008.

Ben-Ghiat, Ruth. *Strongmen: Mussolini to the Present*. W. W. Norton, 2020.

Benner, Katie, and Jennifer Medina. "Trump Administration Sues California Over Immigration Laws." *New York Times*, March 6, 2018. https://www.nytimes.com/2018/03/06/us/politics/justice-department-california-sanctuary-cities.html.

Berkowitz, Eric. "The Subway Mayor." *LA Weekly*, August 18, 2005.

Bernal, Rafael. "Koch-Affiliated Libre Initiative Rolls Out New Public Image." *The Hill*, June 24, 2024. https://thehill.com/latino/4737026-charles-koch-libre-initiative/.

Bernstein, Shana. *Bridges of Reform: Interracial Civil Rights Activism in Twentieth-Century Los Angeles*. Oxford University Press, 2011.

Berumen, Frank. *Edward R. Roybal: The Mexican American Struggle for Political Empowerment*. Bilingual Educational Services, 2015.

Bier, David J. "Testimony of David J. Bier, Director of Immigration Studies, the Cato Institute, Before the Committee on the Judiciary, Subcommittee on Immigration Integrity, Security, and Enforcement, United States House of Representatives, January 22, 2025." https://docs.house.gov/meetings/JU/JU01/20250122/117827/HHRG-119-JU01-Wstate-BierD-20250122.pdf. Video recording available at https://www.cato.org/multimedia/media-highlights-tv/david-j-bier-testifies-hearing-restoring-immigration-enforcement.

"Biography Sketch of Carmela G. Lacayo." Dr. Hector P. Garcia Papers, Collection 5, Box 21. Special Collections and Archives, Mary and Jeff Bell Library, Texas A&M University–Corpus Christi. https://tamucc-ir.tdl.org/handle/1969.6/27040.

Blasier, Cole. *The Hovering Giant: U.S. Responses to Revolutionary Change in Latin America, 1910–1985*, Revised ed. University of Pittsburgh Press, 1985.

Blume, Howard. "New Name, New Life for Belmont School." *Los Angeles Times,* August 10, 2008. https://www.latimes.com/local/la-me-belmont10-2008aug10-story.html.

Bluth, Rachel, and Melanie Mason. "23 Dem AGs Think They've Cracked the Code to Fighting Trump." *Politico,* February 27, 2025. https://www.politico.com/news/2025/02/27/democrats-taking-trump-musk-winning-00206310.

Bonta, Rob. "California Sues Pres. Trump." Interview by Elex Michaelson. *The Issue Is: With Elex Michaelson,* February 14, 2025. YouTube, 25 min., 58 sec. https://youtu.be/PT5D_TyKddk.

Bower, Stephanie. "Statement of Stephanie Bower, Coordinator, Legislative Department, United Farm Workers." *The Knowing Employment of Illegal Immigrants. Hearing before the Subcommittee on Immigration and Refugee Policy of the Committee on the Judiciary, United States Senate, 97th Cong., 1st Sess. September 30, 1981.* https://books.google.com/books?id=Yf6jIcIThtUC&pg=PA78&dq=Stephanie+Bower+Sanctions.

Bowman, Karlyn, and Samantha Goldstein. *The Exit Polls: A History and Trends Over Time, 1972–2020.* American Enterprise Institute Public Opinion Studies, January 2022. https://www.aei.org/wp-content/uploads/2022/01/The-Exit-Polls.pdf.

Boyarsky, Bill. *Big Daddy: Jesse Unruh and the Art of Power Politics.* University of California Press, 2008.

Boyarsky, Bill. "The Rocky Race of Sarah Flores." *Los Angeles Times,* October 11, 1990. https://www.latimes.com/archives/la-xpm-1990-10-11-ti-2694-story.html.

Boyd, Thomas M., and Stephen J. Markman. "The 1982 Amendments to the Voting Rights Act: A Legislative History." *Washington and Lee Law Review* 40, no. 4 (1983): 1,347.

Brennan Center for Justice. "Meet the Members of Trump's 'Voter Fraud' Commission.'" Brennan Center for Justice Expert Brief, July 18, 2017. https://www.brennancenter.org/our-work/research-reports/meet-members-trumps-voter-fraud-commission.

Bronder, Saul E. *Social Justice and Church Authority: The Public Life of Archbishop Robert E. Lucey.* Temple University Press, 1982.

Browning, Rufus P., Dale Rogers Marshall, and David H. Tabb. *Protest Is Not Enough: The Struggle of Blacks and Hispanics for Equality in Urban Politics.* University of California Press, 1984.

Brownstein, Ronald. "The Coalition of Transformation vs. the Coalition of Restoration." *The Atlantic,* November 21, 2012. https://www.theatlantic.com/politics/archive/2012/11/the-coalition-of-transformation-vs-the-coalition-of-restoration/265512/.

Brownstein, Ronald. "Is Donald Trump Outflanking Hillary Clinton?" *The Atlantic*, November 2, 2016. https://www.theatlantic.com/politics/archive/2016/11/trump-clinton-electoral-college/506306/.

Bullock, Charles S., Keith Gåddie, and Justin J. Wert. *The Rise and Fall of the Voting Rights Act*. University of Oklahoma Press, 2016.

Bunting, Glenn F., and Alan C. Miller. "Feinstein Raises Immigration Profile: Senator Says She is Staking Out Middle Ground on Reform." *Los Angeles Times*, July 18, 1993. https://www.latimes.com/archives/la-xpm-1993-07-18-mn-14398-story.html.

Burt, Kenneth C. *The Search for a Civic Voice: California Latino Politics*. Regina Books, 2007.

Cadava, Gerald. *The Hispanic Republican: The Shaping of an American Political Identity, from Nixon to Trump*. Ecco, 2020.

Cadelago, Christopher. "The Untold Story of How Kevin Leon Became Kevin de León." *The Sacramento Bee*, February 23, 2017. https://www.sacbee.com/news/politics-government/capitol-alert/article133464794.html.

Cadelago, Christopher, and Jeremy B. White. "Legislators Rip Trump, but Brown Bides Time." *The Sacramento Bee*, December 6, 2016.

Calavita, Kitty. *California's "Employer Sanctions": The Case of the Disappearing Law*. Research Report Series 39. Center for U.S.-Mexican Studies, 1982.

Calavita, Kitty. *U.S. Immigration Law and the Control of Labor*. Academic Press, 1984.

California Environmental Voters. "California Environmental Scorecard." https://envirovoters.org/scorecard/.

California Latino Legislative Caucus. "The California Latino Legislative Caucus Thanks Pete Wilson on the 25th Anniversary of Prop. 187." November 4, 2019. Video, 3 min., 8 sec. https://latinocaucus.legislature.ca.gov/25th-anniversary-proposition-187-thank-you-pete-wilson.

California Legislative Information. "AB-2940 Retirement: California Employee Savings Program (2007–2008), Bill History." https://leginfo.legislature.ca.gov/faces/billHistoryClient.xhtml?bill_id=200720080AB2940.

California Secretary of State. "November 3, 1992, General Election Statement of Vote." https://elections.cdn.sos.ca.gov/sov/1992-general/assemblymember.pdf.

California State Postsecondary Education Commission. *Equal Educational Opportunity in California Postsecondary Education, Part III*. March 1980. https://files.eric.ed.gov/fulltext/ED190005.pdf.

California State Treasurer. "California Secure Choice Retirement Savings Investment Board: Summary of Senate Bill 1234." October 24, 2016. https://www.treasurer.ca.gov/calsavers/meeting/2016/20161024/staff/4.pdf.

California State Treasurer. "CalSavers Retirement Savings Board." Accessed May 13, 2025. https://www.treasurer.ca.gov/calsavers/.

California State Treasurer. "State Treasurer Fiona Ma, Board, Leaders Announce Official Launch of CalSavers." News release, July 1, 2019. https://yubanet.com /california/state-treasurer-fiona-ma-board-leaders-announce-official-launch-of-calsavers/.

California State Treasurer. "Treasurer Chiang & Senator De León Vow to 'Leave No Worker Behind' at CalSavers Kickoff Event in Los Angeles." News release, November 27, 2018. https://www.treasurer.ca.gov/news/releases/2018/ 20181127/74.pdf.

Camarillo, Albert. *Chicanos in a Changing Society: From Mexican Pueblos to American Barrios in Santa Barbara and Southern California, 1848–1930*. Southern Methodist University Press, 2005.

Campbell, J. Howard. *From Cinnabar to Quicksilver*. New Almaden Quicksilver County Park Association, 2009.

Campbell, Randolph B. *An Empire for Slavery: The Peculiar Institution in Texas, 1821–1865*. Louisiana State University Press, 1989.

Candaele, Kelly. *Building Power: Turning Arizona Blue*. Posted October 29, 2020. YouTube, 10 min., 48 min. https://youtu.be/Fj_LPiwtx_g.

Carpizo, Almendra. "Recordando a el Barrio del Chivo." *The Fresno Bee*, October 25, 2017.

Carrasquillo, Adrian. "'Can I Just Vote for Her Instead of Biden?': Inside Kamala's Scramble to Win the Latino Vote." *Politico*, August 26, 2024. https://www. politico.com/news/magazine/2024/08/26/kamala-harris-latino-voters -00173976.

Castañeda, Antonia. "A History of Mexican Americans in California: Historic Sites. Spanishtown Site, New Almaden, Santa Clara County." Five Views: An Ethnic Historic Site Survey for California. National Park Service online book, 2004. https://www.nps.gov/parkhistory/online_books/5views/5views5h87.htm.

Castañeda, Jorge. *Compañero: The Life and Death of Che Guevara*. Vintage, 1998.

Centro de Acción Social Autónomo. "Guide to the Centro de Acción Social Autónomo Papers, 1963–1978." Collection no. M0325. Online Archive of California. Department of Special Collections, Stanford University Libraries. https://oac.cdlib.org/findaid/ark:/13030/tf587004hp/admin/.

Chatfield, LeRoy. "A Turning Point." Farmworker Movement Documentation Project. Published by LeRoy Chatfield, presented by UC San Diego Library, 2004. https://libraries.ucsd.edu/farmworkermovement/essays/chatfield.shtml.

"Chavez and the UFW: A Review Essay." *Rural Migration News* 16, no. 4 (2010). https://migration.ucdavis.edu/rmn/more.php?id=1578.

Chickering, Roger, Stig Forster, and Bernd Greiner. *A World at Total War: Global Conflict and the Politics of Destruction, 1937–1945*. Cambridge University Press, 2004.

Chinchilla, Norma, and Nora Stoltz Hamilton. *Seeking Community in a Global City: Guatemalans and Salvadorans in Los Angeles*. Temple University Press, 2001.

Chomsky, Samantha. "'But He Can't Work in Stockton': El Malcriado and the United Farmworkers' Shifting Border Politics." *Michigan Journal of History* XV (June 2019): 172–271. https://michiganjournalhistory.files.wordpress.com/2019/06/mjh-volume-xv.pdf.

Clarke, Thurston. *The Last Campaign: Robert F. Kennedy and 82 Days That Inspired America*. Henry Holt, 2008.

CNN. "Election 2024: Exit Polls." National Election Pool/Edison Research, November 5, 2024. https://www.cnn.com/election/2024/exit-polls/national-results/general/president/0.

Cohen, Deborah. *Braceros: Migrant Citizens and Transnational Subjects in the Postwar United States and Mexico*. University of North Carolina Press, 2013.

Congress.gov. "H.R. 4437—Border Protection, Antiterrorism, and Illegal Immigration Control Act of 2005." 109th Congress (2005–2006). https://www.congress.gov/bill/109th-congress/house-bill/4437.

Congress.gov. "S. 506—Fair Housing Amendments Act of 1979." 96th Congress (1979–1980). https://www.congress.gov/bill/96th-congress/senate-bill/506/cosponsors.

Conway, Dennis. "Step-Wise Migration: Toward a Clarification of the Mechanism." *The International Migration Review* 14, no. 1 (1980): 3–14. https://www.jstor.org/stable/2545058.

Cottle, Michelle. "Golden State Warrior: California's New Attorney General, Xavier Becerra, Prepares to Battle Trump." *The Atlantic*, May 2017. https://www.theatlantic.com/magazine/archive/2017/05/golden-state-warrior/521457/.

Coulter, Ann. *¡Adios, America! The Left's Plan to Turn Our Country into a Third World Hellhole*. Regnery, 2016.

Coulter, Ann. "GOP Double-Crosses Voters on Amnesty." *Republican and Herald*, February 22, 2015.

Coulter, Ann. Interview by Jorge Ramos. *America with Jorge Ramos*, May 26, 2015. Video posted August 29, 2015, by Ann Coulter, Facebook. https://www.facebook.com/watch/?extid=CL-UNK-UNK-UNK-IOS_GK0T-GK1C&mibextid=wwXIfr&v=754084668034683.

Coulter, Ann. "Three Generations of Imbeciles." *Casper Star-Tribune*, February 6, 2015. https://www.newspapers.com/image/499257031.

Covered California. "The First 10 Years: Looking Back and Looking Forward." September 8, 2021. https://www.coveredca.com/pdfs/10-year-anniversary/10-YEAR-REPORT-BOOK-regular-edition.pdf.

Cox, Kiana. "Most U.S. Adults Feel What Happens to Their Own Racial or Ethnic Group Affects Them Personally." Pew Research Center, 2019. https://www.pewresearch.org/short-reads/2019/07/11/linked-fate-connectedness-americans/.

Craig, Richard B. "Operation Intercept: The International Politics of Pressure." *The Review of Politics* 42, no. 4 (1980): 556–80. https://www.jstor.org/stable/i261342.

Crawford, James. *Language Loyalties: A Source Book on the Official English Controversy*. University of Chicago Press, 1992.

Danailova, Hillary. "Latino Republicans, Empowered by Election, Flex New Political Might in PA." *City & State PA*, November 15, 2024. https://www.cityandstatepa.com/politics/2024/11/latino-republicans-empowered-election-flex-new-political-might-pa/401065/.

Daniel, Cletus E. *Bitter Harvest: A History of California Farmworkers, 1870–1941*. Cornell University Press, 1981.

Daniel, Cletus E. *Chicano Workers and the Politics of Fairness: The FEPC in the Southwest, 1941–1945*. University of Texas Press, 1991.

Davis, Mike, and Jon Wiener. *Set the Night on Fire*. Verso Books, 2021.

Davis, Richard. "Trump Stole the Democrats' Playbook, to Win Again They Should Steal His." *The Hill*, January 30, 2025. https://thehill.com/opinion/5114895-democrats-steal-trump-playbook/amp/.

Davis, William P. "President Trump's Approval Rating: Latest Polls." *The New York Times*, May 6, 2025. https://www.nytimes.com/interactive/polls/donald-trump-approval-rating-polls.html.

The Dawson News. "Phelps Dodge Corporation, Stag Canon Branch, Welfare Committee Election Ballot General Representatives." Vol. 1, no. 47, December 22, 2021. https://chuckspeed.com/Dawson_Association/dawson_news/Volume 1.pdf.

Decker, Cathleen. "Analysis: Rosier Views on Economy Pose a Challenge for Republicans." *Los Angeles Times*, January 25, 2015. https://www.latimes.com/nation/politics/la-na-republicans-economy-20150126-story.html.

Degler, Carl. *Neither Black nor White: Slavery and Race Relations in Brazil and the United States*. University of Wisconsin Press, 1986.

del Olmo, Frank. "Chavez Union Does Turnabout, Opposes Alien Worker Bill." *Los Angeles Times*, March 27, 1973.

del Olmo, Frank. "A Dissenting Vote on the Endorsement of Pete Wilson." *Los Angeles Times*, October 31, 1994. https://www.latimes.com/la-delolmo-best-1994-story.html.

del Olmo, Frank. "Latino Community, with Church's Help, Is on Move." *Los Angeles Times*, June 12, 1986. https://www.latimes.com/archives/la-xpm-1986-06-12-me-10314-story.html.

del Olmo, Frank. "Latino 'Decade' Moves into '90s." *Los Angeles Times*, December 14, 1989. https://www.latimes.com/archives/la-xpm-1989-12-14-ti-1-story.html.

Delgado, Richard, Leticia M. Saucedo, Marc-Tizoc González, Jean Stefancic, and Juan F. Perea. *Latinos and the Law: Cases and Materials*, Second Edition. West Academic, 2021.

"Department of Defense Security for the Protection of Department of Homeland Security Functions." *Presidential Memoranda*, June 7, 2025. https://www.whitehouse.gov/presidential-actions/2025/06/department-of-defense-security-for-the-protection-of-department-of-homeland-security-functions/.

DeSipio, Louis. *Counting on the Latino Vote: Latinos as a New Electorate*. University of Virginia Press, 1996.

di Stefano, Onofre. "'Venimos a luchar': A Brief History of La Prensa's Founding." *Aztlán* 16, nos. 1–2 (1985): 95–118.

"Dolores Huerta Talks About Republicans, César Chávez, Children, and Her Home Town." Originally published in *La Voz del Pueblo*, January 25, 1973. In García, *A Dolores Huerta Reader*.

Doyle, Kieran. "LA Demonstrations: The Most Explosive Escalation of Tensions Between Demonstrators and Police Since BLM." Armed Conflict Location & Event Data (ACLED), June 12, 2025. https://bit.ly/3FLPkTG.

Duara, Nigel, and Jeanne Kuang. "With Troops and Protests, Trump's Feud with California Moves to the Streets of LA." *Calmatters*, updated June 10, 2025. https://calmatters.org/politics/2025/06/los-angeles-national-guard-trump/.

Echavarri, Fernanda. "Latinx Activists Are Closer Than Ever to Flipping Arizona—If Democrats Don't Take Them for Granted." *Mother Jones*, November/December 2020. https://www.motherjones.com/2020-elections/2020/09/arizona-election-trump-mcsally-kelly-arpaio-sb-1070/.

Ehisen, Rich. "George Skelton: The Dean of California's Capitol Press Corps." *Capitol Weekly*, February 28, 2022. https://capitolweekly.net/oral-histories/george-skelton-the-dean-of-californias-capitol-press-corp/.

Einenkel, Walter. "Rep. Pete Aguilar Gives Amazing Speech on House Floor Denouncing Jim Jordan's Speaker Nomination." *Daily Kos*, October 17, 2023. https://www.dailykos.com/stories/2023/10/17/2199953/-Rep-Pete-Aguilar-gives-amazing-speech-on-House-floor-denouncing-Jim-Jordan-s-speaker-nomination.

Elmore, Maggie Jane. *Claiming the Cross: How Mexican Americans, Mexican Immigrants, and the Catholic Church Worked to Create a More Inclusive National State, 1923–1986*. University of California, Berkeley, 2017.

Equis Research. "May 2025 Poll on Latinos, Trump and Immigration." Survey data collected April 16–May 5. Released May 14, 2025. https://www.weareequis.us/research/may-2025-poll-on-latinos-trump-and-immigration?utm_source=substack&utm_medium=email.

Erden, Bora, Lazaro Gamio, K. K. Rebecca Lai, Blacki Migliozzi, Bedel Saget, Elena Shao, and Ashley Wu. "Maps and Timeline of the L.A. Immigration Protests and the Federal Response." *The New York Times*, June 11, 2025. https://www.nytimes.com/interactive/2025/06/08/us/la-immigration-protests-photos-map.html?smid=nytcore-ios-share&referringSource=articleShare&sgrp=p&pvid=96541E41E6-4F23-410B-9AEE-CC400CBCAF56B.

Escutia, Martha, and Marina Jimenez. "They Called Him Papu: The Life of a Beloved Grandfather." *StoryCorps*, originally aired August 21, 2020, on National Public Radio Morning Edition. https://storycorps.org/stories/they-called-him-papu-the-life-of-a-beloved-grandfather.

Esparza Loera, Juan. "Attorney General-Designee Rob Bonta is Latest Example of César E. Chávez's Impact." *Vida en el Valle*, March 29, 2021. https://ufw.org/vida-en-el-valle-attorney-general-designee-rob-bonta-is-latest-example-of-cesar-e-chavezs-impact/.

Findell, Elizabeth, Ruth Simon, Michelle Hackman, and Tarini Parti. "The White House Marching Orders That Sparked the L.A. Migrant Crackdown." *The Wall Street Journal*, June 9, 2025. https://www.wsj.com/us-news/protests-los-angeles-immigrants-trump-f5089877.

Fine, Janice, and Daniel J. Tichenor. "A Movement Wrestling: American Labor's Enduring Struggle with Immigration, 1866–2007." *Studies in American Political Development* 23, no. 1 (2009): 84–113. https://doi.org/10.1017/S0898588X09000042.

Flores, Henry. *Latinos and the Voting Rights Act*. Lexington Books, 2015. Kindle.

Flores, Lori A. *Grounds for Dreaming: Mexican Americans, Mexican Immigrants, and the California Farmworker Movement*. Yale University Press, 2018.

Florez, Dean. "Is the Capitol for Sale to the Highest Bidder?" *The Sacramento Bee*, June 30, 2002. https://www.newspapers.com/image/647465353/.

Folkart, Burt A. "Enrique (Hank) Lopez; Attorney, Activist." *Los Angeles Times*, October 25, 1985. https://www.latimes.com/archives/la-xpm-1985-10-25-me-14459-story.html.

Forbes Breaking News. "Pete Hegseth Snaps at Aguilar When Pressed on National Guard Deployment to Los Angeles." June 10, 2025. YouTube, 5 min., 18 sec. https://www.youtube.com/watch?v=jq5vNlreDrg.

Fortinsky, Sarah. "Aguilar Delivers Fiery Speech in Support of Jeffries Amid House Speaker Fight." *The Hill*, October 18, 2023. https://thehill.com/homenews/house/4262910-aguilar-fiery-support-jeffries-house-speaker-fight-jordan/.

Fox, Cybelle. "Save Our Senior Noncitizens: Extending Old Age Assistance to Immigrants in the United States, 1935-71." *Social Science History* 45, no. 1 (2021): 55-81. https://doi.ora/10.1017/ssh.2020.40.

Fragomen Jr., Austin T. "The Final Report and Recommendations of the Select Commission on Immigration and Refugee Policy: A Summary." *The International Migration Review* 15, no. 4 (1981): 758–68. https://doi.org/10.2307/2545523.

Fragomen Jr., Austin T. "Permanent Resident Status Redefined." *The International Migration Review* 9, no. 1 (1975): 63–68. https://doi.org/10.1177/019791837500900107.

Fragomen, Austin T., and Michael G. Wenk. "Legislative and Judicial Development of Interest." *The International Migration Review* 6, no. 4 (1972): 435–40. https://doi.org/10.1177/019791837200600405.

Fry, Hannah, and Clara Harter. "California Overtakes Japan to Become World's Fourth-largest Economy. But Tariffs Pose Threat," *Los Angeles Times*, April 24, 2025. https://www.latimes.com/california/story/2025-04-24/californias-economy-overtakes-japan-to-become-4th-largest-in-world.

Galarza, Ernesto. "The Burning Light: Action and Organizing in the Mexican Community in California." Oral history conducted by Gabrielle Morris and Timothy Beard. Regional Oral History Office, the Bancroft Library, University of California, Berkeley, 1982.

Galarza, Ernesto. *Farm Workers and Agri-Business in California, 1947–1960*. University of Notre Dame Press, 1977.

Galarza, Ernesto. "Guide to the Ernesto Galarza Papers, 1936–1984." Collection no. M0224. Online Archive of California. Department of Special Collections, Stanford University Libraries. https://oac.cdlib.org/findaid/ark:/13030/tf2290026t/.

Galarza, Ernesto. *Merchants of Labor: The Mexican Bracero Story*. McNally and Loften, 1964.

Galindo, Erick. "How Dolores Huerta and Cesar Chavez Started the Chicano Civil Rights Movement from a Kitchen in Boyle Heights." *L.A. Taco*, September 7, 2018. https://lataco.com/how-dolores-huerta-and-cesar-chavez-started-the-chicano-civil-rights-movement-from-a-kitchen-in-boyle-heights.

Gamboa, Erasmo. *Bracero Railroaders: The Forgotten World War II Story of Mexican Workers in the U.S. West*. University of Washington Press, 2017.

Ganz, Marshall. *Why David Sometimes Wins: Leadership, Organization, and Strategy in the California Farm Worker Movement*. Oxford University Press, 2009.

García, David, and Raúl Ruiz. "Requiem 29: The Chicano Moratorium (1971)." National Latino Communications Center, NLCC Educational Media (1997), DVD. Reposted September 7, 2017, by Chimalli Media. YouTube, 31 min, 12 sec. https://youtu.be/Vfa-JfeiIjU.

Garcia, Dawn. "Spanish-Language Media, Text Messaging and MySpace: The Creation of a New Counterpublic Sphere in California." Master's thesis, Stanford University, 2008.

García, Ignacio M. *Viva Kennedy: Mexican Americans in Search of Camelot*. Texas A&M University Press, 2000.

Garcia, Juan R. *Operation Wetback: The Mass Deportation of Mexican Undocumented Workers in 1954*. Praeger, 1980.

García, Mario T. *The Chicano Generation: Testimonios of the Movement*. University of California Press, 2015.

García, Mario T., ed. *A Dolores Huerta Reader*. University of New Mexico Press, 2008.

García, Mario T. *Father Luis Olivares, a Biography: Faith Politics and the Origins of the Sanctuary Movement in Los Angeles*. University of North Carolina Press, 2022.

García, Mario T. *The Latino Generation: Voices of the New America*. University of North Carolina Press, 2014.

García, Mario T. *The Making of a Mexican American Mayor: Raymond L. Telles of El Paso*. Texas Western Press, 1998.

García, Mario T. *Memories of Chicano History: The Life and Narrative of Bert Corona*. University of California Press, 1994.

García, Mario T. *Mexican Americans: Leadership, Ideology and Identity, 1930–1960*. Yale University Press, 1989.

Garcia, Matt. *From the Jaws of Victory: The Triumph and Tragedy of Cesar Chavez and the Farm Worker Movement*. University of California Press, 2012. Kindle.

Garcia, Matt. *A World of Its Own: Race, Labor, and Citrus in the Making of Greater Los Angeles, 1900–1970*. University of North Carolina Press, 2001.

Garcia, Richard A. *Rise of the Mexican American Middle Class: San Antonio, 1929–1941*. Texas A&M Press, 1991.

García y Griego, Manuel. "The Importation of Mexican Contract Laborers to the United States, 1942–1964." In *Between Two Worlds: Mexican Immigrants in the United States*, edited by David G. Gutiérrez. SR Books, 1996.

Garofoli, Joe. "Trump's Campaign Ad Is Brash, Angry and Openly Anti-Immigrant." *San Francisco Chronicle*, January 4, 2016. https://www.sfchronicle.com/politics/article/Trump-s-campaign-ad-is-brash-angry-and-openly-6736471.php.

Garza, Humberto. *Organizing the Chicano Movement: The Story of CSO*. Sun House, 2009.

Garza, Melita M. *They Came to Toil: Newspaper Representations of Mexicans and Immigrants in in the Great Depression*. University of Texas Press, 2018.

Geiger, Jeffrey E. *German Prisoners of War at Camp Cooke, California*. Sunbury, 2018.

Geile, Robert T. "NOTE: Bustos v. Mitchell (Saxbe v. Bustos): The Dilemma of Commuting Alien Laborers." *California Western International Law Journal* 5, no. 2 (1975): 184–202. https://scholarlycommons.law.cwsl.edu/cgi/viewcontent.cgi?article=1932&context=cwilj.

Gelatt, Julia, and Margie McHugh. "Immigration Fee Increases in Context." *Immigration Facts*. Migration Policy Institute, February 2007. https://www.migrationpolicy.org/sites/default/files/publications/FS15_CitizenshipFees_2007_02-13.pdf.

Gellman, Irwin. *The President and the Apprentice: Eisenhower and Nixon, 1952–1961*. Yale University Press, 2015.

Gerassi, John. *The Great Fear in Latin America*. Revised ed. Collier, 1967.

Goitein, Elizabeth. "'The Insurrection Act' by Any Other Name: Unpacking Trump's Memorandum Authorizing Domestic Deployment of the Military." *Just Security*, June 10, 2025. https://www.brennancenter.org/our-work/analysis-opinion/unpacking-trumps-order-authorizing-domestic-deployment-military.

Goldmacher, Shane. "The Waxman–Berman Machine Finally Shuts Down." *National Journal*, January 24, 2013.

González, Gilbert. *Labor and Community: Mexican Citrus Worker Villages in a Southern California County, 1900–1950*. University of Illinois Press, 1994.

González Gutiérrez, Carlos. "Fostering Identities: Mexico's Relations with Its Diaspora." *The Journal of American History* 86, no. 2 (1999).

González Gutiérrez, Carlos, and David Ayón. "Mexico and the Mexican Community in the United States." In *Reimagining U.S.-Mexico Relations: From Here to 2024*. USC Center on Public Diplomacy, online publication, 2014. https://uscpublicdiplomacy.org/story/mexicos-public-diplomacy-us-mexico-relations.

Gooch v. Clark, 433 F.2d 74 (Court of Appeals, 9th Circuit, 1970). https://scholar.google.com/scholar_case?case=11345792838603944952&q=Gooch+v.+Clark&hl=en&as_sdt=2006&as_vis=1.

Grad, Shelby. "The Prop. 187 Rebellion Inside the L.A. Times Newsroom." *Los Angeles Times*, November 8, 2019. https://www.latimes.com/california/story/2019-11-08/rebellion-inside-los-angeles-times-proposition-187-pete-wilson.

Graff, Garrett M. *Watergate: A New History*. Simon & Schuster, 2022.

Grant, Colin. *Negro with a Hat: The Rise and Fall of Marcus Garvey*. Oxford University Press, 2008.

Gratton, Brian, and Emily Klancher Merchant. "*La Raza*: Mexicans in the United States Census." *Journal of Policy History* 28, no. 4 (2016): 537–67. http://dx.doi.org/10.1017/S0898030616000257.

Grayer, Annie, Gabe Cohen, and Betsy Klein. "Trump Preparing Large-Scale Cancellation of Federal Funding for California, Sources Say." *CNN*, June 6, 2025. https://amp.cnn.com/cnn/2025/06/06/politics/trump-california-federal-funding.

Green, Hardy. *The Company Town: The Industrial Edens and Satanic Mills That Shaped the American Economy*. Basic Books, 2010.

Greenberg, Amy S. *A Wicked War: Polk, Clay, Lincoln, and the 1846 U.S. Invasion of Mexico*. Knopf Doubleday, 2012.

Greene Sterling, Terry, and Jude Joffe-Block. *Driving While Brown: Sheriff Joe Arpaio Versus the Latino Resistance*. University of California Press, 2021.

Griego, Tina. "Group Seeks to Convert Seven Small Cities Into a Unified Political Force: Redistricting: The Plan to Combine Several Districts into One Faces Formidable Obstacles." *Los Angeles Times*, August 4, 1991. https://www.latimes.com/archives/la-xpm-1991-08-04-hl-257-story.html.

Grisales, Claudia, Barbara Sprunt, and Deirdre Walsh. "Senate Kills Articles of Impeachment Against Homeland Security Secretary Mayorkas." *NPR*, April 17, 2024. https://www.npr.org/2024/04/17/1245377914/senate-articles-impeachment-mayorkas-vote.

Gritter, Matthew. *Mexican Inclusion: The Origins of Anti-Discrimination Policy in Texas and the Southwest*. Texas A&M University Press, 2012.

Guendelman, Sylvia R. "South American Refugees: In the San Francisco Bay Area." *Migration Today* 9, no. 2 (1981): 19–25.

Gutiérrez, David G. "'Sin Fronteras?': Chicanos, Mexican Americans, and the Emergence of the Contemporary Mexican Immigration Debate, 1968–1978." *Journal of American Ethnic History* 10, no. 4 (1991): 5–37.

Guzman-Lopez, Adolfo. "LA Mayor Gets Mixed Reviews on Education." KPCC, March 2, 2009.

Haas, Lisbeth. "Grass-Roots Protest and the Politics of Planning: Santa Ana, 1976–88." In *Postsuburban California: The Transformation of Orange County Since World War II*, edited by Bob Kling, Spencer Olin, and Mark Poster. University of California Press, 1995.

Hall, Matthew, Emily Greenman, and Youngmin Yi. "Job Mobility among Unauthorized Immigrant Workers." *Social Forces* 97, no. 3 (2019): 999-1027. https://10.1093/sf/soy086.

Hamburger, Tom, and Peter Wallsten. "Obama's Grass-Roots Latino Strategy." *Los Angeles Times*, February 2, 2008. https://www.latimes.com/archives/la-xpm-2008-feb-02-na-latinos2-story.html.

Harlow, Neal. *California Conquered: The Annexation of a Mexican Province, 1846–1850*. University of California Press, 1982.

Haus, Leah. "Openings in the Wall: Transnational Migrants, Labor Unions and U.S. Immigration Policy." *International Organization* 49, no. 2 (1995): 285–313. https://www.jstor.org/stable/2706973.

Hawley, Ellis W. "The Politics of the Mexican Labor Issue, 1950–1965." *Agricultural History 40*, no. 3 (1966): 157–76. https://www.jstor.org/stable/3740695.

Hayes-Bautista, David E. *El Cinco de Mayo: An American Tradition*. University of California Press, 2012.

Hayes-Bautista, David E. *La Nueva California: Latinos from Pioneers to Post-Millennials*. University of California Press, 2017.

Hayes-Bautista, David E., Cynthia L. Chamberlin, Branden Jones et al. "Empowerment, Expansion, and Engagement: Las Juntas Patrióticas in California, 1848–1869." *California History* 85, no. 1 (2007): 4–23. https://www.jstor.org/stable/25161927.

Henderson, Timothy J. *Beyond Borders: A History of Mexican Migration to the United States*. Wiley-Blackwell, 2011.

Henderson, Timothy J. *A Glorious Defeat: Mexico and Its War with the United States*. Hill and Wang, 2008.

Hernández, Antonia. "Antonia Hernandez—UCLA 100—Our Stories, Our Impact." Interview posted October 2, 2019, by UCLA Institute for Research on Labor and Employment. Vimeo, 4 min., 37 sec. https://vimeo.com/363970494.

Hernández, Antonia. "Antonia Hernandez Oral History Interview." Interview by Louise LaMothe. American Bar Association Women Trailblazers in the Law Project, Los Angeles, CA, October 22, 2007. C-SPAN, 1 hr., 23 min., 24 sec. https://www.c-span.org/program/american-history-tv/antonia-hernandez-oral-history-interview/226754.

Hernández, Antonia. "Chicanas and the Issue of Involuntary Sterilization: Reforms Needed to Protect Informed Consent." *Chicano Law Review* 3, no. 3 (1976). https://escholarship.org/content/qt35v8r48h/qt35v8r48h.pdf.

Hernández, Antonia. "Interview with Antonia Hernandez." Interview by Stephen F. Knott. New York, March 22, 2007. Edward M. Kennedy Oral History Project, Miller Center, University of Virginia. https://millercenter.org/the-presidency/presidential-oral-histories/antonia-hernandez-oral-history.

Hernández, Antonia. "Podcast FULL INTERVIEW—Antonia Hernández." Interview by Giselle Fernández, "LA Stories Unfiltered," *Spectrum News*, November 1, 2021. Posted by California Community Foundation, November 2, 2021. YouTube, 24 min., 10 sec. https://youtu.be/rdOQsRTx6y8.

Hernández, Antonia. "Statement on Behalf of the Mexican American Legal Defense and Educational Fund ('MALDEF') by Antonia Hernandez, President and General Counsel Before the Committee on the Judiciary, United States Senate." 101st Cong., 2nd Sess. September 18, 1990. https://www.govinfo.gov/content/pkg/GPO-CHRG-SOUTER/pdf/GPO-CHRG-SOUTER-2-4-2-2.pdf.

Hernandez, Daniel. "A Loss of Innocence." *Los Angeles Times*, August 23, 2020. https://www.latimes.com/projects/chicano-moratorium/chicano-moratorium-participants-discuss-movement/.

Hernandez, Marita. "50,000 Worshipers Gather to Mark the Start of Mahony's Latino Plan." *Los Angeles Times*, June 2, 1986. https://www.latimes.com/archives/la-xpm-1986-06-02-me-8415-story.html.

Hernandez, Tim Z. *All They Will Call You*. University of Arizona Press, 2017.

Herrera, Jack. "Kevin de León Took on the Democratic Establishment. It Fought Back." *Pacific Standard*, November 2, 2018. https://psmag.com/social-justice/kevin-de-leon-took-on-the-democratic-establishment-and-it-fought-back.

Herszenhorn, David M. "Senate Blocks Bill for Young Illegal Immigrants." *The New York Times*, December 18, 2010. http://www.nytimes.com/2010/12/19/us/politics/19immig.html.

Herzog, Lawrence A. *Where North Meets South: Cities, Space, and Politics on the U.S.-Mexico Border*. CMAS Books, Center for Mexican American Studies, University of Texas at Austin, 1990.

Higham, John. *Strangers in the Land: Patterns of American Nativism, 1860–1925*. Atheneum, 1965.

Hofstadter, Richard. *The American Political Tradition and the Men Who Made It*. Vintage, Reissue ed., 2011.

Hohl, Donald G., and Michael G. Wenk. "The Illegal Alien and the Western Hemisphere Immigration Dilemma." *The International Migration Review* 7, no. 3 (1973): 323–32. https://doi.org/10.1177/019791837300700306.

Hopper, Jennifer. *Presidential Framing in the 21st Century News Media*. Routledge, 2017.

Hornblower, Margot. "The Man Behind Prop. 227: Meet Ron Unz, the Tycoon Who Waged a Campaign to All but Outlaw Bilingual Education in California." *Time*, June 8, 1998. https://www.cnn.com/ALLPOLITICS/1998/06/01/time/prop.277.html.

Horwitt, Sanford D. *Let Them Call Me Rebel: Saul Alinsky, His Life and Legacy*. Knopf, 1989.

Hubler, Shawn, Jennifer Medina, and Jill Cowan. "Calif. Senator Forcibly Removed and Handcuffed After Interrupting Noem." *New York Times*, June 12, 2025. https://www.nytimes.com/2025/06/12/us/politics/senator-alex-padilla-handcuffed.html?smid=nytcore-ios-share&referringSource=articleShare&sgrp=p&pvid=93BE1BBA-C3D9-4735-803D-0EB4AD36F01A.

Huerta, Dolores. "Interview No. 1577." Interview by Steve Velasquez, Harry Rubenstein, and Peter Liebhold, 2005. Institute of Oral History, University of Texas at El Paso.

Ibarra, Ana B., and Ben Christopher. "We Tracked California's Lawsuits Against Donald Trump. Here's Where the State Won—and Lost." *CalMatters*, January 20, 2025. https://calmatters.org/politics/2025/01/california-lawsuits-against-donald-trump/.

Institute of Governmental Studies. "Redistricting in California: Inventory of the Collection of the California Special Masters on Reapportionment, 1991." https://igs.berkeley.edu/sites/default/files/redistricting_in_california_1991_1.pdf.

Jacobs, Jennifer. "Pitching for Conservative Votes." *Des Moines Register*, January 25, 2015. https://www.newspapers.com/image/113767290/.

Jacobs, John. *A Rage for Justice: The Passion and Politics of Phillip Burton*. University of California Press, 1995.

Jelen, Ted G. "Nevada: The Tea Party Takes on Harry Reid but from the Wrong Angle." In *Key States, High Stakes: Sarah Palin, the Tea Party, and the 2010 Elections*, edited by Charles S. Bullock. Rowman & Littlefield, 2011.

Johnson, Richard. "The 1982 Voting Rights Act Extension as a 'Critical Juncture': Ronald Reagan, Bob Dole, and Republican Party-Building." *Studies in American Political Development* 35, no. 2 (2021).

Johnston, Andrew Scott. *Mercury and the Making of California: Mining, Landscape, and Race, 1840–1890*. University Press of Colorado, 2013.

Jones, Blake, and Dustin Gardiner. "Rob Bonta Finds His Calling." *Politico*, January 22, 2025. https://www.politico.com/newsletters/california-playbook/2025/01/22/rob-bonta-finds-his-calling-00199855.

Jones, Blake, and Dustin Gardiner. "Robert Rivas' Waiting Game." *Politico*, February 4, 2025. https://www.politico.com/newsletters/california-playbook/2025/02/04/robert-rivas-waiting-game-00202277.

Jordan, Miriam. "Univision Gives Citizenship Drive Unusual Lift: Broadcaster Uses Clout to Mobilize Latino Vote." *The Wall Street Journal*, May 10, 2007.

Kahn, Mattie. "Eva Longoria Calls the Shots." *Glamour*, October 29, 2020. https://www.glamour.com/story/eva-longoria-calls-the-shots-profile.

Kamasaki, Charles. *Immigration Reform: The Corpse That Will Not Die*. Mandel Vilar, 2019.

Kaplowitz, Craig A. *LULAC, Mexican Americans, and National Policy*. Texas A&M University Press, 2005.

Karabin, Sherry. "AltaMed Sees Number of Patients Grow." *Los Angeles Business Journal*, July 1, 2024. https://labusinessjournal.com/healthcare/altamed-sees-number-of-patients-grow/.

Kay, Jane. "Tracking a Toxic Trail: Long-Closed Mine Identified as Largest Source of Mercury in San Francisco Bay." *SFGATE*, December 22, 2002. https://www.sfgate.com/bayarea/article/tracking-a-toxic-trail-long-closed-mine-2709557.php.

Kennedy, John F. "Inaugural Address." January 20, 1961. National Archives. https://www.archives.gov/milestone-documents/president-john-f-kennedys-inaugural-address.

Kerwin, Donald M. "More Than IRCA: US Legalization Programs and the Current Policy Debate. Migration Policy Institute, December 2010. https://www.migrationpolicy.org/pubs/legalization-historical.pdf.

Khokha, Sasha. "Immortalized by Woody Guthrie, 'Deportees' Who Died in Plane Crash Are Nameless No Longer." KQED, July 14, 2017. https://www.kqed.org/news/11512311/immortalized-by-woody-guthrie-deportees-who-died-in-plane-crash-are-nameless-no-longer.

Kiser, George C. "The Bracero Program: A Case Study of Its Development, Termination, and Political Aftermath." PhD diss., University of Massachusetts Amherst, 1973.

Klein, Dianne. "State Puts New Edge on Immigration Debate: Residents Increasingly See Illegal Influx as a Source of California's Woes. Pressure for Action Grows." *Los Angeles Times*, September 6, 1993. https://www.latimes.com/archives/la-xpm-1993-09-06-mn-32208-story.html.

Kominski, Gerald F., Narissa J. Nonzee, and Andrea Sorensen. "The Affordable Care Act's Impacts on Access to Insurance and Health Care for Low-Income Populations." *Annual Review of Public Health* 38 (2017): 489–505. https://doi.org/10.1146/annurev-publhealth-031816-044555.

Korach, Natalie. "Why the *LA Times*' Owner Courted CNN's Top Trump Defender." *Vanity Fair*, December 17, 2024. https://www.vanityfair.com/news/story/la-times-owner-courted-cnn-trump-defender.

Koszczuk, Jackie. "Proof of Illegal Voters Falls Short, Keeping Sanchez in House." *Congressional Quarterly*, February 7, 1998. https://www.cnn.com/ALLPOLITICS/1998/02/13/cq/sanchez.html.

La, Lynn. "A Second California Governor Try for Antonio Villaraigosa." *CalMatters*, July 24, 2024. https://calmatters.org/newsletter/antonio-villaraigosa-california-governor-2026/.

La Ganga, Maria L. “Bilingual Ed Initiative Wins Easily.” *Los Angeles Times*, June 3, 1998. https://www.latimes.com/archives/la-xpm-1998-jun-03-mn-56054-story.html.

Landsberg, Mitchell. “L.A. Mayor Sees Dropout Rate as ‘Civil Rights Issue.’” *Los Angeles Times*, March 2, 2006. https://www.latimes.com/archives/la-xpm-2006-mar-02-me-dropout2-story.html.

Langer, Gary. “Trump Has Lowest 100-Day Approval Rating in 80 Years: POLL.” ABC News, April 26, 2025. https://abcnews.go.com/Politics/trump-lowest-100-day-approval-rating-80-years/story?id=121165473.

“Leadership and Popular Movements: The UFW Experience.” Center for the Study of Democratic Institutions, March 12, 1985. Reprinted as chap. 5 in García, *A Dolores Huerta Reader*.

Leal, Jorge Nicolás. “Paving The Road to the White House or to La Panamericana? The Post-Electoral Hopes of the Southern California Viva Kennedy Clubs, 1960–1963.” Master’s thesis, California State University, Northridge, May 2011.

“Letters from Dolores Huerta to César Chávez.” Archives of Labor and Urban Affairs, Wayne State University. Reprinted in García, *A Dolores Huerta Reader*.

Levine, Daniel B. “Oral History.” https://www2.census.gov/about/history/stories/our-stories/daniel-levine.pdf.

Levinson, Jerome, and Juan de Onis. *The Alliance That Lost Its Way: A Critical Report on the Alliance for Progress*. Quadrangle Books, 1972.

Levy, Jacques E. *Cesar Chavez: Autobiography of La Causa*. Norton, 1975.

Linder, Joshua. “The Amnesty Effect: Evidence from the 1986 Immigration Reform and Control Act.” *The Public Purpose* 9 (Spring 2011): 13–31. https://www.american.edu/spa/publicpurpose/upload/2011-public-purpose.pdf.

Liptak, Adam. “Supreme Court Rejects Theory That Would Have Transformed American Elections.” *The New York Times*, June 27, 2023. https://www.nytimes.com/2023/06/27/us/politics/supreme-court-state-legislature-elections.html.

Livingston, Abby. “Eva Longoria Is Famous for Her Acting, but She’s Increasingly Recognized as a Political Player in Texas and Beyond.” *The Texas Tribune*, October 29, 2020. https://www.texastribune.org/2020/10/29/eva-longoria-politics/.

Lodhi, Humera, Shelly Cheng, Parker Kaufmann, Pablo Barria Urenda, and EJ Fox. “AP VoteCast: How America Voted in 2024.” *Associated Press*. Polling conducted October 28–November 5, 2024. https://www.apnews.com/projects/election-results-2024/votecast/.

London, Joan, and Henry Anderson. *So Shall Ye Reap: The Story of Cesar Chavez & the Farm Workers’ Movement*. Thomas Y. Crowell, 1970.

Lopez, Mark Hugo, and Paul Taylor. *Dissecting the 2008 Electorate: Most Diverse in U.S. History*. Pew Research Center, April 30, 2009. https://www.pewresearch.org/race-and-ethnicity/2009/04/30/dissecting-the-2008-electorate-most-diverse-in-us-history/.

López-Córdova, Ernesto et al. "Globalization, Migration and Development: The Role of Mexican Migrant Remittances." *Economía* 6, no. 1 (2005).

Lorence, James J. *The Suppression of Salt of the Earth: How Hollywood, Big Labor, and Politicians Blacklisted a Movie in the American Cold War*. University of New Mexico Press, 1999.

Los Angeles Business Journal. "Tribune to Give Away Hoy in Los Angeles and Chicago." December 7, 2004. https://labusinessjournal.com/news/tribune-to-give-away-hoy-in-los-angeles-and/.

Los Angeles County Auditor-Controller. "Incorporated Areas—Cities." Gateway Cities Council of Governments. https://www.gatewaycog.org/.

Lowenstein, Roger. *Origins of the Crash: The Great Bubble and Its Undoing*. Penguin Press, 2004.

Loza, Mireya. *Defiant Braceros: How Migrant Workers Fought for Racial, Sexual, and Political Freedom*. University of North Carolina Press, 2016.

Lucas, Greg. "The Battle of Los Angeles." Celebrate California, California State Library. Accessed April 24, 2025. https://celebratecalifornia.library.ca.gov/february-24-1942-the-battle-of-los-angeles-2/.

Macías, Jorge Luis. "Sesenta grupos se tomarán las calles contra La Migra en LA." *La Opinión*, February 14, 2025. https://laopinion.com/2025/02/14/sesenta-grupos-se-tomaran-las-calles-contra-la-migra-en-la/.

Madrigal-Lauchland, Vanessa. "The Shifting Meanings of Stockton's Barrio del Chivo." *California History* 96, no. 3 (2019).

Magaña, Lisa, and Erik Lee, eds. *Latino Politics and Arizona's Immigration Law SB 1070*. Springer, 2013.

Mai-Duc, Christine. "In Taking on Jorge Ramos, Donald Trump May Have Tussled with the Wrong Media Star." *Los Angeles Times*, August 26, 2015. https://www.latimes.com/nation/la-na-jorge-ramos-donald-trump-20150826-htmlstory.html.

Manchester, Julia. "7 Most Likely GOP Successors to Trump in 2028." *The Hill*, February 15, 2025. https://thehill.com/homenews/campaign/5139201-potential-republican-successors-to-trump/amp/.

Mansbridge, Peter. "Why Jorge Ramos Took on Trump." *CBC News: The National*, October 21, 2016.

Marcoida, Juan. "CSO San Jose Juan Marcoida 1952 CSO & Radio Program." Interview by Ramon J. Martinez, posted October 17, 2014, by R. J. Martinez. YouTube, 22 min., 8 sec. https://youtu.be/nQ9gboTFaQI.

Marinucci, Carla, and Heather Caygle. "Becerra Appointed California Attorney General." *Politico,* December 1, 2016. https://www.politico.com/story/2016/12/becerra-appointed-california-attorney-general-232063.

Mariscal, Jorge. "Cesar and Martin, March '68." In *The Struggle in Black and Brown: African American and Mexican American Relations during the Civil Rights Era,* edited by Brian D. Behnken. University of Nebraska Press, 2012.

Márquez, Benjamin. *LULAC: The Evolution of a Mexican American Political Organization*. University of Texas Press, 1993.

Márquez, Benjamin. *The Politics of Patronage: Lawyers, Philanthropy, and the Mexican American Legal Defense and Educational Fund*. University of Texas Press, 2021.

Martin, Jonathan. "This California Democrat Might Be the Future of the Party." *Politico,* June 9, 2023. https://www.politico.com/news/2023/06/09/aguilar-pelosi-california-house-democrats-00101113.

Martin, Philip L. "The CAW at 30." Wilson Center Mexico Institute, September 29, 2020. https://www.wilsoncenter.org/article/caw-30.

Martin, Philip L. "A Comparison of California's ALRA and the Federal NLRA." *California Agriculture* 37, no. 7 (1983).

Martin, Philip L. "Good Intentions Gone Awry: IRCA and U. S. Agriculture." *The Annals of the American Academy of Political and Social Science* 534 (July 1994): 44–57. http://www.jstor.org/stable/1048497.

Martin, Phillip. "Mexican Braceros and US Farm Workers." Wilson Center Mexico Institute, July 10, 2020. https://www.wilsoncenter.org/article/mexican-braceros-and-us-farm-workers.

Martin, Philip L. *Promise Unfulfilled: Unions, Immigration, and the Farm Workers.* Cornell University Press, 2003.

Martin, Philip. "Proposition 187 in California." *The International Migration Review* 29, no. 1 (1995): 255–63. www.jstor.org/stable/2547004.

Martin, Phillip L. "Select Commission Suggests Changes in Immigration Policy—A Review Essay." *Monthly Labor Review* (February 1982): 31–37. https://www.bls.gov/opub/mlr/1982/02/art4full.pdf.

Martínez, A. "As National Guard Deploys, Democratic Rep. Nanette Barragán Sees 'Sign of a Dictator.'" *NPR Morning Edition,* June 9, 2025. https://www.npr.org/2025/06/09/nx-s1-5427213/democratic-rep-barragan-trump-immigration-raids-los-angeles.

McCall, Bruce. "Building a Bridge to the Twenty First Century." *The New Yorker,* October 27, 1996. https://www.newyorker.com/magazine/1996/11/04/building-a-bridge-to-the-twenty-first-century.

McCann Ramirez, Nikki. "Biden Says He Regrets Not Signing Name to COVID Checks Like Trump Did." *Rolling Stone*, December 10, 2024. https://www.rollingstone.com/politics/politics-news/biden-regrets-not-signing-name-covid-checks-trump-1235199950/.

McCarthy, Justin. "Hispanics' Support for Obama Climbs After Executive Actions." Gallup U.S. Daily Survey, December 10, 2014. http://www.gallup.com/poll/180005/hispanics-support-obama-climbs-executive-order.aspx.

McElroy, Robert C., and Earle E. Gavett. *Termination of the Bracero Program: Some Effects on Farm Labor and Migrant Housing Needs*. US Department of Agriculture, Economic Research Service, Agricultural Economic Report no. 77, June 1965.

McGreevy, Patrick. "Becerra Tells Senators He'd Stick with Job." *Los Angeles Times*, January 19, 2017. https://www.newspapers.com/article/the-los-angeles-times-becerra-hearing-18/157164305/.

McGreevy, Patrick. "Setback Puts Kevin de León on the Path to Senate Leadership." *Los Angeles Times*, June 18, 2014. https://www.latimes.com/local/la-me-kevin-de-leon-20140619-story.html.

McWilliams, Carey. *Factories in the Field: The Story of Migratory Farm Labor in California*. Little Brown, 1939.

McWilliams, Carey. *North from Mexico: The Spanish-Speaking People of the United States*. Greenwood Press, 1990.

McWilliams, Carey. *Southern California Country: An Island in the Land*. Duell, Sloan & Pearce, 1946.

Mehta, Seema. "How Antonio Villaraigosa Went from a Union Organizer to a Union Target." *Los Angeles Times*, September 25, 2017. https://www.latimes.com/politics/la-pol-ca-villaraigosa-labor-20170925-story.html.

Mendel, Ed. "New State-Run IRA for Private Sector Opens July1." *Capitol Weekly*, June 18, 2019. https://capitolweekly.net/new-state-run-ira-for-private-sector-opens-july/.

Merle, Jean, and Antonio Olivo. "Solis Trounces Martinez in Bitter Race." *Los Angeles Times*, March 8, 2000. https://www.latimes.com/archives/la-xpm-2000-mar-08-mn-6735-story.html.

Middlekauff, Robert. *The Glorious Cause: The American Revolution, 1763–1789*. Revised ed. Oxford University Press, 2007.

Milne, David. "Trump Is His Own Secretary of State." *Foreign Policy*, November 21, 2024. https://foreignpolicy.com/2024/11/21/trump-secretary-state-rubio-hegseth-waltz-gabbard-gaetz-kissinger/.

Miranda, Lin-Manuel, Quiara Alegría Hudes, and Jeremy McCarter. *In the Heights: Finding Home*. Random House, 2021.

Mize, Ronald L. "Workplace Identities and Collective Memory." In *Immigrant Life in the US: Multi-Disciplinary Perspectives*, edited by Donna R. Gabaccia and Colin Wayne Leach. Routledge, 2003.

Mohyeldin, Ayman, "Marco Rubio's Irrelevance in Trump World." *MSNBC*, March 9, 2025. YouTube, 12 min., 12 sec. https://www.youtube.com/watch?v=A6gWmDWP5OQ.

Molen, Sandra. "Voice of the People." *Más Magazine*, October 31, 2008.

Moonesinghe, Ramal, Man-huei Chang, and Benedict I. Truman. "Health Insurance Coverage—United States, 2008 and 2010." *Centers for Disease Control and Prevention Morbidity and Mortality Weekly Report* 62, no. 03 (2013): 61–64. https://www.cdc.gov/mmwr/preview/mmwrhtml/su6203a10.htm.

Moore, Truman E. *The Slaves We Rent*. Random House, 1965.

Mora, Cristina. *Making Hispanics: How Activists, Bureaucrats and Media constructed a New American*. University of Chicago Press, 2014.

Morrison, Patt. "More Than 30 Years Ago, Father Luis Olivares Brought the Sanctuary Movement to Los Angeles." *Los Angeles Times*, November 14, 2018. https://www.latimes.com/opinion/op-ed/la-ol-patt-morrison-mario-garcia-luis-olivares-20181114-htmlstory.html.

Morrison, Patt. "When His Holiness Was in Hollywood: A Look Back at Pope John Paul II's 1987 Visit." *Los Angeles Times*, September 17, 2015. https://www.latimes.com/nation/la-na-pope-john-paul-la-20150921-story.html.

Murphy, Ruth Z. "Current Concerns of the Private Sector." *International Migration Review* 4, no. 3 (1970). https://www.jstor.org/stable/3002324.

Myrdal, Gunnar. *An American Dilemma: The Negro Problem and American Democracy*. Reprint ed. Transaction Publishers, 1966.

National Conference of Catholic Bishops. *National Pastoral Plan for Hispanic Ministry*, 1988. https://archive.org/details/isbn_1555861997.

National Museum of the Latino American Commission. "Final Report to the President and Congress of the United States: To Illuminate the American Story for All." May 2011. https://americanlatinomuseum.org/wp-content/uploads/2019/02/To-Illuminate-the-American-Story-for-us-All.pdf.

Nava, Julian. *My Mexican-American Journey*. Arte Publico, 2002.

Nepal, Sadikshya. "Primer: Evolution of the H-2A Visa Program." Bipartisan Policy Center, September 15, 2021. https://bipartisanpolicy.org/explainer/primer-h2a-visa/.

The New York Times. "The 1990 Census: California." February 26, 1991. https://www.nytimes.com/1991/02/26/us/the-1990-census-california.html.

The New York Times. "U.S. Raid Nets 36 Illegal Aliens In Treasurer-Designate's Plant." October 6, 1971. https://www.nytimes.com/1971/10/06/archives/us-raid-nets-36-illegal-aliens-in-treasurerdesignates-plant-us-raid.html.

Nicholls, Walter J. *The DREAMers: How the Undocumented Youth Movement Transformed the Immigrant Rights Debate*. Stanford University Press, 2013.

Nichols, John. "If Less Than 115,000 Had Switched in Three Battleground States, Harris Would Have Beaten Trump." *The Nation*, December 20, 2024. https://www.thenation.com/article/politics/three-battleground-states-defeated-trump/.

Nichols, John. "A Warrior for Workers." *The Nation*, December 19, 2008. https://www.thenation.com/article/archive/warrior-workers-0/.

Nusbaum, Eric. *Stealing Home: Los Angeles, the Dodgers, and the Lives Caught in Between*. PublicAffairs, 2020.

O'Connell, Daniel J., and Scott J. Peters. *In the Struggle: Scholars and the Fight Against Industrial Agribusiness in California*. New Village, 2021.

O'Connor, Allison, Jeanne Batalova, and Jessica Bolter. "Central American Immigrants in the United States." Migration Policy Institute, August 15, 2019. https://www.migrationpolicy.org/article/central-american-immigrants-united-states-2017.

O'Connor, Karen, and Lee Epstein. "A Legal Voice for the Chicano Community: The Activities of the Mexican American Legal Defense and Educational Fund, 1968–82." In *The Mexican American Experience: An Interdisciplinary Anthology*, edited by Rodolfo O. de la Garza. University of Texas Press, 1985.

Olivas, Michael A. *No Undocumented Child Left Behind*. New York University Press, 2012.

Oreskes, Benjamin. "How the Mayor of a Small Inland Empire Town Became One of Congress' Most Powerful Democrats." *Los Angeles Times*, April 23, 2023. https://www.latimes.com/california/story/2023-04-23/pete-aguilar-congress-latino-democrat-redlands.

Orta, Carlos F. *From Havana to DC: The Rise of Cuban Americans in Florida Politics*. Fig Factor Media, 2024.

Ortego, Phillip D. "The Mexican-Dixon Line: Rights of Passage for Alien Commuter Labor." *El Grito: A Journal of Contemporary Mexican American Thought* 1, no. 4 (1968): 29–33. https://opendoor.northwestern.edu/archive/files/original/b01c474941424ce7b86f475f5c3c1b87.pdf.

Ostrow, Ronald J. "U.S. Inquiry Targets 1982 L.A. Council Redistricting." *Los Angeles Times*, February 26, 1985. https://www.latimes.com/archives/la-xpm-1985-02-26-me-24976-story.html.

Owen, Dean R. *November 22, 1963: Reflections on the Life, Assassination, and Legacy of John F. Kennedy*. Skyhorse, 2015.

Oxnard Press-Courier. "Del Buono Heads Service Group." November 8, 1958.

Oxnard Press-Courier. "New Citizens in Colonia." Editorial, November 26, 1958.

Pack, Robert. *Jerry Brown: The Philosopher Prince*. Stein and Day, 1978.

Palermo, Joseph. "Here's What RFK Did in California in 1968." HuffPost.com, updated May 25, 2011. https://www.huffpost.com/entry/heres-what-rfk-did-in-cal_b_80931/amp.

Palermo, Joseph A. *In His Own Right: The Political Odyssey of Senator Robert F. Kennedy*. Columbia University Press, 2001.

Pappas, Nick. *Crosses of Iron: The Tragic Story of Dawson, New Mexico, and Its Twin Mining Disasters*. University of New Mexico Press, 2023.

Parker, Ashley, and Michael Scherer. "'I Run the Country and the World.'" *The Atlantic*, April 28, 2025. https://www.theatlantic.com/magazine/archive/2025/06/trump-second-term-comeback/682573/.

Partnership for Public Service. "The State of Public Trust in Government 2024." Survey data collected March 25–April 1, 2024. https://ourpublicservice.org/publications/state-of-trust-in-government-2024/.

Patiño, Jr., Jimmy C. "A Time for Resistance: Globalization, Undocumented Immigration, and the Chicana/o Movement in the San Diego Borderlands." PhD diss., UC San Diego, 2010.

Pawel, Miriam. *The Browns of California*. Bloomsbury, 2018.

Pawel, Miriam. *The Crusades of Cesar Chavez: A Biography*. Bloomsbury, 2014.

PBS SoCal. "The Muñoz Family: Civil Rights Activists," October 31, 2011. https://www.pbssocal.org/shows/departures/the-munoz-family-civil-rights-activists.

Peña, Luz, and Juan Carlos Guerrero. "Hidden Crisis: Tragedy in Half Moon Bay." ABC7 News Bay Area, April 6, 2023. https://abc7ne.ws/3Udbu40.

Peña Harden, Margaret Jean. "A Lifetime of Labor Activism: Dolores Huerta and the United Farmworkers." Master's thesis, University of Georgia, 2003.

Perkins, Lucy. "Donald Trump Sues Univision for $500 Million." *NPR*, June 30, 2015. https://www.npr.org/sections/thetwo-way/2015/06/30/418990895/donald-trump-sues-univision-for-500-million.

Perlstein, Rick. *Reaganland: America's Right Turn, 1976–1980*. Simon & Schuster, 2020.

Perotti, Rosanna. "Resolving Policy Conflict: Congress and Immigration Reform," PhD diss., University of Pennsylvania, 1989.

Pertschuk, Michael. *Giant Killers*. W. W. Norton, 1986.

Pew Research Center. "Public Trust in Government: 1958–2024." June 24, 2024. https://www.pewresearch.org/politics/2024/06/24/public-trust-in-government-1958-2024/.

Pew Research Center. "Trump's Job Rating Drops, Key Policies Draw Majority Disapproval as He Nears 100 Days." April 23, 2025. https://www.pewresearch.org/politics/2025/04/23/trumps-job-rating-drops-key-policies-draw-majority-disapproval-as-he-nears-100-days/.

Pfeifer, Michael J. *The Making of American Catholicism: Regional Culture and the Catholic Experience*. New York University Press, 2021.

Piore, Michael J. "The Dual Labor Market: Theory and Implications." In *Social Stratification, Class, Race, and Gender in Sociological Perspective,* edited by David B. Grusky. Routledge, 2001.

Pitt, Leonard. *The Decline of the Californios: A Social History of the Spanish-Speaking Californians,* 1846–1890. University of California Press, 1966.

Pitti, Stephen J. *The Devil in Silicon Valley: Northern California, Race, and Mexican Americans*. Princeton University Press, 2003.

Pollard, Vic. "Valley-dictorian," *The Bakersfield Californian,* May 23, 1999.

Prokop, Andrew. "The Architect: Stephen Miller's Dark Agenda for a Second Trump Term." *Vox,* September 26, 2024. https://www.vox.com/2024-elections/373479/stephen-miller-mass-deportation-camps-trump-agenda.

Pulido, Laura. *Black, Brown, Yellow, and Left: Radical Activism in Los Angeles.* University of California Press, 2006.

Quezada, Jeanette, and Christina Bravo. "'Needlessly Reckless': Local Leaders, Community Condemn South Park ICE Raids." *NBC San Diego,* updated June 2, 2025. https://www.nbcsandiego.com/news/local/community-speaks-after-ice-raids-at-south-park-italian-restaurant/3837706/?amp=1.

Quick, Sonya. "Ambitious Collaboration Boosts Journalism in Los Angeles." *CalMatters,* September 10, 2024. https://calmatters.org/inside-the-newsroom/2024/09/ambitious-collaboration-boosts-journalism-in-los-angeles/.

Rainey, James. "The Eternal Soldadera." In García, *A Dolores Huerta Reader.*

Ramírez, José A. *To the Line of Fire!: Mexican Texans and World War I.* Texas A&M University Press, 2009.

Ramírez, Ricardo. *Mobilizing Opportunities: The Evolving Latino Electorate and the Future of American Politics.* University of Virginia Press, 2013.

Ramos, George. "A House Divided Over Immigration." *Los Angeles Times,* September 27, 1993. https://www.latimes.com/archives/la-xpm-1993-09-27-me-39466-story.html.

Ramos, Henry A. J. *The American GI Forum: In Pursuit of the Dream, 1948–1983.* Arte Publico, 1998.

Ramos, Jorge. *No Borders: A Journalist's Search for Home.* Rayo, 2003.

Ramos, Jorge. *Sin Miedo: Lecciones de rebeldes.* Celebra, 2016.

Ramos, Jorge. *Stranger: The Challenge of a Latino Immigrant in the Trump Era.* Vintage, 2018.

Rappatoni, Linda. "Pope Holds Poignant Dodger Stadium Mass for 60,000," *UPI Archives,* September 17, 1987. https://www.upi.com/Archives/1987/09/17/Pope-holds-poignant-Dodger-Stadium-mass-for-60000/8416558849600/.

Rasmussen, Petra W. and Gerald F. Kominski. "Sources of Success in California's Individual Marketplace under the Affordable Care Act." *Journal of Health Politics Policy and Law* 44, no. 4 (2019): 679–706. https://escholarship.org/uc/item/43x1c7sd.

Rector, Kevin. "California, Other States Sue to Block Trump Executive Order on Birthright Citizenship." *Los Angeles Times,* January 21, 2025. https://www.latimes.com/politics/story/2025-01-21/california-other-states-sue-to-block-trump-executive-order-on-birthright-citizenship.

Reese, Michael, and Dan Schnur. "1992–94: The Preprimary Maneuvering and the Primary Campaign." In *The 1994 Governor's Race: An Inside Look at the Candidates and Their Campaigns by the People Who Managed Them,* edited by Gerald C. Lubenow. Berkeley: Institute of Governmental Studies Press, 1995.

Reinhold, Robert. "In California, New Talk of Limits on Immigrants." *The New York Times,* December 3, 1991. https://www.nytimes.com/1991/12/03/us/in-california-new-talk-of-limits-on-immigrants.html.

Remington, Chris. "Villaraigosa: Give California Mayors Control Over Local Schools." Capital Public Radio, October 4, 2017. https://www.capradio.org/news/insight/2017/10/04/insight-100417b/.

Rendon, Jesus M. "Archbishop Robert E. Lucey and Organized Labor." *Journal of the Life and Culture of San Antonio*. Accessed May 14, 2025. https://www.uiw.edu/sanantonio/Lucey.html.

Rennie, David. "The Political Passion of Eva Longoria." *The Economist 1843 Magazine,* May 3, 2016. https://www.economist.com/1843/2016/05/03/the-political-passion-of-eva-longoria.

Republican National Committee. *Growth and Opportunity Project*. Released on March 18, 2013. Accessed June 4, 2025. https://www.documentcloud.org/documents/624293-republican-national-committees-growth-and/.

Reyes, David. "Santa Ana Rent Strike: A New Role for Latinos." *Los Angeles Times,* February 22, 1985. https://www.latimes.com/archives/la-xpm-1985-02-22-mn-550-story.html.

Rhodes, Jesse H. *Ballot Blocked: The Political Erosion of the Voting Rights Act.* Stanford University Press, 2017.

Rivas-Rodriguez, Maggie. "Ignacio E. Lozano: The Mexican Exile Publisher Who Conquered San Antonio and Los Angeles." *American Journalism* 21, no. 1 (2004): 75–89.

Rodriguez, América. *Making Latino News: Race, Language, Class*. SAGE Publications, 1999.

Román, Stephanie, and Samantha Vargas Poppe. *Latinos and the Great Recession: 10 Years of Economic Loss and Recovery*. UnidosUS Policy and Advocacy, 2019. https://unidosus.org/wp-content/uploads/2021/07/unidosus_latinosgreatression.pdf.

Roper, John Herbert. "The Voting Rights Extension Act of 1982." *Phylon* 45, no. 3 (1984): 188–96. https://www.jstor.org/stable/274403.

Roper Center for Public Opinion Research. "US National Election Day Exit Polls." https://ropercenter.cornell.edu/exit-polls/us-national-election-day-exit-polls.

Rose, Margaret. "Dolores Huerta: The United Farm Workers Union." In García, *A Dolores Huerta Reader*.

Ross, Fred. *Conquering Goliath: Cesar Chavez at the Beginning*. El Taller Grafico, 1989.

Rubin, Jennifer. *Resistance: How Women Saved Democracy from Donald Trump*. William Morrow, 2021.

Rytina, Nancy. "IRCA Legalization Effects: Lawful Permanent Residence and Naturalization through 2001." Paper presented at The Effects of Immigrant Legalization Programs on the United States, October 25, 2002. https://www.dhs.gov/xlibrary/assets/statistics/publications/irca0114int.pdf.

Rytina, Nancy. "Population Estimates: Estimates of the Legal Permanent Resident Population in 2006." DHS Office of Immigration Statistics, February 2008. www.dhs.gov/xlibrary/assets/statistics/publications/LPR_PE_2006.pdf.

Saaliq, Sheikh. "Elon Musk Met with Modi During the Indian Prime Minister's US Visit. What Does He Want from India?" *Associated Press*, February 14, 2025. https://apnews.com/article/india-us-modi-musk-187301d9afe2c6d0edb0542466c2a589.

Sahagun, Louis. "A Day of Rage in East LA," *Los Angeles Times*, part of the newspaper's online "The Chicano Moratorium 50 Years Later," August 23, 2020. https://www.latimes.com/projects/chicano-moratorium/east-la-protest-gave-voice-chicano-movement/.

Sánchez, George J. *Becoming Mexican American: Ethnicity, Culture, and Identity in Chicano Los Angeles, 1900–1945*. Oxford University Press, 1993.

Sánchez, George J. *Boyle Heights: How a Los Angeles Neighborhood Became the Future of American Democracy*. University of California Press, 2021.

Sanger, Sarah. "Interview with Dolores Huerta." *Santa Barbara Independent*, November 30, 2009. https://www.independent.com/2009/11/30/interview-dolores-huerta/.

Saxton, Alexander. *The Indispensable Enemy: Labor and the Anti-Chinese Movement in California*. University of California Press, 1995.

Schey, Peter A. "The Select Commission on Immigration and Refugee Policy: A Lost Opportunity for Progress." *In Defense of the Alien* 4 (1981). https://www.jstor.org/stable/i23140938.

Schor, Paul. *Counting Americans: How the US Census Classified the Nation*. Oxford University Press, 2017.

Securities and Exchange Commission. "Order Instituting Cease-and-Desist Proceedings, Making Findings and Imposing a Cease-and-Desist Order Pursuant to Section 21c of the Securities Exchange Act of 1934," May 30, 2006. https://www.sec.gov/files/litigation/admin/2006/34-53882.pdf.

Securities and Exchange Commission. "SEC Brings Settled Charges Against Tribune Company for Reporting Inflated Circulation Figures and Misstating Circulation Revenues." Press release, May 30, 2006. https://www.sec.gov/news/press/2006/2006-82.htm.

Sentner, Irie, and Myah Ward. "Trump Says Harris Would Turn Every Town into a 'Third-World Hellhole.'" *Politico*, September 28, 2024. https://www.politico.com/news/2024/09/28/trump-harris-wisconsin-00181547.

Shaw, Randy. *Beyond the Fields: Cesar Chavez, the UFW, and the Struggle for Justice in the 21st Century*. University of California Press, 2010.

Shaw, Randy. "Eliseo Medina, Who Reshaped Labor and Immigrant Rights Movements, Retires from SEIU." *Beyond Chron*, September 30, 2013. https://beyondchron.org/eliseo-medina-who-reshaped-labor-and-immigrant-rights-movements-retires-from-seiu/.

Shetty, Abhishek. "Throwback Thursday: Contested USAC Elections of Yesteryear Triggered Racially Charged Protests." *Daily Bruin*, May 2, 2018. https://dailybruin.com/2018/05/02/throwback-thursday-contested-usac-elections-of-yesteryear-triggered-racially-charged-protests.

Shutes, Milton H. "Abraham Lincoln and the New Almaden Mine." *California Historical Society Quarterly* 15, no. 1 (1936): 2–20. https://doi.org/10.2307/25160617.

Sierra, Christine. "In Search of National Power: Chicanos Working the System on Immigration Reform, 1976–1986." In *Chicano Politics and Society in the Late Twentieth Century*, edited by David Montejano. University of Texas Press, 1999.

Sierra, Christine. "Latino Organizational Strategies on Immigration Reform: Success and Limits in Public Policymaking." In *Latinos and Political Coalitions*, edited by Roberto E. Villarreal and Norma G. Hernandez. Praeger, 1991.

Simon, Richard. "Judge Kenyon Enlivened Case with a Gentle Wit." *Los Angeles Times*, June 5, 1990. https://www.latimes.com/archives/la-xpm-1990-06-05-mn-483-story.html.

Simon, Richard, and Frederick M. Muir. "Schabarum Snubs Aide and Backs Judge as His Successor." *Los Angeles Times*, March 16, 1990. https://www.latimes.com/archives/la-xpm-1990-03-16-me-214-story.html.

Skelton, George. "Brown May Be Catching Wave with Prop. 187." *Los Angeles Times*, October 27, 1994. https://www.latimes.com/archives/la-xpm-1994-10-27-mn-55346-story.html.

Skelton, George. "Padilla Was Right to Challenge Noem's Right-Wing Lunacy." *Los Angeles Times*, June 16, 2025. https://www.latimes.com/politics/newsletter/2025-06-16/skelton-monday-politics-newsletter-padilla-noem.

Skelton, George. "Wilson Expands Reasons to Support Term Limits." *Los Angeles Times*, October 12, 1990. https://www.latimes.com/archives/la-xpm-1990-10-12-mn-2252-story.html.

Skelton, George. "Wilson Urges Welfare Cuts, Tax Increases, Austerity: State of the State Address Outlines His Plan for Balancing the Books During a Time of National Recession." *Los Angeles Times*, January 10, 1991. https://www.latimes.com/archives/la-xpm-1991-01-10-mn-11270-story.html.

Smith, Grant H. *The History of the Comstock Lode*. Nevada Bureau of Mines and Geology, 1998.

Smith, Lynn. "Nacho Lozano—'As Chicano as American Pie.'" *Los Angeles Times*, December 5, 1987. https://www.latimes.com/archives/la-xpm-1987-12-05-li-6380-story.html.

Smith, Patrick, Mirna Alsharif, Gary Grumbach, and Dennis Romero. "As Immigration Raids Continue, ICE Protests Spread Coast to Coast." *NBC News*, updated June 11, 2025. https://www.nbcnews.com/news/amp/rcna211980.

Smith, Toby. *Coal Town: The Life and Times of Dawson, New Mexico*. Ancient City, 1993.

Snodgrass, Mary Ellen. *Beating the Odds: A Teen Guide to 75 Superstars Who Overcame Adversity*. Greenwood, 2008.

Sobczyk, Joe. "Trump's First Economic Scorecard Gets Marked with GDP Contraction." *Bloomberg Washington Edition* newsletter, April 30, 2025. https://www.bloomberg.com/news/newsletters/2025-04-30/trump-s-first-economic-scorecard-gets-marked-with-gdp-contraction.

Sonksen, Mike. "A Brief History on the Gateway Cities." Watershed Conservation Authority. Accessed May 14, 2025. https://greenportal.wca.ca.gov/local-voices/a-brief-history-on-the-gateway-cities-2.

Stanley-Becker, Isaac. "Trump's Real Secretary of State." *The Atlantic*, May 14, 2025. https://www.theatlantic.com/politics/archive/2025/05/steve-witkoff-putin-russia-ukraine-diplomat/682805/.

Starr, Kevin. *Embattled Dreams: California in War and Peace, 1940–1950*. Oxford University Press, 2002.

State of the Cities Data Systems. "SOCDS Census Data: Output for Los Angeles City, CA." Accessed February 10, 2025. https://socds.huduser.gov/Census/race.odb?msacitylist=31100*0600044000*1.0&metro=cbsa.

Stegall, Katy. "Federal Immigration Agents Raid San Diego Restaurants, Detain Workers." *CBS 8*, May 31, 2025. https://www.cbs8.com/article/news/local/federal-immigration-raid-san-diego-restaurant/509-6e5d70c1-85e5-4bff-ab9e-f6b2e34ad06c.

Stelter, Brian. "Made-for-TV Crackdown." *Reliable Sources with Brian Stelter, CNN*, June 9, 2025. https://view.newsletters.cnn.com/messages/1749473917864ea73170f0f11/raw.

Sterngold, James. "A Citizenship Incubator for Immigrant Latinos." *The New York Times*, February 1, 2000. https://www.nytimes.com/2000/02/01/us/a-citizenship-incubator-for-immigrant-latinos.html.

Stewart, Jocelyn. "The Advocate: As the President of the Mexican American Legal Defense and Educational Fund, Antonia Hernandez Speaks for Millions." *Los Angeles Times*, September 12, 1999. https://www.latimes.com/archives/la-xpm-1999-sep-12-tm-9130-story.html.

Stone, Walter J., and Ronald B. Rapoport. *Three's a Crowd: The Dynamic of Third Parties, Ross Perot, and Republican Resurgence*. University of Michigan Press, 2005.

Sumagaysay, Levi. "Gavin Newsom Vows to 'Leave No Region Behind' on California Jobs." *CalMatters*, November 21, 2024. https://calmatters.org/economy/2024/11/california-economy-newsom-central-valley/.

Suter, Tara. "Harris Says in Fundraising Email She Ate 'a Family-Sized Bag of Nacho Doritos' on Night of Trump Election." *The Hill*, August 16, 2024. https://thehill.com/blogs/in-the-know/4831686-vice-president-harris-eats-doritos/.

Swan, Jonathan, and Maggie Haberman. "Inside the Explosive Meeting Where Trump Officials Clashed with Elon Musk." *The New York Times*, updated March 17, 2025. https://www.nytimes.com/2025/03/07/us/politics/trump-musk-doge-power.html.

Symonds, Matthew. *Softwar: An Intimate Portrait of Larry Ellison and Oracle*. Simon & Schuster, 2003.

Tapper, Jake. "The Fred Thompson Watergate Myth." *ABC News*, August 8, 2007. https://abcnews.go.com/amp/Politics/story?id=3447219.

Tatalovich, Raymond. *Nativism Reborn?: The Official English Language Movement and the American States*. University Press of Kentucky, 1995.

Taylor, D. Garth. "The Naturalization Trail: Mexican Nationality and US Citizenship." *Latino Research @ ND* 3, no. 2 (2006). University of Notre Dame Institute for Latino Studies. https://latinostudies.nd.edu/assets/95313/original/lr_nd6_web.pdf.

Taylor, Jessica. "Trump Dissolves Controversial Election Commission." *NPR*, January 3, 2018. https://www.npr.org/2018/01/03/575524512/trump-dissolves-controversial-election-commission.

Taylor, Paul, and Mark Hugo Lopez. "National Latino Leader? The Job Is Open." Pew Research Center, November 15, 2010. https://www.pewresearch.org/hispanic/2010/11/15/national-latino-leader-the-job-is-open/.

Tempest, Rone. "A Rapid, Sometimes Bumpy, Rise." *Los Angeles Times*, May 24, 2001. https://www.latimes.com/archives/la-xpm-2001-may-24-mn-2055-story.html.

Thomas, Ken. "Longoria, DNC Finance Chief Partner for Latinos." *Akron Beacon Journal*, May 5, 2014.

Thompson, Gabriel. *America's Social Arsonist: Fred Ross and Grassroots Organizing in the Twentieth Century*. University of California Press, 2016.

Thompson, Marilyn W. "Voting Maps Throughout the Deep South May Be Redrawn After Surprise Supreme Court Ruling." *ProPublica*, June 13, 2023. https://www.propublica.org/article/scotus-voting-rights-act-alabama-redistricting-allen-milligan.

Thomson-DeVeaux, Amelia. "Are Black and Hispanic Americans Abandoning Biden?" *FiveThirtyEight*, May 31, 2023. https://fivethirtyeight.com/features/biden-approval-black-hispanic-voters/.

The Times Editorial Board. "Our Dishonest President." *Los Angeles Times*, April 2, 2017. https://www.latimes.com/projects/la-ed-our-dishonest-president/.

Toosi, Nahal. "The Marco Rubio Guide to Survival Is Not Working Well." *Politico*, February 17, 2025. https://www.politico.com/news/magazine/2025/02/17/marco-rubio-state-department-toosi-00204407.

Torres, Art. "Art Torres Oral History Interview." Interview by Steve Edgington, 2003. CSUF Center for Oral and Public History for the California State Archives State Government Oral History Program. https://archive.org/details/oh2004-06-torres/.

Truax, Eileen. *Dreamers: An Immigrant Generation's Fight for Their American Dream*. Beacon, 2015.

Tumulty, Karen. "The Down-Ballot Officials Who Could Freeze the Trump Train in Its Tracks." *The Washington Post*, September 4, 2018. https://www.washingtonpost.com/opinions/the-down-ballot-officials-who-could-freeze-the-trump-train-in-its-tracks/2018/09/04/f0c94472-ad33-11e8-8a0c-70b618c98d3c_story.html.

Tunney, John. "John Tunney Oral History." Interview by Stephen F. Knott and James Sterling Young. Edward M. Kennedy Oral History Project, Miller Center of Public Affairs, University of Virginia, May 3, 2007. https://s3.amazonaws.com/web.poh.transcripts/Tunney_John_2007.ARCHIVE.pdf.

Udasin, Sharon. “Newsom Asks Congress for Almost $40B in Wildfire Recovery Aid.” *The Hill*, February 24, 2025. https://thehill.com/policy/energy-environment/5161318-california-wildfires-recovery-funding-request-newsom/.

United States Census Bureau. “1990 Census Apportionment Results.” December 1990. https://www.census.gov/data/tables/1990/dec/1990-apportionment-data.html.

United States Conference of Catholic Bishops. “Encuentro.” Accessed February 10, 2025. https://www.usccb.org/committees/hispaniclatino-affairs/encuentro.

University of New Mexico Geospatial and Population Studies. “1930 Population of the United States by Color or Race and Nativity.” Archived October 23, 2023, at https://web.archive.org/web/20231003174443/https://gps.unm.edu/pru/census/1930-population-united-states-color-or-race-and-nativity.

Uranga, Rachel. “Immigrant Rights Activists Vow to Disrupt ICE Raids in California.” *Los Angeles Times*, February 13, 2025. https://www.latimes.com/california/story/2025-02-13/immigrant-rights-activists-vow-to-disrupt-ice-raids-in-california.

Uranga, Rachel, and Ruben Vives. “What Really Happened Outside the Paramount Home Depot? The Reality on the Ground vs. the Rhetoric.” *Los Angeles Times*, June 8, 2025. https://www.latimes.com/california/story/2025-06-08/what-actually-happened-at-the-paramount-home-depot.

Valdez, Luis. “Commentary of Luis Valdez: The Plan of Delano.” Farmworker Movement Documentation Project. UC San Diego Library. Archived November 12, 2024, at https://web.archive.org/web/20241112221829/https://libraries.ucsd.edu/farmworkermovement/essays/essays/Plan%20of%20Delano.pdf.

Valdez, Luis. “Huelga en General.” In “Songs,” National Farm Worker Ministry. Accessed May 14, 2025. http://nfwm.org/resource-center/worshipresources/farm-worker-songs/.

Vankar, Preeti. “Number of Affordable Care Act-Related (ACA) Enrollments in the Marketplace, Medicaid, and the Basic Health Program (BHP) in the U.S. from 2014 to 2024.” Statista, September 16, 2024. https://www.statista.com/statistics/1280656/number-of-us-aca-related-enrollments/.

Vanzi, Max. “California, Tribe Reach Gaming Pact.” *The Washington Post*, March 6, 1998. https://www.washingtonpost.com/archive/politics/1998/03/07/california-tribe-reach-gaming-pact/b4d64c7b-49af-4ba7-8d75-18043e59563d/.

Vargas, Arturo. "Testimony of Arturo Vargas, Executive Director, National Association of Latino Elected and Appointed Officials." *Naturalization Delays: Causes, Consequences, and Solutions, Hearing Before the Subcommittee on Immigration, Citizenship, Refugees, Border Security, and International Law Committee on the Judiciary. House of Representatives,* 110th Cong., 2nd Sess., January 17, 2008. https://tile.loc.gov/storage-services/master/gdc/gdcebooks public/20/23/69/38/47/2023693847/2023693847.pdf.

Vargas Santiago, Luis Adrian. "Uncontainable Zapata: Iconicity, Religiosity, and Visual Diaspora." PhD diss., University of Texas at Austin, 2015.

Varney, Philip. *New Mexico's Best Ghost Towns: A Practical Guide*. University of New Mexico Press, 1987.

Verhovek, Sam Howe. "Immigrants' Anxieties Spur a Surge in Naturalizations." *New York Times,* September 13, 1996. https://www.nytimes.com/1996/09/13/us/immigrants-anxieties-spur-a-surge-in-naturalizations.html.

Vertuno, Jim. "Protests Against Immigration Raids Spread Across the U.S." *Associated Press,* June 11, 2025. https://www.pbs.org/newshour/amp/politics/photos-protests-against-immigration-raids-spread-across-the-u-s.

Vincent, Roger. "Spanish Papers Square Off." *Los Angeles Times,* March 2, 2004. https://www.latimes.com/archives/la-xpm-2004-mar-02-fi-newspaper2-story.html.

Vives, Ruben. "ICE Agents with Assault Rifles Toss Flash-Bangs in Trendy San Diego Neighborhood: Community Fights Back." *Los Angeles Times,* June 2, 2025. https://www.latimes.com/california/story/2025-06-02/an-alarming-show-of-force-san-diego-elected-officials-denounce-hsi-work-raids.

Vives, Ruben. "They Patrol L.A.'s Streets in Search of ICE, Trump Immigration Raids." *Los Angeles Times,* February 28, 2025. https://www.latimes.com/california/story/2025-02-28/volunteers-patrol-neighborhoods.

Vogel, Carole G. *Shock Waves Through Los Angeles: The Northridge Earthquake*. Little Brown, 1996.

Vogel, Nancy. "State Repeals Oracle Contract." *Los Angeles Times,* July 24, 2002. https://www.latimes.com/archives/la-xpm-2002-jul-24-me-oracle24-story.html.

Voss, Kim, and Irene Bloemraad, eds. *Rallying for Immigrant Rights: The Fight for Inclusion in 21st Century America*. University of California Press, 2011.

Ware, Holly. "Newsday, Hoy Axe Two Top Executives." *New York Post,* July 20, 2004. https://nypost.com/2004/07/20/newsday-hoy-ax-2-top-executives/.

Wasserman, David. "Key Takeaways From the 2024 National Popular Vote Tracker." *The Cook Political Report,* December 10, 2024. https://www.cookpolitical.com/analysis/national/national-politics/key-takeaways-2024-national-popular-vote-tracker.

Weintraub, Daniel M. "Wilson Scales Back Request for U.S. Aid for Immigrants." *Los Angeles Times*, April 1, 1993. https://www.latimes.com/archives/la-xpm-1993-04-01-mn-17685-story.html.

Weisberg, Lori, and Alexandra Mendoza. "ICE Agents Conduct Raid at Buona Forchetta, Popular South Park Restaurant." *The San Diego Union-Tribune*, updated May 31, 2025. https://www.sandiegouniontribune.com/2025/05/30/ice-agents-conduct-raid-at-buona-forchetta-popular-south-park-restaurant/.

Weissert, Will, and Adriana Gomez Licon. "Immigration Reform Stalled Decade After Gang of 8's Big Push." *Associated Press*, April 3, 2023. https://apnews.com/article/immigration-asylum-trump-biden-gang-of-eight-3d8007e72928665b66d8648be0e3e31f.

West, Al. "Labor Forgets Fight During Legislature." *Santa Fe New Mexican*, January 11, 1939.

Whitaker, Barbara. "A Quick Climb Up the Los Angeles Political Ladder." *The New York Times*, July 7, 2001. https://www.nytimes.com/2001/07/07/us/public-lives-a-quick-climb-up-the-los-angeles-political-ladder.html.

White, Ben. "GOP to Fix the Economy? Good Luck." *Politico*, November 6, 2014. https://www.politico.com/story/2014/11/republican-economy-2014-election-112618.

Williams, Timothy. "Poverty, Pride and Power: In Line for Federal Help, Pacoima Hides Problems Below Neat Surface." *Los Angeles Times*, April 10, 1994. https://www.latimes.com/archives/la-xpm-1994-04-10-me-44400-story.html.

Wilson, Pete. "State of the State Addresses." The Governors' Gallery. https://governors.library.ca.gov/addresses/s_36-Wilson02.html.

Wolffe, Kate. "California Senate Elects Monique Limón as Next Leader." *Sacramento Bee*, June 11, 2025. https://www.sacbee.com/news/politics-government/capitol-alert/article308254510.html.

Wong, Edward. "Marco Rubio, Secretary of Everything." *The New York Times*, May 1, 2025. https://www.nytimes.com/2025/05/01/us/politics/marco-rubio-national-security-secretary-state.html?smid=url-share.

Wong, Kent. "Dynamic Political Mobilization: The Los Angeles County Federation of Labor." *Working USA* 8, no. 2 (2004).

Woodward, Bob, and Carl Bernstein. *All the President's Men*. Reissue ed. Simon & Schuster, 2014.

Young, Julia G. *Mexican Exodus: Emigrants, Exiles, and Refugees of the Cristero War*. Oxford University Press, 2015.

Zamora, Emilio. *Claiming Rights and Righting Wrongs in Texas: Mexican Workers and Job Politics During World War II*. Texas A&M University Press, 2008.

Zarembo, Alan. "Slow but Steady Approach Has Served Bustamante Well." *Los Angeles Times*, August 30, 2003. https://www.latimes.com/archives/la-xpm-2003-aug-30-mn-cruz30-story.html.

Zepeda-Millán, Chris. *Latino Mass Mobilization: Immigration, Racialization, and Activism*. Cambridge University Press, 2017. Kindle.

Index

Pages numbers in italics refer to photographs and images.

N

About the Authors

DAVID R. AYÓN, coauthor of *Power Shift: How Latinos in California Transformed Politics in America,* has written and taught on the politics and policymaking of Latinas/os, California, the US, Mexico, and Latin America at UC Berkeley, Stanford, UC Santa Cruz, Occidental College, USC, Loyola Marymount, and UC San Diego. His work is featured in *The Oxford Encyclopedia of Latinas and Latinos in Contemporary Politics, Law, and Social Movements; International Relations of California and Texas with Mexico and the World; Contemporary U.S.-Latin American Relations, Foreign Affairs Latinoamérica; Mexico's Democratic Challenges;* the opinion pages of *Los Angeles Times,* and other publications. A senior fellow of the Center for the Study of Los Angeles, Ayón has also served as senior advisor to the Mexico Institute of the Woodrow Wilson Center, as well as to the firm Latino Decisions; directed programs of the Mexico Institute and the USC School of International Relations; and worked as analyst, consultant, political columnist (for Univision.com, 2014–15), and special producer for Spanish-language TV news for elections in the US and Mexico since 1992. Twice a visiting research fellow of the Center for U.S.-Mexican Studies, Ayón was educated at Princeton, Stanford, and El Colegio de México. He is a former director of the U.S.-Mexico Foundation; serves on the editorial board of *Foreign Affairs Latinoamérica,* for which he has also acted as guest editor; and is a life member of the Council on Foreign Relations, serving on its term membership committee.

George L. Pla, founder and CEO of Cordoba Corporation, is an entrepreneur, author, and philanthropist whose work spans business and civic activities that hold the common theme of empowering communities throughout California. George Pla's founding of Cordoba Corporation as a full-service engineering company and his philosophy of leadership were the subjects of a curriculum-based case study by the Harvard Business School. In May 2023, California State University, Los Angeles awarded George Pla an Honorary Doctorate Degree in recognition of his contributions to education and community and business leadership. Dr. Pla's involvement in academic institutions includes serving as a regent emeritus at Loyola Marymount University, as a presidential associate at the University of Southern California (USC), and on the Board of Councilors for USC's Sol Price School of Public Policy. From his early days in grassroots and community activism, to a position in government as the youngest official in California serving in Governor Jerry Brown's first administration, and throughout his career, Pla has been on the forefront of Latino politics in California. He is the coauthor of the formative book on Latino politics, *Power Shift: How Latinos in California Transformed Politics in America*, which recounts the origins and development of ten Los Angeles Latino leaders who transformed politics and government, forging a remarkable Latino-empowerment process. Pla currently serves on the board of directors of the LA28 Olympic Games, as President of the Los Angeles Memorial Coliseum Commission, and as Chair of the Los Angeles Area Chamber of Commerce.